Biblical Keys to
Financial
Prosperity

Kenneth E. Hagin

Unless otherwise indicated, all Scripture quotations in this volume are from the *King James Version* of the Bible.

Second Printing 1996

ISBN 0-89276-524-0

In the U.S. write:
Kenneth Hagin Ministries
P.O. Box 50126
Tulsa, OK 74150-0126

In Canada write:
Kenneth Hagin Ministries
P.O. Box 335, Station D,
Etobicoke (Toronto), Ontario
Canada, M9A 4X3

BOOKS BY KENNETH E. HAGIN

* Redeemed From Poverty, Sickness and Spiritual Death
* What Faith Is
* Seven Vital Steps To Receiving the Holy Spirit
* Right and Wrong Thinking
  Prayer Secrets
* Authority of the Believer (foreign only)
* How To Turn Your Faith Loose
  The Key to Scriptural Healing
  Praying To Get Results
  The Present-Day Ministry of Jesus Christ
  The Gift of Prophecy
  Healing Belongs to Us
  The Real Faith
  How You Can Know the Will of God
  The Threefold Nature of Man
  The Human Spirit
  Turning Hopeless Situations Around
  Casting Your Cares Upon the Lord
  Seven Steps for Judging Prophecy
* The Interceding Christian
  Faith Food for Autumn
* Faith Food for Winter
  Faith Food for Spring
  Faith Food for Summer
* New Thresholds of Faith
* Prevailing Prayer to Peace
* Concerning Spiritual Gifts
  Bible Faith Study Course
  Bible Prayer Study Course
  The Holy Spirit and His Gifts
* The Ministry Gifts (Study Guide)
  Seven Things You Should Know About Divine Healing
  El Shaddai
  Zoe: The God-Kind of Life
  A Commonsense Guide to Fasting
  Must Christians Suffer?
  The Woman Question
  The Believer's Authority
  Ministering to Your Family
  What To Do When Faith Seems Weak and Victory Lost
  Growing Up, Spiritually
  Bodily Healing and the Atonement (Dr. T.J. McCrossan)
  Exceedingly Growing Faith
  Understanding the Anointing
  I Believe in Visions
  Understanding How To Fight the Good Fight of Faith
  Plans, Purposes, and Pursuits
  How You Can Be Led by the Spirit of God
  A Fresh Anointing
  Classic Sermons
  He Gave Gifts Unto Men:
     A Biblical Perspective of Apostles, Prophets, and Pastors
  The Art of Prayer
  Following God's Plan For Your Life

The Triumphant Church: Dominion Over All the Powers of Darkness
Healing Scriptures
Mountain-Moving Faith
Love: The Way to Victory
Biblical Keys to Financial Prosperity
The Price Is Not Greater Than God's Grace (Mrs. Oretha Hagin)

MINIBOOKS (A partial listing)

* The New Birth
* Why Tongues?
* In Him
* God's Medicine
* You Can Have What You Say
* Don't Blame God
* Words
  Plead Your Case
* How To Keep Your Healing
  The Bible Way To Receive the Holy Spirit
  I Went to Hell
  How To Walk in Love
  The Precious Blood of Jesus
* Love Never Fails
  How God Taught Me About Prosperity

BOOKS BY KENNETH HAGIN JR.

* Man's Impossibility — God's Possibility
  Because of Jesus
  How To Make the Dream God Gave You Come True
  The Life of Obedience
  Forget Not!
  God's Irresistible Word
  Healing: Forever Settled
  Don't Quit! Your Faith Will See You Through
  The Untapped Power in Praise
  Listen to Your Heart
  What Comes After Faith?
  Speak to Your Mountain!
  Come Out of the Valley!
  It's Your Move!
  God's Victory Plan
  Another Look at Faith

MINIBOOKS (A partial listing)

* Faith Worketh by Love
* Seven Hindrances to Healing
* The Past Tense of God's Word
  Faith Takes Back What the Devil's Stolen
  How To Be a Success in Life
  Get Acquainted With God
  Unforgiveness
  Ministering to the Brokenhearted

*These titles are also available in Spanish. Information about other foreign translations of several of the above titles (i.e., Finnish, French, German, Indonesian, Polish, Russian, etc.) may be obtained by writing to: Kenneth Hagin Ministries, P.O. Box 50126, Tulsa, Oklahoma 74150-0126.

Contents

Introduction

One of the most difficult tasks in ministering to folks is getting them to understand the truth that God wants them to prosper and do well in life. In fact, God wants them to prosper more than *they* want to! Many good Christian people have never entered into the dimension of prosperity that God intended for them, and one reason they haven't is a lack of understanding in this area.

If you want to *walk* in the perfect will of God and experience His richest and best for your life, you've got to *do* the perfect will of God. That requires honoring and obeying God and His Word.

But in order to honor and obey the Word, a person must first find out what the Word has to say. The Word of God has a great deal to say about prosperity for the believer.

Many Christians are not prospering today because they are not willing *and* obedient to the call of God on their lives or to some specific direction God has given them. Others simply need to get their thinking straightened out so they can think, talk, and act in line with God's Word concerning prosperity.

Still others give financially with wrong motives — just to *get* something in return. Or they give motivated by guilt or fear instead of by faith and love. And some Christians dishonor God and His Word, not only by failing to tithe and give offerings, but in the way they conduct their business affairs.

But this doesn't have to be the case in your life. God *wants* you to prosper financially!

I remember what my life was like before I learned this truth about prosperity from the Bible. My family and I struggled greatly in this area, just barely making it financially for many years. We weren't scraping the bottom of the barrel; we were *underneath* the barrel and the barrel was on top of us! But praise God, the Word works! Prosperity came to us as we learned to act on the Word of God in that area.

Success in God doesn't come overnight. And if you're not prospering in life right now, your prosperity in God won't appear overnight either. But if you'll continually honor and obey God and His Word, it *will* come.

It is my prayer that the teachings in this book will bring God's blessings to your life so you can *be* a blessing to the Kingdom of God and the work of God on the earth.

Kenneth E. Hagin

Chapter 1
Poverty: A Blessing
Or a Curse?

CHRIST HATH REDEEMED US from the curse of the law, being made a curse for us: for it is written, Cursed is every one that hangeth on a tree.

— Galatians 3:13

Christ hath redeemed us!

If we stop reading right there, we'd know Jesus redeemed us. But what did He redeem us from? The rest of the verse says, ". . . *FROM THE CURSE OF THE LAW, being made a curse for us: for it is written, Cursed is every one that hangeth on a tree*" (Gal. 3:13).

> **GALATIANS 3:14**
> 14 That the blessing of Abraham might come on the Gentiles through Jesus Christ; that we might receive the promise of the Spirit through faith.

I couldn't do justice to a study on prosperity without explaining the great Bible truth of redemption. Christ has redeemed us from the curse of the Law! The curse of the Law includes spiritual death, sickness, and poverty.

1

The first curse that God said would come upon man for breaking His Law is found in Genesis 2:17. God said to Adam in Genesis 2:17, "... *in the day that thou eatest thereof* [of the tree of the knowledge of good and evil] *thou shalt surely die.*"

Adam and Eve were permitted to eat fruit from all the trees in the Garden of Eden except the fruit of the tree of the knowledge of good and evil. The curse of spiritual death was to come upon them if they disobeyed God.

Genesis 3:22-24 tells us that man did disobey God, was driven from the Garden, and could eat no longer of the tree of life. Man became the slave of sin and death.

Death has always been a mystery to man. It was not a part of the creation or part of God's original plan. The Bible tells us that physical death is an enemy of God and man. First Corinthians 15:26 tells us that physical death is the last enemy that shall be put underfoot.

When you die physically, your spirit and soul leave your body and go to your eternal home (Luke 16:19-24).

Although several kinds of death are spoken of in the Bible, there are three kinds we should familiarize ourselves with: 1) spiritual death; 2) physical death; and 3) eternal death or the Second Death, which means being cast into the lake that burns with fire and brimstone (Rev. 21:8).

Spiritual death is that which lays hold of one's spirit rather than his body. Physical death is a *manifestation* of spiritual death.

Eternal death or the Second Death is the ultimate finality of death or the home of the spiritually dead.

Spiritual death came to earth first and then manifested itself in the physical body by destroying it. Physical death is a manifestation of the law that is at work within. Paul called it "the law of sin and death" (Rom. 8:2).

When God said to Adam, ". . . *in the day that thou eatest thereof thou shalt surely die*" (Gen. 2:17), He was not referring to physical death but to spiritual death. If man never had died spiritually, he would not have died physically.

What is spiritual death? Spiritual death means *separation from God*.

The moment Adam sinned, he was separated from God. When God came down in the cool of the day, as was His custom, to walk and talk with Adam, He called, ". . . *Adam . . . Where art thou?*" (Gen. 3:9). Adam answered, ". . . *I hid myself.*" He was separated from God.

When Adam and Eve listened to the devil, it resulted in spiritual death. Spiritual death immediately began to manifest itself in the human family. Eventually, Adam and Eve's firstborn son murdered the second-born son (Gen. 4:8).

Man had become an outcast, an outlaw, driven from the Garden with no legal ground to approach God.

Man in his fallen state could not respond to the call of God without a sacrifice. Man was hindered in his response to God because he was more than a transgressor; he was more than a lawbreaker and sinner.

Jesus said to the Pharisees, *"Ye are of your father the devil, and the lusts of your father ye will do. He was a murderer from the beginning, and abode not in the truth, because there is no truth in him. When he speaketh a lie, he speaketh of his own: for he is a liar, and the father of it"* (John 8:44).

The Pharisees were very religious. They did a lot of good things. They went to the synagogue on the Sabbath. They prayed. They paid their tithes. They fasted. They did a lot of other fine things. But they lied about Christ and murdered Him. They had the characteristics of the devil.

This explains why man cannot be saved by his conduct or good works; he must be born again. If man were not a child of the devil, he could just act right and he'd be all right. But since he's a child of the devil, even if he tries to act right, he'll still go to hell when he dies — to the lake that burns with fire and brimstone, which is the Second Death.

Why? Because man as he is cannot stand in the Presence of God. Man had to be saved by Someone paying the penalty for man's sins and giving man the New Birth.

You might take a flop-eared old mule and try to make him into a racehorse, but it won't work. You could dress that mule up by filing his teeth or polishing his hooves. You could feed him the finest food, run him around the track every day, and house him in the finest stable. But on the day of the race when the gun sounds, all he'll do is lope off down the track, because he's a mule. It's just not in him to be a racehorse. In order for the old mule to become a racehorse, he'd have to be reborn as a racehorse, which is impossible.

Man, however, through the New Birth can be reborn! Through regeneration, he can be changed! He can become a new creature in Christ Jesus!

It doesn't matter how much money a man has, how well-educated or religious he is, mere man cannot stand in the Presence of God, because his nature is wrong.

Man is lost today not because of what he *does*, but because of what he *is*. (What he does is the result of what he is.)

An unregenerate man needs life from God because he is spiritually dead. But thanks be to God, *Christ has redeemed us from spiritual death!*

JOHN 5:26
26 For as the Father hath life in himself; so hath he given to the Son to have life in himself.

Jesus Christ had no death in Him. He was not born as we are born. He didn't have spiritual death in Him (John 14:30). Yet Hebrews 2:9 says he tasted death for every man. He took upon Himself our condition of spiritual death. Notice Hebrews 9:26 says He ". . . *put away SIN* [not sins] *by the sacrifice of himself."*

How did He do that? Well, I don't know, but because the Bible says He did it, I believe it.

Now why did Jesus take death that we might have life?

I was born and raised Southern Baptist. Afterward, I was filled with the Holy Spirit and came over among the Pentecostals. I heard for years among the Baptists that Jesus became what we were that we might become what He was.

Now that doesn't mean He became a sinner (that's what we were — sinners!). It simply means He took our place as our Substitute when our sin was laid on Him. That doesn't mean He had in His spirit the personal nature of the devil. It just means that our sin was *laid* on Him.

Remember what Jesus said along this line in John's Gospel.

> **JOHN 10:10**
> **10** The thief [He's talking about the devil, not about God; God is not a thief.] **cometh not, but for to steal, and to kill, and to destroy: I am come that they might have life, and that they might have it more abundantly.**

> **JOHN 5:24**
> **24** Verily, verily, I [Jesus] **say unto you, He that heareth my word, and believeth on him that sent me, hath everlasting life** [or eternal life]**, and shall not come into condemnation; but is passed from DEATH unto LIFE.**

Now in John 5:24, Jesus is not talking about physical death. He is talking again about spiritual death. In

other words, Jesus came to redeem us from spiritual
death and its consequence of eternal separation from
God.

> **EPHESIANS 2:1**
> 1 And you hath he quickened, who were dead in
> trespasses and sins [spiritual death].

Verses 8 and 9 of Ephesians chapter 2 tell us how
that redemption came about in our own lives.

> **EPHESIANS 2:8,9**
> 8 For by grace are ye saved through faith; and
> that not of yourselves: it is the gift of God:
> 9 Not of works, lest any man should boast.

It is not by works that a person is saved. Now certainly, we believe in good works, because the Bible said
we are ". . . *created in Christ Jesus UNTO GOOD
WORKS . . .*" (Eph. 2:10).

Yet right on the other hand, we couldn't save ourselves through good works.

No, our good works are a result of the fact that
we've been born again and have become new creatures
(2 Cor. 5:17). Our spiritual nature has been changed!

In other words, without Jesus, we're just simply
helpless and hopeless. And without Him, we're nothing.
But thanks be unto God, He comes into our lives, if we
accept Him, and makes us new creatures — sons — in
Him!

> **ROMANS 8:14-16**
> **14 For as many as are led by the Spirit of God, they are the SONS of God.**
> **15 For ye have not received the spirit of bondage again to fear; but ye have received the Spirit of adoption, whereby we cry, Abba, Father.**
> **16 The Spirit itself** [or a better translation would be Himself] **beareth witness with our spirit, that we are the children of God.**

Have you passed from spiritual death unto spiritual life? If you have, then God is your Father. Can you look up to Him and say, "Father God"? That's what "Abba, Father" means.

Is God's Spirit within your spirit, bearing witness with your spirit that you are a child of God? Do you have the Holy Spirit in your spirit crying, "Abba, Father?" If you do, you're born again!

If you don't, thank God, you can accept Christ this moment. And when you do, then the Holy Spirit comes in to dwell in you.

In Christ, we have passed from death unto life. How do we know it? We've got the witness in our spirits that Romans 8:14-16 talks about. Our spirit bears witness that we are the children of God. And John said something else about it.

> **1 JOHN 3:14**
> **14 We know that we have passed from death unto life, because we LOVE the brethren. . . .**

And Galatians also has something to say about love and the recreated human spirit.

GALATIANS 5:22
22 But the [first] **fruit of the Spirit** [that is, the fruit of the recreated human spirit] **is LOVE.** . . .

If you've been born again, then you've been made a new creature in Christ. The Bible says you've been translated out of the kingdom of darkness into the Kingdom of light (Col. 1:13).

You've been redeemed from spiritual death. Our text says you've been redeemed from the curse of the Law (Gal. 3:13).

The Curse of the Law Also Includes Sickness and Poverty

The curse of the Law, which is the penalty for breaking God's Law, includes *spiritual death, sickness and disease,* and *poverty.*

A lot of folks understand that in Christ, they've been redeemed from spiritual death and sickness and disease. But they don't realize that they've been redeemed from poverty.

Notice our text again.

GALATIANS 3:13,14,29
13 **Christ hath redeemed us from the curse of the law, being made a curse for us: for it is written, Cursed is every one that hangeth on a tree:**
14 **That the BLESSING OF ABRAHAM might come on the Gentiles through Jesus Christ; that we might receive the promise of the Spirit through faith.** . . .

29 And if ye be Christ's [are you His?], **then ARE YE ABRAHAM'S SEED, and HEIRS ACCORDING TO THE PROMISE.**

Again, "Christ hath redeemed us from the curse of the Law." But what exactly is the curse of the Law? There is one way to find out, and that's to go back to the Law.

The Law refers to the first five Books of the Bible called the Pentateuch. And the first curse that God mentioned was in Genesis: "... *in the day that thou eatest thereof* [of the tree of the knowledge of good and evil] *thou shalt surely DIE*" (Gen. 2:17).

Well, Adam didn't die that day physically when he and Eve ate of the tree of the knowledge of good and evil. It was more than 900 years before he died physically. But Adam *did* die *spiritually*.

So when we say Adam "died," we do not mean that he ceased to exist. We just simply mean that he became separated from God.

In other words, Adam was once alive unto God, but then Adam became spiritually dead. He broke that relationship and fellowship with God through his sin.

So then as we go back to these five Books of the Bible, first we find in Genesis that spiritual death is a curse of the Law. And we find in Galatians that we're redeemed from spiritual death right now in Christ (v. 13). We've passed from death unto life if we're in Him.

We also learn that physical death will be put underfoot, too, when Jesus comes again (1 Cor. 15:26).

We also find in Deuteronomy 28 that sickness and poverty are curses of the Law. Now in connection with sickness, we read that sickness is a curse for breaking God's Law.

> **DEUTERONOMY 28:58-61**
> **58 IF THOU WILT NOT OBSERVE TO DO ALL THE WORDS OF THIS LAW that are written in this book, that thou mayest fear this glorious and fearful name, THE LORD THY GOD;**
> **59 Then the Lord will make thy plagues wonderful, and the plagues of thy seed, even great plagues, and of long continuance, and sore sicknesses, and of long continuance.**
> **60 Moreover he will bring upon thee all the diseases of Egypt, which thou wast afraid of; and they shall cleave unto thee.**
> **61 Also EVERY SICKNESS, and EVERY PLAGUE, which is not written in the book of this law, them will the Lord bring upon thee, until thou be destroyed.**

And we can also read in Deuteronomy 28 that poverty is a curse of the Law.

> **DEUTERONOMY 28:15**
> **15 But it shall come to pass, IF THOU WILT NOT HEARKEN UNTO THE VOICE OF THE LORD THY GOD, TO OBSERVE TO DO ALL HIS COMMANDMENTS AND HIS STATUTES which I command thee this day; that ALL THESE CURSES SHALT COME UPON THEE, and overtake thee.**

Well, what are the curses that are referred to in that verse of Scripture?

DEUTERONOMY 28:16-19,38-40
16 CURSED shalt thou be in the city, and cursed shalt thou be in the field.
17 CURSED shall be thy basket and thy store.
18 CURSED shall be the fruit of thy body, and the fruit of thy land, the increase of thy kine, and the flocks of thy sheep.
19 CURSED shalt thou be when thou comest in, and cursed shalt thou be when thou goest out. . . .
38 Thou shalt carry much seed out into the field, and shalt gather but little in; for the locust shall consume it.
39 Thou shalt plant vineyards, and dress them, but shalt neither drink of the wine, nor gather the grapes; for the worms shall eat them.
40 Thou shalt have olive trees throughout all thy coasts, but thou shalt not anoint thyself with the oil; for thine olive shall cast his fruit.

Poverty Is a Curse; Prosperity Is a Blessing

Now those verses are certainly talking about poverty. But notice what it says in the first part of Deuteronomy 28 about the *blessings* for *keeping* God's Law.

DEUTERONOMY 28:1-14
1 And it shall come to pass, if thou shalt hearken diligently unto the voice of the Lord thy God, to observe and to do all his commandments which I command thee this day, that the Lord thy God will set thee on high above all nations of the earth:
2 And all these BLESSINGS shall come on thee, and overtake thee, if thou shalt hearken unto the voice of the Lord thy God.

3 BLESSED shalt thou be in the city, and blessed shalt thou be in the field.

4 BLESSED shall be the fruit of thy body, and the fruit of thy ground, and the fruit of thy cattle, the increase of thy kine, and the flocks of thy sheep.

5 BLESSED shall be thy basket and thy store.

6 BLESSED shalt thou be when thou comest in, and BLESSED shalt thou be when thou goest out.

7 The Lord shall cause thine enemies that rise up against thee to be smitten before thy face: they shall come out against thee one way, and flee before thee seven ways.

8 The Lord shall command the BLESSING upon thee in thy storehouses, and in all that thou settest thine hand unto; and he shall BLESS thee in the land which the Lord thy God giveth thee.

9 The Lord shall establish thee an holy people unto himself, as he hath sworn unto thee, if thou shalt keep the commandments of the Lord thy God, and walk in his ways.

10 And all people of the earth shall see that thou art called by the name of the Lord; and they shall be afraid of thee.

11 And the Lord shall make thee plenteous in goods, in the fruit of thy body, and in the fruit of thy cattle, and in the fruit of thy ground, in the land which the Lord sware unto thy fathers to give thee.

12 The Lord shall open unto thee his good treasure, the heaven to give the rain unto thy land in his season, and to bless all the work of thine hand: and thou shalt lend unto many nations, and thou shalt not borrow.

13 And the Lord shall make thee the head, and not the tail; and thou shalt be above only, and thou shalt not be beneath; if that thou hearken unto the commandments of the Lord thy God, which I command thee this day, to observe and to do them:

14 And thou shalt not go aside from any of the
words which I command thee this day, to the right
hand, or to the left, to go after other gods to serve
them.

Those are the blessings for keeping God's Law!

The Blessings Are for Us Today

A lot of people argue, "Well, the Lord just said that
to Israel. The blessings for obeying God's laws and commandments don't apply to us."

But while we're on the subject of the Law, turn to
Romans and Galatians.

Remember God said, *"O that there were such an
heart in them, that they would fear me, and KEEP ALL
MY COMMANDMENTS always, that it might be well
with them, and with their children for ever!"* (Deut.
5:29).

Yes, that was written to Israel under the Old
Covenant. But notice what the New Covenant says
about fulfilling or obeying God's laws and commandments.

ROMANS 13:8
8   Owe no man any thing, but to love one another:
for he that loveth another hath FULFILLED THE
LAW.

GALATIANS 5:14
14   For all THE LAW IS FULFILLED in one word,
even in this; Thou shalt love thy neighbour as thyself.

Mark that down and don't let it get away from you. Israel had to keep God's commandments in order to prosper, and under the New Covenant we have a commandment to keep, too, in order to prosper. It's the commandment or law of love.

Notice Paul was writing that to Gentile Christians, not to Hebrew Christians, so we know he's not talking just to the Israelites. So if *we're* walking in love, we've fulfilled the Law.

Let's continue reading in Romans 13.

ROMANS 13:9,10
9   For this, Thou shalt not commit adultery, Thou shalt not kill, Thou shalt not steal, Thou shalt not bear false witness, Thou shalt not covet; and if there be any other COMMANDMENT, it is briefly comprehended in this saying, namely, THOU SHALT LOVE THY NEIGHBOUR AS THYSELF.
10 Love worketh no ill to his neighbour: therefore LOVE IS THE FULFILLING OF THE LAW.

Now go back to Galatians 3:13 and 14 again and you'll see why we're not under the curse of the Law.

GALATIANS 3:13,14,29
13 CHRIST HATH REDEEMED US FROM THE CURSE OF THE LAW, being made a curse for us: for it is written, Cursed is every one that hangeth on a tree:
14 That the BLESSING OF ABRAHAM might come on the Gentiles through Jesus Christ; that we might receive the promise of the Spirit through faith. . . .

29 And if ye be Christ's, then are ye Abraham's seed, and heirs according to the PROMISE.

Well, what is Abraham's promise? What was it that God promised him?

Abraham's promise was threefold in nature. It was first a spiritual blessing. Second, it was a physical blessing. And third, it was a financial and material blessing.

So if the Israelites under the Old Covenant could receive God's blessings by keeping the Law, then if we under the New Covenant would walk in love, *we* would fulfill all the Law too. And the blessings should come on us also.

Notice Paul said, *"That the blessing of Abraham might come on the Gentiles through Jesus Christ . . ."* (Gal. 3:14).

Now when I first got hold of this, not only was I scraping the bottom of the barrel, I was *under* the barrel, and the *barrel* was on *top* of me!

But I believed the Word, praise God, and I kept believing it and preaching it, and I eventually got out from under the barrel, where I could at least start on the bottom! And I've been rising to the top ever since!

Don't think that it is just going to happen overnight, because it isn't. I ran up and down the hills and hollows of east Texas preaching prosperity when I didn't have a dime in my pocket. I had a car that was worn out with four bald tires and no spare at all. I looked like everything in the world *except* prosperous. But I just kept preaching prosperity because I knew it was so. I mean, if the Bible said it, it's so whether I've got it or not!

But, you see, God doesn't always settle up every Saturday night. For example, on the negative side, a lot of people think they're getting by with wrongdoing, because God doesn't always settle up every Saturday night.

And God doesn't always settle up the first of every month either. And He doesn't even always settle up the first of every year. But sooner or later, payday is coming. And, boy, you'd sure like to be around when payday comes if you've sown the right seed!

Now if you're sowing the *wrong* seed, you *don't* want to be around when payday comes. When you can see that you have sown the wrong seed, you'd better repent of it quickly and get it all under the blood. Then God will forgive you and forget it, and you can pick up and go on.

As I said, some people argue, "That prosperity business is all Old Testament though." But we've got ample Scripture that proves that the blessing of Abraham — including prosperity — is ours, too, under the New Testament.

In the Old Testament, according to Deuteronomy, poverty was to come upon God's people if they disobeyed Him. It was the curse that was to come upon them because they'd failed to do all of God's commandments and His statutes.

The Word of God teaches us that we've all sinned; we've all come short of the glory of God (Rom. 3:23). Therefore, the curse of the Law should also fall on us.

But, thank God, Galatians 3:13 said, *"Christ hath redeemed us from the curse of the law, being made a curse for us. . . ."*

Notice it said, *"Christ . . . [was] made a CURSE for US. . . ."* It didn't say, "Christ was made a curse for *Himself."*

No! He was made a curse for *us!* He became our Substitute. The curse fell on Him instead of upon us, and He bore it for us so that we could be free.

2 CORINTHIANS 8:9
9 For ye know the grace of our Lord Jesus Christ, that, though he was rich, yet for your sakes he became poor, that ye through his poverty might be rich.

Jesus Christ was rich. Yet for our sakes, He became poor, that we through His poverty, might be rich.

"Well," some people said, "that just means *spiritually* rich."

But, no. The only way Christ became poor was from the material standpoint. He didn't become poor spiritually, because the spiritually poor couldn't raise the dead! If they could, everybody would be doing that.

The spiritually poor could not turn water into wine. No, Jesus certainly wasn't poor spiritually.

Also, the spiritually poor couldn't have fed five thousand people with a little boy's lunch. But Jesus did. The spiritually poor could not have wrought the healings and the miracles that Jesus did.

God Wants His People To
Have Abundant Provision

Jesus became poor *materially* for us. He was our Substitute. And the Scripture says God will meet our needs according to His riches in glory *by* Christ Jesus (Phil. 4:19). Paul said that writing to the Church at Philippi, but it applies to believers everywhere.

PHILIPPIANS 4:19
19 But my God shall supply ALL YOUR NEED according to his riches in glory by Christ Jesus.

You see, this is talking about supplying *all* your need, including your financial and material needs as well as other needs. In fact, in this particular chapter in Philippians, Paul is talking about financial and material things, because in the previous verses, it says that these people had given of their material substance.

Let me say this. In Second Corinthians 8:9, it says, *"For ye know the grace of our Lord Jesus Christ, that, though he was rich, yet for your sakes he became poor, that YE through his poverty might be RICH."*

People misinterpret that word "rich." Someone said, "You mean God is going to make all of us millionaires?"

I didn't say that. The word "rich" according to the dictionary means *a full supply.*

In other words, it means *abundant provision.* Well, isn't that what Philippians 4:19 says, *"But my God shall supply ALL your need according to his riches in glory by Christ Jesus"*?

It didn't say, "But my God shall supply *half* of your need. . . ." No, it says *all* of them. It promises a full supply.

Jesus Himself said in Matthew 6:33, *"But seek ye first the kingdom of God, and his righteousness; and all these things shall be added unto you."*

Again, this verse didn't say, ". . . and all these things shall be *subtracted* from you."

No! These things shall be *added* unto you. Now what are "these things"? They are material things — something to eat, something to wear, and so on. In other words, "these things" is talking about the material things of life.

So many people think it is a mark of spirituality to go through life with the top of your hat out, the soles of your shoes worn out, the seat of your pants worn out, and just barely getting along.

But that isn't what Jesus said. He said, ". . . *all these things shall be ADDED unto you,"* not taken away from you.

Understanding the Law of Giving

In Luke 6:38 when Jesus said, "Give and it shall be given unto you," He was talking about more than one area. He was also talking from a financial standpoint.

The rest of that verse says, ". . . *good measure, pressed down, and shaken together, and running over, shall men give into your bosom. For with the same mea-*

sure that ye mete withal it shall be measured to you again." I believe Jesus spoke the truth.

Notice Jesus said, *". . . shall MEN give into your bosom. . . ."* Now God is behind it, of course, but *men* will give unto your bosom.

I remember one time I was holding a meeting in Dallas, Texas. A friend of mine lived there. He came to my meeting, and I took him to his house after one of the services. He handed me a $100 bill. You've got to realize, back then a $100 bill looked like $2,000 today.

This man taught the older men's Bible class in quite a large church in that town. He said, "Brother Hagin, you know I pay my tithes and give offerings at my church. This money that I'm giving you is beyond tithes and offerings. I want you to know that."

My friend continued, "We had a fellow in our church — an evangelist — who preached a meeting for us. The very first night he preached on Luke 6:38. Then he didn't preach on that, but he read the same text every night for two weeks before he preached.

"When we came to the close of the meeting, he said, 'Now the pastor does not know that I'm going to do this, but I want to take up an offering for this church to purchase a new air-conditioning system.'"

This was many years ago when money was money. I mean, it was more than forty years ago. The church's air-conditioning system had gone out, and they needed to buy a new one. The previous system was so old and outdated, they were also going to have to put in some more air ducts. It was going to cost them about $10,000.

My friend continued, "This evangelist just said, 'I'm going to lay my Bible right here on the altar. I'm going to open it to Luke 6:38. I don't want anybody to give anything that he can afford to give. I want you to give what you *can't* afford to give and come and lay it on that verse. Believe it. Then say, "Lord, I'm acting on that verse. With what measure I mete, it shall be measured to me again."'"

Well, giving something you *can't* afford to give is a bigger measure than giving something you *can* afford to give. You remember in Mark 12:42 and Luke 21:2, Jesus stood where the people were casting in their money, and that poor widow woman came by and put in two mites.

Jesus said, "She gave more than all of them" (Mark 12:43; Luke 21:3). Why? Because she gave everything she had.

So my friend who taught the men's Sunday school class said, "Three businessmen had talked to me and asked me to pray. They talked to me at the close of Sunday school as we were going into the main auditorium for morning worship.

"Their businesses were just in disarray. In fact, bankers and financial advisors told two of them to take bankruptcy. The other man's business was not quite that far gone."

My friend said, "I knew if those men gave anything, it would be something they couldn't afford to give because they didn't have anything to give!

"But one of the businessmen told me afterward that he marched down there to that altar and put his last three hundred dollars on the Bible. Another one of the businessmen who was in trouble financially gave five hundred dollars. And the other man who was just on the verge of bankruptcy gave two hundred dollars."

The Sunday school teacher said, "I am a witness to the fact that in thirty days' time, every one of them was out of the red and in the black in their businesses."

They honored God, and God honored them!

Now they didn't give just to get. That would be self-ish. They wanted to see the work of God go forward.

Keep things in the right perspective. In other words, keep your attitudes and motives right.

Yet, on the other hand, when you give, you still have a right to believe God for a return on your giving.

Honor God With Your Faith, Your Giving, And Right Motives

For instance, in one church I pastored, one of my deacons said to me, "You know, Brother Hagin, I've been saved thirteen years. I have paid my tithes all these years, but if anything has ever happened to me extraordinarily in the way of finances, I don't know it."

This deacon had a good job in the oil field with one of the oil companies, and he made good money. Of course, he still had his good job, so that was a blessing. And when the company gave raises, he got one. But nothing *extraordinary* in the way of finances had ever happened to him.

He told me, "I'll be honest with you, Brother Hagin. I never have heard anybody really teach on the subject of tithing and giving offerings. They just said you're supposed to do so, so I just did it."

Well, again, his motive was all wrong. This man just did something because somebody else told him to do it. It wasn't that he even believed it! In fact, he told me, "Really, I was afraid *not* to tithe and give offerings."

You see, he was giving out of fear and not out of faith, so naturally it didn't work.

I said to him, "First of all, if you'll repent, the Lord will forgive you for not having the right motive.

"And, second, from now on when you put in your tithes on Sunday morning, you thank the Lord, first of all for your salvation — that you are a child of God.

"Keep your motive right. Say, 'Lord, I'm giving because I love You, not because I'm afraid of You. And I'm not paying my tithes just because somebody told me to do it or just because somebody preached it. I may not understand it, but I see that it is in the Word.

"'So I'm paying my tithes because I love You. And I love the church, and I want to see it go forward and succeed. That's why I'm paying tithes and giving offerings. And I expect You to honor Your Word, and I thank You for doing it. You said, "Them that honor Me, I'll honor."'"

When God said that in the Old Testament, He was talking about bringing in the firstfruits. Proverbs 3:9 says, *"Honour the Lord with thy substance, and with the firstfruits of all thine increase."* He said, "Them that honor Me, I'll honor" (1 Sam. 2:30).

Then I told the deacon to say, "Lord, You said, 'Give and it shall be given unto you.' So I'm putting this in the offering by faith."

Then I told the man to come back and tell me what happened.

It wasn't thirty days before he came back, just grinning. "It's working!" he said.

For years his paying tithes and giving offerings had not worked. Now why? *Because he didn't do it in faith.* His motives and his attitude were all wrong. But when he got his motives and attitude right, he got blessed.

Don't Be Robbed of Your New Testament Blessing!

The Bible said in Hebrews 7:8, *"And here men that die receive tithes; but there he receiveth them, of whom it is witnessed that he liveth."*

Now almost any time you get something good from the Scriptures, people will say, "Well, that's just for the Jews. That's not for us nowadays." But the Book of Hebrews is in the New Testament, and the writer of Hebrews was writing to Hebrews under the New Covenant. And he said, *". . . here men that die receive tithes; but there he receiveth them, of whom it is witnessed that he liveth."* That's talking about Jesus!

From the natural standpoint, it looks like "men that die" receive tithes, but actually *". . . he [Jesus] receiveth*

them, of whom it is witnessed that HE LIVETH." Well,
Jesus said, *"I am he that liveth, and was dead; and,
behold, I am alive for evermore . . ."* (Rev. 1:18)!

So you see, Abraham's blessing — the blessing for
keeping God's commands, His Word — is ours because
of Jesus Christ! He is the One who lives and is alive
forevermore! Abraham's blessing includes financial
prosperity, and it's for us today.

> **GALATIANS 3:14,29**
> **14 That the blessing of Abraham MIGHT COME
> ON THE GENTILES THROUGH JESUS CHRIST;
> that we might receive the promise of the Spirit
> through faith. . . .**
> **29 And if ye be Christ's, then ARE YE ABRAHAM'S
> SEED, AND HEIRS according to the promise.**

Abraham's blessing is ours! But we need to understand exactly what was Abraham's blessing. Well, we
know it was a threefold blessing. First, God promised
Abraham that He was going to make him rich (Gen.
12:2,3; 13:2).

Someone said, "You mean, God said He is going to
make all of us rich?"

Yes, that's what I mean.

"Well, do you mean He's going to make all of us *millionaires?*"

No. Again, that word "rich" according to the dictionary means *a full supply.* I believe there is a full supply
spiritually, physically, and in every way in Christ Jesus.

Thank God for abundant provision through Christ Jesus!

I held a meeting in 1954 for Brother A. A. Swift in New Jersey, just across the river from New York. He was an Assemblies of God minister and an executive presbyter of the Assemblies of God denomination.

I stayed in the home of Brother Swift. He was about seventy at the time, and I was thirty-six. He had received the baptism of the Holy Ghost in 1908 and had gone out as a missionary to China in 1911 with his wife and two children.

There was no missionary organization in Pentecostal circles at that time, so Brother Swift had no support from those circles. There was a mission in London, England, that supported him, however. The only problem was, that organization didn't believe in speaking in tongues.

Brother Swift told me that as he would go to his place of prayer, God kept dealing with him that really he was receiving money under false pretenses. He couldn't preach the baptism in the Holy Ghost and speaking in tongues to the people because the organization supporting him didn't believe in it. Privately, however, he got several people in that country filled with the Spirit.

He said, "Lord, what am I going to do?"

The Lord said, "Just send in your resignation to the organization."

That organization paid him $103 a month. That meant $1,236 for the year. He said, "Lord, what am I going to do? Nobody else is going to support me and my wife and two children here in China!"

The Lord said, "Turn the church over to one of the organization's other missionaries. Go over to another city and start a new work."

Just think about it! He was supposed to start a new work in China in 1912! It was tough enough to start a new work in *America* in 1912. It's still tough enough today. You've got to do it by faith.

So Brother Swift said, "I did what the Lord said, but I still questioned the Lord, 'What are we going to do? We don't have any support.'

"The Lord spoke to my heart and said, 'Didn't you know I promised to make you rich?'"

I'd received revelation along this line myself, but Brother Swift just confirmed it. I hadn't preached it yet. I wanted to prove it out first.

I'd seen that truth in 1950 when the Lord showed it to me. And it was working fine for me personally. As I just began to suggest some things to Brother Swift about it, he said, "I see God has been talking to you. Now let me tell you what God said to me in 1911 when I resigned from that missionary organization.

"God said, 'Didn't I promise to make you rich?'" (Really, there were some areas I didn't see until Brother Swift filled me in on them.)

Brother Swift answered the Lord, "No, I didn't know You promised to make me rich. If You did, I'd sure be glad to know it. Where is that found?"

The Spirit of God showed him where it was written in the Bible.

GALATIANS 3:13,14
13 Christ hath redeemed us from the curse of the law, being made a curse for us: for it is written, Cursed is every one that hangeth on a tree:
14 That the blessing of Abraham might come on the Gentiles through Jesus Christ; that we might receive the promise of the Spirit through faith.

So Brother Swift told me, "I turned in my resignation and went over and started this other church. And for the first six months of 1912, it looked like my wife and I and our two children were going to starve to death in China. It looked like it wasn't going to work."

You see, you can't always go by what it looks like. There always comes a test to your faith. The trial of your faith, the Bible said, is more precious than gold.

Like I said, God doesn't settle up the first of the year or the first of the month or even every six months.

But Brother Swift said to me, "Before 1912 was out, I checked up on it, and God had given me $3,750 in American dollars."

Now $3,750 in 1912 was a lot of money! Brother Swift *had* been getting $1,236, so the amount the Lord gave him was three times as much as he had received from the mission that had supported him.

You know, dear friends, Brother Swift was glad to find out that God promised to make him rich. Did God make him a millionaire? No, but Brother Swift and his family were abundantly provided for. They had a full supply.

Some folks have thought it was a sin to have money. But, you know, most people are not poor because they've *honored* God. Rather, they're poor because they've *dis*honored Him.

Some folks have said to me, "Brother Hagin, I'm afraid of money, because don't you know the Bible said, 'Money is the root of all evil'?"

No, the Bible didn't say that. The Bible said, *"For the LOVE of money is the root of all evil . . ."* (1 Tim. 6:10).

The *love* of money is the root of all evil. It is not wrong to have money; it is wrong for *money* to have *you*. It is wrong for money to be your master.

God wants His people to have their needs met and to have a full supply. So believe His Word that says we are redeemed from the curse of poverty. Exercise your faith and keep your motives and attitudes right in your giving. As you do, you'll get blessed because Abraham's blessing belongs to you!

Chapter 2
Qualifications for Walking In Prosperity

God wants to prosper His children. He is concerned about us and wants us to have good things in life. He said in His Word, *"If ye be willing and obedient, ye shall eat the good of the land"* (Isa. 1:19). But God doesn't want us to put "eating the good of the land" first.

Moses was an example of someone who didn't put those things first. For example, Moses, who was raised by an Egyptian, refused to be called the son of Pharaoh's daughter when he grew up.

> **HEBREWS 11:24-26**
> **24 By faith Moses, when he was come to years, refused to be called the son of Pharaoh's daughter;**
> **25 Choosing rather to suffer affliction with the people of God, than to enjoy the pleasures of sin for a season;**
> **26 Esteeming the reproach of Christ greater riches than the treasures in Egypt: for he had respect unto the recompence of the reward.**

Think about what Moses refused! He was the son of Pharaoh's daughter — and he was in line for the throne! Moses had prestige, honor, and wealth. He had all the things the world had to offer. Yet Moses esteemed the reproach of Christ as greater riches than all the treasures of Egypt. Moses saw a difference between the people of God and the people of the world.

Some people are more interested in making a dollar than they are in serving God. But spiritual things must come first if you are going to be spiritual. You must esteem the things of God — spiritual things — more than earthly things.

One qualification for prospering is to esteem earthly things lightly. You cannot put earthly things above spiritual things and expect to prosper as God desires you to.

No, it's not wrong to have money. It's wrong for *money* to have *you*. It's wrong for money to be your ruler or master or for you to consume finances on your own lusts.

God *wants* you to prosper financially! But your prosperity depends on your putting first things first. There are qualifications involved.

In the Old Testament, God told the Israelites to keep His statutes and walk in His commandments (Deuteronomy 28). Well, that's spiritual prosperity to put God's Word first and to walk in the truth. God desires the same today.

Under the inspiration of the Holy Spirit, John writes, *"Beloved, I wish above all things that thou mayest prosper and be in health, even as thy soul prospereth"* (3 John 2). In the next two verses, John goes on to say that he had no greater joy than to hear that God's people are indeed walking in the truth of God's Word.

God told the Israelites, "Walk in My statutes and keep My commandments. Do that which is right in My sight, and I'll take sickness away from the midst of you, and the number of your days I will fulfill" (Exod. 15:26; 23:26). That's *physical* prosperity or divine healing and health.

The Lord also talked to the Israelites about their "basket and store" being blessed, their barns being filled, and about them being the head and not the tail (Deut. 28:1-14; Prov. 3:10). That's *material* prosperity. But notice their *physical* and *material* prosperity depended upon their *spiritual* prosperity.

3 JOHN 2
2   Beloved, I wish above all things that thou mayest PROSPER and BE IN HEALTH, EVEN AS thy SOUL PROSPERETH.

John is talking about financial or material prosperity, physical prosperity, and spiritual prosperity. Notice that material and physical prosperity are dependent upon spiritual prosperity.

Put First Things First

The first Psalm is so beautiful and further confirms that God wants His people to prosper.

PSALM 1:1-3
1   Blessed is the man that walketh not in the counsel of the ungodly, nor standeth in the way of

sinners, nor sitteth in the seat of the scornful.
2   But his delight is in the law of the Lord; and in
his law doth he meditate day and night.
3   And he shall be like a tree planted by the rivers
of water, that bringeth forth his fruit in his season;
his leaf also shall not wither; and whatsoever he
doeth shall PROSPER.

So you see, God wants us to prosper. However, our
need is to evaluate things as they should be evaluated —
to esteem earthly things lightly and to put first things
first.

Everyone thinks the preacher ought to be that way.
For example, if a pastor happened to take the pastorate
of a church where he makes more money, many people
would think, *He just took that church so he'd be better
paid.* Yet they themselves would think nothing in the
world about taking a better job! They would probably
even think nothing about moving off to another location
where there wasn't a good church — only one in which
they'd all backslide!

Years ago back in the Depression days, I was in a
particular town on business and ran into a certain fellow on the street. He had a good job making good
money, but he'd been offered a job in another town making $50 more a month. That was a lot of money back
then. I knew many men with families who didn't even
make $50 a month. But this gentleman was already
making a good salary and had the chance to make an
even better one.

He told me, "Did you know I was moving?"

He was a member of a Full Gospel church, and I happened to know that there wasn't a Full Gospel church in the town where he was moving.

I said to him, "What kind of church is there in that town?"

"What do you mean?" he asked.

"Is there a Full Gospel church there?" I asked him.

He answered, "I don't know; I never thought about it."

I said, "No, you were only interested in the extra fifty dollars a month. But wait a minute.

"I knew you before you came into Pentecost. I happen to know that you'd spent all of your money on medical bills for your wife. Doctors thought she had cancer of the stomach.

"But when she received the baptism of the Holy Ghost, without anybody even praying for her, she was healed.

"I also happen to know that you had spent thousands of dollars on one of your sons who had a physical ailment. But since you began attending a church where divine healing is taught, your boy has been in good health."

"Yes," the man said.

"Well," I said, "I also happen to know that there's not a Full Gospel church in that town." (It would have been different if he had been to going to that town to start a Full Gospel church, but he wasn't. He wasn't capable of starting a church.)

The man said, "You know, I never thought about that."

I said, "You'd be taking your family out of a good Full Gospel church, where the Gospel is being preached and where you've been blessed immeasurably, all for fifty dollars more a month. I won't tell you not to do it, but I will tell you to pray about it."

The next time I saw this fellow, he said to me, "I'm not going; I don't believe it's worth it."

Another man and his wife came to a meeting I was holding in Dallas. The woman's mother, who had gone to be with the Lord, was a member of a church I'd pastored years before. She had been a wonderful Christian and a great blessing to my wife and me.

I knew that this wife hadn't always been a Christian. Years before when she would visit her mother, her mother told me she wasn't saved. But she had later gotten saved, received the Holy Spirit, and attended a fine Full Gospel church.

But when I saw this woman with her husband at my meeting and asked, "Where do you attend church now?" the woman said, "Oh, we don't go anywhere."

"What do you mean? I thought you were a member at such-and-such church."

"Oh, there's not even a church there anymore," she answered. "It was closed down for a while until another pastor came and took over it. Then the pastor backslid and quit preaching. We just go here and there to church every so often. While you're in town, we're coming to your meetings."

I asked: "Well, where do you pay your tithes?"

"We don't pay our tithes," she answered. "We used to pay them, but we quit. We used to pay our tithes to the pastor, but he backslid."

"Well," I said, "you don't have to backslide just because he did."

I didn't know whether they appreciated me telling them that or not, but I continued: "You need to get in a church somewhere and work for God and worship the Lord. You need to get hooked up instead of going from church to church. A rolling stone never gathers any moss.

"Besides that, we need each other. We need the fellowship of one another."

Someone said, "I can stay home and be as good a Christian as anybody."

You can't do it. The Bible says, *"Not forsaking the assembling of ourselves together, as the manner of some is; but exhorting one another: and so much the more, as ye see the day approaching"* (Heb. 10:25).

We see that day approaching — the coming of the Lord. We need one another. No, we don't go to church because we're in love with the pastor or the pastor's wife or the Sunday school teacher. We should go to church because we love God and want to worship Him.

Some people lose their children to the devil because the parents don't put first things first. The children grow up physically and get away from God because the wrong example was set for them.

But you can't just tell children what to do. The Bible says, *"TRAIN up a child in the way he should go: and when he is old, he will not depart from it"* (Prov. 22:6). You have to set the right example. You have to be a person of faith yourself. To do that, you have to put first things first.

F. F. Bosworth said, "Some people wonder why they can't have faith for healing. They feed their body three hot meals a day, and their spirit one cold snack a week."

Folks could have faith for healing or for anything the Word of God promises — prosperity, a healthy, happy family, long life — if they would just put first things first.

Determine in your heart to put spiritual things first and to esteem earthly things lightly. Put God first, even before your own self. You'll be blessed spiritually, physically, and in every way — you and your family as well.

> **ISAIAH 1:19**
> **19 If ye be willing and obedient, ye shall eat the good of the land.**

I left my last church in 1949 and went out into what we call field ministry. I went from church to church holding revival meetings. I'd been out there for a year, and I got hold of the verse that said, *"If ye be willing and obedient, ye shall eat the good of the land"* (Isa. 1:19). But, boy, I sure wasn't eating the good of the land!

I had worn my car out. I had to sell it for junk. I had three notes at three different banks, and I got just enough from the sale of the car to pay the interest on the notes, renew them, and buy the kids a few clothes.

I had all of this written down, and I went to the Lord in prayer about my financial situation. I was away from home holding a meeting. I was fasting, and every day I talked to the Lord about my situation.

I said, "Lord, You see that I obeyed You when You told me to leave that church I was pastoring and to go out on the field. I did what You said to do. And You said, 'If you'll be willing and obedient, you'll eat the good of the land.'

"Now, Lord, here's what my church paid me, *plus* they furnished the parsonage — the best parsonage we'd ever lived in. All the utilities were paid, and probably half of what we ate was paid for because people just constantly brought food to the parsonage for us."

And then I said to the Lord, "They also sent us to every convention we needed to attend. The church paid our way there and back, and a lot of times, they'd buy me a new suit and my wife a new dress." They wanted us to go to those conventions looking good because we were representing them.

I showed the Lord the figures I had written down. "But now, Lord," I continued, "here is my gross income for *this* year. This is every penny I received this year." It was $1,200 *less* in actual cash than what I received the previous year.

Besides that, now I had to pay traveling expenses, my own rent, and utilities just from the money I received holding meetings in the field. Besides *that*, I had to pay my own way to the conventions that were necessary for me to attend.

So, you see, all that took a big chunk out of my salary — about half of it.

I added, "Lord, see how much better off I would have been if I'd stayed where I was? And they wanted me to stay. The church board said, 'Brother Hagin, if you'll stay with us, we'll just vote you in as pastor indefinitely. Just stay here till Jesus comes.'"

Actually, I would have liked to have done that because we were the most comfortable we'd ever been in all of our years of pastoral work.

We were living in the best parsonage. We were getting the most salary we'd ever received. The church was doing well. But the Lord said, "Go," so I went.

I said, "Now, Lord, I obeyed You. If You hadn't spoken to me, I was perfectly satisfied from the natural standpoint to stay where I was." (I said from a *natural* standpoint, not from a *spiritual* standpoint, because when we're spiritual, we want to obey God. But the flesh is not always willing.)

I told the Lord, "I obeyed You. But now we're living in a three-room apartment. My children are not adequately housed. They're not adequately clothed. They're not adequately fed. We're *sure* not eating the good of the land."

You Must Be Willing *and* Obedient

I was telling this to the Lord and quoting Isaiah 1:19. And about the third day, the Lord said to me in just the same way He talks to other believers — we call it the still, small voice. He said, "The reason you're not eating the good of the land is that you don't *qualify*."

I said, "What do You mean, *I don't qualify*? I obeyed You. That scripture said if you would be willing and obedient . . ."

"That's what it says," the Lord answered. "You qualify on the *obedient* side, but you don't qualify on the *willing* side. So you don't qualify."

I don't mind telling you ahead of time, God's Word is always true! The Bible said, ". . . *yea, let God be true, but every man a liar* . . ." (Rom. 3:4). And if *you're* not eating the good of the land, it may be because you don't qualify.

So the Lord told me, "Yes, you obeyed Me, all right, in leaving that church, but you weren't *willing*."

Now don't tell me it takes a long time to get willing. I know better! When the Lord said that to me, I got willing in ten seconds! I just made a little adjustment in my spirit. Then I said, "Lord, now I'm ready. I'm ready to eat the good of the land. I'm willing. *I* know I'm willing. *You* know I'm willing. And *the devil* knows I'm willing."

Of course, a part of being willing and obedient is keeping your motives pure. God sees the heart of man, and He knows what attitudes are motivating him (1 Sam. 16:7). If a person's motive is not right, he needs to repent and make the necessary adjustments. God is not going to bless someone whose motives are impure. No, that person has to be willing and obedient and have the right motives.

I got the willing and obedient part settled. And I knew I had the right motive. But on the other hand, if I was going to eat the good of the land, the Lord still had to change my thinking. My thinking had to get straightened out and come in line with what the Word says on the subject of prosperity.

These are some of the reasons why people are not eating the good of the land. And it could simply be because they're not abiding in the Book that tells them how to do it!

Learn To Think in Line With God's Word

You see, a lot of times, our thinking is wrong. It's not in line with the Bible. And if our *thinking* is wrong, then our *believing* is going to be wrong. And if our *believing* is wrong, then our *talking* is going to be wrong.

You've got to get all three of them — your thinking, your believing, and your speaking — synchronized with the Word of God.

God has given us His Word to get our thinking straightened out. In my case, God knew my thinking was wrong because, you see, in the denomination I'd been brought up in, we were taught that it was wrong to have anything. I began my ministry in this particular denomination, and they were great about praying for the pastor: "Lord, You keep him humble, and we'll keep him poor." And they thought they were doing God a favor!

Then in 1937 I was baptized in the Holy Ghost and spoke with other tongues. I got the left foot of fellowship from my denomination and came over among the Pentecostals.

They were *doubly* that way about praying for the pastor. In other words, they doubled up on their praying: "Lord, You keep him humble, and we'll keep him poor!"

And you always heard preachers say, "I don't want any of this world's goods," because they thought there was something wrong with this world's goods.

But turn to Psalm 50, and I'll show you why it's not wrong to have this world's goods.

> **PSALM 50:10,12**
> **10 For every beast of the forest IS MINE, and the cattle upon a thousand hills. . . .**
> **12 If I were hungry, I would not tell thee: for THE WORLD IS MINE, and the fulness thereof** [that means that everything that's in the world is God's].

Mark those verses in your Bible. Meditate on those verses and confess them.

The Lord showed me these verses because He had to get my thinking straightened out. I thought it was wrong to have anything. I thought a person ought to go through life with the seat of his britches worn out, the top of his hat worn out, the soles of his shoes worn out, and live on Barely-Get-Along Street way down at the end of the block right next to Grumble Alley!

That's the kind of thinking many people in the church world have today. But they're not thinking in line with God's Word.

Chapter 3
Our Authority
In the Area of Finances

As I continued to wait before the Lord about my finances, spending time in the Word with prayer and fasting, He said to me, "Go back to the Book of beginnings."

Now that I was willing and obedient, He was showing me how to get my thinking straightened out. I knew what He was talking about when He said the Book of beginnings — He meant the Book of Genesis.

The Lord went on to tell me that He made the world and the fullness thereof. He created it. He said to me, "Then I created My man, Adam." And the Lord saw that it was not good for man to be alone, so He created Eve.

The Lord said to them, "I give you dominion over all the works of My hands" (Gen. 1:26, 28). Over how much? Over *all* the works of His hands!

GENESIS 1:1, 26-30
1 In the beginning God created the heaven and the earth. . . .
26 And God said, Let us make man in our image, after our likeness: and let them HAVE DOMINION

> over the fish of the sea, and over the fowl of the
> air, and over the cattle, and over all the earth, and
> OVER EVERY CREEPING THING THAT CREEP-
> ETH UPON THE EARTH.
> 27 So God created man in his own image, in the
> image of God created he him; male and female cre-
> ated he them.
> 28 And God blessed them, and God said unto
> them, Be fruitful, and multiply, and replenish the
> earth, and subdue it: and HAVE DOMINION over
> the fish of the sea, and over the fowl of the air, and
> OVER EVERY LIVING THING THAT MOVETH
> UPON THE EARTH.
> 29 And God said, Behold, I have given you every
> herb bearing seed, which is upon the face of all the
> earth, and every tree, in the which is the fruit of a
> tree yielding seed; to you it shall be for meat.
> 30 And to every beast of the earth, and to every
> fowl of the air, and to every thing that creepeth
> upon the earth, wherein there is life, I have given
> every green herb for meat: and it was so.

After the Lord showed me these scriptures in Psalm
50:10-12 and Genesis chapter 1, He said, "There's
another scripture that says, *'The silver is mine, and the
gold is mine, saith the Lord of hosts'"* (Haggai 2:8). He
then said, "They're all Mine, not because they're in My
possession, but because I created them.

"But who do you think I created the cattle upon a
thousand hills for? Who do you think I created the silver and the gold for?

"Who do you think I created the world and the fullness thereof for? For the devil and *his* crowd? No. I
made them for My man Adam.

"But," the Lord continued, "My people have wrong thinking."

You see, the devil can run a night club, and he and his crowd don't mind spending thousands of dollars to put up an electric sign to let everyone know what it is. But if somebody puts up a nice sign for the church, there are people who will object to that. The devil's got them hoodwinked.

How come the devil and his crowd have most of the silver and gold since the Lord made it for Adam? Did you ever wonder about that?

The Lord said, "The silver and gold are not all here for the devil and his crowd. I made it all for My man Adam, but then he committed high treason against Me."

Adam sold out! Adam committed treason. He surrendered it all to Satan.

LUKE 4:5-8
5 And the devil, taking him [Jesus] up into an high mountain, shewed unto him ALL THE KINGDOMS OF THE WORLD in a moment of time.
6 And the devil said unto him, All this power [authority] will I give thee, and the glory of them: FOR THAT IS DELIVERED UNTO ME; and to whomsoever I will I give it.
7 If thou therefore wilt worship me, all shall be thine.
8 And Jesus answered and said unto him, Get thee behind me, Satan: for it is written, Thou shalt worship the Lord thy God, and him only shalt thou serve.

When the Lord created Adam, Adam was *in one sense* the god of this world because God created the world and the fullness thereof and turned it over to him (Gen. 1:26,28).

But we read in Second Corinthians 4:4 that *Satan* is the god of this world. Well, Satan wasn't the god of this world to begin with. So how did he *become* the god of this world? *Because Adam committed treason and sold out to him.* Now Adam didn't have a *moral* right to disobey God and sell out to Satan, but he had a *legal* right to do it.

Notice Luke 4:6 and 7. We know Adam turned his dominion over to Satan because Satan said to Jesus, ". . . *All this power will I give thee, and the glory of them: FOR THAT IS DELIVERED UNTO ME; and to whomsoever I will I give it. If thou therefore wilt worship me, all shall be thine.*"

Some folks said, "Well, that wasn't even Satan's to give." But if it wasn't Satan's to give, then it wouldn't have been any temptation to Jesus. And if it wasn't a temptation, then why does the Bible say He was *tempted* (Luke 4:2)?

It's ridiculous to think Jesus wasn't actually tempted by the devil. Although we know that Jesus is deity, we must also realize that in His humanity, He was tempted (Heb. 4:15). Satan showed Jesus all the kingdoms of the world in a moment of time and said to Him, "All this authority will I give Thee and the glory of it, for *it is delivered unto me.*" Who delivered it to him? *Adam did!*

The Lord told me all this and related it to faith for finances. As I was praying and waiting before Him, He said to me by the Holy Spirit: "The money you need is down there. It isn't up here in Heaven. I don't have any American dollars up here. I'm not going to rain any money down from Heaven because if I did, it would be counterfeit. And I'm not a counterfeiter."

Afterward, I remembered what Jesus said in Luke 6.

> **LUKE 6:38**
> **38 Give, and it shall be given unto you; good measure, pressed down, and shaken together, and running over, shall MEN give into your bosom. . . .**

You see, when men give unto you, God's behind it, all right, but that verse says, ". . . *shall MEN give into your bosom. . . .*" That's why the Lord said, "The money you need is down there. I'm not going to rain any money down from Heaven. I don't have any money up here. If I did rain money out of Heaven, it would be counterfeit. And I'm not a counterfeiter."

After the Lord showed me this, He said, "Whatever you need, you just claim it."

We Have Been Given Authority in Christ

The reason we have a right to claim our needs met is, Jesus came to the earth and defeated Satan. We're *in* the world but we're not *of* the world (John 15:19), yet we still have to live in this world. So we must use our

God-given authority to enforce Satan's defeat and enjoy the blessings of God that we have in Christ, including financial prosperity.

> **COLOSSIANS 1:12**
> **12 Giving thanks unto the Father, which hath made us meet** [or able] **TO BE PARTAKERS OF THE INHERITANCE OF THE SAINTS IN LIGHT.**

That's something that belongs to us in *this* life!

Now notice the next verse. *Here* is the inheritance of the saints in light that the Father gives as a result of Jesus' defeating Satan.

> **COLOSSIANS 1:13**
> **13 Who** [the Father] **HATH DELIVERED US FROM THE POWER OF DARKNESS, and HATH TRANS-LATED US INTO THE KINGDOM OF HIS DEAR SON.**

Notice this scripture says, ". . . *HATH delivered us*. . . ." In other words, Jesus is not *going* to deliver us; He already *has* delivered us.

The rest of that verse says, ". . . *from the POWER of darkness, and hath translated us into the kingdom of his dear Son.*" Notice that word "power" again. There are several different Greek words that are translated "power" in the New Testament. This one in Colossians 1:13 means *authority*.

In other words, God hath delivered us from the *authority* or *dominion* of darkness. Well, what's the

authority or dominion of darkness? That's Satan's kingdom. Remember what Jesus said through the apostle
John in First John 5:19: ". . . *the whole world lieth in
wickedness.*" He's talking about spiritual darkness and
spiritual death.

We're *in* the world, all right. But we're not *of* the
world. The whole world lieth in darkness, but God hath
delivered us from the power of darkness, and hath
translated us into the Kingdom of His dear Son (Col.
1:13)! That's our inheritance!

Now turn to Colossians chapter 2.

> **COLOSSIANS 2:13-15**
> **13 And you, being dead in your sins and the uncir-
> cumcision of your flesh, hath he quickened** [or
> made alive] **together with him** [Christ], **having for-
> given you all trespasses;**
> **14 Blotting out the handwriting of ordinances
> that was against us, which was contrary to us, and
> took it out of the way, nailing it to his cross;**
> **15 And having spoiled** [put to nought or reduced to
> nothing] **principalities and powers** [the evil forces of
> the enemy], **he made a shew of them openly, tri-
> umphing over them in it.**

Hallelujah! *We* are the triumphant ones because of
what Jesus did. He didn't do it for Himself; He didn't
need it. What Jesus did, He did for *me.* He did it for
you. He did it for *us!* He became our Substitute. He took
our place. And when He defeated the enemy, praise
God, it was written down to our credit that *we* defeated
the enemy in Him. Therefore, we have the authority to

tell Satan to take his hands off what belongs to us —
including our finances.

Yet some folk are going around talking about the
"warring" Church. They don't know that Jesus has
already whipped Satan!

"Yes," someone said, "but don't you know Paul told
Timothy to be a good soldier [2 Tim. 2:3]. Therefore,
we're soldiers, and we're in the army."

Yes, but it's an *occupation* army! In other words, we
just come in "mopping up" behind what Jesus has
already won! Hallelujah! It's a *triumphant* Church, not
a *warring* Church!

You see, Jesus made a show of principalities and
powers openly. That is, He made a show of them before
three worlds — Heaven, earth, and hell — *triumphing*
over these powers through the Cross (Col. 2:15)!

I wish I could get that over to Charismatics. Too
many Charismatics are like young mockingbirds that
have just been hatched. They don't even have their eyes
open yet, but their mouths are wide open. Anybody can
just poke anything in the world down them!

And like little birds, those Christians will believe
almost everything they hear and swallow it. But, no.
Close your mouths and open your eyes, and measure
what you hear by the Word of God! The Word declares
we are more than conquerors and that we have overcome the world through Jesus Christ. The Word
declares that we are redeemed from the curse of the
Law — from poverty, sickness, and spiritual death.

The Word also says we have been given authority over the devil in Jesus' Name and that we can use that authority and claim our financial needs met. So learn to think and speak in line with what the Word says. You can have what the Word says you can have, and you are who the Word says you are. You are born of God!

1 JOHN 4:4
4   YE ARE OF GOD, little children, and have overcome them: because greater is he that is in you, than he that is in the world.

Now in the Old Testament, there are long pages of genealogy — and it was necessary for the Israelites to have their genealogy recorded. There were pages and pages of "So-and-so begat So-and-so" (all those names you can hardly pronounce!).

After a while, you can get tired of reading all those names, and you just want to skip over them and start reading something else!

But in the New Testament, we can write our genealogy in four little words: "I-am-of-God." Hallelujah! If you have been born again, say this out loud: "I am of God!" (1 John 4:4).

I was watching a so-called Christian television program some time ago. It was one of those talk shows, and there was a woman on the show as a guest. She sang, and then the host talked to her. She said that she had to leave her husband and divorce him because she had to find out who she was. I thought, *She ought to get saved so she'd* know *who she is*!

"I don't know who I am" or "I've got to find out who I am." Unsaved people talk like that, because we who are saved *know* who we are! We are of God! We have been born again. We are new creatures in Christ Jesus!

Look in First John again in the third chapter.

> **1 JOHN 3:1**
> **1   Behold, what manner of love the Father hath bestowed upon us, that we should be called the SONS OF GOD: therefore the world knoweth us not, because it knew him not.**

That's who we are! We know *exactly* who we are. According to the Word, we are "of God"! We are sons of God. We are new creatures in Christ Jesus. His Spirit bears witness with our spirit that we are the children of God (Rom. 8:16).

When I heard that woman say, "I've got to find out who I am," I turned that program off to see if I could find a good western to watch. I mean, I thought a good western would be more edifying!

Praise God, *"Ye are of God, little children . . ."* (1 John 4:4). *That's* our genealogy!

Those Born of God Are Overcomers!

Now look at that next statement in First John 4:4: *". . . and have overcome them. . . ."* Overcome who? All those demons and evil spirits that John talked about in verses 1 through 3. He said, "You've overcome them."

"Well," someone asked, "if I've overcome them, how

come I'm having so many problems with them?"
Because you don't *know* it! You don't *know* you overcame them! And because you don't know it, you don't
act on it!

Notice it didn't say you were *going* to overcome them.
This verse clearly says, that we *have* overcome them.
That's past tense: ". . . [ye] *HAVE overcome them . . .*"
(1 John 4:4). How can that be? Because of the rest of
that verse: You've overcome them because greater is He
that's in you than he that's in the world!

> **1 JOHN 4:4**
> **4 Ye are of God, little children, and have over-
> come them: BECAUSE GREATER IS HE THAT IS
> IN YOU, THAN HE THAT IS IN THE WORLD.**

Paul wrote to the Church at Colossae and said it's
"*. . .Christ in you, the hope of glory*" (Col. 1:27).

> **COLOSSIANS 1:27**
> **27 To whom God would make known what is the
> RICHES OF THE GLORY OF THIS MYSTERY
> among the Gentiles; which is Christ IN you, the
> hope of glory.**

This is the mystery: Through the Holy Ghost, Christ
indwells us, and we are the Body of Christ. He is the
Head, and we are the Body.

Now, can your head have one experience and your
body another experience? No, it's impossible. In the
same way, the Lord Jesus' victory is *our* victory. When

He overcame demons and evil spirits and put them to nought, that's all marked down to our credit. Notice it says, *"YE . . . have overcome them . . ."* (1 John 4:4).

Why do folks have so much trouble with evil spirits then? Because of folks' wrong thinking! They don't know that in Christ, they've overcome demons and evil spirits. And because they don't know it, they don't act on it. But believers do have authority over Satan. They just need to believe and exercise that authority in every area of their lives, including the area of finances.

Jesus Defeated the Works of the Devil — Including Poverty and Lack

There's another passage of Scripture that would help us in our thinking along this line.

> **1 CORINTHIANS 2:4-6**
> **4   And my speech and my preaching was not with enticing words of man's wisdom, but in demonstration of the Spirit and of power:**
> **5   That your faith should not stand in the wisdom of men, but in the power of God.**
> **6   Howbeit we speak wisdom among them that are perfect [mature]: yet not the wisdom of this world, nor of the princes of this world, THAT COME TO NOUGHT.**

Remember what we read in Colossians 2:15: *"And having spoiled principalities and powers, he made a shew of them openly, triumphing over them in it."*

Jesus spoiled principalities and powers! If you look in the margin of a good reference Bible, it will tell you,

"He put to *nought* principalities and powers." He reduced them to nothing. In other words, He reduced them to nothing as far as their being able to dominate us. Therefore, they can't dominate us financially either.

Since these principalities and powers are dethroned, why then are they still ruling in the world? *Because the world doesn't know that they're dethroned.* They don't know about it, and, therefore, they can't act upon it!

That's the reason Jesus said He was anointed by the Spirit (and so are we) to *preach deliverance*!

Someone asked, "What do you mean, *preach deliverance*?"

Preach to the captives, "You're delivered! Jesus delivered you! These powers have come to nought! They're dethroned powers!"

1 JOHN 4:4
**4   Ye are of God, little children, and HAVE OVER-
COME THEM: because greater is he that is in you,
than he that is in the world.**

"Well, I'm *trying* to overcome them," someone said.

No, you don't *try*. You just accept by faith what Jesus did. What He did, He did for you! Christ's victory is your victory. Glory to God!

Exercising Our Authority

That's why when the Lord told me to claim the money I needed, I understood what He meant. He was telling me to believe and exercise my spiritual authority in the area of finances.

The Lord had said to me, "The money that you need is not up here in Heaven. I don't have any money up here. The money that you need is down there. It's Satan who's keeping it from coming, not Me.

"Satan is going to stay there till Adam's lease runs out." (Then, thank God, Satan is going to be put in the bottomless pit for a little while, and finally cast into the lake of fire.)

The Lord said to me, "Don't pray about money like you have been. Whatever you need, claim it in Jesus' Name. And then you say, 'Satan, take your hands off my money.' And then say, 'Go, ministering spirits, and cause the money to come.'"

This was way back in 1950. And from that day to this, I've not prayed about money. I'm talking about for me individually — personally. Now when it comes to RHEMA Bible Training Center, that's a different thing. We present the needs of the training center to people to help us, because that's not just *my* responsibility.

It's the same way with the local church. It's not just one person's responsibility. We *all* should believe God, not just the pastor.

And yet, right on the other hand, the pastor has a responsibility, too, because he's in authority. He has to do certain things and make certain decisions in the church. And that's a great responsibility.

Angels Are Ministering Spirits

In 1950 when I began to see how faith worked in the area of finances, it was all new to me.

In fact, I said to the Lord, "What do You *mean*? I can understand the part about how we can exercise authority over the enemy, claim the finances we need, and tell Satan, 'Take your hands off my money.' But, what do You mean about the part, 'Go, ministering spirits, and cause the money to come'?"

The Lord said, "Didn't you ever read in My Word where it says that angels are ministering spirits sent to minister *for* those who are heirs of salvation?" (Heb. 1:14).

Because I thought it said "minister *to* us," I had to get my Bible and read it. Isn't it strange how we can read Scripture for years and years, and read right over things and not get what the Word said?

> **HEBREWS 1:13,14**
> **13 But to which of the angels said he at any time, Sit on my right hand, until I make thine enemies thy footstool?**
> **14 Are they not all ministering spirits, sent forth to minister FOR them who shall be heirs of salvation?**

Notice verse 13 says, *"But to which of the ANGELS. . . ."* So He's talking about angels. Now look at verse 14: *"Are they not all ministering spirits. . . ?"*

Now notice what it said. *"Are they not ALL* [How many of them? *All* of them.] *ministering spirits. . . ?"*

They are spirit beings. They are ". . . *ministering spirits, sent forth to minister FOR them who shall be HEIRS OF SALVATION"* (Heb. 1:14).

Well, that's us! These angels are ministering spirits that are sent forth to minister *for* us. "For" us means they were sent to do something *for* us!

Now over in Satan's kingdom, we could say that Satan is the chief. And, you see, all these demons and other spirits are doing *his* work. You hear folks say sometimes, "Satan influenced me to do that." Well, he might not have been there present at the time, but one of his ambassadors were. These demons and evil spirits influence people. They'll even influence Christians, if Christians will let them.

Well, just as demon spirits influence people, good spirits or ministering spirits can influence people too.

I Put Into Practice What I Received

After the Lord showed me this, I went to the church where I was holding the meeting and stood there on the platform. I'll be honest with you, since this was a new revelation to me, my knees were shaking.

I was trembling, not because I was afraid like someone would be afraid of a rattlesnake or a bad storm. I'm talking about a holy, reverential fear. Remember the Apostle Paul said, *"And I was with you in . . . fear, and in much trembling"* (1 Cor. 2:3). What I experienced was a different thing entirely from tormenting fear. It was a holy fear.

You see, what the Lord had shown me was new to me, and my head was telling me, "That's not going to work." I just stood on the platform, and I said privately, "Well, now, let's see. It takes one hundred and fifty dollars a week to meet my budget." (That doesn't sound big now, but that was big then.)

I was supposed to be at that church one week. So I said, "In Jesus' Name, I claim one hundred and fifty dollars this week." And then I said, "Satan, take your hands off my money in Jesus' Name." Then I also said, "Go, ministering spirits, and cause the money to come." That's it — that's all I did.

Then I said to the pastor, "Now, Brother, don't make any special pull for money. When you get ready to take up my offering, just say as little about it as you can. Don't say a lot about it."

"Well," the pastor said to me, "you know our custom. We take up an offering on Tuesday, Friday, and Sunday nights for the evangelist. We're accustomed to taking up pledge offerings. If I just say, 'This is Brother Hagin's offering' and pass the plate, you won't get over a dime."

I said, "If I just get a dime, you won't hear me say a word."

I had preached in that same church a year before. This was a different pastor this time, and the only other difference in the church was they had two more church members this year than the year before. The church was about the same size. They hadn't gotten anybody saved.

The last year when I preached at this church, they paid me $57.15 a week for two weeks. That's $114.30 total. And when they gave me that offering, they thought they'd hung the moon!

The pastor who was there then had taken up to thirty or forty minutes for that offering, saying, "Who'll give another dollar? . . ." (Don't misunderstand me. That's all right to do if the Lord leads you to do that. In fact, I have been anointed at times to take up such an offering.)

But now that I'd seen how faith worked for finances, I said to this pastor, "Don't take up any pledge offering."

"Well, uh . . . If that's the way you want it," the pastor said.

"That's the way I want it."

The meeting started and was going well, and the pastor asked me: "Could you stay longer?"

I said, "I've got another meeting coming up, but I was going to take a little time off between meetings to go home."

But in the process of time, he persuaded me to stay on through Wednesday night of the following week, which gave us about a ten-day meeting.

So I changed the amount I had claimed — the amount I needed to meet my budget. Instead of $150, now I was claiming $200. I didn't pray about it. I claimed what I needed in Jesus' Name, and said, "Satan, take your hands off of my finances." Then I said, "Go, ministering spirits; cause the money to come."

When the ten-day meeting ended, I had the $200 plus $40-odd dollars over that amount!

The pastor said, "That beats anything I've ever seen in my life!"

You remember, this church thought $50 a week was *big*. They would have thought $75 a week was wonderful, and $100 a week — they would have thought that was a miracle!

The Word Works!

I left for home that Wednesday night after the service. I was down in east Texas, and we lived up in north Texas. I left home the following Saturday and drove down to Alabama for my next meeting.

I had been behind on my house rent for four months, so I paid up as far as I could, left money for my wife, and had just enough money to buy gas to get down to Alabama.

When I arrived in Alabama, I was tired. I would have stopped overnight along the way, but I didn't have any money to rent a motel room. I didn't have a dime in my pocket.

It was after midnight when I got there, so I went to the parsonage to see the pastor. He took me to the home of one of the deacons. The pastor wanted me to preach the next morning, but I said, "Oh, no. No, I've driven for about fifteen to sixteen hours on little two-lane roads, going through just about every little ole town. I'm too tired to preach."

We got up the next morning and went to church, and he introduced me to the congregation.

They had seventy-two in Sunday school and seventy in the congregation for the morning service. I mean, they counted anything that moved!

I was sitting there on the platform, and I don't know to this day what that pastor preached — I was having such a battle between my head and my heart. My head said, "Boy, you played whaley."

Do you know what that means? It just means that you've played the fool, so to speak, just like Jonah did who found himself in the *whale's* belly!

My head was telling me, "You came down here, and you won't even get enough money to get back home. Why, look at that little bunch of people sitting out there. You shouldn't have come down here. You won't get enough money to get back home."

It took me awhile to get my head quiet. You see, you can get quiet physically, but it's more difficult to get quiet mentally than it is to get quiet physically. Have you found that out yet?

I was quiet physically — I was sitting there not moving a muscle. But I finally got my head quiet, and I sat there and very quietly said, "I claim one hundred and fifty dollars a week in Jesus' Name. Satan, take your hands off my money. Go, ministering spirits, and cause the money to come." I didn't even say it out loud. I sort of whispered it because the preacher was preaching.

After the service, I said the same thing to this pastor: "Don't make any pull for money. Just pass the plate and say, 'This is Brother Hagin's offering.'"

"Brother Hagin, you won't get a quarter," this pastor said.

"Well," I said, "if I don't, I won't say anything about it. You'll never hear me gripe or say a word about it."

The meeting got to running real well, and we ran it three weeks. Three weeks times $150 a week would be $450. But I wound up with $965. Hallelujah! I also received a new set of tires on top of that! The car I had recently bought was used, and the tires were already bald. But I got a new set of tires.

I was putting into practice the revelation the Lord had given me. Anytime you get a revelation from God, don't just run out and preach it. Even though the Lord showed me that revelation in 1950, I didn't start preaching it till four years later in 1954.

Prove All Things

If you get any revelation from God, friends, check it in line with the Word, and then put it into practice for yourself before you start preaching it. If it won't work for you, it won't work for anybody else.

Then not only that, but share your revelation with those who are over you and who are older than you in the ministry. Like I said, I got that revelation and practiced it, but I never said a word about it — I never preached it to anybody. I'd just talk about it a little bit to some fellow pastors.

But as I already mentioned, I shared this revelation with Brother A. A. Swift, who was about seventy at the time. I was only thirty-six when I held a meeting for him. This man was a pioneer of the Pentecostal Movement and was recognized as a leading Bible teacher.

He got out his notes and gave them to me. And that's where I got most of my material for the book *Redeemed From the Curse of Poverty, Sickness, and Spiritual Death.*

He told me, "You go ahead and use these notes. Just go ahead and preach it everywhere you go."

So that's when I started preaching what the Lord had shown me four years before. And I've been preaching it ever since. But I had a leading teacher in the Pentecostal Movement — a man twice as old as I was — to judge it. Also, I proved it out over a four-year period before I taught it to others.

Some people think if they've got a revelation, they have to "run off" with it. They want to tell it. They also want everybody to agree with them.

If folks don't agree with them, they get mad and get in the flesh. And they think that's the Spirit of God. Oh, bless their darling hearts.

The Lord had given me the same revelation this Pentecostal preacher had received years before. The Bible says, "Are they not all ministering spirits?" (Heb. 1:14). Say out loud: "Thank God for the ministering spirits."

After I received the revelation from the Lord about faith for finances, I would *purposely* go to small churches — to country churches and out-of-the-way places — to prove it out. And I'd say the same thing to the pastor: "Don't make any pulls for money."

Did you ever notice that our ministry never makes any great pulls for money? For example, did you ever notice that in *The Word of Faith* magazine, we never say anything about money or ask you to contribute anything to *The Word of Faith*?

We do send out a letter about four times a year letting folks know the ministry's needs. We just let you know what we're doing and give you an opportunity to get in on it if you want to. But we don't put any pressure on people.

Put Pressure on the Word, Not on People

Some folks have told us that the way we do things won't work. It's sort of like the science that says the bumblebee can't fly. According to science, bumblebees can't fly. But the bee doesn't know that, so it just goes ahead and flies!

Our ministry is not in trouble financially. We're not bragging on ourselves; we're bragging on the Lord. Our ministry has never been in trouble financially. We may have had some lean periods, but we were never really in trouble. There's a difference.

The RHEMA Bible Training Center campus sits on more than ninety-five acres of property. We've been building ever since we moved to our present location. We have twelve buildings on campus, a multi-building storage facility, plus a complex of ninety-six apartments that we've turned into student housing.

In recent years, a fellow from up north visited us. Although my wife and I had known him for some time, he'd never been to Broken Arrow. We took him and his wife around the RHEMA campus on a golf cart. As we were riding around, suddenly, he got to laughing. He got to laughing so hard, he nearly fell out of the golf cart!

Finally, he regained his composure. I said, "What's the matter with you?" I thought he was laughing at *me!*

He said, "Folks up in my part of the country have said, 'Faith doesn't work.' I just got to thinking, Brother Hagin, that if you could ever get it to work, there's no telling what you could do!" Bless their hearts. I feel so sorry for people who say faith doesn't work. I could weep about it, really.

Faith in God and His Word that is acted upon will bring results every time. I could tell you story after story of how the Word worked for me even in the midst of dire circumstances.

Yet there is a man-ward side and a God-ward side to receiving the blessings of God. You remember we read Isaiah 1:19: *"If ye be willing and obedient, ye shall eat the good of the land."*

Before you can effectively exercise your faith for finances or *any* of God's blessings, you must be willing and obedient. Then you must think and believe in line with His Word and walk in the light of it. When you do, your faith will bring into manifestation what God has provided for you in His great plan of redemption.

Chapter 4
The Bible Way To Release
Your Faith

For verily I say unto you, That whosoever shall say unto this mountain, Be thou removed, and be thou cast into the sea; and shall not doubt in his heart, but shall believe that those things which he saith shall come to pass; he shall have whatsoever he saith.

— Mark 11:23

Thou art snared with the words of thy mouth, thou art taken with the words of thy mouth.

— Proverbs 6:2

The Bible says that it is God's will that His children prosper (3 John 2). And God has made provision for every one of us to have our needs met and to walk in prosperity.

But there are *keys* to appropriating the divine promises. In 1949, after I left the last church I pastored to go into field ministry, the Lord gave me the revela-

69

tion of faith for finances. I had been seeking Him because our needs weren't being met. Isaiah 1:19 says, *"If ye be willing and obedient, ye shall eat the good of the land."* But we sure weren't eating the good of the land!

I argued with the Lord that I *had* been obedient to do what He had told me to do. He said, "You qualify on the *obedient* side, but you don't qualify on the *willing* side. So you don't qualify."

I made the necessary adjustment in my spirit immediately. Then I knew I was willing *and* obedient.

You Must Renew Your Mind With God's Word

After I became willing, the Lord still had to get my thinking straightened out. You see, in my denomination, we had always believed it was God's will that we be poor and not have anything. So I had to get my mind renewed to think in line with what God's Word said about prosperity.

Then the Lord told me not to pray about finances the way I had been praying. Before, when a need arose, we'd always get by somehow. But we struggled financially.

The Lord said I was to claim whatever it was I needed in Jesus' name, to command Satan to take his hands off my money, and to send out ministering spirits to cause the money to come. This was the revelation I received from the Lord about faith for finances.

You see, faith operates the same way in every area. I had used faith to get saved. And I was raised up from the deathbed by believing and acting upon Mark 11:23 and 24. But until I received the revelation of faith for finances and learned how to release my faith in that area, I didn't know how to appropriate getting my needs met.

The 'Saying' Part of Faith

Mark 11:23 says, "... *whosoever shall SAY . . . and shall not doubt in his heart, but shall believe that those things which he SAITH shall come to pass; he shall HAVE whatsoever he SAITH.*" What shall he have? Whatsoever he saith!

Now notice Proverbs 6:2. In the margin of my Bible, that verse reads, "Thou art *taken captive* with the words of thy mouth." In other words, you said the wrong thing, and as a result, you were taken captive.

What you say will either set you free or keep you bound. It's important what you say.

Years ago God showed me something from the Word about the saying part of faith. In 1951, I was holding a four-week meeting in a little town called Graham, Texas.

One day after a morning session, I just stayed in church and prayed. I decided I would read the Book of Mark on my knees at the altar, so I did.

I'd been on my knees quite a bit praying, too, as I was reading, so I got tired. Finally, I just sat down between the altar bench and the platform and finished reading the Book of Mark.

As I was sitting there meditating on the Great Commission in Mark 16, I began to really feel tired, so I just lay down on my back. As I was lying there with my hands under my head, just sort of staring at the ceiling, my mind got quiet.

Suddenly, on the inside of me — in my spirit — I heard these words: "Did you notice in Mark 11:23 that the word 'say' in relation to the believer is in that verse in some form *three times*, and the word 'believe' is in there only *once*?"

I rose up to a seated position and said, "No. No, I didn't notice that." And I had preached from that verse and had quoted it many, many times.

So I just turned the pages of my Bible back to Mark chapter 11 and read Mark 11:23.

> **MARK 11:23**
> **23 For verily I say** [you don't count the first "say" because that's Jesus talking] ... **That whosoever shall SAY unto this mountain, Be thou removed, and be thou cast into the sea; and shall not doubt in his heart, but shall believe that those things which he SAITH shall come to pass; he shall have whatsoever he SAITH.**

I counted them off on my fingers, and I counted "believe" one time and "say" in some form three times — "say," "saith," and "saith."

I said out loud to the Lord, "That's right! I never noticed that before." Then on the inside of me, in my spirit, I heard these words: "My people primarily are not missing it in their believing. They have been taught to believe and have faith. Where they're missing it is in what they are *saying*. And you'll have to do three times as much preaching and teaching about the *saying* part of faith as you do about the *believing* part in order to get people to see it."

And I've found that to be the case. The Word of God has a lot to say about what you say.

ROMANS 10:8
8 But what saith it? The word is nigh thee, even IN THY MOUTH, and in thy heart: that is, the word of faith, which we preach.

Believing *and* Confessing Get the Job Done

You see, for the Word to work for you, it's got to be both in your mouth *and* in your heart. It can't just be in your mouth. Folks can say things, but if they don't really mean them — if their heart doesn't agree with what they're saying — it won't work.

Or they can believe something in their heart, but if they don't vocalize it — if they don't say it — it won't come to pass. Faith that receives the promises of God will only work by believing *and* saying.

The Scripture also said, *"We HAVING the same spirit of faith, according as it is written, I BELIEVED, and therefore have I SPOKEN; we also BELIEVE, and therefore SPEAK"* (2 Cor. 4:13).

Notice it says, *"We HAVING . . . ,"* not, "We're *trying to get it."* And it's not, "We're *praying for it."* No, we already have faith. If you're saved, you already *have* that spirit of faith.

Since we *have* that spirit of faith, we ought to *speak* the things we believe. Never talk failure. I don't know about you, but I don't believe in failure. Never talk defeat. I don't know about you, but I don't believe in defeat. I believe in victory, praise God.

You talk about your trials, you talk about your difficulties, you talk about your lack of faith, you talk about your lack of money, and your faith will just absolutely shrivel.

But if you'll talk about your wonderful Heavenly Father — if you'll talk about the Word of God, then your faith will grow in leaps and bounds. Praise God forevermore!

If you talk about sickness, it will develop sickness in your system. If you talk about your doubts, your doubts will become stronger, and they will destroy your faith.

If you talk about your lack of finances, it will stop the money from coming in. Folks need to learn that. But if they'll believe in their heart what the Word of God said and confess it with their mouth, they'll get results.

As I said, in the early days of my ministry, I hadn't been getting any results in the area of finances. I understood faith for healing, but at that time, I didn't understand that faith worked the same way for finances too.

But, thank God, He showed me how to appropriate what belongs to me in Christ. He gave me the understanding of how faith for finances works and told me to claim what I needed.

We're talking about claiming what the Word says is yours. We're not talking about claiming something that's off the wall. Somebody may say, "Well, I'm going to claim ten million oil wells!" God didn't promise you ten million oil wells. You can only believe and confess in line with God's Word. Don't get off in left field.

We're talking about claiming what the Word says is yours. Is it wrong to claim the New Birth? Is it wrong to claim the baptism in the Holy Spirit?

Is it wrong to claim an answer to prayer if God promised to answer you? No, because the Word says, *"my God shall supply all your need according to his riches in glory by Christ Jesus"* (Phil. 4:19). When we believe and confess in line with God's Word, we can appropriate what belongs to us in Christ.

I was holding another meeting in west Texas about a year after I received this revelation on faith for finances. The meeting was just before Christmas. After Christmas, I was scheduled to go to Vernon, Texas, to minister. I was staying in the parsonage in west Texas, and I was traveling alone. Oretha was at home because the kids were in school.

Ordinarily, the minute my head hit the pillow at night, I was asleep. But I couldn't sleep that night. The Lord was dealing with me about going somewhere else — about not going to Vernon to minister.

I put off obeying the Lord. I said, "Lord, I couldn't cancel with that pastor at this late date. I'm already scheduled to go there. The meeting here is over, and I'm going to take off one week for Christmas and start with the church in Vernon the next Sunday."

The next night I had the same problem falling asleep. And the same thing happened the third night. Finally, to get some rest I said, "All right, Lord. I'll call the pastor in Vernon tomorrow. If he lets me off the hook, fine. If he doesn't, I'm going to go, because my word's out, and I'll never change my word.

"You said in Your Word in Psalm 15 that one of the characteristics of a spiritual pilgrim is that he sweareth to his own hurt and changeth not. So if that pastor doesn't let me off the hook, I won't change, because You — *Your Word* — told me not to."

> **PSALM 15:4,5**
> 4   . . . a vile person is contemned [scorned]; **but he** [the Lord] **honoureth them that fear the Lord. HE THAT SWEARETH TO HIS OWN HURT, AND CHANGETH NOT.**
> 5   He that putteth not out his money to usury, nor taketh reward against the innocent. He that doeth these things shall never be moved.

So the next day, just as I started to pick up the phone to call this pastor, the phone rang. I answered it and the operator said, "I have a long-distance telephone call for Reverend Kenneth Hagin." I said, "This is he." Then that pastor in Vernon came on the line!

"Brother Hagin?"

I said, "Yes. *I* was just about to call *you*. I started to pick up the phone when it rang just now."

He said, "What were you going to call me about?"

I said, "You go ahead and tell me what you're calling about because you got to me first! Then I'll tell you why I was going to call."

"Well," he said, "you're scheduled to come to my church after you go home for Christmas."

"Yes. That's what I planned to do. But why did you call?"

"Well," he said, "I'll be here the first Sunday night, but an emergency has arisen, and I have to go to Kansas City. I'll be gone the first week of your meeting. I trust that's all right with you. I'll be back the following Sunday night."

I said, "Fine."

"Now," he said, "what were you going to call me about?"

I said, "Well, the last three nights, God has been talking to me," and I told this pastor that the Lord was dealing with me about postponing the meeting and going somewhere else to minister. Then I told him, "But I didn't want to put you off."

"Oh, Brother Hagin," he said, "*I* didn't want to put *you* off."

Then the pastor said, "I can understand why the Lord has been talking to you. Because of this emergency that's come up, we've been on the phone back and forth with someone in Kansas City for the last two or three days. And I actually need to be there *two* weeks. So that's fine. That's perfectly all right. You go right on somewhere else to minister. But you will come back to my church, won't you?"

"Yes," I said, "when the Lord leads me to, I'll come back to your church. We'll not cancel the meeting; we'll just postpone it." (I got back to his church two years later!)

"Now then," I said to the Lord after I hung up the phone, "we've got that settled. You know I'm going to be off at Christmastime, and I'll be spending a little extra money at Christmas for gifts. I'm sure You want me to go to Brother Johnson's church because he's talked to me personally, inviting me to come. He's written me a letter, phoned me, and sent me a telegram.

"He has just built a new sanctuary that will seat eight hundred people comfortably. He told me, 'I can put a thousand in it easily enough, and I promise you a full house every night.' (We didn't have very many of those big churches back then.) Lord, I'm sure that's where You want me to go because I'll be to spending extra money for Christmas, and they've got a lot of people."

"No, I don't want you to go there."

"Where do You want me to go?"

"To Brother Robinson's church way down in the upper part of the big thicket of east Texas."

I tell you, you could get back in those woods where Brother Robinson's church was and think you'd come to the "jumping off" place! Brother Robinson had a country church that ran sixty to seventy people in Sunday school. That included kids, babies, and anything that moved!

I said, "Lord, surely You don't want me to go down there — not me. I'm going to these big churches now. Surely You don't want . . ."

"Yes, that's where I want you to go."

The Word Works in Any Situation Or Circumstance

"Well, now," I said to the Lord, "this is wintertime, and that's country down there. Whatever crops they had, they're all gone." I continued, "It takes one hundred and fifty dollars a week to meet my budget, and I expect my budget to be met there just like it is anywhere else."

The Lord said, "You do the going, and I'll do the doing. That's where I want you to go."

I contacted Brother Robinson and told him I'd come immediately after the Christmas holidays.

I stayed at home for the holidays as long as I could because I was gone so much of the time. I got to Brother Robinson's church on a Sunday afternoon just before church time. There was a little parsonage right next to the church. Brother Robinson and I were standing in the kitchen of the parsonage talking.

He said, "Brother Hagin, I started to call you. I know you've got a family, and it's wintertime, and you've been off for Christmas.

"But, you see," he continued, "we have two main crops here in east Texas. We have a tomato crop that is harvested in the latter part of May and in June. But the hail got the tomato crop, and we had a tomato-crop failure."

Then he said, "Our other crop is cotton. It's harvested in the fall. But the boll weevils got the cotton, and we had a cotton-crop failure too.

"We can't promise you a dime, Brother Hagin. I started to phone you and let you know that you'd better not come because we can't promise you a dime."

I said, "I didn't ask you for a dime. I never said anything to anybody about money, did I?"

"No, no," he said. "You didn't."

"But," I said, "as long as you brought up the subject, may I say something?" (I never said anything to folks to correct them unless they brought the subject up themselves.)

I said, "Don't make any pull for money. Just simply take up the offering."

He said, "Well, we take up an offering on Tuesday, Friday, and Sunday nights for the evangelist."

I said, "Okay, but say as little as you can about my offering.

"And while I'm at it, don't talk about the negative side of things. You see, you were talking about the lack. Talking about lack of finances keeps finances from coming in. Don't get up there and say, 'Well, we had a tomato-crop failure, and we had a cotton-crop failure.'

When you do that, you're telling the people they're not able to give."

What You Say Defeats You or Puts You Over

I told this pastor, "If you're going to say anything when you take up the offering, say this: 'The world and the fullness thereof are the Lord's. The cattle on a thousand hills are the Lord's. The silver and the gold are the Lord's. And what belongs to the Lord, belongs to us, so we're all able to give. Now we're going to receive an offering for Brother Hagin.'"

He did that. I had claimed $150 a week. I had planned to stay one week, but I stayed ten days. So then I claimed $200 for the ten days. And I got $240 some-odd dollars!

At first I didn't know why the Lord wanted me to go to that church, but when the meeting was over, I saw why He'd sent me down there. We had thirty-two people come to the altar to be filled with the Holy Ghost. Out of the thirty-two who came to be filled with the Holy Ghost, thirteen were grown men. And of the thirteen grown men, twelve were heads of families.

When I laid hands on them, they were instantly filled with the Holy Ghost. And in ten days, that pastor got twelve brand-new families in his church! Hallelujah!

Not only that, but we were meeting out in the country in a one-room church building. They ran seventy in Sunday school and had all those different Sunday school classes in one room on Sunday morning! You could hardly hear what was going on. And they only had one wood stove in the middle of the room to heat the whole building.

Then over in the parsonage they had a wood stove in what we'd call the living room. And they had a kerosene cookstove that they couldn't get parts for. It didn't burn right, and everything the dear pastor's wife cooked tasted like kerosene!

I said, "Brother Robinson, why don't you get a butane system? You could put four small heaters in the church and really warm the thing up. And then you could get a cookstove in the parsonage."

"We were going to do that," the pastor answered. "Mr. So-and-so over in Crockett, Texas, owns a butane-appliance store. He's a good Baptist deacon, and so I talked to him about it. He said, 'Brother Robinson, I'll install the system, furnish the stoves for the church and the parsonage for just exactly the amount I've got invested in them. Then I'll give you ten percent myself, out of my own pocket.'"

I said, "Why in the world didn't you do that?"

"Well, we had the cotton-crop failure and the tomato-crop failure," he replied.

So at the next church service, I simply got up on the platform and said to the congregation, "Folks, listen. I've been staying over there in the parsonage, and that stove over there is worn out. You can't get parts for it. It's old, and I don't mean this as an insinuation about Sister Robinson because she's a good cook, but everything she cooks tastes like kerosene."

Then I told them what the man said who owned the butane business. "Not only that, but after he installs the system, he'll put a big tank out there behind the church, install the heaters in the church and in the parsonage, *plus* furnish the butane for the church and the parsonage thereafter — forever — free of charge!

"Glory to God!" I continued. "Let's do that. I'll give such-and-such amount of money on it."

And I'll tell you, I hadn't intended on taking up a pledge offering, but as fast as you could snap your fingers, people began jumping up all over the building, saying, "I'll give this." "I'll give that." And in just a few seconds' time, we had the whole amount we needed!

Yet they had a tomato-crop failure and a cotton-crop failure! You see, you can't keep talking about the negative circumstances and do anything for God.

After that, I began to talk to pastors about the revelation on faith for finances that I'd received from the Lord. "Well, now," many pastors said, "that'll work for you, because you're out there on the field. But that wouldn't work in pastoring."

Well, I hadn't received the revelation while I was still pastoring. I was out in the field ministry when I received that understanding. So I said to the Lord, "Lord, I know You told me that the last church I pastored would be the last church I'd ever pastor. But if You could arrange it some way or another so that I could temporarily pastor, I'd like to, because I want to prove out this revelation."

I was holding a seven-week meeting in Dallas in 1953. The pastor said to me, "Brother Hagin, I'm going to be gone all summer on a leave of absence. Would you stay here and pastor the church? The associate pastor will do the visitation and the other work. All you've got to do is preach Sunday morning, Sunday night, and Tuesday and Friday nights. An evangelist is going to be here two weeks out of the summer. But for the rest of the time, you'd preach."

"Well," I said, "I'll pray about it." I prayed about it, and the Lord said, "This is your opportunity. You've got three months here to pastor." So I said, "All right. And I'll also run teaching services on faith every Monday through Friday morning all summer."

(Incidentally, I was at that church teaching every morning for twenty-three weeks altogether — we took Saturdays off — and I never did run out of things to say on the subject of faith! You can't exhaust the subject of faith.)

My family and I arrived the last Sunday of May, the Sunday before the pastor left. The pastor encouraged the people to be faithful and to pay their tithes. I was sitting on the platform and just very quietly, I exercised my faith for finances for the church.

I said, "When the pastor comes back at the end of summer, I claim that every bill will be paid, and we'll be in the black, not in the red. Satan, take your hands off of our money. Go, ministering spirits and cause the money to come."

All summer I didn't have to pray any more about

finances — I just said it that one time. I put into practice what the Lord had taught me about faith for finances.

And in your own life, just say it once. And whenever you think about it, just praise God for the answer.

That pastor also had a daily radio program that ran every day, including Saturday. It wasn't the church's radio program; it was his.

But so often, people out there in the listening audience think that because the program is being broadcast live from a church, that means the church is sponsoring the program. Therefore, this pastor hadn't received a good response of people sending in money, so he had gotten behind financially.

It doesn't sound big now, but forty years ago, $3,750 was big money. That's how much the pastor was behind paying his radio bills.

So the radio station said, "You have to pay, or we're going to cancel your radio program. You've got to pay every week for that week's broadcast. You can't go in the red anymore."

Because I had held a revival earlier in this church that lasted seven weeks, I knew the church's policy and practice for collecting the radio offering. The church board had said, "We'll make Tuesday night radio night whether we're in revival or not."

During that seven-week revival, I noticed they would never take less than forty-five minutes and up to an hour and a half on Tuesday nights raising money for the radio program! Then I had to preach after that!

And on the radio show, the pastor and his staff were always talking about the trouble they were in. "We may not be on next week," they'd say. "So send your money in." But who'd want to send their money in to a radio program that won't be on next week! So I claimed the whole amount he needed to pay the radio bill.

The following Tuesday night after the pastor left, the associate pastor got up on the platform and took an hour or so on the radio offering. (I hadn't had a chance to talk with him yet.) He said things like, "We don't want the pastor to come back and find that we've lost his program." Finally, he got enough to pay for that week's broadcast plus $10 toward the $3,750 that they were behind.

So later I said to him, "Now, dear Brother, don't do that anymore." I'd been left in charge of the operation of the church, so I said, "And don't say on the radio, 'We're going off the air.' Just act like we've got plenty of money."

"But if I do that, people won't give anything," he answered.

I said, "If they don't, I'll pay it myself." Actually, I didn't have enough money to buy an old set of hens and chickens!

"Well, okay. I'll do it. You're in charge," the associate pastor said.

I said, "Okay. Next Tuesday night, you just take as little time as you can on the offering. Just say, 'Now you remember, Tuesday night is radio night. This offering goes toward the pastor's radio program. We're going to pass the plates now.'

"And when you get on the radio, don't say, 'We're going off the air.' Just act like we're going to stay on forever. Encourage folks to give because they should give. They need to be blessed. Encourage them to help us by sending in money to support the program."

This church had what they called a radio pastor or minister. I don't know why they called him that; he didn't preach. He just answered the mail. Anyhow, he came to me and said, "Brother Hagin, this beats anything I've ever seen. The mail has doubled; the offerings have *doubled*."

When the pastor got back at the end of the summer, we had a business meeting with the board, the secretary, the treasurer, and so forth. Someone read the report and said we'd gotten the radio program out of the red. It was all paid. Anybody in the ministry will tell you that support usually *drops off* in the summertime.

Then not only that, but the church secretary and treasurer also read in the report: "Every bill is paid, and we have twelve cents left over."

They didn't know a thing about how I had prayed. I simply smiled and said, "Well, all I claimed was that we'd be in the black. And we're in the black — we've got twelve cents!"

The pastor said, "You don't understand. Brother Hagin, this is a miracle. Ask any board member. This is the first time we've ever operated in the black in the summertime. We've got an expense fund that we have to dip into *every summer*! I've been here eight years, and never in the history of the church have we operated in the black in the summertime."

I just said it one time. I just claimed once that we'd be in the black. Then I didn't pray about finances the rest of the summer. I just had a high-heeled time in the Lord!

Get Convinced in Your Heart

Someone said, "Boy, I wish I could get that to work for me."

It doesn't work by wishing. If it did, everybody would be there. It works by getting convinced in your heart first. It won't work just by saying, "Well, I'm going to try that. Brother Hagin said to do this, so I'm doing it because Brother Hagin said so."

It won't work that way. No, get the Word in your heart. Get the revelation of it in your spirit. Be convinced in your own heart; *then* say it. And it will work!

God's Word works! Say out loud: "God's Word works for *me*. And I am a doer of the Word, not just a hearer."

But, you see, it will not do you any good just to say the Word unless you absolutely believe it from your heart. And you'll only believe it from your heart as a result of meditating in the Word until it becomes a reality on the inside of you. Then you can exercise faith for finances. You can say with your mouth what you believe in your heart, and results will be forthcoming.

Chapter 5
Honor Your Pastor
And Receive God's Blessings

Render therefore to all their dues: tribute to whom tribute is due; custom to whom custom; fear to whom fear; HONOUR TO WHOM HONOUR.

Owe no man any thing, but to love one another: for he that loveth another hath fulfilled the law.

For this, Thou shalt not commit adultery, Thou shalt not kill, Thou shalt not steal, Thou shalt not bear false witness, Thou shalt not covet; and if there be any other commandment, it is briefly comprehended in this saying, namely, Thou shalt love thy neighbour as thyself.

Love worketh no ill to his neighbour: therefore love is the fulfilling of the law.

— Romans 13:7-10

Let the elders that rule well be counted worthy of DOUBLE HONOUR, especially they who labour in the word and doctrine.

89

> *For the scripture saith, Thou shalt not muz-*
> *zle the ox that treadeth out the corn. And, The*
> *labourer is worthy of his reward.*
>
> — 1 Timothy 5:17,18

Through the years there has been great debate about what or who is an "elder." If you'll rightly divide the word of truth (2 Tim. 2:15), you can see that as the early Church grew and developed, elders were no longer just older men. Elders were pastors, called and equipped by God to have oversight of the flock.

The word "pastor" is only used one time in the New Testament: *"And he gave some, apostles; and some, prophets; and some, evangelists; and some, PASTORS and teachers"* (Eph. 4:11).

But even though that's the only place the word "pastor" is used, we can see the same ministry gift of the pastor called by other names.

The same Greek word that's translated *pastor* is also translated *shepherd.* The Word of God talks about Jesus being the Chief Shepherd (1 Peter 5:4).

Also, Paul says in First Timothy 3:1, *". . . If a man desire the office of a BISHOP, he desireth a good work."* The word "bishop" is also translated *overseer.* But the word "bishop" is also used in association with the office of pastor.

> **1 PETER 2:25**
> **25 For ye were as sheep going astray; but are now returned unto the SHEPHERD and BISHOP of your souls.**

So then "pastor," "shepherd," "overseer," and "bishop" are the same offices called by different names.

In the New Testament, both Jesus and Paul used the example of a flock of sheep to refer to a church or a body of believers. Well, who has the oversight of a flock of sheep? The shepherd does.

Notice in Acts 20:28, Paul said something in his farewell message to the "elders" of the church at Ephesus.

> **ACTS 20:28**
> **28 Take heed therefore unto yourselves, and to all THE FLOCK, over the which the Holy Ghost hath made you OVERSEERS, to feed THE CHURCH OF GOD, which he hath purchased with his own blood.**

Paul was talking to the elders of the church at Ephesus. He said, "The Holy Ghost made you overseers." Who are "overseers"? They're *shepherds*. Who is a shepherd? He's a pastor, so Paul was talking to *pastors*.

Notice the last part of Acts 20:28: ". . . *to all the flock, over the which the Holy Ghost hath made you overseers, to FEED THE CHURCH OF GOD. . . .*" Therefore, these people were preachers and teachers, not just some businessmen that somebody appointed to be "elders" in the church.

Businessmen don't have any anointing to serve in the office of a pastor. When we say elder, shepherd, overseer, or bishop, we're talking about a *pastor*.

Let's look again at our text.

1 TIMOTHY 5:17
17 Let the ELDERS that rule well be counted worthy of DOUBLE HONOUR, especially THEY WHO LABOUR IN THE WORD AND DOCTRINE.

Remember our other text: *"Render therefore to all their dues: tribute to whom tribute is due; custom to whom custom; fear to whom fear; HONOUR TO WHOM HONOUR"* (Rom. 13:7).

Pastors Are Laborers in the Word and Doctrine

Look at First Timothy 5:17 again: *"Let the elders that rule well be counted worthy of double honour, especially they who labour in the word and doctrine."*

Notice that according to the last phrase, we are to render to everyone his due, "especially those who preach and teach the Word."

First Timothy 5:18 says, *"For the scripture saith, Thou shalt not muzzle the ox that treadeth out the corn. And, THE LABOURER IS WORTHY OF HIS REWARD."*

You see, Paul is talking about the pastor — the shepherd.

LUKE 10:7
7 ... for the labourer is worthy of his hire. ...

Now let's look at First Thessalonians 5.

1 THESSALONIANS 5:12,13
12 And we beseech you, brethren, to know them which labour among you, and are over you in the Lord, and admonish you;
13 And to ESTEEM THEM VERY HIGHLY in love for their work's sake....

We should esteem very highly the office of the pastor and those who labor in the Word and doctrine, and we should consider them "worthy of their hire."

1 CORINTHIANS 9:7-14
7 Who goeth a warfare any time at his own charges? who planteth a vineyard, and eateth not of the fruit thereof? or who FEEDETH A FLOCK, and eateth not of the milk of the flock?
8 Say I these things as a man? or saith not the law the same also?
9 For it is written in the law of Moses, THOU SHALT NOT MUZZLE THE MOUTH OF THE OX THAT TREADETH OUT THE CORN. Doth God take care for oxen?
10 Or saith he it altogether for our sakes? For our sakes, no doubt, this is written: that he that ploweth should plow in hope; and that he that thresheth in hope should be partaker of his hope.
11 If we have sown unto you spiritual things, is it a great thing if we shall reap your carnal things?
12 If others be partakers of this power [or authority] over you, are not we rather? Nevertheless we have not used this power [authority]; but suffer all things, lest we should hinder the gospel of Christ.
13 Do ye not know that they which minister about holy things live of the things of the temple? and they which wait at the altar are partakers with the altar?

14 Even so hath the Lord ordained that THEY WHICH PREACH THE GOSPEL SHOULD LIVE OF THE GOSPEL.

Now notice Galatians 6:6.

GALATIANS 6:6
6   Let him that is taught in the word communicate UNTO HIM THAT TEACHETH in all good things.

That's a little bit blind to us. But *The Amplified Bible* says, "Let him who receives instruction in the Word [of God] share all good things with his teacher — contributing to his support."

The Living Bible says, "Those who are taught the Word of God should help their teachers by paying them." Another translation says, ". . . by sharing with him all good things."

Honoring the Pastoral Office

We read Galatians 6:6, *"Let him that is taught in the word communicate unto him that teacheth in all good things."* I just read that one verse to establish something I'm going to say to you about honoring the office of the pastor.

But more specifically, I want to talk to you about honoring *your* pastor, not necessarily honoring him as a man, but honoring the office that he holds. You should have respect and reverence for that office. This is an important scriptural key to financial prosperity in your own life.

We have an example in the New Testament of someone who reverenced the office of the high priest. Do you
remember on one occasion in the Acts of the Apostles,
Paul had a hearing before the Sanhedrin council, and
the high priest commanded that Paul be smitten? In
other words, someone slapped Paul. The high priest
wasn't dressed as a priest at that time, so Paul didn't
know he was a high priest.

When Paul was slapped, he said, ". . . *God shall
smite thee, thou whited wall: for sittest thou to judge me
after the law, and commandest me to be smitten contrary to the law?"* (Acts 23:3).

When he said that, some who stood by said,
". . . *Revilest thou God's high priest?"* (Acts 23:4).

Immediately, because Paul honored that office (not
the man — the *man* had done wrong), Paul apologized!
He said, ". . . *I wist not, brethren, that he was the high
priest: for it is written, Thou shalt not speak evil of the
ruler of thy people"* (Acts 23:5).

In other words, Paul was saying in effect, "If I had
known that he was the high priest, I wouldn't have said
that." Why? Because Paul reverenced that *office.*

How God Regards Ministry Offices

You can understand something about God's nature
and His mind by looking at Old Testament types and
shadows. In the Old Testament, the Levites stood in the
office of the priest, and they carried on all the priestly
work. And certain Levites were high priests who served

a longer period of time than the others who were just what we'd call regular priests.

The Levitical priests ministered and served for only twenty years — from thirty to fifty years of age. They retired at age fifty. And God made a plan so that when they retired at age fifty, they were financially secure. The other people brought tithes unto the Levites and paid them.

And, of course, the Levites had cattle and lands and so forth. So when they retired, they had plenty to support them.

There's Blessing in Honoring What God Honors

I've been in the ministry since 1934. Let me tell you something that I have learned about honoring those God has placed in the office of pastor. This is not something I *think*. It's not something somebody told me. It's something I *know*! The reason you should honor the office of the pastor and honor the man who stands in that office is that those who do will prosper in life!

The Apostle Paul talks about the laborer being worthy of his hire (1 Tim. 5:18). In other words, we are to see to it first of all that the pastor is amply taken care of financially.

We read in Galatians 6:6, *"Let him that is taught in the word communicate unto him that teacheth in all good things."*

But notice verse 7: *"Be not deceived; God is not mocked: for whatsoever a man soweth, that shall he also reap."* A lot of times, folks take that scripture out of context. You've heard, for example, an evangelist take that scripture and preach it to sinners.

However, that scripture was written to the Church! Paul wrote this letter to be read throughout the churches in Galatia. He's saying to Christian people, "Don't be deceived. God is not mocked. Whatsoever a man soweth, that shall he also reap."

Sowing and reaping is in connection with verse 6 that says we should communicate or give to him who teaches the Word.

I notice those churches that give to ministers always prosper. They prosper because they're sowing the right kind of seed.

Churches and Church Members Reap What They Sow

I also notice what happens to those churches that muzzle the ox and put God's servant on such a low wage that he can hardly get by.

Churches that muzzle God's servant never prosper. Spiritual blessings are withheld from them and financial blessings are withheld from them because they're in violation of God's Word.

You see, the *church* sows seed just as individual church members sow seed.

Many years ago, I knew of one local church that was very prosperous. It was a large church for the day. It doesn't sound too big today, but back then, 40 or 50 years ago, if you ran 2,000 people on Sunday night, that was tremendous for a Full Gospel church.

Most of us would run maybe 100 or 200 people on a Sunday night. But during revivals on weeknights, this church would run 800 to 1,000 people. So this was a big church.

One young man, who was the associate pastor at that church, was a good friend of mine. Once when he and I went to a convention together, he was greatly troubled about something. He told me: "Our church will have a guest minister in to speak. And we always give him the Sunday night offering. Weeknight offerings go to meet the expenses." (They put the guest minister up in a motel or hotel and fed him while he was there, plus they paid for advertising and utilities.)

This young pastor continued, "The offering on Sunday nights runs between three hundred and three hundred and fifty dollars."

Remember, this was forty or fifty years ago. We didn't have all the money we have now; we're more affluent today. That amount doesn't sound big now, but that was a lot of money back then.

He said, "I knew what the offering ran on Sunday nights, and when we invited a preacher to speak, that whole amount was supposed to be given to the guest minister. But the church board said, 'That's too much. Let's just give him one hundred and fifty and put the rest in the church treasury.'"

Well, you might as well take your gun, hold up a fellow, and rob a filling station as do something like that! That's robbery!

You see, the Bible said, "Don't be deceived. God is not mocked. Whatever you sow, you're going to reap" (Gal. 6:7). Churches reap what they sow too.

After that, the church just went downhill to almost nothing. In fact, one of the associate pastors told me several years later, "There hasn't been anybody baptized in the Holy Ghost in this church in three and a half years." Think about that!

A church congregation is going to reap what they sow. And many churches wonder why they're not prospering.

"I don't understand why God doesn't bless us," somebody will say. "We ought to get a different pastor."

But what are you doing with the pastor you *have*? Folks in authority in the church ought to see to it that the pastor is supported before anything else is supported. And I'll guarantee you that if they do, God will bless them.

I remember holding a meeting in a certain church down in Texas where I had held a number of meetings before. The pastor of that church said to me, "It was suggested to the church board that they set up a parsonage fund."

Now this was many years ago. A pastor usually had a parsonage furnished him with all utilities paid, and then he also received about $150 a month income.

But somebody suggested that because the pastor entertained so many people, a fund should be set up to help him with some of the expenses. This particular pastor was in a larger city, and preachers often came by to see him. You could be out a lot of money entertaining that many people.

So it was suggested to the board, "Let's set up a parsonage fund for the pastor to use to entertain people who visit him, to buy wedding gifts, and so forth. That way, he doesn't have to buy them out of his own pocket."

The fund was also to be used for furniture for the parsonage and to buy an automobile because the pastor had been making calls in his own automobile. He would still have his personal automobile, but this other automobile would be used for church work, because he was constantly on the run, visiting people.

Well, the board sort of hesitated, so someone suggested, "I'll tell you what you could do. Just try it for a year." This person knew that whatever a church sows they're going to reap! That goes for individual members too. So the board set a certain portion of the church income aside for this parsonage fund.

One of the men later told me, "I'll tell you, when we made the decision to start a parsonage fund, almost overnight, our church income doubled."

They held a business meeting the next year, and this man said, "Let's *up* that amount. We've been giving the pastor a certain percentage. Let's give a *bigger* percentage to the parsonage fund this year."

They did that, and God just kept blessing them. And one of the men told me that they met the following year and upped the percentage *again* for the parsonage fund.

He said, "We weren't running that many more people in church, but God just kept blessing us."

The board members said, "The more we put in the parsonage fund and bless the pastor, the more God blesses us." They caught on to something, praise God!

You see, they were giving honor to whom honor was due according to the Bible.

Honor God by Esteeming, Honoring, And Obeying His Word

In the Old Testament God said, ". . . *them that honour me I will honour . . .*" (1 Sam. 2:30).

Well, how are you going to honor God? You're going to honor God by doing His Word. That's one way to honor Him. And He'll honor you individually for honoring Him. He'll also honor a church for honoring Him.

That's why I want to encourage you to see to it that your pastor and those who have the oversight over you are well cared for.

One way you can do that is to always remember your pastor and his wife at Christmas. And find out when their birthdays are. I realize that many people have small churches, and sometimes they can't do as much as others. But you can do *something*.

You folks who are in authority in a local church, take note of this and attend to it. The pastor is not going to tell you these things because you might think, *He's just saying this for his own benefit.*

But you know I'm not saying it for my benefit because I'm not going to get anything out of it! I'm just telling you to support and honor your local pastor because I want *you* to be blessed.

You can honor your pastor by giving him a gift at Christmastime. Also, send your pastor and his wife to conventions every so often. For example, we hold our own Campmeeting and Winter Bible Seminar every year. Send them to events like these. Put back a certain amount of money especially for conventions, or take up special offerings to send them.

I pastored for nearly twelve years, and there were certain conventions I needed to attend. One was a state convention our denomination held every year.

My church would take up a special love offering the Sunday beforehand to send me and my wife to the convention, pay our motel bill, and buy our meals while we were there. And many times they'd buy me a new suit and my wife a new dress to wear to the convention.

Now why did they buy us a new set of clothes? Because we were going to that convention representing them. So when you send your pastor and his wife to a convention or special meeting, buy him a new suit and his wife a new dress.

Why? Because they're going to that meeting as your representatives, representing *you*!

If folks look at your pastors and they look bedraggled, those folks are going to say, "What kind of a bunch are they pastoring anyway?" And they're going to judge you.

No, you should want your pastor and his wife to look good, because they want *you* to look good!

I'm not teaching this just to be teaching. I'm telling you some very important facts. Those of you who are in the place of authority in your church, if you'll see that these things happen, I'll guarantee you that the blessings of God will rest upon you and your congregation in a greater way than they ever have before.

I received the baptism of the Holy Ghost and spoke with other tongues as a young Baptist boy preacher, and got the left foot of fellowship from among the Baptists. That's when I came over among the Pentecostals.

I can remember that in those days our churches were small. They didn't promise you anything by way of a salary. You *had to* use your faith for your salary and for the operational expenses of the church.

Then, of course, you had to encourage the people to believe God too. But the Sunday morning tithes and offerings more or less belonged to the pastor. Sunday night's offering was usually a church offering, and Wednesday night's offering was for whatever expenses we had. The church operated on this kind of a financial plan. The leaders of that denomination didn't "muzzle the ox that treadeth out the corn."

You 'Muzzle the Ox' by Robbing God's Ministers

I noticed in the early days when I was pastoring, one of the Full Gospel denominations nationwide was establishing one brand-new church every day, and two on Sunday! In fact, they expanded over a ten-year period, averaging seven new churches every single week.

Then the higher-ups in the denomination decided that they needed to put all the pastors on salary and that $100 a week was enough.

I remember one of the district superintendents of that denomination went to preach in a certain church that was quite large.

They'd run about 2,000 people on Sunday night. The congregation on Sunday mornings wasn't as big, maybe 1,500 to 1,800 people.

The pastor of that church didn't take the Sunday morning tithes and offerings for himself. They'd take up Sunday morning tithes and offerings for their two associate pastors. But the senior pastor just simply said to the people, "I'm going to be standing at the front door shaking hands with people as they go. I'm just trusting God. If you want to leave anything in my hand, that'll be fine. If you don't, that'll be fine too."

So people would just hand him something — whatever they wanted. And probably, he received several thousand dollars a year.

But then along came this district superintendent who preached in this pastor's church. He took the pastor out to eat and said, "You ought to put yourself on a salary. Now be humble and set a good example. Put yourself on a salary of $100 a week. That's big enough." Nobody usually got more than that back then.

"No," this pastor said, "I'm not going to do that. Did you notice I have the biggest church in the state? We get more people saved, more people filled with the Holy Ghost, and more people healed than practically anywhere in the state. We have more people in attendance. And I don't set myself on any salary."

The pastor continued, "Before I started preaching, I was a business man. I've had any number of offers from businesses to work for them. They'd offer me $19,000 to $24,000 a year to manage their businesses." (Now you understand, we're talking about late Depression days.)

The pastor said, "If I'm worth $19,000 a year to the world, I'm worth $19,000 a year to God."

Well, I'm not saying whether or not I agree with what the senior pastor did, and people did talk about it. They were against it. But I noticed that every single one of those churches who muzzled the ox that treadeth out the corn began to go down in number and in spiritual things. They didn't move so much in the manifestation of the power of God and the Holy Ghost.

The Practical Side to Faith for Finances

You see, there's a practical side to walking in the blessings of God for your life individually as well as corporately — as a church. And I'm presenting to you that practical side.

Sometimes people get the wrong idea when you begin to teach and preach faith. They think that if a minister is walking by faith, then they don't need to bless him.

For example, I remember once I went to teach at a convention for some people. I was just one of the speakers there. I spoke every day for several days, about four or five days total. When we were all getting ready to leave because the meetings were over, the people who were sponsoring the meeting told all the special speakers to go to a certain place where they would be reimbursed for their traveling expenses.

My wife and I had traveled at our own expense to get to that meeting. We were going on to another meeting, and I'll be honest with you, I didn't have enough money to get to my next meeting.

Well, we went along with the rest of them to get reimbursed for our traveling expenses.

When the people who sponsored that meeting came to me, they said, "Well, you preach faith — you're a faith preacher, so just go ahead and believe God." And they didn't give me a thing.

I was left stranded. You see, the Bible teaches faith, all right, but what they did was not faith because it wasn't in line with the Word. For instance, what about the scripture that says, *"Render therefore to all their dues . . ."* (Rom. 13:7)?

I remember thinking, *I don't know what I'm going to tell my wife, because I don't have enough money to get to the next meeting.* I didn't have any credit cards in those days. I didn't even have enough gasoline to get to the meeting I was scheduled to hold. I'd used all my money just to get to this special convention. And I'd had a long way to travel to get there!

The sponsors of that convention told me to just go ahead and walk by faith, so they didn't reimburse me. But, actually, in this case, there was some obligation involved on the part of the people who had invited me to speak at the convention. If it hadn't been for one of the businessmen attending the meeting, I would have been stranded. But he walked close enough to God that God could speak to him.

This businessman didn't know what had happened, and I didn't tell him. (I didn't tell a soul, actually.) He said, "Brother Hagin, the Lord told me to give you this one-hundred-dollar bill."

I said, "I believe it. Thank you." And that $100 got me to the place where I was going.

Then later some of the higher-ups in the organization that sponsored the convention asked me, "Brother Hagin, did they give you anything for preaching there?"

I said, "Well, I don't want to rat on somebody."

They said, "But we want to know."

I said, "Well, no, they didn't give me anything. They said, 'You're a faith teacher — just go ahead and live by faith.'"

"Who said that?"

I told them, and they said, "Well, we'll take care of that." And in a little while I got a check from that group for several hundred dollars.

You see, those people at that convention ought to have given it to me to begin with. They "muzzled the ox that treadeth out the corn."

Yet right on the other hand, any of us — even the preacher — can be in the wrong in the area of finances and rob people if he doesn't render what is proper. He, too, could muzzle the ox that treadeth out the corn.

When the Ox Is Muzzled, The People Are Robbed Too

When I started preaching, I was just seventeen years old. I learned much better and faster after I got filled with the Holy Ghost (even though a person does have the Holy Ghost and the witness of the Spirit in the New Birth).

I started pastoring my first church at eighteen. It was a country church about eight and three-quarters miles from the courthouse square.

The first year I preached out at that country church, I wore out four pairs of shoes because I walked so much to get to the church.

Now you understand, they weren't real expensive shoes. Those were Depression days. J. C. Penney's had three grades of shoes. You could buy one grade for 98 cents, another grade for $1.98, and the third grade of shoe for $2.98, and that was the best shoe they had.

I tried to get in the middle and buy the $1.98 pair. But I wore out four pairs in one year and didn't get enough money to buy even one new pair.

You see, I never did take up any offerings. We didn't even have an offering plate. I pastored there nearly three years and never received one single offering because I thought, *Oh, I'm going to live by faith. I'm a faith preacher and teacher.* I didn't know I was living by ignorance!

There's a vast difference between faith and ignorance! Faith is based on the knowledge of God's Word!

I did, however, have enough sense to know that if I invited somebody to come and hold a revival, I was obligated to give him an offering. So we'd just take some man's hat and pass it in order to give the visiting minister an offering. Otherwise, we never received an offering in church. I just never said a word about it.

I remember one day I needed $3 the very next day. That doesn't sound big now, but to me that $3 looked like $3,000 today!

As I was walking to church that evening, I prayed about that $3 because I had to have it. But we didn't take up offerings in our church because I was living by "faith." As I said, I was actually living by ignorance!

At that time, we had a little red-headed lady who played the piano in the church. And right in the middle of a song that evening (she didn't even wait till the end of the song), she just stopped playing, jumped up, and said, "I'm going to take up Brother Hagin an offering if it hairlips the devil!" I'd never heard anybody make a statement like that in my life! But that's what she said right in Sunday night church!

Then she said, "The Lord told me Brother Hagin needs three dollars." Boy, she was right on!

Since we didn't have an offering plate or bucket or anything, she got some man's hat and passed it around.

We didn't even have any music because she was the only pianist we had. She just passed the hat around.

Almost all of the offering was change because those were Depression days, and nobody had any folding money. I counted it out and came up with three dollars and a dime!

I don't remember hitting the ground going home! I floated all the way home, I was so thrilled! That was the only offering I received in three years.

Then I got the baptism of the Holy Ghost and spoke with other tongues. I was already *born* of the Spirit, but then I got *filled* with the Spirit. Then I began pastoring a little Full Gospel church.

I pastored this small Full Gospel church for about six or eight months until I was called to a larger Full Gospel church. I pastored this larger Full Gospel church for about two years. So it had been more than two years since I'd left that small church.

The Lord began to deal with me because I hadn't taught the people at that smaller church about tithing and giving. You see, I'd never said a word to them about money.

The Lord said to me, "You robbed those people. You did them wrong."

I had to ask the Lord to forgive me. Then He said, "I want you to go back and ask that congregation to forgive you, and I want you to acknowledge that you were wrong. Then I want you to teach them on the subject of tithing and giving."

"Now, Lord," I said, "I'm not going to contact that pastor. I've been gone about two years. If I contact him and tell him, 'The Lord wants me to come back there and preach,' he may think, *Why, he's trying to get back in here and take this church over!*"

I said to the Lord, "That pastor has the same Holy Ghost I have. *You* talk to him."

We make a mistake sometimes by thinking that when the Lord tells us something, nobody else knows anything about it. But why be so stupid? We aren't the only ones who have the Holy Ghost. The same Holy Ghost is in all of us who are born again.

About two weeks later, I got a letter from that pastor. Since those were late Depression days, we didn't have a telephone. And even if we'd had one, we wouldn't make a long-distance call on it because that would run up the bill.

So this pastor wrote me a letter. As I said, it was about two weeks after I'd prayed and repented before God, saying, "Give me an opportunity, and I'll go back and ask the church to forgive me."

In his letter, this pastor said, "Brother Hagin, I could be wrong, but it seems to me the Lord's been dealing with me about your coming back here and preaching. Maybe you could hold a revival or something. If you feel led to come, contact me."

I wrote him a letter and said, "Yes, I can come." I *didn't* tell him, "Yes, I'm anointed to come and speak to your church, and God already talked to me about it." I simply said, "Yes, I can come to your church."

He contacted me again and gave me a date to come to his church, and I accepted.

When I went back to that church, the first thing I did when I got up before the congregation was tell them exactly what the Lord had said to me. I said, "I have to repent. I had to repent before God because I failed Him. My unwillingness to teach on the subject of tithing and giving wasn't anything in the world but an ego trip, and I called it faith.

"No," I continued, "I thought I was living by faith, but I missed God when I didn't teach you to tithe and give; therefore, I robbed you. God wanted to bless you, but He couldn't because you hadn't invested anything."

Give God Something To Work With

The Bible says, "*. . . whatsoever a man soweth, that shall he also reap*" (Gal. 6:7). In other words, if he sows nothing, he's going to reap nothing. That church sowed nothing, so they reaped nothing.

So I said, "I want you to forgive me. I ask your forgiveness. I've already repented before the Lord, and thank God, He forgave me. Now I want you as a congregation to forgive me. I did you an injustice. I did you wrong!"

Then I said, "I'm going to teach you now what I should have taught you while I was here."

Isn't that a different way to start a revival meeting — to teach on the subject of tithes and offerings? But I did it!

Thank God for the Word — for *all* of the Word of God. The Word of God teaches us to tithe and to give offerings. But it also teaches us give honor to whom honor is due.

The Word of God is God speaking to us. And when we come in line with God's principles for success and prosperity, including honoring our pastor and the office he stands in, we will reap a sure harvest of blessings!

Chapter 6
Sowing and Reaping and The School of Obedience

But this I say, He which soweth sparingly shall reap also sparingly; and he which soweth bountifully shall reap also bountifully.

— 2 Corinthians 9:6

There is a law of sowing and reaping both in the natural and the spiritual realms. And it's a law that works! Yet many believers have not realized and understood the importance of this biblical principle, especially in the area of finances.

We know we can receive our needs met by faith in God's Word just as we can receive healing or any other blessing found in God's Word by faith.

But right on the other hand, you could be blessed materially through a manifestation of the Holy Ghost, too, like the widow woman in the Old Testament. God spoke to her through the prophet Elijah, and although there was a famine in the land, her oil cruse just kept pouring out oil and the meal barrel just kept giving her meal (1 Kings 17:16). That was just as good as money.

Well, that was a supernatural manifestation. And there are supernatural manifestations for us very often in the area of finances when we faithfully obey God and sow seed.

The manifestations of the Holy Spirit are as *He* wills; we can't *make* them happen. But whether there is a manifestation of the Holy Spirit or not, we always have the Word to act upon.

Yet there's another side to faith in God's Word for finances. In other words, you can't reap a crop naturally or supernaturally without *sowing seed*. You can't just go out into the backyard and say, "I'm going to pick some tomatoes" if you haven't *planted* any tomatoes! Or you can't say, "I'm going out into the field to pick cotton tomorrow" and expect to pick any cotton if the ground hasn't been prepared and the seed sown. If cotton hasn't been *planted*, you're not going to pick any cotton!

I think that folks often miss it in this area when it comes to faith for finances. They want God to bless them, all right, and it's amazing how He'll have mercy on them and help them sometimes. But oftentimes, they're trying to exercise faith principles to reap a crop when nothing has been planted!

From my experience throughout my many years of preaching faith, I think more people fail when it comes to faith for finances than anything else. The reason is that they're trying to exercise faith for finances, but they haven't planted any seed.

LUKE 6:38
38 GIVE, and IT SHALL BE GIVEN UNTO YOU;
good measure, pressed down, and shaken together,
and running over, shall men give into your bosom.
For WITH THE SAME MEASURE THAT YE METE
WITHAL IT SHALL BE MEASURED TO YOU
AGAIN.

You see, the Bible plainly said, "Give, and it will be given unto you. With the same measure with which you sow, it shall be measured back unto you." Jesus Himself said it.

Let's look again at our text.

2 CORINTHIANS 9:6
6   . . . He which soweth sparingly shall reap also
sparingly; and he which soweth bountifully shall
reap also bountifully.

If you want a bountiful crop, you've got to sow bountifully.

It Pays To Obey God's Unchanging Word

If a person will just obey the Bible, he will reap many wonderful results. For example, God plainly said to Israel, ". . . *if thou shalt hearken diligently unto the voice of the Lord thy God, to observe and to do all his commandments which I command thee this day, that . . . all these blessings shall come on thee, and overtake thee . . .*" (Deut. 28:1,2).

And God is the same today; He hasn't changed. We don't have a different God in the New Testament than they had in the Old Testament. For example, if God didn't want people to tell lies in the Old Testament, He doesn't want people to lie in the New Testament.

Somebody said, "Oh, prosperity is just for the Old Testament." But not telling a lie is not just for the Old Testament, and not stealing is not just for the Old Testament!

> **MALACHI 3:10**
> **10 BRING YE ALL THE TITHES INTO THE STOREHOUSE, that there may be meat in mine house, AND PROVE ME NOW HEREWITH, saith the Lord of hosts, IF I WILL NOT OPEN YOU THE WINDOWS OF HEAVEN, AND POUR YOU OUT A BLESSING, THAT THERE SHALL NOT BE ROOM ENOUGH TO RECEIVE IT.**

I personally have come to the conclusion that there are spiritual laws, just like there are natural laws. And when one follows those laws and puts them into practice or action, they work no matter who the person is.

We all know that in the natural there are natural laws. There's the law of gravity, for instance. And the law of gravity will work for everybody.

Suppose somebody wanted to demonstrate that the law of gravity doesn't work. He climbs up on top of a building and says, "The law of gravity is no longer in force, and I'm going to jump off this building to prove it."

Well, he'd better jump where there's some grass, and he might make it! If he hits concrete or asphalt, it's going to be tough on him because when he jumps, he's going to go *down* whether he's saved or unsaved!

Whether you're saved or unsaved, pretty or ugly, a man or a woman, or a boy or a girl, the law of gravity is going to work for you!

I'm thoroughly convinced that in the spirit realm there are laws too. And when you come in contact with those laws, they're going to work for you no matter who you are.

Now don't misunderstand me. How much more do those laws belong to those who are God's children! They're God's laws, and how much more will His laws work for those who have more light concerning their operation!

Spiritual Laws Will Work for Anyone

One thing that got me started thinking along these lines happened in the last church I pastored.

There was a man who came to church with his wife and three children. He was not a Christian, but she was saved, filled with the Holy Spirit, and was a Sunday school teacher in the church.

Her husband told her, "I'll go to church with you and the children, and I'll go with you to Sunday school *until* somebody says something to me personally about being saved. Then I'm quitting."

I taught an auditorium Bible class, and this man never missed my class. He never missed a Sunday morning, Sunday night, or Wednesday night service. When we were in revival, he never missed a revival service.

Usually the Sunday night service was an evangelistic service. Back then, you had a bigger crowd on Sunday night than you did on Sunday morning. And when we'd give the invitation during the Sunday night service, often those with soul-winning hearts would leave their seat and go minister to someone they felt under conviction, but resisting. They were real soul-winners.

I didn't know this man had said, "As soon as somebody says something to me about being saved, I'm quitting." But I was led by the Holy Spirit to get this group of soul-winners together, and I said to them, "Don't any of you ever talk to So-and-so about being saved."

"Why not?" they asked.

"Because you'll run him off."

You see, the Holy Ghost can tell you things. I don't mean He told me that in words; I just had an inward intuition that it was so.

Some of the folks in that group really didn't know when God was leading them or when He wasn't leading them, and they were overly zealous.

So I had to just practically forbid them to say anything to that man about being saved.

"But what if the Lord leads me?" one of them asked.

"If He leads you, I'll know it."

Wouldn't that be strange if God Almighty, full of wisdom, would set a pastor over a congregation and then start doing something in the crowd and never tell the pastor about it?

It would be strange if God put him there as overseer

and then start working among the people and doing things without telling the overseer what He's doing.

So no one spoke to this man about being saved. His wife came by the parsonage one day and said, "Brother Hagin, you know my husband is not a Christian. He wanted me to talk to you. He feels a little uneasy around you."

Her husband was a contractor, and he and another man were partners in business. They were building a building downtown. I don't know if they had underbid on that building or not, but their business was in danger, and the banker told them the only thing they could do was to take bankruptcy.

The woman continued, "My husband and his partner are not Christians. But I'm saved, and I go to this church. My husband's partner is married, and his wife is saved and goes to such-and-such a church.

"My husband said, 'I told my partner that I believe if we'll start paying our tithes and giving offerings, God will prosper us.'"

His partner had said, "Yes, but I'm not a Christian."

This woman's husband said, "I'm not either, but my wife is, and your wife is. I'll put in my tithes and offerings at my wife's church, and you put in your tithes and offerings at your wife's church."

His partner agreed, so the woman asked me, "Brother Hagin, would that be all right with you?"

Well, of course, we would like to have the extra money for the church, but I'll be honest with you, I was still very immature. (I'm learning and growing all the time, aren't you?) And at that time, I really doubted that it would work since he was not born again.

But I didn't tell his wife that because I didn't want to discourage her. You don't want to discourage folks. If you can't *help* them, please don't *hinder* them.

So I simply said to her, "Yes, we will accept his tithes and offerings."

I'm a witness to the fact that in thirty days' time, their business turned around, and they were out of the red and in the black!

This woman's husband was still unsaved, but he got to where he would talk to me some. He had bought out his partner a few months after they turned the business around.

The man said to me, "I got all of our employees together and testified to them how God blessed the business when I started paying tithes. I encouraged them to pay their tithes too. Of course, I can't fire them if they don't, but I encouraged them to pay tithes."

Some of them asked him, "What's tithes?"

He told them, "That's ten cents out of every dollar that belongs to God." And then he'd testify to them about how God brought his business out of ruin by his paying his tithes.

He even tried to get sinners that he hired to pay their tithes! Not only that, he even got one of my deacons to start paying his tithes faithfully!

Again, don't get me wrong. I'm not saying that a spiritual law will benefit a sinner indefinitely.

God won't honor that. A person can't continue to violate the Word in one area and expect it to continue to work for him in another area.

God will honor His Word. And He'll honor the person who endeavors to walk in all the light that he has at the moment.

About a year later, this businessman got saved. One night in church, he just came to the altar, got saved, and was filled with the Holy Ghost.

About nine months before this man got saved, I looked at the books where we kept records of the giving in the church. I saw that in that particular month, sixty percent of the church income came from this man and through church members who worked for him. God made him a blessing to us even before he got saved!

But God saved him, and the man is saved to this day. He still puts his tithes in his home church, but he also supports this ministry. He has for years and probably will continue to do so till he dies and goes to Heaven.

I tried to figure that out — how a sinner could be blessed by giving tithes and offerings! This man who paid his tithes to our church was a sinner when he first started paying his tithes and giving offerings. And God blessed him because he found a spiritual law that works.

I just finally had to come to the conclusion that there's a law of sowing and reaping. Somehow this man got in contact with that law, began practicing it, and it worked for him and his family.

Cooperate With God's Laws and Prosper!

So in your own life, just go ahead and obey the Bible in the area of finances. Pay your tithes and give offerings. Act on God's Word in faith, and God will bless you because He's faithful and true to His Word.

Then beyond cooperating with God's laws concerning tithing and giving offerings, be open to receive further light from God's Word concerning giving to others. Also, be sensitive to the Holy Spirit who will very often direct you specifically to give.

Now don't do something just because somebody else did. Don't operate on the other fellow's experience. Operate on what you know the Bible said, and operate on what the Holy Ghost is saying to *you*.

At RHEMA Bible Training Center, we've had guest ministers come and speak to the student body. One minister told about an experience he had way back in the beginning of his ministry when he didn't have a very good automobile. He gave it away, and God gave him a new one.

Some of the RHEMA students, bless their hearts, thought they'd get new cars, too, so they gave their cars away and walked the rest of the school year!

Somebody said, "But *that minister* did it and it worked."

"Yes," I said, "but God *told* him to do it. Did God tell you to do it?"

"Well, no. I just thought I'd get a new car."

It doesn't work that way.

The School of Obedience

Somebody else talked about the fact that he gave a house away. He gave a $40,000 house away, and God gave him a $250,000 home.

Somebody said, "Boy, bless God! I'm going to give mine away too. I'm going to get me a new house!" He gave his house away and then he and his family were out in the cold. I know of that actually happening. There they were without a thing.

"Why didn't that work?" they came to me bawling.

"Well, did God tell you to give it?"

"No, but So-and-so said *he* did it."

Don't you do something just because So-and-so did it. Be sure the Spirit of God is telling *you* to do it.

It's *Always* Right and Timely To Practice the Word!

On the other hand, you've got the Bible. If you know what it says, you don't have to have any leading to pay tithes and to give offerings. You know you're supposed to do that. The Bible tells you to do that. You don't have to have any leading to give. Jesus said, *"Give, and it shall be given unto you . . ."* (Luke 6:38).

You don't have to have any leading to sow because the Bible said, *". . . He which soweth sparingly shall reap also sparingly; and he which soweth bountifully shall reap also bountifully"* (2 Cor. 9:6). The Bible says that, so just do it. But when you get out beyond *that*, it's when you obey the Spirit of God that things happen.

For many years in the ministry, God had never told me to give a car or anything like that away. But I gave offerings and sowed seed, and I prospered financially.

As my wife and I moved to different places over the years, God has given us a number of different homes. I could tell you some miraculous things that have happened in that area.

For instance, once I was looking at a house and didn't have the money at all. But I was convinced the Spirit of God was moving, and by faith, I told a man I'd take the place. I needed $1,000 for a down payment, and back then, $1,000 was $1,000! It was miraculous how God brought that down payment in.

Several years ago, God did finally say something to both me and my wife (I didn't just act apart from her) about giving something away. I knew when He quickened it on the inside of me. He said to give one of my automobiles away. So we just gave it away — a brand-new automobile.

When I first told Oretha what the Lord had quickened to me, she said, "I got the same thing in my spirit."

Then later the Lord also led me to give our ministry airplane away. And about four months after that, a fellow I didn't even know wrote a letter to the ministry and said, "We feel led of the Spirit to send your ministry this check for $500,000." Glory to God!

I'm well satisfied that if I hadn't obeyed God, that wouldn't have happened. Yet I didn't have that in mind when I gave away the airplane to another ministry. I really didn't expect to get anything. I just knew I was obeying God.

"Well," somebody said, "I wish I could get something like that to happen to me."

I'll tell you where you've got to start. You've got to start by obeying the Lord and His Word with your nickels, dimes, and quarters.

Practice Faithfulness Where You Are

I remember one particular incident that took place in 1940 at Christmastime. There was a fellow, a young evangelist, in town from off the field. He was older than I was in age but younger in ministry. In other words, I'd been preaching longer than he had. In fact, he was just starting out, and he and his wife had five children.

Some of his folks and his wife's folks were members of my church. So while he was off at Christmastime, he attended our church. I tried to get him to preach, and I would have given him an offering for preaching.

You realize those were Depression days. And you'd give $5 to a fellow who preached for you on a Sunday night.

Somebody said, "That beats anything I've ever seen! Only $5!"

But let me tell you what finances were like in Depression days. For example, I remember one fellow who worked for the railroad company whose monthly salary was only $37.50 *a month*. He had three children, so there were five of them in the family. He paid house rent, fed his family, and drove an automobile on $37.50 a month!

So, you see, $5 for an evening's preaching was nice by comparison! And I would have given this young evangelist an offering, but he wouldn't preach. He said, "Brother Hagin, I'm just sort of embarrassed to preach here in front of my kinfolks." So I went ahead and preached that night. Then I was shaking hands with folks when the service was over, and the Lord said to me, "I want you to give him $10."

"Dear Lord," I said, "I can't give him $10. Don't You know this is Christmastime?"

I could go back and show you my books. I still have them. You see, I only averaged $43.15 a month myself. Well, $10 was about a week's pay!

"Lord, I can't give him $10," I continued. "I won't have anything left for Christmas. I haven't even bought my wife a Christmas present yet."

"I want you to give him $10."

There I was shaking hands with people and smiling, and all the while I was having an argument between my head and my heart! (You just don't know what's going on inside a fellow sometimes!) I was shaking hands with people, talking to them, smiling and greeting them, and my head and heart were having a fight.

The Lord was talking to me in my heart, but my head was saying, *No, that won't work. Don't do that. Man, what are you going to do? You haven't bought your wife a Christmas present yet!*

Finally, I just got that $10 together, and everybody was gone by then. The young evangelist was standing outside talking to somebody. I just shook hands with him and left it in his hands. I didn't even have a $10 bill — just dollar bills and some change.

It wasn't very long afterwards that I heard his mother-in-law tell somebody, "You know, my son-in-law was off at Christmastime. He has five children, and he just had enough money to pay his rent and his utilities. He didn't have a dime left — not a dime — to buy his kids anything for Christmas. He couldn't buy Christmas dinner. And somebody gave him $10." (Whether you realize it or not, $10 would go a long way back then.)

I didn't jump up and down and holler, "That was me! I did it!"

No, I just stayed quiet and said to myself, *Thank God. I'm so glad I obeyed God.*

In the process of time, I was shaking hands with folks at church before an evening service. Our church was right on the highway. In those days all the highways went right through town; we didn't have any freeways.

A Greyhound bus pulled up and stopped right in front of our church, and I saw a fellow get off the bus, get a suitcase, and begin walking toward the church. I recognized him as a minister. I had never really officially met him, but I knew who he was because I had seen him at conventions.

I wondered, *What's he getting off here for?* It was about time to start church, so I greeted him, and he told me who he was.

I said, "Yes, I know who you are."

He said, "I've never officially met you, but I knew who you were too."

I said, "Well, since you're going to be with us tonight, why don't you preach for us."

He said, "Okay. But I need to go over to the parsonage, change my shirt, and freshen up."

"Go ahead," I said. "We'll be singing. Just come on over and preach."

We were going to give him $5 out of the church treasury. That was the custom. But while he was preaching, the Lord said to me, "I want you to give him $12.50 out of your own pocket."

That doesn't sound big now, but that was more than a week's pay back then. Actually $12.50 a week for pay would be about $50 a month. I only averaged $43.15 a month, so that was a little bit more than a week's pay.

You may make $500 a week now, but to me that $12.50 was just as big then as $500 would be to you now.

I have a good memory, but I don't know to this day what that fellow preached on because I was having an argument between my head and my heart.

"I can't give him $12.50," I told the Lord. "I just can't do it. I can't afford to." I didn't have any bank account, not even a checking account.

I never did settle it during the service. We went back over to the parsonage after the meeting, and I was still having a fight between my head and my heart.

The minister was getting ready for bed, and I began counting out $12.50. Most of it was in change (nickels, dimes, and even pennies — that's how we got it in those days!).

So I was counting that out and getting it ready for him. My wife was in the kitchen fixing us a bite to eat when the Lord said to me, "Now the reason this minister got off the bus here is that he's run out of money, and this is as far as he could go."

The Lord said to me on the inside, just as plainly as anything: "He's going down to Winnsboro next Sunday to preach and try out for a certain church there. They're going to elect him as pastor over there." This minister came back into the room where we were, and I told him, "Hold out your hands," and I gave him the $12.50.

He put it in his coat pocket, and we began talking about something else. And the devil said to my mind, "Now you've played whaley" (that's just a good Texas-Oklahoma colloquial expression that means you've goofed). The devil said to my mind, "You've missed it and made a fool of yourself." After all, I had given away my week's pay. And the devil said, "You gave it away, and now you're just out the $12.50."

Just to confirm what the Lord had said, I asked the minister, "Where are you going after this?"

"Brother Hagin," he said, "my wife and two children are down at her parents' house in Winnsboro. I went to the bus station in the last town I was in and said, 'This is how much money I have. How far will it take me?' I thought I'd take the bus that far and hitchhike the rest of the way."

He continued: "The bus brought me right here to your town. I asked the bus driver to let me off in front of the church here. I didn't have a dime left — that was as far as I could go. I planned on hitchhiking to Winnsboro, but with this money, I can buy a ticket."

Then he said, "Next Sunday I'm supposed to preach over at a certain church to try out to be their pastor."

I said, "Brother, that's all you have to say. Now I want to tell you something. You're the next pastor over there." And sure enough, he was!

Now pay attention to something here. About two years after that happened, my wife and I went to minister to a lady on her deathbed. Her husband had taken her by ambulance to three clinics across north-central Texas. Doctors at each one of these clinics had said the same thing: "We can't do anything for her. She's too far gone. Among other things, she has an incurable blood disease in the last stages. She's dying; she'll be dead in a few days."

To *Obey* the Voice of God, You Must *Know* the Voice of God

My wife and I went to minister to that dear lady. We didn't know her. One of our church members knew her. And as we went into her room to pray for her, we knelt by the bed, and the same Voice that spoke to my heart and told me to give that one minister $10 and the other minister $12.50 said to me, "Get up. Don't pray. Just stand up and say to her, 'The Lord told me to tell you that you're healed. Get up!'"

I did, she did, and God did! Hallelujah! That was on a Thursday, and she was in our church on Sunday, dancing and shouting the victory.

On our way back home from ministering to that woman on Thursday, my wife and I were rejoicing that God used us to raise up a woman from the deathbed. Just about that time, just like somebody was sitting in the back seat, the Lord said to me, "I couldn't have used you here if you hadn't obeyed Me on that $10 and the $12.50."

I'd forgotten all about that. It had been about two years since I'd given that money to those two ministers. I had to stop and think, "What do You mean, that $10 and the $12.50?"

The Lord brought it back to my remembrance, and I said, "Yeah, I remember that."

He said to me, "If you hadn't obeyed Me on that, I couldn't have used you here."

We all want God to use us. Wouldn't you like God to use you to raise up somebody from a deathbed? Well, friends, how are you going to know the Voice of God when He tells you how to get people off a deathbed if you don't know His Voice when He tells you to give away $1 or $5?

You see, that's the way you start learning God's Voice. But if He can't trust you with $5 or $10, how's He going to trust you to raise somebody from a deathbed? You could very easily call learning to hear God's Voice in giving *the school of the Holy Ghost* or the school of obedience because it all works together!

There is a law of sowing and reaping that many believers have yet to tap into, and as a result, they have not prospered like God wants them to. But there is another principle of obedience to the Voice of the Holy Spirit that will also bring rich rewards if you practice it.

Start where you are. Be faithful to obey the Word by paying your tithes and giving offerings. And be obedient to the leading of the Holy Spirit to direct you specifically to give. You can't out-give God. If you sow seeds bountifully in faith and obedience, you will reap a bountiful harvest of blessings!

Chapter 7
Godliness Is Profitable
In All Things

*But refuse profane and old wives' fables, and
exercise thyself rather unto godliness.*

For bodily exercise profiteth little [or as the
margin says, bodily exercise profiteth for a little
time]*: BUT GODLINESS IS PROFITABLE unto
all things, having promise of the life that now is,
and of that which is to come. . . .*

*Meditate upon these things; give thyself
wholly to them; that thy profiting may appear to
all.*

— 1 Timothy 4:7,8,15

The Bible says godliness is profitable in all things.
That's talking about prosperity for the whole man —
spirit, soul, and body. The Bible also says that the
profit godliness brings is for this life *and* the life to
come. And the profit that godliness brings in this life is
more than just finances and material profit. There's
more to it than that, but financial prosperity is certainly a part of it.

Notice particularly verse 8: *"For BODILY EXER-CISE PROFITETH LITTLE: but GODLINESS IS PROFITABLE UNTO ALL THINGS, having promise of the life that now is, and of that which is to come."*

The reason bodily exercise only "profiteth little" is that it only profits in one area. Bodily exercise does profit, but it only "profiteth little." It is wrong to take the physical and put it on the same level with the spiritual. That is where many folks miss it. Keep the physical in its place and it's right and blessed.

But godliness is profitable. That simply means it pays off. Anything that is profitable pays off.

In 1944, I was preaching down in east Texas, where one of the pastors there had a sixteen- or seventeen-year-old son. The son was a little short fellow and sort of stooped-shouldered with a hollow-looking chest.

The pastor's son asked me, "Is it wrong to take up physical fitness and exercise?" You see, he wanted to build up his chest and his biceps.

Some of the old-time Pentecostals thought just about everything was wrong. Some even thought it was wrong to wear deodorant. *I* always thought it was wrong *not* to!

When the pastor's son asked me if it was wrong to take up physical fitness, I told him, "Why, certainly not."

He said, "I picked up a book at a newsstand, a magazine on physical fitness, that told how to order certain equipment."

I went back to that town, about fifteen months later, to hold a meeting. I was staying in the parsonage with these same folks. This pastor's son pulled off his shirt to show us he had expanded six inches around his chest! He'd also developed his biceps.

This young man could have developed other parts of his body, but he was just interested in developing his chest and the upper part of his body. He stood up straight instead of stooped because he'd built up certain muscles.

However, although that exercise paid off for him by building him up physically, it didn't build him up spiritually or mentally. That is the reason that bodily exercise profiteth little.

But godliness is profitable *unto all things*! It pays off in everything ". . . *having promise of the life that now is, and of that which is to come.*"

Now a lot of folks try to tell you that we don't have any promise in this life. They tell you that we just get saved and then we're to go through life with our nose to the grindstone, living on Barely-Get-Along Street way down at the end of the block, right next to Grumble Alley. And they think that is a sign of godliness!

But, no. God said, ". . . *godliness is profitable unto all things, having promise of THE LIFE THAT NOW IS* . . ." (1 Tim. 4:8). We've got promises in *this* life. The rest of that verse says, ". . . *AND of that* [life] *which is to come.*" So godliness pays off here *and* hereafter.

"Godliness" just simply means *living for God*. Now what do we mean, "living for God"? Living for God means doing just exactly what Paul said in verse 12.

1 TIMOTHY 4:12
12 Let no man despise thy youth; but be thou an example of the believers, in word, in conversation, in charity, in spirit, in faith, in purity.

Be an example for believers in word, in conduct or manner of life, in love, in spirit, in faith, and in purity. That's living for God. And living for God is profitable!

Yet the way some people talk, living for God doesn't pay off in this life. But notice that Paul said, ". . . *having promise of the life that NOW IS.* . . ." That's present tense. You see, too many times, Christians only think about what a great day it will be when we all get to Heaven. And don't misunderstand me, that *will* be a great day, thank God! But these folks seem to imply that God's promises are all for the next life.

But notice that Paul said living for God is profitable in this life and in the next one, too, ". . . *having promise of the life that NOW IS, AND OF THAT WHICH IS TO COME*" (1 Tim. 4:8)! What does it mean, godliness is "profitable"? You see, God has an investment in us as believers, and He wants to realize some returns on His investment! We talk about *our* inheritance. But *God* has an inheritance in *us*, and He desires that it produce a high profit, because He said, "Godliness is *profitable*."

Then notice in the latter part of First Timothy 4:15: ". . . *that thy profiting may appear to all.*" That's talking about in this life!

You know that in this life when a person gets a little money, sometimes he wants to invest it. And he usually wants to invest it where it brings the best dividends.

I believe that God not only desires for us to be saved (and thank God, He *has* remitted our sins), but He also wants us to bring glory unto His Name *after* we are saved. That will help bring God great dividends for His investment in us!

In the Bible, the Apostle Paul writing to the Church at Corinth said something along this line.

> **1 CORINTHIANS 3:9**
> 9 . . . ye are God's husbandry, ye are God's building.

That can be a little bit blind to us because that word "husbandry" doesn't mean so much to us today. But a modern translation reads, "Ye are God's *garden*." Another translation said, "Ye are God's *farm*."

Well, you expect a farm to produce, don't you? You expect a garden to produce; you expect it to be *profitable*. There wouldn't be any profit in planting a garden or tilling or working a farm if it didn't produce anything.

You know, friends, godliness is not a hindrance to success. It's exactly the opposite. *Godliness is profitable unto all things!* It's profitable unto protection, promotion, perpetuity, and prosperity. Hallelujah!

Godliness Ensures *Protection*

First of all, godliness will ensure *protection*.

You see, if we're God's, we belong to Him! And He will protect us. You remember Paul said in First

Corinthians 6:19, ". . . *your body is the temple of the Holy Ghost which is in you, which ye have of God, and ye are not your own."*

You see, you don't belong to yourself. You're not your own. You were bought with a price; you belong to God.

Since we belong to God, then we ought to expect Him to take care of us. As I said, godliness ensures *protection.*

Now that doesn't mean that we're to act foolish and think we'll just automatically be protected. For example, Acts 27 says Paul had to appeal his case to Caesar and was on his way to Rome to do so. As they boarded the ship for Rome, Paul said, ". . . *I perceive that this voyage will be with hurt and much damage, not only of the lading and ship, but also of our lives"* (v. 10).

Now notice Paul didn't say, "God *showed* me" or "God *told* me." No, Paul *perceived* it. You see, each one of us ought to have a certain amount of spiritual perception.

Paul perceived that their voyage would be "with hurt and much damage." But those who were sailing with Paul didn't pay any attention to him because the south wind was blowing softly. So they set sail for Rome anyway.

> **ACTS 27:14-20**
> **14 But not long after there arose against it a tempestuous wind, called Euroclydon.**
> **15 And when the ship was caught, and could not bear up into the wind, we let her drive.**
> **16 And running under a certain island which is**

> **called Clauda, we had much work to come by the boat:**
> **17 Which when they had taken up, they used helps, undergirding the ship; and, fearing lest they should fall into the quicksands, strake sail, and so were driven.**
> **18 And we being exceedingly tossed with a tempest, the next day they lightened the ship;**
> **19 And the third day we cast out with our own hands the tackling of the ship.**
> **20 And when neither sun nor stars in many days appeared, and no small tempest lay on us, all hope that we should be saved was then taken away.**

All hope that they would be saved was gone. They'd thrown all of their merchandise overboard to try to save themselves. Then Paul stood forth in the midst of their hopeless situation (v. 21).

After seeking God and the Lord speaking to him (in fact, the Lord sent an angel), Paul said, ". . . *I exhort you to be of good cheer: for there shall be no loss of any man's life among you, but of the ship. For there stood by me this night the angel of God, WHOSE I AM, and whom I serve"* (vv. 22,23).

In other words, Paul said, "I belong to God." Hallelujah!

Just think about it! God saved the whole bunch of them just because Paul belonged to God. I don't know whether or not there was anybody else on board who belonged to God.

But God saved all of them because of one godly man. The angel told them, "Now the ship is going to be lost.

But if you'll do what I tell you, there will not be the loss of anyone's life."

Paul said, "I belong to God!"

> **ACTS 27:23**
> 23 For there stood by me this night the angel of God, WHOSE I AM, and WHOM I SERVE.

Then Paul went on to tell them what the angel told him.

> **ACTS 27:24,25**
> 24 Saying, Fear not, Paul; thou must be brought before Caesar: and, lo, God hath given thee all them that sail with thee.
> 25 Wherefore, sirs, be of good cheer: for I BELIEVE GOD, that it shall be even as it was told me.

Now notice this passage of Scripture again. There's another little clause here that I want to emphasize. After Paul said, ". . . *there stood by me . . . the angel of God, whose I am, and whom I serve,*" Paul also said, "I believe God!" (v. 25).

Paul said three things: I *belong to* God, I *serve* God, and I *believe* God!

Not only did Paul belong to God, but Paul said, "I serve God."

That's very positive. Notice he didn't say, "I'm *trying* to serve God. The Lord knows I'm doing the best I can." No, talk like that is just a human cop-out.

In Paul's second letter to Timothy, Paul said, "The time of my departure is at hand" (2 Tim. 4:6). Paul knew it was time for him to leave this world. But notice what he said: *"I have fought a good fight, I have FINISHED MY COURSE, I have kept the faith"* (v. 7).

Notice Paul *finished* his course. He didn't halfway finish it! You see, if you're going to serve God, you're going to put God first above everything else. That means that whatever He tells you to do, you don't quit in the middle of the stream.

That's what it means to be godly — to live for God and serve Him wholeheartedly. There's reward or profit for living a godly life. Living for God will affect you in every way, including in the realm of finances.

The Lord didn't say the going is always going to be good. In fact, the Word of God says, "The afflictions of the righteous are many" (Ps. 34:19). Now that's translated from the Hebrew language, and that word translated "afflictions" is talking about troubles and trials.

In Psalm 91, God said, "I'll be with him in trouble." Well, you see, if you never had any trouble, why would He say He'd be with you in trouble? No, serving God doesn't mean you're not going to have any trouble.

Some people get the idea if you live by faith and walk by faith, you just sort of float through life on flowery beds of ease. They think you'll never have any persecution or opposition or trouble. They get the idea that the blessings of protection, promotion, perpetuity, and prosperity will just sort of fall on them like ripe cherries off a tree. But that's not what the Bible said.

Psalm 34:19 says, *"Many are the afflictions of the righteous: but the Lord delivereth him out of them all."*

You see, we're living in a world where Satan is called its god (2 Cor. 4:4). Although we're *in* the Kingdom of God, we also live *in* this world. But we can be thankful we are not *of* this world.

Godliness ensures divine protection! That simply means *God will see you through!*

Godliness Ensures *Promotion*

Godliness pays off! It's profitable! It will ensure protection, and it will also ensure *promotion*.

When I talk about promotion, I'm not talking necessarily about promotion according to the world. Yet right on the other hand, your promotion or your profiting shall appear to all according to First Timothy 4:15. "All" means everybody in the world and everybody in the Church as well. All means *all!*

Godliness ensures promotion. You know, God has been *unable* to promote many folks. He wanted to bless and promote them. He wanted them to develop and grow. He wanted their profiting, including financial prosperity, to appear to all.

But, you see, they didn't apply themselves. They were too lazy or slipshod. Too many times they had a cotton string for a backbone. We need people, especially young people, with a crowbar — an iron bar — as a backbone. We need young people who will say, "I'm going to stand my ground no matter what!"

I certainly wasn't perfect growing up. I knew nothing about holiness; I'd never heard the word. I was born and raised in a denomination that taught that you can't help but sin — that you've got to sin every day.

I got born again the twenty-second day of April, a Saturday night, at twenty minutes till eight o'clock in the south bedroom of 405 North College Street in the city of McKinney, Texas.

But I went right back to the same church I was going to because there was no Full Gospel church in our town. And I was an oddity to all the people in my church because I had changed. You notice that Paul said to Timothy, ". . . *be thou an example of the believers, in word, in CONVERSATION. . .* " (1 Tim. 4:12).

To many of us, the word "conversation" means *speaking words*. But Paul just got through saying, ". . . *be thou an example of the believers, in WORD . . .*" (v. 12). Then he said, ". . . *in conversation. . . .*" So the word "conversation" has to mean something different.

If you'll look it up, you'll find out that this Greek word translated "conversation" here means your *conduct*. In other words, be an example in the way you conduct yourself. Or be an example in your *manner of life*!

As a teenager, I spoke to different groups among other denominations, especially to youth groups. And the young people would all say to me, "Kenneth, what makes you different from us? You don't go to the dances" (yes, they even put on worldly dances in church!).

I didn't go because I don't believe in that. I didn't then, and I don't now. I don't believe in putting on any kind of a dance, especially in church. Now the Holy

Ghost comes on me sometimes, and I begin to dance in the Spirit. That's a different thing entirely. That's the kind of dancing I believe in.

But these young people said, "You don't go to the dances with us. You don't smoke cigarettes." Kids in their early teens and even younger kids sometimes think doing that makes them grown up.

I was fifteen when I got saved. When I was about thirteen, sometimes when somebody else was smoking, I would smoke. I could hardly inhale it, and then I would just puff the smoke out.

But, you know, the first thing I promised God when I got born again was, "I'll never smoke another cigarette." Some way or other, my spirit just knew things my head didn't know, and I knew smoking wasn't right. So I promised Him I'd never smoke another cigarette. And I never have.

I didn't even go to picture shows (they called movies "picture shows" in those days). The only ones that seem to be any good now are those they had back then! Most of these modern-day ones are full of junk! You need to be careful to be an example along these lines. Be an example in your manner of life or conduct.

Those young people who were questioning me were all church people. They said, "Kenneth, you don't drink." (They'd even have church and Sunday school parties and dance, drink, smoke, cuss, and have sex.)

"You don't do any of those things," they said to me. "What makes you different?"

"Well," I said, "I'm a new creature."

"A new what?" they'd ask, and that would give me the opportunity to preach. You see, they opened the door. I didn't just go around spouting off. But if they opened the door, I was ready. So don't go around trying to push something off on somebody. But if they ask questions and open the door, you be ready to answer them.

Pay careful attention here. I'm still talking about promotion — promotion in every way, including financially. I'll tell you about a secret I learned years ago as a Baptist boy.

After I got born again, I missed a whole year of school. When I became bedfast, I'd already completed two years of high school, but I just skipped by; I got a C minus on two subjects. And in my day, if you failed one subject in the second year of high school, you had to take the whole year over, not just that one subject.

Well, there were two subjects, English and mathematics, that I'd made C minus on. They graded us A, B, C, or D. The grade D meant you were failing, and a C minus meant you just barely skimmed by.

The teachers in both the English class and the mathematics class said to me, "You actually made a D, but you lacked two points of making it with a C minus. You just skimmed by." Neither one of them knew what the other teacher had said, but they both said about the same thing. They said, "I thought maybe I'd missed a point or two on some test through the year, so I just gave you the C minus."

But then I got born again, and, of course, I began reading the Bible. Having been in Sunday school all my life, some of the things I read refreshed my thinking because I remembered the stories I'd heard as a young boy.

I'd walk to school every morning. Those were Depression days and there wasn't much traffic, and sometimes a whole bunch of us would just walk right down the middle of the street.

But while everybody else was talking and laughing, I would talk to the Lord. You know you can talk to Him out loud, but you can talk to Him on the inside, and He hears that too.

Now let me prove that by the Scripture. In First Corinthians 14, Paul said, *"If any man speak in an unknown tongue, let it be by two, or at the most by three, and that by course; and let one interpret"* (v. 27).

Then notice what he said in verse 28: *"But if there be no interpreter, let him keep silence. . . ."* That is, you don't say anything out loud.

Now notice the rest of the verse: *". . . and let him speak to himself, and to God."* So you can talk to God right on the inside of you.

And so every morning on my way to school, I'd remind the Lord and myself of His Word, making my faith confessions.

I didn't know that's what I was doing, but when you sum it up, that's what I did. I reminded Him about Daniel and the three Hebrew children in the Book of Daniel who were in school over in Babylon.

And, of course, according to the Hebrews' religious custom, the Hebrews didn't eat certain animals. The food that was supplied to Daniel and the three Hebrew children in Babylon was against their religion. So they went to the dean of the school and said to him in effect, "It's against our religion to eat these certain foods, and we don't want to violate our consciences."

The dean answered, "You know, you're going to get me in trouble."

"Well," they said, "just put us on bread and vegetables for ten days."

He did, and at the end of ten days, their countenances were brighter and they looked better than all the others who were eating the regular foods that were supplied to them.

So the dean said, "Just go ahead and eat what you want to eat."

Well, when Daniel and the three Hebrew boys graduated, the Scripture says, *"And in all matters of wisdom and understanding, that the king inquired of them, he found them ten times better than all the magicians and astrologers that were in all his realm"* (Dan. 1:20). God promoted them.

So I'd remind the Lord of that Scripture. I said, "You can bless me like that too. Now I'm going to do my part, don't misunderstand me. I'm not going to shirk my duty. I'm not going to be absent from school (and I never missed one day or one class).

"Lord, I'm not going to whittle my time away," I continued. We had a study period in study hall. I spent every one of those periods studying.

And I never took one single book home to study for the next two years of high school. I didn't do any studying except at school, and I made nothing less than a straight-A report card. I stood at the head of the class.

God Rewards Faithfulness

You can do the same thing. If you'll believe God, He'll promote you too. That means He'll move you forward.

When you live for God, He'll promote you. He's on your side. He's not against you. Now if you just whittle away your time, it won't work. You see, if I'd just messed around in school, throwing paper wads all day and sleeping during the study-hall period, then I would have had to do some studying at home. And then if I hadn't studied at home, I would have failed.

I remember in foreign language class, I made an A minus. And the teacher said to me right in front of the whole class: "Kenneth, actually I guess I should have given you an A, because nobody else in the class made anything above a C. You were so far ahead of the rest of them, I thought, *Maybe he's not that far ahead of them, so I'll give him an A minus.*

"But I may have missed it," she said. "I probably should have given you an A. I wanted to say that in front of the whole class."

But, you see, the point I want to make is that I moved up ahead of all of them in class, and I didn't do any studying at home. I didn't write any themes at home. I never even took a book home with me. But I applied myself at school, and I believed God.

You can apply yourself, and God will promote you. But if you whittle away your time and you don't put God first, you'll get in trouble.

Notice again our text that says godliness, or living for God, is profitable. That's true in the financial realm, but it's also true in every other realm. *It pays to live for God.*

You'll remember that Jesus said, *"But seek ye first the kingdom of God, and his righteousness; and all these things shall be added unto you"* (Matt. 6:33). Notice He said, *". . . all these things shall be ADDED unto you,"* not taken away from you!

Godliness Ensures *Perpetuity*

Living for God is profitable in this life because it ensures or guarantees protection and promotion. It also guarantees *perpetuity* to those who live for God.

Let's look at what the Bible says about those who *don't* live for God.

> **PSALM 55:23**
> 23 . . . bloody and deceitful men shall not live out half their days. . . .

Well, that does away with the theory that everybody's got an appointed time to die, and when that time comes, he's going to die anyway no matter what. Here in this verse it says, "Bloody and deceitful people won't even live out half of their days."

Sometimes people say, "Well, I'm not a person out for blood." But what about deception? It says, ". . . *bloody and DECEITFUL men shall not live out half their days. . . .*" That's what deceitful means — to deceive people.

Deceitful people are on your side one time, and the next time they're against you. One time they're one way, and the next time they're another way. They're very deceptive. We sometimes call them "two-faced."

God said that not only those who are out killing people won't live out half their days, but deceitful people won't live out half their days either.

> **JOB 17:9**
> **9   The righteous also SHALL HOLD ON HIS WAY, and he that hath clean hands shall be STRONGER AND STRONGER.**

"*The righteous also shall hold on his way. . . .*" In other words, he'll stay right in the way of God and walk in the way of God. And he'll get stronger and stronger. Hallelujah!

Well, now, if you'll go back to what Paul said to Timothy, that's exactly what Paul was talking about. He said, "Be an example in word, in manner of life or in conduct, in love, and *purity*."

We walk in purity by walking in the Word and by walking in love.

> **PROVERBS 2:1-5**
> **1   My son, if thou wilt receive my words, and hide my commandments with thee;**

2 So that thou incline thine ear unto wisdom, and apply thine heart to understanding [knowledge];
3 Yea, if thou criest after knowledge, and liftest up thy voice for understanding;
4 If thou seekest her as silver, and searchest for her as for hid treasures;
5 Then shalt thou understand the fear of the Lord, and find the knowledge of God.

Look at verses 3 and 4 again: "*. . . if thou criest after knowledge, and liftest up thy voice for understanding; If thou seekest her as silver, and searchest for her as for hid treasures.*"

We could say it like this: "If you would be just as diligent about crying after knowledge and lifting up your voice for understanding as you would about looking for hidden treasure. . . ." If you knew where there was a treasure hidden, you'd go and dig for it, wouldn't you?

Verse 1 says, "*. . . if thou wilt receive my words, and hide my commandments with thee.*" Paraphrasing that, it says, "If you'll receive the Word of God and hide His *commandment of love* with thee," because that commandment of love fulfills all commandments!

PROVERBS 3:1
1 My son, forget not my law; but let thine heart keep my COMMANDMENTS.

Understand this, *all* the commandments of God are fulfilled in the law of love. You don't have to worry about any other commandment than the law of love because if you walk in love, you'll fulfill all the commandments of God. That's the reason Paul told Timothy, "Be an example in charity or in love."

> **ROMANS 13:10**
> **10 Love worketh no ill to his neighbour: therefore love is the fulfilling of the law.**

What are the benefits of godliness?

> **PROVERBS 3:2**
> **2   For length of days** [shortness of days? No! *Length* of days]**, and LONG LIFE, and peace, shall they add to thee.**

I'm glad I saw this truth years ago. *"My son, forget not my law . . ."* (Prov. 3:1). The law of love is this: Love worketh no ill to his neighbor. Love is the fulfilling of the Law. The rest of Proverbs 3:1 says, *". . . but let thine heart keep my commandments."*

If you walk in love, you will fulfill all of God's commandments!

If you're walking in love, you won't break any command that would curb sin. What will walking in love do for you? Is there any benefit or profit to it? Yes! It will bring you profit spiritually, mentally and emotionally, physically, financially, and in *every* area!

In the margin of my Bible, it says the Hebrew words for "long life" are "years of life." In other words, "For length of days, and *years of life*, and peace, shall they (remembering God's law and keeping His commandments) add to thee" (Prov. 3:2)!

Godliness ensures perpetuity — long life!

PROVERBS 10:27
27 The fear of the Lord PROLONGETH days. . . .

"Fear" in this verse doesn't mean you fear God like you would a rattlesnake or a tornado. It's talking about reverential trust!

Again, in the margin of my Bible, the word "prolongeth" in the Hebrew means *addeth*. The fear of the Lord will add days to your life!

PROVERBS 10:27
27 . . . but the years of the wicked shall be SHORT-ENED.

"Well," somebody said, "I knew people who were wicked, and they lived a long time."

Well, they still shortened their days! If they hadn't lived that way, they could have lived longer and better!

I don't know about you, but I set out years ago to get God's best in life. And I saw this truth right here among all the other truths. Thank God for His Word.

You understand that it's conditional whether or not days are added to your life — whether or not you live a long life. God promised it, all right, but it's up to you to reap the benefits of God's promise. It's up to you whether or not it's so in your case.

Godliness Ensures *Prosperity*

Godliness not only ensures protection, promotion, and perpetuity, but, thank God, godliness also ensures *prosperity*!

Of course, when you use that word prosperity, people think about the natural realm — about financial and material prosperity. That's true, but it actually means to prosper in spirit, soul, and body.

Did you ever notice that according to what John said in his third Epistle, your physical, material, and financial prosperity depends on your *spiritual* prosperity?

> **3 JOHN 2**
> 2   Beloved, I wish above all things that thou mayest **PROSPER AND BE IN HEALTH** [that's physical prosperity], **EVEN AS THY SOUL PROSPERETH.**

You know, when it comes to the realm of the natural, so many people don't see the truth that God wants them to prosper financially and walk in divine health. They think, "God wants to bless us *spiritually*, all right. But we may have to go through life poverty-stricken and barely able to get by."

But that's not true, and we see that fact over and over in the Word.

> **2 CHRONICLES 26:5**
> 5   And he sought God in the days of Zechariah, who had understanding in the visions of God: AND AS LONG AS HE SOUGHT THE LORD, GOD MADE HIM TO PROSPER.

If you'll read all of that account, you'll find out that God is talking about material and financial prosperity.

Besides that, remember what God said to Joshua in the very beginning of Joshua's ministry when he'd taken over to be the leader in place of Moses.

JOSHUA 1:8
8   This book of the law shall not depart out of thy mouth; but thou shalt meditate therein day and night, that thou mayest observe to do according to all that is written therein: for then THOU shalt make THY way PROSPEROUS, and then thou shalt have GOOD SUCCESS.

We could paraphrase that verse like this: "This *Word of God* shall not depart out of thy mouth; but thou shalt meditate therein day and night, that thou mayest observe to do (*do* the Word; don't just be a *hearer* of the Word) according to all that is written therein: for then thou shalt make thy way prosperous. . . ."

Did you notice what God said? He said *you'll* make *your* way prosperous. Now we understand, of course, that God would be behind your prosperity. He's the author of it. But it's up to *you* whether or not you make your way prosperous.

It's up to *you* whether or not you prosper mentally. It's up to *you* whether you prosper in school or on your job. It's up to *you* whether you prosper financially and materially. It's up to *you*!

God tells you what will happen when you put His Word first: ". . . *THEN thou shalt make thy way PROSPEROUS, and then thou shalt have GOOD SUCCESS.*"

Dealing Wisely in the Affairs of Life

I like another translation of Joshua 1:8: "You'll be able to deal wisely in the affairs of life."

Well, you couldn't have good success if you didn't deal wisely in the affairs of life.

And God tells you exactly how to deal wisely so you can have success! It says the Word of God shall not depart out of your mouth — you'll meditate therein day and night. You'll observe it and do it, then you'll make your way prosperous. You'll have good success. Glory to God!

To tell you the real truth about it, most folks who are not prosperous are that way because they haven't honored God. They've *dishonored* God. But if they honor God, they will prosper.

For example, some people are always behind in paying their bills. I guess most of us have been there at sometime or another before we could see certain truths the Word of God taught. But some are *always* behind with their bills — behind with their rent, behind with this payment and that payment.

You see, so many people are always behind and can't get caught up. Then they can't do what they ought to do about spreading the Gospel — sending out missionaries and getting the Word of God out to others.

Reasons Why Some Don't Prosper

Certainly, God wants us to prosper, but we have our part to play. And if we honor God, He will bless us.

We already read in Joshua 1:8 *how* to prosper: by meditating on the Word day and night that we may observe to *do* it. So we know it's God's will that we prosper.

On the other hand, however, you can get in the ditch on the other side, believing God is going to prosper you no matter how you're living.

Some people think that all they have to do is "honor" God by giving and God will give back to them. But, no, He won't, because God honors His Word — *all* of it, not just a part of it.

God expects you to walk in the light that you have from His Word. We already found out from the Word that our financial and physical prosperity is dependent upon our *spiritual* prosperity (3 John 2).

I know of people who thought God was going to prosper them in their giving (and they gave for that very purpose — just to get something in return). But they weren't living right. In fact, they got their money by being crooks! They were givers, all right, but God didn't honor their giving.

I know of one particular man years ago who was a millionaire (that was like being a billionaire today). He had a palatial home in those days that was way beyond what anybody else had in those days.

Back then, not too many people had Mercedes, Lincolns, or Cadillacs either. Yet he and his wife, son, and daughter all had their own expensive cars. He also had his own private jet.

This wealthy man was very liberal in his giving, yet he eventually lost everything he had. He didn't prosper.

Why didn't this man prosper? He paid his tithes; he gave offerings. He didn't prosper because many of his business deals weren't quite right. In other words, they were crooked or shady. And God couldn't honor that.

That man's shady business dealings affected him spiritually. They affected him financially, and they affected him physically. Both he and his wife were very sickly.

You see, the whole package of God's blessings goes together. But if we're not careful, we'll put all our emphasis on money.

Certainly, God's Word talks about material prosperity because the Bible says, ". . .. *whatsoever he doeth shall prosper*" (Ps. 1:3). But let's look again at the second verse of that first Psalm.

> **PSALM 1:2**
> **2 But his DELIGHT is in the LAW OF THE LORD** [God's Word]; **and in his law doth he meditate day and night.**

That goes right along with a statement Jesus made in Matthew chapter 6.

> **MATTHEW 6:33**
> **33 But seek ye FIRST the kingdom of God, and his righteousness; and all these things shall be added unto you.**

Did Jesus say, "But seek ye *second* the Kingdom of

God"? No! He said, ". . . *seek ye FIRST the kingdom of God, and his righteousness; and all these things shall be added unto you."*

Now we expect God to honor His Word and to do His part. But as I said, we have a part to play too. We can't give just to get.

Don't misunderstand me. There is a sense in which we *do* give to get. But we don't give *just* to get. The "getting" is not our main motive. We need to maintain balance in this area. And we need to be an example to others in this area too.

Remember Paul told Timothy, ". . . *be thou an example of the believers, in word, in conversation, in charity, in spirit, in faith, in purity"* (1 Tim. 4:12). Paul was telling Timothy to be an example to other believers.

God wants us to be examples, but there are three things that are problem areas with many people, and that's why they're not prospering. Sometimes it's just one area that's causing the problem. Sometimes it's two of the three areas. And with some people, it's all three of them.

Reason Number One: Laziness

Number one, some people haven't prospered because they're *lazy*. They want to sponge or live off the other fellow.

People come to RHEMA Bible Training Center sometimes and try to do that. Now I know there have been some people whom the Lord has told not to work while attending RHEMA.

They volunteered in various areas of the ministry helping us, and God took care of them. But if the Lord didn't tell you not to work, then *work!* Don't be lazy. Do something!

My wife and I were in a certain restaurant once, and a fellow waited on us who was well qualified to do some great things. He was a college graduate, yet he was there at that restaurant waiting on tables.

Well, he wasn't lazy. He was doing something. And God will prosper him and bless him. He won't have to wait on tables forever. But, you see, he didn't just sit around and wait for something big to turn up. He put his hand to something.

People have told me that they were waiting for something to turn up in the way of a job. But the only thing that will turn up is more bills because they're just sitting around not doing anything!

I was holding a meeting in another state back in 1958. The pastor of the church where I was holding the meeting asked me, "Brother Hagin, would you talk to Brother So-and-so?"

"Certainly," I said. "If I can help him, I will."

The pastor went on to explain that this man and his family had gotten saved and started coming to church there. And they had gotten some of my books. Then the man in the family quit a good job and said he was going to live by faith and that God was going to take care of him. I call that ignorance gone to seed!

The poor children in that family were suffering. The

wife was doing some laundry, ironing, and housework for different church members just to try to get a few dollars.

Some of the church members would take up money to help the children while the father was just staying home, sleeping every day, waiting for something to happen.

This pastor had two men in his church who owned factories, and one of them offered this man a job for good pay for that day.

"No," the man said, "that's not exactly what I'm looking for. You know, I'm believing God." This man had been lying around that way for two or three years! And the church was taking care of him and his family!

That man wasn't any more believing God than I'm an astronaut who landed on Mars day before yesterday! He was nothing in the world but a lazy bum! He was just plain lazy. And a lot of folks haven't prospered because they're lazy. That's the very reason that particular man hadn't prospered.

Reason Number Two:
Extravagance and Excesses

Then number two, others haven't prospered and won't prosper because of *extravagance.*

No, it isn't even the devil. I know it's a whole lot easier if you can lay it off on the devil, saying, "Well, the devil got me into this debt."

No, if you've been extravagant, the devil didn't get you into it. You ran up those bills on those credit cards yourself. And the devil didn't sign a single one of them!

In fact, you knew when you bought those things that you were going to have to make payments. And you knew that the interest is excessive — sometimes twenty-one percent. But you just kept buying anyway.

The devil didn't get you into that. That's called extravagance. And God can't bless that.

Reason Number Three: Poor Management

The number three reason folks are not prospering is closely related to reason number two: *poor management*.

Some folks just don't know how to manage money. Some *know* they don't know how to manage money, so they let their spouse manage it for them, and they prosper as a result. If you don't know how to manage money, you can get yourself in a mess!

One reason some people are poor managers is they buy everything they see. They put it on a credit card, and they get into trouble. Then they want to borrow money to get out of trouble.

They may even preach and teach prosperity, yet they're not prospering. No, and there's another little saying that goes with that: They're not *going* to prosper until they straighten up! They don't have to have the devil cast out of them. They just need to get some sense and some discipline. The Bible teaches us to discipline ourselves.

"Yes, but I really *wanted* that item." Well, the Bible teaches us to keep the flesh under (1 Cor. 9:27). When you get into trouble with credit cards and act extravagantly, that's the flesh; that's not the devil.

Many times when folks act like that, they didn't really need the things they bought anyway. They were already up to their necks in debt.

But God wants us to prosper!

I like something that John Wesley, the founder of the Methodist church, said along this line. He said, "Make all you can; save all you can; and give all you can."

Pay your tithes and give offerings. Make all you can. If you get a better job and can make more money, that's fine. Do it. But don't spend it all. Pay your tithes and give offerings, and save all you can.

I remember the years when I was in The Voice of Healing. There were about 120 of us who were evangelistic preachers in The Voice of Healing. I had been holding meetings in churches, and the Lord said to me at that time, "Stay in the churches."

So for the next thirteen years, I held meetings in churches. Then the Lord said, "Get out of the churches and go hold meetings in auditoriums and neutral places. If you do go to a church, put on your own meeting."

I had my ledger on my desk. I kept a record of all my finances. And I saw something very interesting over a period of months.

Before that, for a thirteen-year period, I had been in the churches. I'd held meetings about once a month for two or three weeks — sometimes longer.

I saw that every three months, out of every three meetings, there was one meeting that I would make money way over and beyond my budget. The next meeting, I'd just barely make my budget, and the third meeting, I wouldn't meet my budget. But because I made more than my budget the first month, I saved the extra money. I didn't spend it. That way, I had it made. I never did get into trouble financially.

But I saw others who were co-laborers in the ministry, people used of God in the gifts of the Spirit, and miraculous and spectacular things happened in their ministry. They judged their budgets by their big months — by the months when they made over and beyond their budgets. I know that because they'd tell me and others about it.

And I even knew one Voice of Healing minister who rented offices three different times. He bought equipment and desks. He hired a couple of secretaries. He did that based on his "big months," and he wasn't even operating as big as I was. He couldn't make the payments and lost it all. He did that three times, and each time, he lost it all.

You see, he thought when he had that big month, it was going to be that way from then on. I knew a number of others who did that very thing.

Well, I thanked God for the big month, but I knew that every month wasn't going to necessarily be big, especially in the ministry. That's the reason I had my budget, and I stayed with my budget.

The next month I just barely met my budget. I didn't go below my budget, but I received just in the neighborhood of my budget.

Then that third month, I fell below my budget. Yet it didn't hurt me because I'd saved the extra money from the month I went above my budget. And I went a whole lot more above my budget the first month than I went below my budget the third month!

But if I had based my budget and had started spending on the basis of that big month, I would have been in trouble.

Honor God by Walking in the Light of His Word

We've dishonored God a lot of times by laziness, extravagance, and poor management. But God said, "Those who honor Me, I will honor."

There are a number of ways we can honor God in the area of finances. We can honor Him by believing His Word and by being a doer of His Word. That includes faithful tithing and giving.

We also honor God by honoring our pastor and those who have the oversight over us. And we honor God by walking in godliness and by being good stewards of what He's given us by properly managing our finances.

God desires that His children prosper and succeed in life. And He has provided us biblical keys — scriptural laws — to put into practice that will positively change our circumstances. As we are faithful to walk in the light of God's Word, we can expect Him to bless us in *every* area of life, including the area of finances.

THE MAPMAKER'S CHILDREN

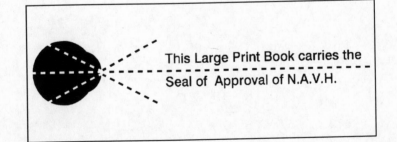

This Large Print Book carries the
Seal of Approval of N.A.V.H.

THE MAPMAKER'S CHILDREN

SARA MCCOY

THORNDIKE PRESS
A part of Gale, Cengage Learning

GALE
CENGAGE Learning·

Farmington Hills, Mich • San Francisco • New York • Waterville, Maine
Meriden, Conn • Mason, Ohio • Chicago

GALE
CENGAGE Learning®

Thorndike Press® Large Print Core.
The text of this Large Print edition is unabridged.
Other aspects of the book may vary from the original edition.
Set in 16 pt. Plantin.

LIBRARY OF CONGRESS CATALOGING-IN-PUBLICATION DATA

McCoy, Sarah, 1980-
  The mapmaker's children / Sarah McCoy. — Large print edition.
    pages cm. — (Thorndike Press large print core)
    ISBN 978-1-4104-8345-4 (hardback) — ISBN 1-4104-8345-2 (hardcover)
    1. Cartographers—Fiction. 2. Artists—Fiction. 3. Underground
Railroad—Fiction. 4. Fugitive slaves—United States—Fiction. 5. United
States—History—19th century—Fiction. 6. Conception—Fiction. 7. Large type
books. I. Title.
PS3613.C38573M37 2015b
813'.6—dc23   2015024656

Published in 2015 by arrangement with Crown Publishers, an imprint of
Crown Publishing Group, a division of Penguin Random House LLC

Printed in Mexico
1 2 3 4 5 6 7 19 18 17 16 15

To Daddio, Curtis McCoy,
the best role model of courage, faith,
and loving fatherhood

PROLOGUE

New Charlestown, West Virginia
February 2010

The old house on Apple Hill Lane shuddered against the weighty snow that burdened its pitch. The ancient beams moaned their secret pains to the wintering doves in the attic. The nesting duo pushed feathered bosoms together, blinked, and nodded quickly, as if to say, *Yes-yes, we hear, yes-yes, we know,* while down deep in the cellar, the metal within the doll's porcelain skull grew crystals along its ridges. Sharp as a knife. The skull did all it could to hold steady against the shattering temperature for just one more minute of one more hour.

The front door banged open, and a gust of snowy wind ran madly through the house's heart chambers.

"The newspapers and TV weathermen called it Snowmageddon!" said a silver-

7

haired man, not yet old by the house's standards. He was followed by a woman bundled in thick knits and gloves. "There's another on the way. An Alberta clipper storm, driving down from Canada, apparently. Did we have to do this today?"

"We've waited long enough, Dad," said a younger man, entering last.

"I know you're eager to flip this place, but there's no reward in being hasty," the elder chastised. "Never mind that there's a blizzard out!"

"I've already scheduled the construction crew. The same one that did the market. They come next week. I want this place ready by spring. People are always looking for new places in the spring — new starts. And they want to move in by summer. We need to capitalize on that. If we wait, we could have this house sitting all next winter. People will start to wonder what's wrong with it."

"But nothing's wrong with it. It's a beautiful old place," said the woman at last, placing her ungloved hand on the banister. Her voice and touch, a tickle of warmth against the house's bones. The house reciprocated in kind, and she smiled down at the curve of the warm wood in her palm. "The history is gold — worth waiting for."

8

The younger man shifted his weight on the floorboards, which groaned. "All respect to you, Ms. Silverdash, but I don't really understand what you're doing here — this is a business deal between me and my dad and whoever has the bankroll to buy."

"I completely understand, Mack." She removed her hand from the banister, and the house chilled at the absence of her touch. "Morris invited me because we've been able to place nearly every Apple Hill home on the West Virginia National Register of Historic Places, and it's greatly increased the real estate value of the homes, the street — the whole town, in fact. But Mr. Potts, God rest his soul, was so averse to anyone coming in, and I honored his wishes. However, now that the opportunity has opened up . . . But I understand — you're right; it's not my place."

The younger man ran his hand through his hair, the early silver of his father already threading his crown. "Aw, Ms. Silverdash, it's just . . ." He sighed, and it plumed the air between them.

"Now, listen to me, son," the elder said, stepping forward. "I won't have you disrespecting Ms. Silverdash. She's got a master's degree in history, which is far more knowledge about this kind of thing than you

— or I, for that matter — have."

The younger snapped tall, affronted. "What's that supposed to mean? Because I didn't finish school, I'm an idiot?"

"That's not what I said, Mack. I'm simply advising us, from a *business* perspective, to listen to an expert here — wait a few weeks and have Niles do an appraisal. The renovation crew can't do a damned thing until the ice melts, anyhow. It's not school smarts, it's common sense. Ridiculous to schedule them now."

But Mack had turned away, his mind far off on some distant thought, some ancient memory. "My whole life, you always did this — took *her* side over our family."

The elder looked to Ms. Silverdash, then rolled his eyes and shook his head.

"And *you* always make reckless decisions, then expect others to clean up your mistakes without taking any responsibility," he muttered.

"Like you?" Mack snapped back. "Mr. Noble. Mr. Chivalrous. Mr. Marry the Woman I Knocked Up on a Friday Night and Raise My No-Good Son! That's what you're thinking."

The air around them crackled.

"I'm sorry," Ms. Silverdash whispered.

"This is a family matter. I shouldn't be here."

The front door stuck, and she had to give a good pull to loosen its grip. Wind sucked at her knitted bonnet and howled low, *Noooo, don't go.*

"You," growled the elder, "ungrateful, self-ish —"

"Just say it, Dad. *Bastard.* Your biggest regret."

His father stared. The house felt his heartbeats, thudding like the hooves of the horses that had once raced to its threshold. The doves in the attic shielded themselves with their wings. The skull below lost its resolve, and the preexisting crack widened, a lightning pattern across its brow.

He lifted a finger. "You are my *son.* You don't know the first thing about real love until you have children of your own."

Mack stood rigid.

"When you're ready to apologize, you know where to find me," said his father. "Until then, I'm not giving you a dime. If you're determined to renovate without my counsel, you're going to have to buy out my investment."

With that, he stormed out of the house, leaving his son alone in the draft. Mack's lips trembled with unspoken regret. Only the house witnessed, voiceless to tell the story.

Outside, the sky had darkened. The bank of storm clouds opened. More snow.

SARAH

That winter wasn't as cold as the previous, but unlike before, the well froze solid. The bucket's rope had snapped like a forest twig just before Christmas. Sarah's father, John Brown, had promised to fish it out when he returned in the spring, but the freeze had yet to abandon its hold. So Sarah and her elder sister Annie had been tasked with melting snow into the timber kitchen barrel, a chore vital to their survival. She'd often look down into the jug and incant, *Sarah Brown, Sarah Brown, Sarah Brown.* The syllables would echo back until they rang foreign as a new song, just like the words around her did now.

"The water. It's in the water. The water . . ." said Dr. Nash. "Burn the drinking gourd."

He pulled her cheeks down with his

fingers, forcing the veil away, her eyes wide. Too sharp: the room, the bed, her parents at the foot, Annie to her right, Dr. Nash's face, clean-shaven as an apple. Her father's jowls were marble stiff and fortified with white whiskers.

"You've got a lot of living to do, Miss Sarah. Come on now, and get to it."

Dr. Nash released her, and she let her chin fall to the right. The smell of her sister close by: garden heliotrope and candle wax on her skin, buttermilk on her breath. Sarah inhaled deeply.

"W-w-will she live?" her mother stammered.

She hadn't always been afflicted. Watson, Salmon, and Oliver said she spoke clear as a bell before Annie accidentally knocked a pot of scalding water onto their infant sister Kitty, who'd died before morning. Sarah had been too young to remember her or their mother's confident tongue.

"Yes, but . . ." Dr. Nash turned his back to Sarah's bed and lowered his voice. "She is damaged. The dysentery within was too severe. She will not bear children."

Each word rang out like the crack of a horsewhip. Had she been asleep, the words might've passed without splintering the air and changing everything.

"Barren?" Mary gasped.

Damaged . . . too severe . . . not bear children . . . Sarah said it back to herself, trying to soothe the razor edges of meaning.

Her mother sobbed. "Who will love her now?"

The air near Sarah's cheek chilled. Her sister had gone to their mother's aid. "I'll make us spearmint tea, Mama."

The mention induced nausea. Sarah couldn't bear something so sweet — too contrary to everything else, like a teaspoon of maple syrup added to a mug of vinegar.

Who will love her now? Sarah Brown, Sarah Brown, Sarah Brown, who will love you now?

She pushed deeper into the pillow, where her tears were lost before they were found.

Hours later, she woke. Her mouth, dry and bitter as a splinter. She was thirsty. For once, there was no tea or soup or family member ladling out either. The storm trapped in her belly for weeks had passed. She swung her legs over the mattress. The pain of weight shot from her hips to her ankles, but she willed her knees to hold strong and gingerly made her way to the kitchen.

At the door separating the kitchen from the scullery, a tail feather of light stroked the farmhouse floor. Voices murmured. Not the high twitter of Annie, little Ellen, or her mother but the slow rumble of coming thunder. Men in secrecy. It was a common melody in the Brown household, but she'd never been close enough to hear the chorus.

"Look hard, Miss Rolla," instructed a man.

"You're almost there," said Sarah's father. "See, that line is Canada — the Promised Land. Freedom! A conductor awaits you on the threshold. All that's incumbent upon you is to get to the ferryboat. Our driver can only take you to the Plattsburgh junction; then you must follow this map. We can't give it to you, lest you be caught and the slave masters discover our stations. Please, my dear, practice your keenest memorization."

"My what?" asked Rolla.

"Remember in your mind," clarified her father's associate. "So that day or night, you'll know the way."

"I'm trying, Mr. Hill, but lines, numbers, words, maps — they all look alike," she explained. "You ain't got something with pictures? I does good with pictures."

Sarah recognized the heavy sound of her father's disappointed sigh. It snagged and raked against his beard brambles.

16

A child cooed, "Mauma, mauma."

"Hush now, Daisy-love."

Sarah's knees pinched as she bent to peer through the kitchen door where her brother Watson had once cracked it with an angry kick.

Two black females and a child in slave clothes. Runaways. One stood at the table, flanked by Sarah's father and two men she didn't recognize. Sarah knew her father was deeply invested in the Great Abolition Calling. Her brothers had fought and died in Kansas Territory for it, but the Brown women had never been privy to their plans and actions. John thought it too dangerous. A woman's role was to be the helper — to tend to the household and raise strong children in service to God's purpose. Or that was how he interpreted the Scriptures.

"Maybe if I put the candle close enough, it'll burn into my mind's eye," said Rolla.

Sarah had been on her deathbed and had risen a new person, tired of being on the outskirts, tired of waiting for fate to decide if she lived or died, tired of powerlessness. If she was damaged and never to have the family of her sisters and mother, what was there left to fear? In a quick drink of tainted water, it could all end. She was not about to let that moment draw near again without having fully lived first — without having found her new purpose.

She pushed open the kitchen door, ignoring her father's shocked gasp, and went straight to the table.

"I can make a picture for you." She flipped over the line map and took hold of the charcoal.

She'd been to Plattsburgh many times. While her father did business in secret rooms, her mother, Mary, walked Sarah and her siblings through the village, shopping, after which they'd go picnicking along the banks of Lake Champlain. Sarah could picture the landscape by heart and did so now. Her hand moved in smooth sweeps and jagged strokes, the scenic landmarks rising off the page like a mirage. She'd never thought herself an artist before, never had the opportunity or inclination to try. But now drawing came as naturally as a smile and felt twice as good.

The men watched. Even her father remained uncharacteristically mute.

"There's a river shaped like an ear," said Sarah.

"I sees it," said Rolla.

"It curves from the forest junction to the water and riverboat landing." Her hand arced gracefully. "All you have to do is follow it. When you see an oak tree with three gnarly eyes and roots that dip like long fingers into the river" — she drew the tree — "you'll know the dock is twenty paces over the lip of the city. You can't see Lake Champlain at first, but don't stop. It's there."

She added rippling waves to finish the illustration, then pushed the page into the sphere of candlelight.

Mr. Hill, the man who'd encouraged Rolla to look hard, now did so himself. "It's true to the way. A pictograph." He turned his face to her with a smile. "Well done, Miss — ?"

"Sarah."

"My second to youngest," said John.

Mr. Hill nodded to her. "A talented artist could be very useful to our cause. There are many passengers who'd benefit from drawings like this, and outsiders would observe nothing but an inventive scene. Do you agree, Miss Rolla?"

"Why, yessum. Yes, I do." She tapped her forehead and closed her eyes. "I can see it like I's already standing there."

John cleared his throat. "Sarah, you ought to be in bed. You're not fully well."

"I was thirsty, Father," she explained.

"There's tea in the kettle. Pour yourself a

cup, and be quick about it. Then I'll help you back up to bed."

There was pride in his voice, like the babble of water under ice, and it warmed and quenched Sarah far more than any tea.

John and Mr. Hill conferred with the third man, who Sarah understood to be an Underground Railroad conductor. She poured her cup while the slave women prepared to move.

"Let go, Daisy," the younger woman pleaded with the child on her lap.

Daisy cuddled one of their old rag dolls. Annie had just finished restuffing it with lavender. It helped little Ellen sleep.

"It ain't yours," she continued, fighting the child's strong clutch.

Sarah could see that Daisy was on the brink of tears and would cry out the moment the doll was removed. The sound would wake her mother and sisters, attuned to the sorrow of babes.

"She can keep it," said Sarah.

The young woman lowered her gaze to the floor. "No miss'um. We couldn't be takin' your family's belonging."

"It's mine. I want her to have it." This was partially true. It had been Sarah's when she was Ellen's age, passed down like the rest of their toys, clothes, games, and storybooks.

Youthful possessions they each treasured, then outgrew and forgot.

Ellen had other dolls, ones with painted faces and newly sewn dresses. She wouldn't miss this one made of calico rags and dried herb wadding.

"It'll give the baby a quiet companion during the journey."

The woman stopped her struggle with the child and dared look up. "Thank you. Mighty kind."

No longer fighting to hold her grip, Daisy cooed and sucked on one of the rag doll's strips, seeking to consume the honeyed scent and growing sleepier with each inhalation.

Sarah ran her finger over the girl's soft, yellow-rose cheek. "There's secret magic inside." The child's eyes batted closed in sleep.

"Chamomile does a similar trick." The woman smiled.

Sarah lifted her teacup. "I pray that by this hour tomorrow night, all of us are sleeping safe and soundly to start afresh in the dawn."

"No finer blessing be upon us," said Rolla, coming to the side of her fellow travelers. "We wish the sames on you, Miss Brown."

"Sarah," her father called from the

doorway, and she obeyed.

Upstairs, he tucked her back under the chilled covers and placed the teacup on the bedside table. The steam rose in blurred brushstrokes.

"Are you cross with me, Father?" she asked.

He'd said not a word, and the silence worried her.

"How can I be cross when you've been of service to the Lord's calling?"

She could not see his grin beneath the beard but imagined it by the squint of his eyes.

"Sarah, might you be able to do that again — paint a map in pictures?"

She knew she could and nodded.

"Good. I'll bring you supplies tomorrow, but you must make me a promise." His countenance darkened then, narrowing to the daggers of light that speared congregations, businessmen, and family alike.

"This is to remain a secret, not to be spoken of to your mother, sisters, or brothers, and certainly no one outside of our family trust. These drawings — they are fraught with grave danger. For you, our kin, and, most notably, those undertaking this Pilgrim's Progress. Do you understand?"

Outside, the slave baby cried out,

22

awakened by the cold air, then was quickly muffled within the wagon.

Mary's feet thumped the floor next door, followed by the sound of her approaching steps. Nightcap askew and rubbing bleary eyes, she asked, "Is everyone well? I heard a cry?"

"We are well, dear," said John.

"One of the hunting dogs." Sarah looked to her father for approval. "Dreaming of the chase in his sleep, no doubt."

They did sound alike, and for all the proof that remained, it could've been either.

EDEN

New Charlestown, West Virginia
August 2014

"A dog is *not* a child." Eden clutched the railing, her face swollen like a day-old bee sting.

Her husband, Jack, stood at the bottom of the staircase. In his arms drooled a dog the size and color of a pumpkin. Threaded between the handles of the briefcase at his feet was a pink rose gone limp from the summer heat.

"I thought . . ." he began.

She shook her head. What had he thought? That he could simply stop somewhere and bring home a substitute. It was thought*less*.

The August sun shone through the screen door, splashing light onto the burnished oak floors. She put a hand over her eyes. *Too much. Too bright.* She still wasn't used to having a door beyond the door. The renovating architect said all the homes in New

24

Charlestown had similar. Their Adams Morgan brownstone might've been cramped and in the middle of city chaos, but she'd loved its hunter-green door, shellacked by centuries of paint and heavy as lead. When she shut it, there was a sealed kiss. A perfect match of wood to wood.

"Please." Eden squinted beneath her bladed hand. "The door. I'm not even dressed." She tugged Jack's Sting T-shirt down over her bare thighs.

He began to turn, but she stopped him.

"Wait — do it on your way out. Take it back." She nodded at the dog.

"I can't take it back. He was the last one in the box. I got him from a gypsy on Route 7."

Annoyance burned in Eden's chest. She resisted the urge to correct him. There might've been gypsies in England, but the term was simply pejorative in the United States. He'd been here long enough now. He should know. And how could he have taken on such a responsibility without one word to her? It was like she didn't exist anymore, impotent as the nursery room under this roof.

The dog reached up to sniff the starched collar of Jack's button-down and lick the five o'clock shadow at the base of his jaw.

25

Jack didn't wear aftershave but somehow still smelled of musky cedar and spearmint. Winter garden smells she'd once romanticized as coming from his English country home.

During the early years of their marriage, when he showered each morning, the steam billowing into the bedroom was so heady with his scent that it often woke her from the deepest sleep. She'd pull him back to bed, naked and warm, and let herself forget time, work, and restraint — let herself be submerged in all that was Jack Anderson and the family she hoped they could create.

Starting a family was on her bucket list, after running a marathon and scuba diving. Jack and she had done the Cherry Blossom ten-miler in D.C. to get into shape for the wedding, then snorkeled on their Virgin Islands honeymoon. Close enough. She'd crossed off both on the list and immediately started baby making; however, when it came to conception, "close enough" was anything but.

She'd had two miscarriages at the beginning. Quiet tragedies. A stain in her underwear, blood in the water, gone in a minute. Thimble hearts that beat, then stopped. She'd still mourned as if she'd known their faces.

During the first, Jack had looked at her with such brimming despair. His eyes like two deep wells of sorrow. She'd hated seeing her own pain reflected back.

"My first didn't take, either," Eden's mother had said on the phone, pausing to inhale her Newport on the other end. "God will give you a child when He thinks you're good and ready."

Eden had cringed and bitten her tongue. Her mother had been raised Catholic and had converted to Judaism when she'd married Eden's father; then they'd converted the family to Presbyterian. Somewhere along the way, she'd cobbled together her own strict tenets of faith. One of which was that you didn't mess with procreation.

"New souls are governed by God, not test tubes," she'd said years ago when a picketed fertility clinic made the national news.

Her rigidity and emotional distance had always been so, made even more apparent when Eden's father had a heart attack at a business dinner in Manhattan. He died with a mouth full of strawberry cheesecake. Eden had been twenty-one, a senior at Georgetown University, her brother Denny twelve. Their mother benevolently waited until Denny was in prep school to sell their childhood home in Larchmont, New York, and move to a chalet in Santa Fe, New Mexico.

Eden didn't tell her when the second pregnancy went the way of the first. In fact, she didn't speak of it to anyone.

"Please," she'd begged Jack through the locked bathroom door. "I don't want you in here."

After the bleeding stopped, she took a shower so hot it made her skin pink and speckled. She cried furiously under the water jets until the steam choked her quiet; then she placed her soiled underwear in the trash atop the used Q-tips and dulled razor blades. She knew she'd never be able to work out the stains. She slipped into her white terry-cloth robe and emerged at nearly midnight, her dark hair dripping a wet trail.

Jack sat on the ground, his head leaned back against the wall, mouth open, snoring. She put a hand to his chin to wake him, and he fumbled to stand.

"The baby's gone. Let's not talk about it."

He nodded and reached to pull her into his chest, but she took two steps back, her bare feet smearing the droplets on the ground. The pain was too acute; his compassion felt like peroxide on an open wound. She couldn't bear it, even if it would make the healing easier.

His arm dropped to his side. "What can I do?"

Nothing, she thought. He could do nothing. It was her body. Her fault.

Following that, her body had seemed to give up completely. They'd spent nearly two years attempting to conceive naturally, without success. She'd tried yoga, massages, Reiki, a phase where she exercised, a phase where she barely lifted a toe. Her homeopath prescribed more red meat, then no meat, Chinese herbs that smacked of stewed stinkbugs, acupuncture, goji berries, organic tinctures in strange dark bottles, teas, and vitamins. When none of those seemed to cure her, she moved on to modern medicine: a fertility specialist, who recommended drugs to induce ovulation and daily hormone injections that made her sob over a missed green light, a cookie dropped to the floor, bow-tied pigtails on little girls. The ob-gyn had instructed her to minimize stress, and the holistic healer said city living was subconsciously traumatic.

So they'd moved to New Charlestown and she'd sacrificed everything: her position at the public relations agency; her lifelong love of pulling on a pair of sneakers and running for miles; birthday parties and anniversaries of friends; her ability to think in a straight line; her ability to enjoy a moment without worrying that she could lose the very thing she wanted most and the only thing she couldn't achieve through sheer determination.

Five rounds of in vitro, plus the move, and their savings were depleted. Even with Jack's promotion to Aqua Systems marketing VP, they'd agreed that if it didn't work this time, they'd have to stop and wait a year or more, to save up. Eden was empty in other ways, too: her heart was bankrupt.

She'd *felt* pregnant after the last embryo transfer. Her breasts were tender, her appetite unsettled, her ankles achy. The same signs she'd had with her two earlier pregnancies. So when the doctor had placed the sonogram wand over her belly, she'd been smiling, searching the grainy black-and-white monitor for the bean she just knew was there. Instead, a black cavern reflected back. Barren.

She was thirty-six. Jack was thirty-nine. A year from now seemed as incurable as a death sentence. They were miserable and had been for a long time. What was the point, she wondered. No child's face to look into and say, *That's you and that's me in one person.* There was Jack and there was Eden and years of silent disappointment between.

A loud chirping began from a crevice in the floorboards.

"You've let a cricket in," Eden sighed. A thumping in her temples echoed the sound.

The dog in Jack's arms shook his woolly ears and lifted his nose in the direction of the tweets, sniffing out the tiny intruder. His round black eyes, barely visible through the dense coat of curls, settled on her. He tilted his head and let his tongue loll out, smiling.

The tangled frustration in Eden's chest tightened to a knot. An impulse surged: to hold him for a minute and feel the soft heartbeat against her own. But even that was a stabbing reminder. So she crossed her arms tightly, her wrists pinched against her ribs.

"We don't know the first thing about raising . . ." The words cut her to the quick. She gulped. "A dog."

Jack ran his fingers through its wild sprigs of fur, and it licked at his palm appreciatively.

"He could be diseased," she argued to him, to herself. "Rabies or pinworms or worse. We've never had a pet. Why start now?" She cocked her hip and felt the smart of the old injection site, still tender after so many weeks. "And what are you trying to say by bringing that home, Jack?" Tension zipped up her spine. Her cheeks flamed. The lingering synthetic hormones acted like kerosene on her natural temper. She bulged her eyes at him. "Just *what*?"

The chirping tempo increased.

Jack frowned. "Calm down, Eden."

"*Don't* tell me to calm down," she snapped. "I'm not a child — I'm your wife, and I'm tired of everybody telling me what to do without listening to a word I say!" Her voice pitched, and she didn't fight it.

The dog tucked his nose into Jack's sleeve cuff.

"You're frightening him."

Truthfully, Eden's rage had been rising ever since the doctor's appointment two weeks prior. She'd wanted to break every instrument in the room. Throw the needles like darts. Smash the sonogram machine. Rip the paper gown to shreds. Scream at Jack, at Dr. Baldwin, at fate and God for being so damned cruel.

What she'd done instead was hold her breath and nod while the men jabbered words of regret and what came next: *surrogacy, adoption, cryopreservation, maybe a break was all they really needed.* Eden hadn't said a word. She'd lain there staring at the exam room's fluorescent lights, feeling her lungs pinch. It was as if she'd been forced underwater and had yet to come up for air.

Now the dam broke and she yelled as loud as she could: "*Frightening?* He's a damned dog, Jack! A dog! He doesn't know what frightening is! This" — she slammed her fist against the banister — "is *not* frightening!" She had to bite the inside of her cheek to keep from sobbing and tasted copper.

The chirping stopped, but the dog whined, legs swimming frantically. Jack set him down on the ground and he skittered into the kitchen, knocking over the briefcase and crushing the rose beneath it.

Jack exhaled. His eyes narrowed at her, then speared down to the floor.

It felt wonderful — the purge — for five seconds, before Eden regretted the whole thing. "I'm sorry," she muttered.

This wasn't her. She was acting more like a teenager now than she had as a teenager: dramatic outbursts, pounding fists, her way or the highway, irrational, hysterical. She hated it. Hated herself in the moment, and yet she couldn't control the percussion of her heart from reaching that climactic cymbal. She was twisted up in pain, regret, a marriage that wasn't weathering the storms and maybe shouldn't have existed from the start. It'd made her ugly, hard, and mean.

Now she'd scared an innocent orphan dog to boot. What kind of monster was she?

"Denny texted me while I was dealing with the airlines," said Jack. "Did he get in touch with you?"

Eden had turned off the phones, not wanting her rest interrupted. She figured anybody phoning the house was peddling something she'd just as soon avoid. She hadn't been downstairs yet to see the indicator light on the answering machine.

Jack pressed Play.

"Hey, E, it's Denny," came her brother's voice.

She finally stepped off the stairs, to the ground floor.

He was working at a restaurant-bar in Philadelphia, waiting tables during the day and playing sets for the patrons at night. When Eden thought of him, she heard songs so full of emotion that they vibrated her bones and made her nostalgic for a childhood that had been anything but enviable.

"Your cell rang through to voice mail, so I was hoping to catch you at home. Just wanted to, y'know, talk to my big sis . . ."

What sounded like a siren went by in the background. "Late set at the café. Didn't get off until dawn — heading home now." He paused and sighed, the air pushed through the receiver raspy. A flutter in Eden's stomach. Something was up, but then he quickly got off, saying, "Kay — so call me back."

Jack picked up the phone. "I'll say you're not well — caught a bug."

Eden shook her head. "No, it's fine. I'll call him myself. Tomorrow."

Jack nodded. "Tell him I'm waiting for him to pay a visit and see the new house."

"Uh-huh," said Eden.

Like she wanted her little brother to witness what they'd become: dirty dishes atop unpacked boxes; the smell of Jack's Bombay Bistro takeout and new paint; her unbathed, unshaved, undone self in one bedroom and Jack in another down the hall. Initially he'd moved into the guest bedroom because his snoring kept her up. Her fertility specialist said sleep was a vital part of her optimal health. Jack hadn't asked to come back to their bed after the last transfer failed, and she was grateful.

In the kitchen, claws scraped wood. Eden found the dog rooting behind a tower of brown boxes in the pantry. Jack had requested that the perpendicular walls dividing the kitchen, pantry, and former maid's quarters be sledgehammered for expansion, but the architect had refused, explaining that they housed a major support beam. Apparently, if you mucked with the structure, everything would collapse. So they'd left the old walls as they were.

Now the dog trembled and hid his face deep in a wooden cranny where the house had separated from the baseboard, leaving a gap, an almost-but-not-quite match.

She couldn't immediately fix the floor, but she could remedy the dog's anxiety. "Hey, little fellow," she coaxed. "Come on out of there. Does he need water or to go to the bathroom?" she asked Jack.

"He went before we came in." Jack scratched at the five o'clock shadow. He looked worn out.

What day was it? On Mondays, he flew to Austin then back to Aqua Systems' headquarters in D.C. for a Friday roundtable with the company CEOs. It wasn't Friday already? She could swear she'd heard the Presbyterian church's bells ringing the day before. Though they'd been in the house for three months, she still wasn't used to their chime and woke with a start at every Sunday call to worship. The ringing had been endearing when she'd imagined sitting by the nursery window feeding her child to their tune. Now she found them mocking. She'd pull her pillow over her head and whisper, *Shut up, shut up, shut up* with each bell toll.

"Why are you home?" It came out as more of an accusation than she'd intended.

He pushed a heavy box aside and bent down. "She's all growl and no bite, ole boy."

Eden straightened her shoulders defensively but let it go. She'd expended her supply of fighting strength.

"What've you got there?" Jack picked up the dog, and as he did, a cricket the size of a paper clip bounded from its clutch. "I'll be damned, he caught the cricket."

"Kill it quick," said Eden.

The cricket leapt down the hole again.

"Great," Eden huffed. "Lost it."

"My flight to Austin was canceled. Storms," Jack explained. "They've put me on an eight A.M. departure tomorrow. I thought I'd come home with a surprise." He nodded back to the entryway and the thorny rose sticking up sideways from under his briefcase. "The puppy was a bonus." He met her stare, her eyes daggered. "My mistake." The dog pulled toward the wall, sniffing madly. "I'm sure someone in town would love him. A good family."

"Lord knows we're not," she said, then wished she could squash each word. *Shut up, Eden, just shut up,* she told herself.

Jack put the dog down, and it plunged back into the fissure. He paid no mind, leaving them in the pantry: Eden, dog, and cricket. The refrigerator door opened. A beer top popped. The metal bottle cap clinked on the marble counter.

"What about him?" Eden called.

"I'll figure it out," Jack said, his voice trailing off toward the living room. That was his way of saying he didn't want to talk anymore. He wanted to sit on the couch and zone out to ESPN soccer.

The dog's ears pooled on the floor, his snout inches below. There could be a spider or snake down that hole, thought Eden. Jack was just going to drink his beer while the dog got bitten? It was plain negligent.

"For heaven's sake." Eden pulled the dog from the crevice. This time, the cranny came, too.

With a hoary groan, the pantry floor opened. The cleft was not the house deteriorating beneath them. It was purposeful: a handle. The earthy dampness of long-harbored air plumed in a strange coolness. Instead of bounding into the shallow pit, the dog sat obediently beside Eden, his furry muzzle warm against her knee.

"Jack?" Eden's voice was barely louder than the cricket's chirp. The room choked on dusty phantoms.

In the darkness below glowed an orb. A moon-shaped child's face, decapitated.

It's a sign, she thought. I'm going to die in this place, this town, this marriage if I don't get out *now.*

She screamed and dropped the door in the floor.

FROM THE
NEW CHARLESTOWN SPECTATOR:
A JOURNAL OF CIVILIZATION

INSURRECTION AT HARPERS FERRY

October 18, 1859 — Rumors reached this place at 6 o'clock this morning of a Negro insurrection at Harpers Ferry some two days prior. Wagonloads of rifles were seized, along with plans to distribute weapons to slaves in the surrounding country for a national mutiny!

A band of white and Negro men took possession of the United States Armory on Sunday evening. They cut and destroyed the telegraph wires, so while we, innocent residents and neighbors, heard the gunshots and hostile shouts outside our doors, we had no concrete details or means to report — till now.

Upon hearing word of the assault, Governor Wise sent Virginia militia to Harpers Ferry and a dispatch to the capital with an emergency plea for President Buchanan to provide federal assistance, which the President immediately granted Monday. Several U.S. Marine companies advanced south on orders to take the Harpers Ferry Bridge by midnight at all hazards. The mission was well accomplished, as we are here, on Tuesday, reporting the facts from cease-fire.

Captain John Brown has been arrested as the leader of the rabble uprising and is interned at the Jefferson County jailhouse. While Captain Brown is mortally wounded, Governor Wise has sworn that the hand of justice will be put forthwith to him and his accomplices so that our countrymen will see that the State of Virginia acted in accordance with the law; and furthermore, that we are a peace-loving nation, white men and slaves living in prosperous harmony. Rebellion of any sort will fail as irrefutably as that at Harpers Ferry.

SARAH

North Elba, New York
October 21, 1859

"Quickly," Mary instructed the girls. "Get the last of the smoked sausage and cheese."

Little Ellen ran outside to the root cellar while Sarah crammed clean bandages and a fresh shirt into a burlap sack.

Owen had burst through the front door, stinking of swamps and sweat and blood caked so thick to his face that Mary Brown had thought him some grisly assailant and nearly ran him through with the fireplace poker. But then he'd begged, "Help me, family," and had fallen to his knees, and they knew him to be the only missing member of the Harpers Ferry raiders.

Mary, Sarah, and little Ellen had stayed behind to run the Brown farm while the rest of the family had gone down to Harpers Ferry to aid in John's great insurrection. They had hoped to spark the beginning of the end of slavery, but now all were dead, in custody, or taking flight as fugitives, like Owen. Even Sarah's sister Annie and sister-in-law Martha were in hiding somewhere between Maryland and New York. Mr. Sanborn, one of John's Secret Committee of Six, had sent word to Mary that the young girls were distraught in spirit but well in body. It had provided some comfort to them over the last week of silent anticipation. The future hovered dark and merciless on the horizon, slowly moving closer like a storm. Deluge imminent.

"Hold still," Mary told Owen as she threaded the needle straight into his forehead. He sat on the kitchen stool, the bloody rags used to clean his wound underfoot. "It must be stitched up before you go — if it festers, you'll take a fever and die on the journey or be caught."

He'd run. When their father, John, had denied General Lee's truce of surrender and the marines had stormed their barricaded firehouse, they'd known without asking: he'd run as swift as he could out the back, without stopping even to look behind as the sword came down on their father.

Owen was Sarah's half brother, born to John's first wife, who'd died in childbirth. He'd never been the bravest or the most loyal, but he was always the first to sense danger and avoid it. And though he was not her blood, Sarah's mother had raised him from nappies and coddled him more than her own at times, for the sake of his lost mother. She did the same now, not inquiring of him all the questions on the tip of Sarah's tongue: How had he come all the way up from Virginia? How had he been spared the bullets that took her brothers Watson and Oliver? Why was he not sitting beside Father in the Jefferson County jailhouse? Instead, Mary used the last of their medicinal catgut to sew fine, embroidery-like stitches so that not even a scar would remain to remind him of this disastrous affair.

They'd received all the newspaper reports. In the dark of night on October 16, John's raiding men had severed the telegraph wires to prevent anyone from alerting the authorities, seized the B&O train en route to the Harpers Ferry station, and successfully taken the U.S. Armory. Once there, however, they'd waited, expectantly, for an army of uprising slaves that would never come to their support. Just as those who argued for passive patience and civil discourse had warned John, blood only precipitated more blood. True to prophesy:

the first man to bleed had not been a slave-holding enemy but a free black man, a baggage handler, Hayward Shepherd, who died by one of John's own men, his would-be liberator. Words and action once more in brutal opposition.

There'd been countless messages from prominent business colleagues and Underground Railroad friends, everyone from the author and philosopher Amos Bronson Alcott to the renowned abolitionist Frederick Douglass. Most of the investors in the raid were on their way to safety in Canada or abroad. Though their goals had been righteous, their means of anarchy would not go unpunished.

Home alone in North Elba, Mary, Sarah, and little Ellen had stayed up each night sick with worry that all would perish, that angry slave catchers would come to take vengeance on them, that the law would come to do the same. Their North Elba neighbors were silent, however. Despite being a community whose roads and homes had been built on abolitionary blueprints, they stayed away, shunning the "unlawful" actions while the newspapers ran headlines: HARPERS FERRY VIGILANTES' BLOOD SPILT; THE SOUTH WILL HAVE JUSTICE; UNITED STATES MARINES CRUSH SLAVE REBELLION;

CAPTAIN BROWN MORTALLY WOUNDED
BUT IN CUSTODY!

The world seemed to turn its back on them, the family Brown. Even Owen, still bleeding from a Harpers Ferry wound, was now distancing himself from the event, their mission, the work with the Underground Railroad, and their lifelong beliefs in a world of free equality.

Little Ellen returned breathless, tears streaming. "I can't find the cheese!"

Mary finished sewing Owen's wound, then went out the back kitchen door, to the cellar. Ellen followed, wringing her rag doll to shreds.

Sarah was determined not to let Owen leave without answers. She was just about to demand them when he shoved a wad of paper at her.

She smoothed the dirty page and immediately recognized the faded loops and lines of her pictogram. Her father had asked her to draw a map for the uprising slaves in the surrounding plantations. A visual path to the circle of tall pointed grasses in the woods, code for their hidden arsenal of spears. Plaited railroad tracks through the woods were to lead them secretly to Harpers Ferry township to join John Brown and his men. A beautiful lightning bolt over the

U.S. Armory building symbolized the ignition of freedom against southern slave masters. She'd been so proud of the drawing. Her father had praised her for its beauty and covert brilliance.

John had planned to have Underground Railroad associates in Boston print copies of the image with the Bible verse Galatians 5:1: *Stand fast therefore in the liberty wherewith Christ hath made us free, and be not entangled again with the yoke of slavery.* They'd intended to pass the tracts round the Virginia area plantations under the guise of religious proselytizing, but the funding had not come as hoped.

Her father's Boston associates were wary. Helping runaways escape to freedom was one thing; attacking a federal institution was quite another. Technically, it was an act of treason, and a majority of the law-abiding abolitionists in New England withheld their financial support of this Brown scheme.

A local printer who owed John a favor agreed to print a few dozen replications of Sarah's map. Sarah had seen only her original. The copy Owen handed her was a messy blur of imprecise ink.

"The southern lawmen have copies." Owen stuck a grimy finger to the page. "They're looking for the man who drew this

47

map and swear he'll hang for treason, too."

"I —" Sarah began, but Mary and Ellen returned.

Owen quickly crumbled the page into his palm. "I must go." He took the sack of food and provisions without thanks.

"To Canada?" asked Mary.

"No." Owen fingered his stitched forehead, then looked away. "I'll send word when it's safe. If you don't hear from me, it's better." He marched toward the door, stopped, and locked eyes with Sarah. "No more. Whatever they say or do." He shook his head. "Let them advance without further sacrificial Browns. We've spilled enough blood. It's over, Sarah."

He took one of Father's old hats off the hook, pulled it tightly down over his forehead, and left.

Mary didn't ask Sarah what he'd meant. She merely shut the door behind him and led Ellen up to change for bed. But Sarah knew. He was telling her to stop drawing the maps for the UGRR. He was telling her to follow his lead and run away. The half of him that was not the same as her was weak. Sarah was stronger than that. She was the daughter of John Brown and her mother, who was alive, struggling through every minute of this nightmare by her side.

Upstairs, Mary stuttered a lullaby to calm Ellen: "Hush, baby doll, I pray you don't cry. I'll give you some bread and some milk by and by . . ."

Sarah gritted her teeth. "You're wrong, Owen. It's just beginning."

EDEN

New Charlestown, West Virginia
August 2014

The slam of the front door woke Eden with a start. She'd had a horrible night's sleep. Nightmares full of every incarnation of baby doll heads: a baby doll head growing out of her garden lettuce; a baby doll head where the moon ought to be; a dog chasing a bouncing baby doll head; Jack casually holding it like an apple and telling her it was *nothing but a bit of rubbish* — oh wait, that last one *had* happened.

He'd completely dismissed her, the same way he had her questions to Dr. Baldwin. She'd spent hours on the Internet trying to cull any secret tip, cure, or old wives' tale from the pregnancy chat rooms and obstetrics threads. Then in one fell swoop, he'd cast off her queries and made it sound as if she were asinine. It infuriated her.

Of course she didn't believe in ghosts,

mojo, or spooky-wooky bunkum, but she did believe in the supernatural, and omens fell into that category. Where exactly the dividing line was drawn, she wasn't sure. What she was sure was that she'd found a porcelain baby's head, cracked through the skull, in a pit that by all rights should've been discovered by their pricey architect, if not before. She'd seen the *Amityville* movies. Given what they'd been through, it seemed the house was mocking her. And Jack had done absolutely nothing, because he no doubt agreed.

They'd put in seven good, earnest years of trying to make their union fruitful and had failed. She'd failed. It was time to cut her losses. She couldn't live like this the rest of her days, being reminded of that every time she looked at Jack or walked into the house's pantry, for God's sake. She'd be like that doll head: locked up in the pit, forgotten, powerless, still on earth but dead.

She shivered at the thought. First step, call the PR agency and see if she could get her old job back. If so, she could rent a one-bedroom apartment or stay at a hotel in the city until she found her own place. But with what money? She rolled over and rubbed her forehead. Their joint account was practically empty. Why, oh why, hadn't she set up a secret savings like her mother had advised? At the time, Eden had taken the suggestion as another rebuff — doubt in Eden's ability to sustain the marriage. Maybe she'd seen something of the disappointments to come. Mother's intuition. Another gift Eden had not earned.

Downstairs, the metallic screen door rattled, shaking the whole house. The clock read 9:01. Jack must've missed his flight again, she told herself, but as the morning light threaded the slats of her bedroom blinds, her mind churned at that unlikelihood. What did she think: that she could go back to sleep? With someone or some*thing* walking around downstairs banging doors?

Sudden hot fear had her kicking off the bedsheets. At the bedroom door, she paused.

Unfamiliar footsteps scampered below. Jack's gait was slower, the amble of a tall man with legs that made a confident, wide arc. Was it the tiny body of the doll scuttling for its stolen head? She broke out in a sweat imagining the form bumping into the baseboards, the dog sniffing at its dusty rags.

She wiped the moisture from her upper lip. Nonsense, she reprimanded herself. She wasn't a scared eight-year-old anymore, wearing earplugs to bed to keep from hearing footsteps in the night. Her father had said it was the tree limbs on the roof gable, so she'd rolled the spongy plugs between her fingers and inserted them into her ears, waiting as they slowly expanded to fill each canal. Whatever bumps occurred, she was unaware, and she liked the peace that ignorance bestowed. Eden hadn't thought of those earplug years in ages. They would've helped with Jack's snoring, but that was neither here nor there.

With exaggerated force, she swung open the door and charged headlong into the sunlight. "Who's there?" she called over the banister.

The footsteps stopped.

Eden started down the staircase, then remembered her appearance. If it was a serious intruder, a lone woman scantily clad might give him illicit ideas. So she hung back, cursing herself for being in the exact position she scoffed at in suspense films. *Why is she running upstairs? What an idiot!* she'd said to Jack, who'd replied, *You've got to have a chase. She can't outwit the enemy in the first scene.*

She caught a glimpse of herself in the framed reflection of their wedding photo on the wall. No longer the young, coiffed businesswoman she'd once been: now her hair was a rat's nest; her eyes, two dark hollows. A macabre sight. Perhaps she did have the upper hand.

"Hello, I hear you."

Prancing around the corner came the little orange dog, followed by a child — flesh and blood.

Eden gasped.

The girl held a can of cat food with the top peeled back like a potato chip, and Eden registered the rank odor of compressed meat. She turned her head to keep from gagging.

"He's paying me to do it," said the girl.

The child was obviously lost or mentally unstable.

"This is a mistake."

"Are you Mrs. Anderson?" She cocked her head like a spring sparrow.

Eden nodded. Her stomach dipped at the cat food smell. Coming off the in vitro hormones seemed to have more side effects than going on: nausea, wild dreams, paranoia, hot flashes. But then, she'd been on the doses for so many years, she couldn't recall how *normal* felt.

"I live next door," the girl continued. "Mr. Anderson came over this morning and made me a deal." She pulled the lid off the can and set it on the ground.

The dog padded over, took one lick of the mealy meat, and turned away. It was still here, and Jack was gone. This was *not* taking care of it.

"He's paying me fifty dollars on Friday if I feed and walk your dog while he's off wherevers. See?" She held up a shiny silver key. "I'm not a burglar. He told me to come because of your allergies. Doctor says I'm allergic to pollen — just the March and April kind. My face swells up like a fat strawberry. It sucks."

"My allergies?" asked Eden. She rubbed her forehead, trying to clear the cobwebs of this nightmare.

"To Cricket — dander, my doctor calls it." The girl nodded at the dog, who had gone on to turn the can sideways. Chunks were pressed between the wooden floor slats like brown Play-Doh. She'd have to mop with Pine-Sol to get rid of the stench.

"Uh-huh. That's what Mr. Anderson said?" Eden ran a hand through her hair, and her shirt rode up high on her thighs. First things first: get decent. "I'm sorry, what's your name?"

"Cleo."

"Cleo. That's pretty. I'm Eden. As you can see, you kind of caught me off guard. I'm still in my pajamas." She pulled the Sting

55

T-shirt down. "Can you give me a minute?"

She went upstairs and stomped around the boxes of clothes in her bedroom. How dare Jack do this to her — leave for the week, give their house key to a child stranger, and ask her to take care of it all for him. If he were standing there now, she'd tell him what a careless, *ridiculous* idea . . . fifty bucks for a kid to feed the dog cat food? Was that even safe? The child could poison the thing, and then what — then she'd be left to deal with a dead dog while Jack was off playing cowboy in Texas. The nerve.

The longer it took her to find her clothes, the more spun up she became. Her heart pounded. Her cheeks flamed. Her only calming thought was that he'd learn quickly after she was gone that someone had to clean up his messes; soon she'd look back on this moment after two martinis at an agency lunch and say, *Thank God that's over, thank God I'm here now, thank God.*

She pulled on a hibiscus-printed maxi dress, combed her hair once through, and went downstairs again.

"Now then," she said, but the girl was gone, as was the dog.

She went out on the front porch. To the right on Apple Hill Lane, a woman in a wide-brimmed hat knelt on a gardening cushion, weeding her yellow begonias. Directly across the street, a man who looked too young to be retired sat on his front porch drinking from a mug and leisurely reading a newspaper. A couple of moms in workout clothes chatted as they pushed strollers at a pace that made Eden tired to watch. She hurried inside and shut the wooden door. The moms with their strollers passed. Their peppy voices filtered through the wall.

"Stomach flu. The kids are passing it round like candy. Phil and I haven't slept in a week. Vomit everywhere!" one of the moms explained.

The other chuckled. "These are the days we'll laugh over when we're old and the kids are grown and *their* kids are barfing buckets on their Persian rug."

Eden remembered what her mother had said when she told her they were trying to get pregnant a month after the wedding. "I'm glad to see you came to your senses quick. That Mary Tyler Moore was all show. Career girls — drivel. The truth is, everyone wants to live forever. It's a narcissistic need that began with Adam and Eve in the Garden — to see your seed produce its own. Children mean immortality. Give a man that and he'll stick by you no matter what forbidden fruit may come."

She'd brushed it off as her mother being her usual pessimistic, holier-than-thou self. This was a new era. Women could have it all: a successful career, a perfect household, a devoted husband, *and* a thriving family. And she'd almost proved it. Eden had never expected that her own body would be her biggest obstacle. Jack could have children for years to come — just not with her. Better she left him before he left her for someone young with a belly full of immortal possibilities.

The cat food lay sideways in the middle of the floor. Eden picked up the tin and spotted a note from Jack atop the phone stand.

E, the girl next door is going to take care of Cricket. We'll figure out a more permanent solution when I return. Get some rest and I'll call you from Austin.

Love, J.

"What kind of name is Cricket?"

If they were going to name the dog, she would've liked a hand in it. Achilles, Fitzgerald, Cornwall, Manhattan — a conversation starter. Or at the very least, something they came up with together. But

58

then, what did it matter? Soon there would be no more *together* anyhow.

She crumbled the paper into the pulpy meat tin and tossed it in the garbage. The doll's head sat on the marble counter, farther down from where she'd left it. It gazed directly at her with a snide smile. Eden held her breath a beat, though she hadn't meant to.

"Damn it, Jack," she cursed aloud, exhaling the fear out with it.

In full daylight, the head was smaller than she'd remembered, smaller than in her dreams. Maybe four inches wide and six from crown to neck. Chipped to balding at the crown, the painted hair around the face still parted perfectly in wavy dark locks, giving way to a peachy forehead and rouged cheeks, loved off in patches; tired eyes were rimmed with dirt, the right one black, the left one olive, the harsh break just above it. Eden wondered why they were so oddly painted.

She picked it up, and something within clinked. The piece of porcelain from the chip, she figured, and turned it upside down to try to jiggle it free. When it wouldn't fall out, she worried she'd break the whole thing — shaken baby syndrome. So she let it be and wet a paper towel to clean the dirt off.

The rose of the doll's cheeks shone through. The pursed lips gave way to a demure grin. This was loved, she thought, it *belonged* to someone.

"Where's your little girl now?" She finished bathing it, then set it on the windowsill so as not to risk it rolling off the countertop.

Outside the kitchen window, Cleo's ponytail bobbed up and down in the communal backyard. Eden shielded her eyes with the blade of her hand as she exited. The vegetal smell of warm summer dirt was nearly overpowering, a familiar scent from her childhood in Larchmont. She'd grown detached from it while living in the city.

The dog scampered through the rows of white-tipped basil blooms, snow peas hanging like green icicles, verdant fountains of lettuce. He stopped every few paces to smell a flower or eat a leaf. When he saw Eden, he left the garden and bounded to her feet, licking her bare toes.

"What on earth," she said, pulling her foot away. He moved on to the other. His tongue, like dewy pear skin, tickled. "You crazy dog," she said, her voiced lilted with squelched laughter. She swished her long skirt to shoo him off, but he paid her no mind, his tail wagging from beneath the floral print. "You don't know where those feet have been, Cricket."

Upon hearing his name, he lay down and inclined his head up to her, one fuzzy ear dangling to the dirt. She pulled the ear up and scratched behind it.

"Cricket," she whispered again, and it seemed to fit. His dark eyes searched her face. An old soul within.

Eden had never had a pet as a child. Her mother didn't want to clean up after one. Her father said he would love a dog but they were so frequently traveling, it wasn't practical. "We'd have to kennel it for weeks at a time, and that's not fair, right?" he'd argued.

Even then, Eden recognized the irony. They didn't blink at boarding their children at sleepaway camps for the same amount of time.

The closest thing she'd had to a pet was the brown Tenderheart Care Bear she pretended was a dog when she was six years old. She fed him bowls of rock candy, brushed his fur with her hairbrush, let him sleep on her pillow, and took him with her everywhere her parents left her. Then one day she made the mistake of taking TCB on the Slip 'N Slide. His cotton body absorbed the water, grew fat and sodden, then rotted from the inside out. Her mother threw the doll away while Eden was at her weekly piano lesson. It was like losing the closest friend she'd ever known. Denny wouldn't come along for another three years. She wondered if the owner of the doll's head carried a similar memory of loss.

"I promised your husband I'd feed him," said Cleo, "but looking through your pantry, there isn't even a macaroni." She shot Cricket a look of dramatic pity, which put Eden on the defensive.

What was she doing going through their kitchen? Jack had paid her to take care of the dog, *not* to nose around. She huffed, but Cleo took no notice.

"We only got cat food," she went on, "and he doesn't seem to take to it, so either you give me money to buy dog stuff at Milton's Market or you need to get some." Cleo plucked a purple clover by her ankle. The color nearly matched her eyes.

She was a pretty kid, if sassy, thought Eden. There was a rawness about her: unspoiled produce in Mother Nature's basket. Eden couldn't remember how it felt to be that bud-young.

A bee landed on the tip of a basil bloom, and Cricket sniffed it.

"Watch out," Eden said. "That'll sting you." The dog opened his mouth as if to taste the stem.

In one motion, she swept the pup up. He was light as her childhood teddy bear, the bones of his rib cage thinner than her fingers beneath the fluff. He licked the salty night sweat on her wrists and let his body go limp in her arms.

"So what's it going to be?" Cleo twirled the clover blossom between her thumb and forefinger. "I have to go to the bank on Main at lunchtime. Milton's is there. I can stop."

It wasn't a bad idea. Even if Cricket wasn't staying, Eden couldn't starve the poor animal, and she couldn't blame him for rejecting that god-awful cat food.

"Okay," she said and carried the pup back into the house with Cleo at her heels.

She wasn't sure where her purse was but remembered a crumpled twenty-dollar bill she'd found in Jack's trouser pocket the last time she'd bothered to do the wash. She went to the catchall basket in the laundry room just off the kitchen, fishing one-handed through the loose change, sticks of metallic-wrapped gum bent to odd shapes, crumpled takeout recipes, and a half-eaten Tums peppermint roll until she found the money.

"Here you go," she said, holding out the

crinkle of green, but Cleo's attention was diverted.

"What the hay?"

At first, Eden wasn't sure what she meant; then she followed the child's gaze to the dismembered skull. Before Eden could open her mouth to explain . . .

"Are you and Mr. Anderson voodoo people?"

"No! It's not —" Eden began, but Cleo interrupted *again.*

" 'Cause I don't want no hex. I got enough heaped up on my head. Gives me a neck-ache just thinking about." She didn't seem afraid. Irritated, rather.

"No! We're, I don't know, Presbyterian or something, I guess. No voodoo or hexes. It's an old toy we found — in this house!" She picked it up. "Rubbish." Maybe Jack wasn't being that insensitive.

Like a rattle, the head seemed to chatter back in response as she moved it. She set it back on the windowsill. "Just somebody's forgotten thing."

"Where'd you find it?"

"In the pantry. Under the floor. A cellar of some sort."

"Can I look?"

Eden didn't see why not. Not much there, in her opinion. "To the left. Against the far wall. There's a baseboard with a notch in it."

"Yep, looks like a root cellar," Cleo called out. "We don't got one of those next door 'cause our place was a barn before it was a house. But Ms. Silverdash has one. She keeps her treasures in it — old letters, books, and photos. Says things *preserve* better down there."

"It would make a good place. Who knows how long that doll has been there. All things considered, it's amazing how well it's held up. I agree with this — uh, Ms. Silverdash."

"I'll ask the Nileses." Cleo exited the pantry, scribbling on a pocket pad with a golf pencil. "They own an antiques shop halfway up to the Bluff. It used to be a sawmill till nobody needed sawing no more. When Mrs. Niles passed, Mr. Niles bought the building and filled it up with crazy stuff: rusted kitchen gadgets looking like they could torture a tomato, broken plates, china bowls, plus everything in between, including kids' toys. They say they're pickers. My grandpa says, 'Like boogers.' Maybe so, but if I ever have a question about old stuff, they usually know the answer.

"Once, half a teacup come up from the dirt in the backyard. You could barely make out a letter on the side. An *A, R,* or *H* —

one of the ones with a bridge. I took it over to Vee — that's Mr. Niles's daughter. She's official, got her antique appraiser's license and everything. Ms. Silverdash wanted her to come check out your house before it got sold in case it was a historical site or something but . . ." She seemed to catch herself again and shrugged it off. "The teacup ended up being, like, over a hundred years old."

An appraiser? Eden's mind alighted on the idea. What if the house wasn't just an old house? If it was a historical site, with the repairs they'd done, it could bring in triple or more if sold to a museum or local historical society. The wheels of her mind churned. Jack and she could split it fifty-fifty. Enough to get her going on her own.

Cleo slid her pad and pencil back into her pocket. "I'm good at figuring out whodunits. Don't you worry, we'll get to the bottom of this doll's head case."

Eden didn't think this was exactly a "whodunit" kind of thing, but she wasn't about to snuff the girl's drive. She studied the porcelain skull once more.

Beyond the right eye was a halo of green, as if it had been painted over in black. Artfully drawn and lightly downcast, the eyes gave the doll's face a melancholy expression. The sadness was part of her beauty. But where was the rest? Even pictographs from ancient civilizations had *bodies* attached to faces. No little girl, now or a thousand years ago, would be comforted by a floating head. From what Eden could tell, it appeared to have been purposely removed. There were holes at the base of the ceramic neck for attachment but no torn fabric or clinging threads, no damage or wear to the lower half. Only the forehead crack. Why would someone remove a doll's head? And, moreover, why would they leave it in a root cellar?

Cleo took the money. "What kind of kibble and . . ." She nodded toward the bare pantry. "Do you want me to get anything else?"

Inside was a bottle of barbecue sauce, a tube of raisins, a couple cans of beans, and an empty Kashi box. In May, when they'd moved in, Eden had held the idealistic belief that the garden would supply much of their needs.

From the time she was a child, she'd had an affinity for gardening. Though her mother had complained of having to scrub grass stains from her clothes and dirt from under her fingernails, she'd let Eden till and weed a little two-foot patch of earth in their yard. When friends asked what might possess a child to invest such time and energy in dirt and seedlings, her mother had shrugged, saying, "It's my own fault. I named her Eden."

Their New Charlestown real estate agent, Mrs. Mitchell, had sent photographs of the Queen Anne's preplanted, seasonally thriving garden along with the listing.

"A majority of the garden is on your side of the official property line," she'd said when they met, pointing to the plot map and the corresponding photo. "But there's also a lemon tree and heaps of blueberry bushes on the neighboring property. That's Mr. Bronner's — he's president of Bronner Bank and one of New Charlestown's founding families," she'd boasted.

It had been the one aspect of the move that trumped city living. They'd have a garden bursting with produce. The prospect renewed a childhood longing. The week they moved in, Eden had harvested asparagus and radishes, cut them up, and drenched them in rich olive oil, red wine vinegar, sea salt, and cracked pepper.

Jack had been thrilled. His father had been on the forefront of organic farming before the car crash that left Jack an orphan and sent him off to his only living relation, an

68

uncle in Cornwall, England. So it came as a swift kick to Eden's ego when after eating and applauding her homegrown salad, Jack said he was ready for the main course. "A protein?"

Truthfully, she hadn't thought that far, too preoccupied with her vines of veggies; her mind was seemingly always one step behind because of the IVF hormones. She wasn't about to admit to Jack that she was still hungry, too.

Instead, she'd bristled. "If what I have to offer isn't enough, maybe you should grab takeout on your way home from now on."

And from that day forward, he'd done just that. Bombay Bistro boxes piled high in the garbage, reeking of yogurt raita gone tangy.

"Hmm," she said now, running her hand over the empty pantry shelves. "Thanks, but I need to go buy a bunch anyhow. This" — she gestured to the twenty in Cleo's hand — "is for the dog." Cricket rolled his head into the crook of her arm, pressing his clammy puppy nose to her skin. "Get Casey's Organics."

Casey's Organic Dog Chow Company had been one of her best clients, and its familiar label was the only dog food she could think of on the spur of the moment.

"I'll bring back the change," said Cleo.

"Keep it," said Eden. She was suddenly in a magnanimous mood.

"Oh no, Mrs. Anderson, I couldn't do that. I'm not looking for a handout."

That wasn't what Eden had meant, but she appreciated Cleo's entrepreneurial spirit.

"Shipping and handling fee. And please, call me Eden. Mrs. Anderson isn't me." She'd never changed her maiden name on the Social Security documents and had continued to work as Eden Norton. Changing her business cards and e-mail seemed a cumbersome process. When she was out with Jack's investors, she was simply *Eden, Jack's wife.* Nobody called her Mrs. Anderson.

Cleo glared warily, pocketed the bill, then started toward the door, which reminded Eden.

"Hey, by any chance, do you know who lived here before us?"

Cleo shrugged. "Old Man Potts."

"Did he have children?"

Cleo shook her head. "He had one leg. Lost the other in an automobile wheel when he was my age. He lived with his sister until she married off, and then he was alone. Ms. Silverdash says the word for him is a *reclusive.* A mind-your-own-bees neighbor, if you know what I mean."

"I do."

"Hey." Cleo gestured to Cricket, in Eden's arms. "You aren't going to break out in hives or swell up, are you?"

Eden rolled her eyes. "I'm not allergic to dogs."

She wondered what on earth had possessed Jack to make up such a lie.

Cleo nodded. "I figured." She started toward the back door, chattering as she went. "Potts didn't have but a nickel left when he died and owed a heap to the bank, so the house and everything in it went to pay back the debt. Mack Milton bought the place at auction. Him and his dad were going to do one of them house-flip deals, but then they got in a big fight just before construction started. This house sat boarded up for, like, forever! Kids said it was haunted, but Ms. Silverdash said the only things haunting New Charlestown are old secrets and new grudges." She cleared her throat. "I gotta go. I'll bring your dog food later."

It dawned on Eden that she ought to introduce herself to Cleo's mother. She didn't want to have an awkward scene: *Why is my daughter running your errands? Shouldn't you have checked with us first?*

Again, she blamed Jack for giving her one more thing she had to attend to properly.

"Is your mother home now?" asked Eden. "I should let her know about hiring you."

Cleo stopped, hand on the doorknob, and turned her cheek to her shoulder without fully facing Eden.

"My parents are gone," she said. "I live with my grandpa."

Eden's breath caught. She'd assumed Mr. Bronner of Bronner Bank was Cleo's father and that her mother, like Eden's own, was some former debutante turned homemaker. The pretty picture the real estate agent had painted cracked, and she stood for a long minute attempting to mosaic together a new one.

Mr. Bronner was her grandpa. Was Cleo's mother or father his child? Being married to Jack, she understood the difficulty of a parentless childhood. He'd been thirteen when his parents died in the accident. He'd grown up with a bachelor uncle, and she often wondered if Jack's seeming apathy regarding their infertility was a product of that parental role model or lack thereof. But then, she and Denny had had the conventional two parents, two kids and a white-picket-fenced home, and they hadn't fared much better.

She ought to have had a thoughtful response ready. At her PR agency, she could persuade a blade of grass to buy a green dress, but when it came to the emotions that pierced deepest, she was often at a loss.

"Oh," she said and blinked once, twice. "Oh."

FROM THE
NEW CHARLESTOWN SPECTATOR:
A JOURNAL OF CIVILIZATION

VISITORS TO THE EXECUTION OF
JOHN BROWN

December 1, 1859 — The execution of Capt. John Brown is to take place tomorrow, Friday, before the hour of 12 o'clock, for crimes committed during the raid on the United States Armory at Harpers Ferry. Having been judiciously tried, Brown was convicted of the capital offenses of treason, murder, and conspiracy with no cause. We hope for a prompt execution, exemplifying to the nation that we, in the State of Virginia, acted calmly without influence of passion or alarm.

In Capt. Brown's final address to the Court, he remarked: "I feel entirely satisfied with the treatment I have received on my trial. Considering all the circumstances, it has been more generous than I expected."

The prisoner claims to have intended to peacefully run off slaves; and if men were sacrificed, it was the fault of those who interfered with him.

Such an apology is absurd. Northern

newspapers may champion the concerns of abolitionism, but here in the South, these sixteen white men and five Negroes have merely proven the foolish gains of fanaticism: death and utter ruin. It is to be hoped that the good civilians of Virginia will stay away from the execution proceedings and, instead, attend to their happy homesteads of family and slaves. As propriety deems fit.

SARAH

Jefferson County Jailhouse, Charles Town, Virginia
December 1, 1859

The Jefferson County guard took the knapsack from Sarah's mother.

"I found a jackknife sewn up in a baby doll stomach and a note telling the prisoner where a horse was tied for the getaway. Lady swear she ain't never known it was there." He scoffed. "What she 'spect me believe? Doll swallowed it on its own accord?" He shook his head. "People trying to smuggle all kinds of unlawfuls, so I got to check everywhere."

He plunged a rusted sword into the bread they'd baked from the last bit of ginger, sorghum, and salt in the pantry.

Since the raid on Harpers Ferry in October, the Brown women hadn't the time, stamina, or courage to go to the general store, so their supplies had dwindled considerably. Not that any of them had noticed. Their appetites were gone. Their cheekbones looked more pronounced than ever, making the girls' likenesses to their father striking. Little Ellen was the only one to retain her plumpness. They indulged her youthful ignorance by giving her spoonfuls of butter mixed with maple syrup from the autumn sugar-bush flow. The sound of her giggling and begging for more was a balm to their despondent spirits. In another time, John would've argued that the child would be spoiled, but he wasn't there to speak and, soon, never would be.

The day before their scheduled departure for Virginia, Sarah had found her mother hysterically rummaging through the empty cupboard.

"Gingerbread is his favorite. We must bring gingerbread. We must, we must . . ."

So she and Annie had helped cull together the necessary ingredients for a single loaf, which they'd carried from New York. The loaf that this young soldier was now stabbing to crumbs.

"No hidden weaponry on the visitors, sir," he reported to his superior, who grunted as if surprised.

The soldier pulled together the ends of the handkerchief and handed it back. Mary cradled the mangled bread as if it were a newborn, staring down, pallid as a ghost.

Sarah stepped forward, but the soldier moved into her path. His hands grazed her forearms, and a blush rashed over his rutty cheeks.

"Not as yet." He looked to his superior, who gave an encouraging nod.

"Can't be too careful, Private Pennington," the older man said. "Yankee girls —" He spat chewing tobacco into a spittoon on the floor. "They lie to their grandmamas and sass their daddies."

Sarah clenched her jaw. Her gut burned.

"If we've done anything to cause offense, we do apologize," said Annie.

Their father had praised Annie as meek. Sarah had never embraced the "turn the other cheek" tenet. It was the one area in which she dared to find her father duplicitous, his words incongruous with his actions. On the eve of her father's execution, these southerners were wasting the precious time the Brown women had left. Yes, she'd lie and sass and do quite more than that if she could. She exhaled as loudly as possible and held her ground.

Private Pennington produced a weathered black Bible.

"Mrs. Brown, Misses Browns, I need you

to swear to God and under oath of law as stated by the United States of America and the abiding Commonwealth of Virginia that you do not conceal any weapons in the folds of your petticoats" — he batted his eyes at Sarah, and she rolled her own in response — "or in the linings of other personal apparel that might be used to aid and abet the escape of the outlaw John Brown, convicted of treason against the Commonwealth of Virginia, first-degree murder, and inciting insurrection."

The Bible's edges were coming unthreaded, just like her father's. She wondered if they'd confiscated it and she was now agreeing to these outlandish condemnations on the very book her family had entrusted their lives upon.

"Please put your right hand on the Word and swear it so," he instructed.

Her mother and Annie placed petite gloved hands on either end. "We swear."

No weapons in her petticoats, but she brandished bitterness and a picture map. While her mother and Annie had slept away the dark hours of their carriage drive from the Washington train depot to the jailhouse in Charles Town, Virginia, Sarah had kept her eyes to the road and sketched every observable landmark she could catch by the flash of the horses' canter.

She'd ripped off a ruffle of her muslin underskirt to draw on, then rolled the finished map into the top of her boot. As soon as there was a covert moment, she planned to pass it on to her father so he might follow the escape routes, just like all those he'd saved.

Slavery was an abomination. Every member of her family and plenty more in the northern states believed that to be true. Thousands had made their way south to Jefferson County to voice their discontent and support her father. So many, in fact, that a curfew had been issued for nearby towns, and they'd had to have a military escort from the train station to the jailhouse. Only government-sanctioned individuals were allowed to visit John. None of his notable colleagues from the North had been authorized.

It was up to Sarah to save him, and she was determined that her picture map show him the way to safety on foot. But now this son of the South was asking her to swear on the Holy Word that she had brought nothing to aid her father's life and work on earth? How dare he force her to lie! She knew that if she unclenched her jaw, she'd not be able to bridle her tongue again. She took after her father in that regard, whereas Annie and Mary were fretful spirits. The two had been inconsolable the entire train ride from North Elba.

"He is to be hung in the middle of town like a criminal," Mary had sobbed, clutching their father's letters to her breast. "No mercy or shame for what they do to a good man acting in the name of the Almighty!"

Annie had cried into her black taffeta sleeve, tears leaving stains even blacker than the material. "I tried to keep watch, Mama. I did every day," she said over and over.

Due to her illness and slow recovery, Sarah had remained in North Elba with Mary and little Ellen while Annie and Oliver's wife, Martha, went down to the Kennedy farm in Maryland to cook and provide a convincing appearance to neighbors while the men prepared for the raid. After its abysmal end and half a month in hiding, the two finally arrived home in North Elba as ghostly changelings of the girls they'd been when they'd left, retching with the memories of those few days. Watson and Oliver were dead. Owen on the run. Father wounded and imprisoned.

By November, Dr. Nash had confirmed that Martha's physical ailments were much more than heartache. She was pregnant with

Oliver's child. She had taken to bed then and had not stepped one foot to the floor since. They feared the worst for her and the unborn. The mourning of widowhood was poisoning her to death. Now these enemies would make Sarah's mother drink from the same blighted cup.

It was all too much for Sarah. "Vile devils!" she'd exclaimed in the train passenger cabin. "If I were a man, I'd take up a spear and run the judge through the middle. Damned slave owners!"

In one swoop, her mother had cuffed her cheek, strong enough to sting but soft enough that Sarah knew there wasn't any venom in it. Annie had looked on in horror. Mary had never struck any of her children before. The rod had always been firmly in their father's hand.

" 'Whoso keepeth his mouth and his tongue keepeth his soul from troubles.' Proverbs 21:23," Mary recited, smooth as a song. "You remember that while we're in Virginia, Sarah. Even Jesus was wrongly persecuted and *hung* on the cross. Your father was much aware of the high price for salvation. You best be, too."

And so Sarah had sworn to bite her tongue.

Private Pennington shook the Bible in her

direction. "Sweareth?"

She flared her nostrils, put her hand to the leather binding, and nodded once.

"Her throat's been aching," Annie said quietly. "She swears."

Sarah harrumphed at the lie. Her throat was fine, thank you.

The superior officer took a large metal loop from his belt. The keys clinked like teeth in the cold.

"Come along then. Follow me," he instructed, and the trio walked single file behind him into the maze of prison cells.

Sarah took up the flank. She dared to run bare fingers over the corroded iron bars, stinging cold and smelling of blood.

Her father was the solitary prisoner now. Despite his word of fair treatment and care by the local physician, he'd remained infirmed for his months in captivity. His wounds from the raid had been severe. For his sentencing, they'd had to carry him into the courtroom on a stretcher. He could rise to his feet before the judge and jury only by the strength of three decent men who'd volunteered to bear him up.

"Better he hang fast than die slow, the way he is now," Sarah's brother Salmon had told her in private. Not having participated in the Harpers Ferry raid or any of John's warring in the Kansas Territory, he was the only living son able to attend the trial.

Salmon had not spoken unkindly. Sarah saw that now. Their father lay on a sturdy cot. A davenport desk was within arm's reach; pen and ink were at his disposal, as well as a bowl of stew larger than any Sarah had been afforded in months. Her mouth salivated at the sight of meat and potatoes.

This time tomorrow Father will be worm's meat, thought Sarah, and her hunger pains turned to nausea. She rubbed at the gap above her corset, which she had just begun wearing.

She'd received the hand-me-down bindings and corresponding petticoats as a birthday gift that September. Her mother had sewn a new frock from plum fabric originally ordered to refurnish two settees whose seams had split. Sarah didn't mind that the dress looked like a sofa. She'd seen a likeness of the authoress George Eliot wearing a similar pattern and thought it terribly handsome on a woman. The deep-bruise purple was an omen of mournful days to come.

She hung her head low and considered her stomach cramping beneath the whalebones as penance for allowing hunger and daydreams to consume her thoughts while her father suffered.

"John," her mother called through the bars.

The guard allowed them entrance, and Mary knelt at his side. Tiers of taffeta circled her like a raven rose. Crumbs from the broken gingerbread fell to the floor, and mice in an unseen nest began to squeak as loud as jaybirds. Annie mirrored her mother on the opposite side of the cot.

Sarah stood looking down at the trio, balling her hands to keep them steady. Her nails dug into her exposed palms and formed red half-moons.

Her father opened his eyes, incandescent against the pallor of his skin. She took a step back; the vibrancy of his stare had always been proof to her that he was what they claimed: a divine prophet.

"Mary," he whispered. "Dear Mary." He took her hands with his withered claws, and she kissed his fingers despite their grotesqueness.

Annie wept. He cupped her cheek, then looked to Sarah, his gaze like the flash of gunpowder. She willed herself steadfast.

"Children, you will make men proud," he began, then lapsed in a series of phlegmy coughs. When he stopped, his eyes had closed, and Sarah thought that, like the prophet Elijah, God had seen fit to take him before the sickle fell.

Their mother ran her fingers over his chest, throat, and mouth, and he returned.

"It smells like Christmas," he said. "Our Savior's birth."

"Gingerbread," Mary whispered and pulled the handkerchief lump from her lap.

He smiled weakly. "How did you know? I had a vision that the angels welcomed me with ginger cakes."

Her mother's tears ran like sap. She lifted a soft wad of bread to his mouth. After he'd taken the bite, she turned to Sarah. "Water."

"Might you please give him something to drink?" Sarah asked the armed guard.

He looked round the cell, inspecting each of the women. Detecting no threat of intended escape, he nodded and strode off down the corridor, keys clanking with each step.

Once the guard was gone, her father pulled himself up on his elbows. "Closer, family." His voice was ardent and commanding — the voice she'd known her entire life. All three drew near.

"Listen carefully. Never be ashamed of our cause. I wish that my funeral attendants not be any of these policing pharisees but the barefoot and impoverished slave children of Virginia. Hold them close to you, my dears. Be their angels. The abolishment of slavery does not end with me. You must carry on. I have given this same revelation to your living brothers by letter. You girls, Ruth, and little Ellen are the mothers of the next generation, which I pray will know no nation that places shackles on another man and stands on his back. 'Do not be unequally yoked with unbelievers. For what partnership has righteousness with lawlessness? Or what fellowship has light with darkness?' Promise me, daughters."

"I promise." Annie kissed the underside of his palm and laid her head on the wool blanket over his chest.

This was an easy vow for Sarah to make. She could never have children, would never mother the next generation. No man, equal or unequal, would yoke her.

"You have my promises in life and in eternity, Father."

She bent low by his side and pulled the muslin map free from under her skirt, but before she could slip it to him, he winced at some inward pain and rolled onto his side.

"We are each here to serve His divine will. I have done all that this mortal body will allow. I'm happy to leave this world having fulfilled my purpose. My deepest regret is that I won't be here to watch my children discover theirs and see the blasphemy of slavery abolished."

The clanking of keys returned, and the guard's booted footsteps were not alone. Two men in fitted frock coats followed. Sarah stood up quickly and hid the picture roll beneath the overhang of her shawl.

"Preacher Hill and his son," announced the guard. He'd forgotten the water.

Mary rose at the company, as did Annie. The three women turned to greet the visitors, and Sarah gasped with recognition. She had met the preacher before — the night she'd first discovered her artistic aptitudes and joined the Underground Railroad's mission.

"George, Freddy," her father welcomed them.

"Hello, John," said Mr. Hill. "May I presume you are Mrs. Brown?" He clicked his heels ever so slightly to Mary.

She extended a hand. "Preacher Hill."

"Call me George. This is my son Frederick. Our pleasure to make your acquaintances." He bowed to Mary, then to Annie and Sarah but made no indication of recognizing her. How could he, though, she thought, without giving away their vowed secrets. She nodded courteously and feigned demure interest in the floor.

"George and his family have been blessings to me in this place," John explained. "He pastors New Charlestown Church — a brother in Christ and a *friend.*"

They knew he meant more than a casual ally. Their father had no friends that did not share his beliefs absolutely. He didn't see the point of befriending those who thought slavery right or, even worse, tolerable. *Because thou art lukewarm, and neither cold nor hot, I will spew thee out of my mouth.* That was one of his favorites, and when he quoted it, he always spat for emphasis.

"These officiated ministers of the court have shifty vision. I have no need of exoneration from the likes of them. But George is virtuous. A more trustworthy man, I know not in the entire state of Virginia."

Sarah knew that to be true.

The guard tapered his eyes and adjusted the rifle at his side.

Sarah took a reflexive step back. Yet unaccustomed to wearing the skirt cage in small spaces, she banged against the table and knocked a pencil to the floor. She attempted to retrieve it, but between the corset and the crinoline, that was a doomed endeavor. Frederick — Freddy, as her father had called him — saved her the strain.

89

"They roll faster than a waterwheel," he said setting the pencil firmly back on the table. "Wiser to make them square so they don't run away without meaning to." He winked.

Something in Sarah cinched tight as plaited hair. Did he know her secret — her work in drawing maps for the Underground?

"My two middle daughters," John said, introducing them. "Annie and Sarah. My eldest, Ruth, remains with her family, and my youngest, Ellen, is in the care of friends. Too young for this wretched affair."

Both of the Hills dropped their heads to their chests in similar fashion.

"Indeed," said George. "Wretched."

Sarah looked up to fully appraise the men while their attention was diverted. Like her father, George wore a beard that concealed a majority of his face, but Freddy was clean-shaven. His cheeks were pale as churned buttermilk and round about the edges; his black hair was clipped short, with a hint of curl at the widow's peak. Had they lived together in North Elba, she was sure he'd sit in a grade somewhere between herself and Annie.

Her gaze moved up from his collar and met his squarely. Unlike her father's steel-blue eyes, Freddy's were intensely warm:

hazel or brown — green, perhaps. She couldn't tell. They changed with the flux of the candle's light.

"Best be on with the ladies, Preacher," announced the guard. "Getting late."

Heat rose quickly to Sarah's cheeks. She couldn't leave yet. She hadn't given her father the map. Her heart thudded too fast, but the air remained at her throat, obstructed from reaching her lungs by the blasted corset! She had to do something before it was too late. So she did the only thing she could: she let herself go . . . straight down to the floor.

"Sarah!" screamed Annie. She bent to her sister's aid and fussed with the upturned skirt ruffles. "The stays are too tight. She's not used to it."

That was somewhat true. An excellent smokescreen, in any case. The delicacy of a woman's underthings flustered the guards and kept them from noticing while she slipped the muslin map to her father's hand beneath the blanket.

Her mother stammered, "She's not been well. Dysentery this spring."

Sarah thought she might *truly* be ill then. Talk of corsets and petticoats was one thing, but her damaged health was quite another — no business of these Virginia men.

"My poor Sarah," said Mary.

The pity made her queasy.

Freddy gave her cheek a light smack with his open palm. He lifted his hand to do it again, but she grabbed it with ungloved hand.

"Mr. Hill," she said firmly. "Would you kindly not do that."

She had completed her mission and so was finished with the charade. She would not stand to have this young man thwacking her as if burping a nursing baby!

Freddy sat her upright while Annie moved the rungs of her skirt so that her legs were not exposed. The guard finally brought a cup of water and hardtack. Her mother fed her the cracker. The dryness choked her, and she reached for the water.

"Drink slowly," Freddy instructed, his words blowing strands of hair loose over her ears.

"We had a lighter lunch than usual," Annie told them.

Another lie. They'd eaten nothing. Sarah swallowed hard. The pulpy lump worked its way down sluggishly. Worried it'd hit her stomach like a rock in a cotton gin, she followed Freddy's instruction, then handed him the empty cup.

"Thank you, I'm fine now," she insisted

and pulled herself up out of Freddy's embrace. The back of her neck was hot and pinpricked where his breath had been.

"She needs sustenance," said her father. "All of you do. Go with George now."

"Priscilla, my wife, has a hearty cawl waiting over the fire," said George. "Corn pones, freshly made. We're honored to host you in New Charlestown."

"Very kind of you," said Mary. "But I can't say good-bye just yet. I *can't.*"

"Dear," John said to calm her. "God has counted the minutes of my life, so you are free of that duty. Besides, I'd like some time alone to prepare. Jesus Christ's hours in the Garden of Gethsemane were vital to his forbearance."

No one dared argue with that, though Mary did tremble so fiercely that George took her by the arm to keep her from falling.

Still Mary did not move from John's bedside, until he commanded, "Go, Mary. Don't make me worry after you in my final hours. I will see you in the morning. God bless you and the children."

At that, Mary collected herself. "God have mercy on you." She let go of George's steady arm and kissed John's forehead. Then, calling meekly for both daughters, she proceeded out of the jail cell without turning back.

Sarah and Annie kissed their father good night as they would have at home. It was easier that way — to adhere to routine and do what they'd always done, convince themselves that by virtue of action, the world might set itself right. That in the morning, birds and sunlight would be welcoming visions and not harbingers. That tomorrow was simply tomorrow.

"Good night, Father," said Sarah. His rough beard scratched her cheek. She'd never embraced him without that sting.

"Thank you, Sarah," he replied, and in his words she heard the chimes of Resurrection Day. He would use her map to escape in the night. She would've bet her soul on it.

The military stagecoach drove Sarah, Annie, and Mary away from Harpers Ferry, over a creek branching off the Shenandoah River, through a forest sounding of bullfrogs, to a community of modest brick buildings tucked between the Blue Ridge cliffs.

A gabled white church stood in the center, its steeple rising like an icicle grown backward. Sarah envisioned the prayers of the townsfolk dripping to heaven. It seemed entirely possible by the way the starlight glinted off the needle point, twinkling bright and causing her gaze to shift heavenward. Maybe all those constellations were towns like this one, with prayers melting into some unseen pool. The universe turned upside down. Maybe some soul stood out there, looking up at them, whispering dreams and making legend of earth's face as hopefully as they did the man in the moon. Her head ached at the thought — the known suddenly unknown, reality gone hazy as the Milky Way.

No one had spoken during the entire carriage ride. If fatigue, hunger, and the cold of the open coach hadn't been enough to mute them, despair would have finished the job. What was left to say? They rode huddled together under a wool military blanket, Sarah and Annie on either side of their mother. The girls' breaths plumed long and gray in the darkness, while their mother's came in dandelion tufts. It reminded Sarah of a Hans Christian Andersen story her father had brought back from Europe when she was a child.

Little Gerda arriving at the Snow Queen's palace. So Sarah did as Gerda had and whispered the Lord's Prayer, wishing her breath, too, would take the shape of angels

95

and battle the guarding snowflakes.

"Thank you, Sarah." Her mother squeezed her hand tight after she finished.

Sarah hoped God wouldn't punish her for having used the prayer indecorously. She hadn't heard a word of what she'd said, preoccupied with make-believe tales and the comforting cadence of recitation.

The carriage passed through the town's main thoroughfare before coming to a halt on a side street. The team of horses nickered violently against their bits and clomped their hooves on the compacted dirt. The soldier driving rapped on the rooftop, then threw down their luggage. It landed with a soft thud in a row of boxwoods cut to either side of a short picketed gate.

"This here's New Charlestown," he called out, then jumped down to open their door. "The Hills' house." He pointed to a brick home up the lane with a pinhole of lantern light winking from the shaded window.

George and Freddy had been following and now circled their quarter horses around to a barn equal in size to the house.

The soldier helped Annie and her mother out of the carriage, but Sarah refused his hand, gathering her skirts in her fists and stepping out with as much fortitude as she could muster.

George and Freddy emerged from the darkness, a lean setter the color of red tea trotting alongside them. It gave a low growl at the soldier, who quickly climbed back up onto the carriage.

"On your word, Preacher."

"On my word." George tipped his hat.

The soldier nodded, turned the team, and headed back to the jailhouse at a faster trot than that which had brought them. The three-beat rhythm soon faded into the sound of the wind stirring fallen poplar leaves to a flurry.

"Welcome," said George when the gust died down.

The dog nuzzled its snout into Freddy's leg until he reached down to run his fingers under its chin.

"This is Gypsy." George nodded toward the dog. "Found her digging through a pile of rations on the ship we came over on. Freddy was but a lad of seven — snatched her up before the cook used her in the haggis. Hasn't left Freddy's side since. Come, let's get out of this gloomy cold. Priscilla and my daughter, Alice, are anxious to greet you."

Though his words welcomed them forward, his body walled their path. The women trembled against the wet chill of snow trapped too high in the atmosphere to fall as it threatened.

"I must warn you, however, our Alice is more . . . *simple* than other girls of her age. What she lacks in mind, she makes up for in heart. She may welcome you with fervor. I pray you take no offense."

"A loving spirit is more admired than wit," said Mary.

George led her and Annie up the walkway.

Gypsy sniffed at Sarah's skirt. She'd placed the leftover hardtack in her coat pocket and had forgotten about it. She patted Gypsy's muzzle, and the dog nestled her skull into the greeting.

"She likes you," said Freddy, their luggage weighing his arms down. "Gypsy doesn't give the time of day to most, unless she doesn't like them — in which case, she lets you know mighty quick."

"I'd welcome any newcomer who carried biscuits in her pocket, too."

"Ay, the key to her allegiance," said Freddy. "Pocket crumbs. As soon as you run out, she'll snub you proper." He winked again, and Sarah wondered if it was habitual or another cue that he knew more about her than she of him. In any case, she found it boldly unsettling.

She turned her attention back to Gypsy,

running her hand over the dog's head. *I really do like you,* she thought, and she could've sworn Gypsy's gaze glimmered understanding.

Ahead, the door opened. Light splashed into the darkness, revealing an evergreen wreath with bright holly berries above the door lintel. It was Christmas season. Sarah had forgotten.

"Tidings, new friends!" called a girl's voice, but Sarah saw no child in the threshold, only two silhouetted women of equal height.

George kissed the one to the left. Mrs. Priscilla Hill.

"Welcome to our home." Mrs. Hill cupped both of Mary's hands.

Without any regard to etiquette, the other woman wrapped her arms around Annie's neck.

"Priscilla, Alice, I'm happy to introduce Mrs. Captain Mary Brown," George began, making formal introductions, "Miss Annie Brown, and . . ." He paused for Sarah to take her stand with the trio. ". . . Miss Sarah Brown."

Alice released Annie and threw her arms about Sarah. They were doughy soft but strong and smelled like a peach left too long on the windowsill, cloyingly pungent. It

99

reminded Sarah of Ellen after a day of play in the summer garden. Sarah wondered if Alice had been born this way or had come to it: through disease, like her own affliction, or by experience, like her mother's. In either case, she liked the Hills even more for being forthright. It was a dangerous position for them. Harboring the family members of a convicted criminal and exposing their daughter to the scrutiny of strangers. Others might argue that Alice ought to be institutionalized. Sarah knew of such places.

Freddy took their bags upstairs with Gypsy at his heels. George hung his hat on a peg beside the door, then offered to do the same with their coats. Their woolens were frosted. Shedding them was a weight lifted, and Sarah was warmer without hers.

A brick fireplace crackled heat in the parlor. Alice stood beside it, fidgeting over a basket. The wooden floor creaked with Sarah's approach, and Alice turned with a smile too animated to go unnoticed. She looked older than Sarah, older than Annie, too. But her countenance was that of a child. So unabashed as to make its recipient afraid — not of the girl but of a world that didn't abide such forthright joy. A world of slaves and soldiers, wars and coffins. A world that shot Sarah's brothers and would hang her father in the morn.

"Come." Alice beckoned with an outstretched fist. "For you. A gift."

The hearth cast an orange glow over her skin and lit her eyes to mystic embers. Into Sarah's palm, she released a confetti of blue flower petals, each individually dried to a delicate crisp.

Sarah had pressed tea roses between the pages of heavy volumes many springs ago; but she'd not marked which books and so had stood in her father's library overwhelmed with frustration. She had a similar feeling when she tried to fathom time. She and Annie had once spent an entire day determined to mark every hour so as not to forget.

They'd declared aloud on the strike of each hour, "I vow never to forget this hour on this day in the year of our Lord."

But they had forgotten. In fact, she hadn't thought of that day in years, until now, and she couldn't remember anything about it except the declarative statement. What else had they done? It was lost to her, like the roses. Yet here, in her hand, were blooms plucked, pressed, and remembered.

Sarah moved a finger through the petals so that they crackled like burning kindling, their fragrance made heady by the stoking.

"Hyacinth and wisteria. Welcome," said Alice.

The others entered the parlor, and Alice dispensed from her basket similar handfuls to Mary and Annie.

Annie examined the flowers closely. "Is that purple or blue hyacinth?"

Alice smile even widened. " 'Tis purple. Do you know the fairy language of flowers?"

Annie winked. "Your message is well delivered. Thank you, Alice."

Alice stayed close to Annie's elbow until she seemed to burst with a question: "Will you sit by me at dinner?"

"Yes, how rude of us," said Priscilla. "You've been traveling all day and straight to Captain Brown. You must be exhausted. Please, let's eat, then let you rest."

They followed the Hills into the dining room. When Priscilla sat, everyone else did, too. George at the head of the table with Freddy at the foot, Sarah to Freddy's right. His boot was so close to her own that she dared not twitch an ankle.

It'd been a long time since they'd eaten at a formal dinner, even one as modest as this. There was an air of refinement: the tinkle of silver spoons against the bowls; the linen napkins pressed like Alice's flowers; the hurricane lamps haloing each of them like a Duccio painting, all shimmering golds and dazzling reds. Sarah's brother had brought home a miniature replica of *The Last Supper* from his European travels with their father. Sarah could see the painting in her mind's eye, and it made her stomach growl.

Since the raid, they'd skipped meals or eaten muddled bowls of vegetable porridge with eggs. While the guinea hens in the backyard were plentiful, the Brown women hadn't had the energy or conviction to chase them down, then pluck, gut, and roast them. So they'd let the birds populate and run into the woods, eating only the diminutive eggs.

With the men gone, they'd supped beside the potbelly, which smelled of browned butter and burning maple. They hadn't had a cook or servant in Sarah's life. Her father distrusted anyone behind the walls, and the job of a servant too closely mirrored the charges of slavery. The cooking, the mending, and the raising of children was the sanctified duty of John's wives and daughters, his sons' wives and daughters. He made that clear.

They each had a God-given purpose, like the mechanisms of a pocket watch: the

Brown Clock. A hammer or wheel couldn't decide to pause its business or the hour and minute hands would fall behind and render the whole thing useless, he'd explained. Sarah was led to assume that the women were the wheels; her brothers, the hammers; and her father, the clock face with its marking hands. He fancied himself a great parable teller. The Brown Clock was one of her least favorites. Sarah didn't like the idea of being a wheel. Going round and round without getting anywhere.

At the table, Annie prattled on about the eminent friends of her father's mission, the Alcotts — *". . . a university professor at Harvard Divinity . . . their daughter Louisa May published a delightful novel of fairy stories, a family of philosophers and thinkers they are . . ."* — who were kind enough to watch Ellen while they were away.

Sarah winced, knowing that George was fully acquainted with her father's friends, more so than Annie or anyone else — and what senseless prattle on such a night as this! George nodded along, graciously allowing them to stay away from the topic on the forefront of all their minds: tomorrow.

From beyond the servant's door came a voice: "Stew's near ready, suh."

"Excellent. Come, Siby." George beckoned. "I want to introduce you."

Cautiously, she came through the door into the lamplight. A griffe. Her skin was a soft fawn. Her eyes, lightest hazel. Her curly brown hair was pulled back in a kerchief, a hint of honey showing through. She looked the same age as Alice, maybe a little older but not by much.

"This is our Siby," said George.

She curtsied.

Annie turned to Mary in horror, while Sarah's head tick-tocked between Siby and George. No — it couldn't be — an abolitionist slave owner? A hypocrite of the most offensive sort!

The Hills guessed what their horrified expressions meant. "No, no, no," George, Priscilla, and Freddy said in unison.

"Siby is free. She lives with us, yes, but earns wages. She's part of our family —" George explained, then drew a long breath. "Yes, that's what you've heard the plantation owners say, and I'm sorry to use the similar parlance, but we don't just mean it in theory. We live by it. She's free. Her family, the Fishers, were slaves of my father-in-law's, given to us as a wedding gift."

Priscilla's gaze went to her feet.

George continued, "But as soon as they came into our possession, we freed them."

He smiled confidently, an attempt to alleviate their concerns.

Annie's brow remained furrowed.

"Siby's parents and two younger siblings live down the road in their own house and of their own free will."

Siby nodded emphatically. "I live with the Hills 'cause it's a good job, and there ain't many a'those round here for a person of my distinction." She turned both her arms over. "My pa be dark as an apple seed. But me, Clyde, and Hannah — the baby twins — took after Ma. High yeller. My grandmauma be a light-skinned slave down in Georgia, and my grandpa be Master's son." She shrugged with a smile. "But I's born free, thanks to Mister George." She tilted her head up proudly at that. "Pa work the river. That's how he come to our family name, Fisher. I's happy to do the cooking and cleaning for the Hills. Ma at home now 'cause Miss Prissy say all chil'ens needs their mammy during the swaddling years."

Priscilla looked up from her shoes then. "And a fine job she does."

Siby blushed a rosy yellow. "You's partial 'cause she done mammied you up."

From her father's war against slavery, Sarah knew that asking the enslaved to hope for freedom was one thing, but giving it to them in word and deed was quite another. Her father had wagered his life on hope being powerful enough to incite action at Harpers Ferry, but it hadn't been. The problem was, freed or slave, they all had ties to white families. Some, like Siby's mother, by blood. It was a weighty demand for them to lift a spear against people they'd lived beside all their days. Those who'd been tortured and mistreated were afraid to hope, afraid for their families on the plantations. Those treated kindly weren't willing to disrupt the peace for an outcome that would likely be worse. So it hadn't surprised her that her father had succeeded in recruiting a mere handful of Negro vigilantes. The southern families were as tangled as a blackberry and raspberry briar patch.

Now Priscilla winked at Siby, and Sarah felt the sisterly chemistry between them.

"I never learned to make corn bread as tasty as yours and your mama's," said Priscilla.

"That's Gospel truth!" George thumped the table. "I love my Prissy, but she makes an awful dry pone."

"It's 'cause I make it in da fashion of a pie — round." Siby fidgeted with her apron at the compliments. "Gonna be mealy if y'all don't give it some butter and stew to sop up." She went back to the kitchen.

Alice pulled an alabaster doll with painted yellow hair, red lips, and eyes shining bright as peas from the floor to the table. "Pa, may Kerry come to dinner, too?"

Priscilla looked from the doll around the table. She reached for George's hand, and he ran his thumb over her knuckles.

"Kerry is an early Christmas gift from our Auntie Nan," he explained.

"Pa says her face looks like one of our Kerry Pippin apples. See?" She held it up to the guests.

George cleared his throat. "She may join us so long as she sits quietly without interruption."

"Mama and I are going to needlepoint her a bib of apple blossoms," Alice whispered across the table to Sarah.

Mary had just finished sewing their best hand-me-down doll a new dress. Little Ellen had begged for the pearlescent saffron silk described by a fabled princess in the town puppet show. Make-believe. They'd explained that although spoken, written, or dreamed, some things did not actually exist. "But I can see it in my mind," Ellen had contended, and who were they to argue? They blamed themselves for her extravagant proclivities. She was five and they mollycoddled her, but soon enough she'd eat from the Tree of Knowledge.

Here, now, was Alice Hill, stricken with perpetual youth. A blessing, a curse.

"Apple blossoms are the loveliest," said Sarah. "Three years past, a cold snap dropped snow in April after the apple orchards were in bloom. You couldn't tell the flurries from the flowers. The wells tasted of cider through summer from the melted ice."

Sarah didn't know what compelled her to tell the story, but from Alice's delighted face, she was glad she had.

"Angels from the realm of glory," Alice whispered, then took up her empty cup. "A toast to Christmas!"

George squeezed Priscilla's hand again, then raised his empty glass, too. "To Christ's mercy in all seasons. The merry and the mournful."

Mary's lip trembled. Annie stared at the *H* monogrammed on her chinaware. The candles dimmed, wicks into melted wax.

The grandfather clock in the hallway pealed the hour. Yes, thought Sarah, keep the wheels of the evening turning, the clock hands ticking, the hours moving forward. He's going to live. He's going to be gone when they open the tomb, the bed shroud empty. But each toll of the bell foreboded the undeniable truth: her father was John Brown, not John Christ.

EDEN

"Anybody home?" called Cleo from downstairs. "Mrs. Anderson!"

Eden was in her bedroom. She'd called her PR agency and had a lengthy discussion with one of the VPs — a man who had told Eden that as soon as she was ready to come back, her desk would be waiting. Guess not. Four months later and it had been filled by a "brilliant new gal just out of Georgetown" who'd done "wonders" with Eden's client list. It wasn't fair to them to switch back now, he'd argued, and he'd dared to say that he was jealous of Eden's quaint new life away from the city fracas. She wanted to send Gomer Pyle to pour gasoline on his desk while she struck a match.

It burned.

She'd hung up in a full-body sweat and had been doggedly Googling real estate

111

values of historical marker buildings ever since. She'd also called the Niles Antique Mill and left a message requesting someone to come do an appraisal. Immediately.

"Miss-us Ander-son!"

"Coming!" Eden yelled, bookmarking the page of a New Charlestown property called the Lee-Manning House. Listed on the National Register of Historic Places, it had sold for a mighty sum and now functioned as a bed-and-breakfast. That was just the kind of thing Eden had in mind.

"Oh, hey, I knew you were home."

Downstairs, Cleo knelt beside Cricket, rubbing his head between her palms.

"I got groceries." She stood and went to the kitchen without waiting for Eden. "Milton's didn't have Casey's brand, so I went over to Ms. Silverdash's bookstore to look up another on her computer and to ask about the doll's head, which she was *very* interested in hearing more about. She said you could bring it to her anytime and she'll have a look. She knows everything about New Charlestown. She's got a degree in history and literature. Her store is an anti-quarian" — she pronounced the word carefully — "but she sells brand-new books, too.

"She found this one, *The Holistic Hound.*"

Cleo held up a glossy cookbook. "It's got, like, fourteen different one hundred percent organic recipes. Ms. Silverdash said to give it a try until we can special order from Milton's. I told her how I got hired on to dog-sit for y'all. Well, Mrs. Hunter, who Grandpa says has ears like an Ozark bat, heard that from way across the bookstore and came over with one of her twins — all they do is grunt and holler." Cleo prattled on while pulling items from a brown paper sack.

"So Mrs. Hunter started asking questions about what your house looked like inside. And don't you worry, Mrs. Anderson — I said your house could be featured in *Coastal Living* magazine. That shut her up. Ms. Silverdash told me she was mighty impressed that I got a summer job. She's anxious to meet y'all."

It irked Eden that someone was asking questions about her home and that Cleo had given a fractional glimpse inside. *Coastal Living* magazine — what did that even mean? They were landlocked in West Virginia!

Cleo gestured to the line of ingredients on the counter: a head of broccoli, two potatoes, brown rice, ground chicken, and a can of stock. "Ms. Silverdash said the

Canine Casserole looked like the easiest one to start." She opened the book to a page marked by a yellow Post-it. "Basically, mix everything together and cook."

Eden pinched the bridge of her nose. She was all for eating right, but honestly.

Jack had his father's organic agricultural formulas and innovator patents in a bank lockbox, and Eden liked supporting the Anderson family. Jack had so few legacies. An organic diet *was* recommended by her fertility specialist, so she'd made sure to buy the right labels. All the celebrities were doing it now, too, making it easier to find a vegan muffin than a Twinkie. Truthfully, she would've subscribed to a diet of bugs if the doctors had said it would help, plus most of the organic entrées came ready to eat. She wasn't much of a chef.

Eden rifled through the boxes stacked at the far end of the kitchen until she found the shiny red Dutch oven. A wedding gift off her registry, though she'd never actually used it.

"Are you up for helping me make this Canine Casserole?" She tried not to sound as desperate as she felt. She did not cook. She microwaved. Cooking required knives, fire, perils. There might even be an age limitation.

"How old are you?" she asked Cleo.

"I'll be eleven in January."

When Eden was eleven, she'd already been fully responsible for Denny, so she figured it was old enough for Cleo to be head chef in the kitchen. Eight or nine was a different story. But going on eleven? Well, that was a hopscotch jump from thirteen, and thirteen was practically an adult. People used to get married and have babies at thirteen. Eden couldn't immediately think of an example but knew she'd read it somewhere.

She put the pot on the stovetop burner and waved a hand over it like a magician. "Ta-da!"

Cleo frowned. "We should rinse it out first."

Filled with dust bunnies and packing peanuts, it had been a pop of red in her Adams Morgan kitchen design but nothing more. Cleo had a point: she had to start into this cooking thing on the right foot. Sanitized.

Eden washed the pot.

"Mr. Morris says a casserole ain't nothing but a savory pie. He owns Morris's Café. Best pies in the county. They won so many pie ribbons at the Dog Days End Festival that he's a judge now. He doesn't have the patience for the delicates. Fancy frostings and dippity doodads. It was his wife's café, and Miss Lenore never made 'em that way," Cleo explained while breaking broccoli florets off the base. "His youngest son, Mett, runs things now. Mr. Morris eats lunch next door at Ms. Silverdash's most days — avoiding the counter crowd, he says, but we know he's really steering clear of his oldest son, Mack. Mack delivers the groceries to Mett then." Cleo shook her head solemnly. "Ms. Silverdash says if Miss Lenore was here now, it'd be her heart that broke, not her head. Ms. Silverdash would know. They were best friends."

"Where'd she go — and what's wrong with her head?" Eden asked, encouraging Cleo to go on, and took a seat on a kitchen stool. If the townsfolk had dirt on her, she could hear a little on them.

"Miss Lenore passed away from a stroke when I was seven. Shook everybody up awful bad, then people in town started talking . . ."

"Talking about what?" Eden pushed, though she knew it was none of her business.

Cleo cut the potatoes and put them in the pot. "Long time ago, Ms. Silverdash was keen on Mr. Morris. He moved to town when they were in high school, and my grandpa said that all the girls mooned over him, but he liked Ms. Silverdash best. Mr. Morris was supposed to take Ms. Silverdash to the end-of-school dance, but she had a tooth pulled and her mouth swelled up like a catfish. She didn't want him to miss the dance, so she made Mr. Morris take her best friend, Miss Lenore. He proposed to her two months later. Ms. Silverdash said it was meant to be — love has its own ways. They hitched up at the courthouse. That's how a lot did it back in the day, Grandpa said. Like the pies — no fuss.

"Ms. Silverdash went on to be in the first class of women at the University of Virginia. People in town gave her a heap of grief. They said girls who were too smart end up spinsters and Ms. Silverdash was living proof. Which is dumb."

Cleo took a breath to pour out some brown rice, and Eden jumped to get in her two cents. "You don't need a husband to be successful," she assured the girl. "Ms. Silverdash owns her own bookstore, a big achievement for a man or woman. She's happy."

Cleo added the stock with a sigh. "Well, not so much these days. The bookstore's in trouble. Too many bills and not enough hands to help do all the things Ms. Silver-dash needs doing. Mr. Morris says she's got her ears gummed up — won't listen to reason and let him help. He's a business-man. An investor like he done for the café, Milton's Market, and just about half the town. Even my grandpa's bank back before I was born. But Ms. Silverdash won't let him. Says it'll send tongues wagging to high heaven and being a Bronner, I understand that." Cleo scowled, then put the lid on the pot.

Eden couldn't out-and-out pry, but this town was not entirely matching the real estate agent's idealistic portrait. Trouble behind the scrim. Starting right here in her kitchen with the doll's head and Cleo.

"So . . . you live with your grandpa?" It was the best roundabout way she could think of to ask after Cleo's absent parents.

"And Barracuda." She nodded. "He's a Korat cat. Gray with long teeth. Grandpa got him when Grams was doing chemo. When she first tried to hold him, he bit straight into her. So she called him a bar-racuda and said some things don't care to be smothered with tenderness, but that don't mean they don't want it just the same. True, 'cause to this day, Barracuda won't sleep anywhere but on my gram's sewing chair. He misses her."

"I bet you do, too."

She shrugged. "I was still in diapers when she died. Ovarian cancer. Folks tell me lots of stories, though, so I feel like I know her."

"My father died, too." It came out without her having meant to say it.

Cleo's freckled nose blushed, and she swiped it with the back of her hand. "I bet you miss him."

"He was a good guy." Eden smiled. Deep down, she wished her father had been more of the hero she'd always wanted him to be, wished she could've gone on without knowing the truth about him.

"I don't have a dad."

Silence crowded the room, but what could Eden say? *I'm sorry* didn't feel appropriate. *That's too bad,* even worse.

"It doesn't bother me to be a bastard." She seemed to read Eden's mind. "My mom moved home so Grams could help raise me. That was before the cancer."

Steam puttered from the sides of the lidded pot.

"Canine Casserole just needs to simmer." A hay-colored wisp of hair fell across Cleo's brow, and she scratched at it. "Is it cool if I come over to walk Cricket after dinner? Grandpa and I watch *Jeopardy!* during. We

119

play along. Grandpa gives me a nickel for every answer I guess right. I got one of those giant pickle jars. When it's full, I'm going to open my own account at the bank. Write checks and buy stuff — like an airplane ticket."

"Oh, yeah, where to?"

Cleo sucked her bottom lip for a moment, then shrugged. "I got some places in mind."

Cleo was the most atypical ten-going-on-eleven-year-old child Eden had ever met. From her violet eyes to her guileless sass, Eden liked her. She felt bad that the girl had never known her father, but her relationship with Mr. Bronner seemed to make up for it. Based on the stories, she immediately liked Ms. Silverdash, Mr. Morris, and Cleo's grandparents. She even liked Barracuda. The one person that remained a mystery was the mother.

Single parenthood held a stigma, no matter what people said. A decade back would've been even worse, especially in a small town like this. So what had happened to her? At ten years old, Cleo was already devoid of her biological father and the two pivotal women in her life.

When Eden's father died, she still had her mother. Remote as she was, she'd made fried eggs for breakfast, picked them up from school, taken them to swimming and music lessons. She'd invested time in their childhoods. And that, in its own way, was love. So as reluctant as Eden was to call once a month, she winced at the thought that one day she wouldn't have to. Her mother was *her mother.* Good or bad, you only got one in a lifetime, right?

"If you like to travel, I have a ton of tourism books. Jack and I used to go places," Eden offered and realized how very long it'd been since they'd taken a vacation.

She found a box with cartoon books drawn across the label in a conga line. Who had done that? Neither she nor Jack had any artistic flair — or whimsy, for that matter. Pulling back the packing tape, she found that the *Frommer's Mexico* guide was the first on the stack.

"We went to Puerto Vallarta. You'd like it. It's just like the pictures." She fanned the bright photo pages and unfolded the inner map. "Consider it a lending trade. *The Holistic Hound* for *Frommer's Mexico.*"

The doorbell rang a tinny *ding-dong,* and Cricket took off yapping.

Cleo accepted the book. "Looks like you got company."

The silhouetted visitor tilted his head anxiously left to right, and Eden recognized the subtle gesture as only family could. Denny.

SARAH

New Charlestown, Virginia
December 1, 1859
Siby's cooking lived up to its fame, and
Sarah was grateful when she snuck her an
extra corn bread wedge. "Case your
stomach be giving you trouble in the night,"
she said after showing the women to the
guest room.

When they were changed for bed and the
candle had burned down to a nub, Annie
brought forth a tincture in a black bottle
from her bag.

"I ordered it from the *Albany Advertiser.*"

"A snake oil potion?" their mother asked.

"No, Mama. Balsam made by Dr. Karl
Von Meier of Germany, a famous doctor. It
will help us sleep and give us the fortitude."

A cup and plaster jug sat on the vanity.
Annie filled it: half water, half balsam.

"That should be enough to share."

Their mother ignored her, standing in her

123

nightgown by the frosted window, gazing up at the shrouded sky.

"What if it snows," she whispered. "They can't hang a man in a snowstorm — can't bury the dead in frozen ground." Mary's eyes were bloodshot and dark as train soot. She needed sleep, if only an hour or two.

Annie gave Sarah a desperate look. "We must hold strong to our faith," she said, and Sarah agreed with that.

Their mother collapsed inwardly, defeated. She took the cup and drank.

"It has proven itself," said Annie. "I gave it to Sarah, and it cured her."

This was news to Sarah. She clutched at her throat, shocked that her sister would keep this secret from her. "You had me drink that, unknowingly?"

Annie straightened her shoulders and scowled. "The balsam saved you."

"What if it had poisoned me to death?"

"Then you would've been no better or worse than the first," Annie replied.

Sarah winced at the mention. There'd been another daughter Sarah, born an unlucky thirteen years before her. She'd died in the first dysentery epidemic, which had also taken their brothers Charles, Peter, and Austin. Sarah had always hated the idea that she was a replacement. Annie had no such morbid past. There had been no Annie Brown before her.

Her sister had meant that she'd have been no better or worse in physical affliction than the first Sarah, but what Sarah's head knew and her heart felt were at odds: *You would've been no better or worse than the first. No better than the first.* And then her mother's words returned and cut fresh like a razor. *Who will love her now?*

She turned away from Annie and her mother. Her stomach cramped on the lamb stew, unaccustomed to being so full.

Annie turned the empty cup. "Mama, you weren't supposed to drink it all!"

Mary moved with shaky legs, lay down on the bed, and began to snore.

Sarah put a hand to her mother's cheek. "Her face is warmed through. Blasted, Annie!"

"Don't swear." Annie took the rigid tone of their father. "She's fine." She sat on the bed and gave their mother's legs a jostle. The snore caught on itself, then found its cadence again. "It's got a bit of the spirit in it is all."

"Spirit!"

Annie got up and went to the vanity.

"You've got our mother drunk on balsam

the eve of our father's hanging?" Sarah hissed.

Her sister mixed more water and balsam, then drank it down for Sarah to watch. She puckered her lips when she was through. "I thought it'd be more ambrosial."

"Father would —" Sarah stopped, not knowing how to finish the sentence.

John had preached that drunkenness was the thoroughfare to every kind of evil debauchery in the land. But she'd seen him have a tipple with colleagues on cold North Elba nights. Medicinal use fell outside of the devil's employment. She remembered how the days of her dysentery ran together in hazy, feverish trances, recalled the miasmas of time occurring after meals of Indian pudding and tea, which she now knew were laced with balsam.

"We all need rest." Annie held the cup out.

Sarah shook her head. Her mother and sister saw this tribulation as inescapable, but she knew better. Her father had entrusted in her *more* knowledge than they or any of the other women in his life, and she would not let him down now.

Annie put the cup away and slipped into bed beside their mother. "Stubborn Sarah . . ." She yawned, eyes already closed under the balsam spell. "Good night."

The candle was down to its last minute of wick and wax. Sarah found an extra blanket inside a wooden chest. She wrapped herself in it, smelling a season long past, sunshine and vegetables from the laundry line. She posted herself by the window to watch and wait for something. Even if that something was as improbable as the dawn was certain.

Father, she thought, *if you must perish, I promise I won't let you down.*

Children were created to carry forward a father's legacy. That's what he'd taught them. It was nature's way: the vine showed the seedling how to grow tall; the hatchlings learned to fly from their mother's breast; the fish swam against the current to spawn. "And God blessed them and God spake unto them, 'Be fruitful, and multiply, and replenish the earth.' " Genesis. Her father's favorite book. The end of God's solitary existence. The beginning of Creation. She understood now. Today could not have meaning without the promise of ending. Birth and death, beginning and ending — they were one in the universe's memory.

But who would remember *her* tomorrow?

The taper had burned to nothing and fizzled. Outside, the clouded sky gave way and the winter moon shone open as bone.

She exhaled, leaving a halo of condensation on the windowpane.

Gypsy bayed and hurried between the house and the barn.

The bedroom was inky black and smelled of liniment and bodies, but the world beyond the window was lit and waiting. Sarah pressed her nose to the glass, watching the dog trot through the staked rows of dormant tomato plants. Her coat gleamed like a penny coin. She yelped again at something out of view, then circled back toward the house.

Suddenly, Sarah realized that if her father had escaped and chose not to follow her map, he would still know the way to them here at the Hills' home. How could she stay within when her father could be below, salvation in hand? Sarah's heart beat fast, hope renewed.

She collected the napkin of corn bread and tiptoed out. No pink of candlelight shone from beneath the bedroom doorways. She made her way down the staircase, through the servant's door, into the kitchen. The hearth coals glowed in sleepy smolder. To the left was a narrow passageway: Siby's room and the cooking pantry. Sarah made a beeline for the back door.

Outside, the blanket insulated her body much better than her coat had earlier. The ground frost stung her bare feet, until she found a set of muck boots by the garden trowels. She slipped into them and ventured to where she'd seen Gypsy minutes before. Taking the corn bread from the napkin, she clicked her tongue softly against the roof of her mouth like she did when feeding the guinea hens at home.

Their yard at home was buried beneath frost and snow and layers of winter, but here, in the month of Christmas, the ground was still bearing. A blueberry bush held a smattering of fruits. Every dollar from the UGRR backers had gone toward the purchasing of wood and flint for the raid spears, as ordered by her father. There was not a coin to spare for store-bought artist paints, so Sarah had learned to make long-lasting stains from harvest juices. Beet juice produced a pink paste; orange and carrot peels, a vibrant yellow; blackberries, a purple black to rival the deepest dim; even a blade of grass left its green memory on paper. Nature was more than appearance. It was a bounty of colors, free for all but understood best by those who read colors and shape. A blueberry wave: *waterway to freedom.* Pink hearts: *loving people.* Yellow: *safety.* Black: *danger is near.* Green: *life is here.* Sarah walked the garden rows. In addition to blueberries, she saw orange squash, red beetroot, green sorrel and kale . . .

A horse neighed suddenly. Sarah dropped to her knees in the garden shadows.

Freddy and a man walked toward the barn, leading a speckled mare by the reins.

"Much obliged to you, Mr. Fisher," said Freddy.

Mr. Fisher's face glinted indigo under the night light. "Glad to help, Mr. Hill."

Siby's pa. Sarah was touched by the way Freddy addressed him, respectfully and with obvious affection. Her father's vision before her: white and black men, walking side by side as equals.

"We thought it best to have two horses pulling the wagon," Freddy explained. "In case we need to move at a quicker pace. A lot of strangers in town. Amazing how people don't give the time of day to a man doing a good work, but everybody shows up to see him suffer." Freddy shook his head and whipped the horse's reins across his palm. "Mankind. We're a savage bunch. Sometimes I wonder if Gypsy and Tilda look on us with pity."

Mr. Fisher sighed loud enough for Sarah to hear from her crouch. "I wonder the same. Mr. George be a man of forgiveness, mercy, and tolerance. I know he preaches them things to the white folk in New Charlestown, but do other towns hear them parts of the Gospel? Sho' don't seem like it." He ran his hand over the horse's haunches. "My pa, long time 'go, told me God gave animals a different kind of vision from us peoples. They ain't got as many colors in their head, so they ain't confused as easily. They sees straight through the rainbow. When I was a young'un, I used to wish I could see for a minute like theys do." The horse nuzzled his shoulder. "A rainbow be pretty, but if a man try to take hold of it, he learns fast it ain't nothing but mist in hand." He patted the horse's jowl and pushed it back forward. "Speaking of, I hope this fog rolls off for good tonight, otherwise passengers be late."

Both men stopped their stroll to look up to the sky. Sarah followed their gazes. Surrounded by cloud banks, the moon shone through but not a speck of starlight.

"Coming by land or river?" asked Freddy.

"Rumor's they be from Alabama parts, following the Drinkin' Gourd."

Freddy exhaled heavily, surveying the sky. "They'll be late, to be certain, then."

Passengers, the Drinkin' Gourd: UGRR code. She was right! The Hills and the Fishers shared her father's secret — hers

131

now, too — and Sarah had seen how secrets bonded people more than blood or love or faith. Her father's Secret Committee of Six were men above all others. Men he'd been willing to leave his family for. Men he was willing to hang for.

"Margie and Siby put together vittles for the Hill women. I'll have her add a little extra for them's that's coming."

To get Tilda moving again, he clicked his tongue, then continued in a low voice: "Mr. Freddy, we didn't want to be intruding or being of opinion, but I wouldn't count myself no kind of Christian if I didn't tell you." Mr. Fisher stopped then and lifted his face confidently. "You folks be doing a fine thing here with the Browns. My brother be a freed man out west, and he put to pen the good that Captain Brown be trying to do in the territories. Lots of blood spilt, and he hanged for what? For my peoples and Margie's peoples down in Georgia, so they be free as us. I wouldn't have picked up a weapon to fight in Harpers Ferry, no suh, but no mistaking . . ." Fog curled its way around the moon, cloaking them in shadow. "The signs be saying change."

Something cold and clammy slithered across Sarah's bare knee in the dirt. On nervous edge already and fearing a snake, she jumped from her hideaway, into full view.

Gypsy wagged her tail in greeting. Yellow crumbs clung to her shaggy beard.

"Miss Brown?" Freddy came close to see her better.

As if her family hadn't endured enough humiliation, now this. Sarah reluctantly pulled the blanket tight around herself, throwing the triangular edge over her shoulder like a scarf before squaring her shoulders. "Yes, it is I, Mr. Hill."

Freddy turned to Mr. Fisher. "May I introduce Miss Sarah Brown, Mr. Fisher."

Mr. Fisher bowed. "Miss Brown."

Sarah lifted her head high. "A pleasure to meet you, Mr. Fisher. Please thank your daughter Siby for the most delicious meal I've had in months. As for the moon" — she inhaled deeper than was natural so the gesture could be seen through the sheath of bedding — "Mr. Thoreau insists that a sturdy walk through nature, at any hour or unpredictability, comforts an anxious body and mind."

She felt stronger by evoking Henry David Thoreau and hoped Freddy was educated enough to know of him; otherwise it was a lost rationale.

"Your Mister Thoreau be wise, indeed,"

133

said Mr. Fisher, taking a step back. He pointed a finger to the sky. "But Cold Moon Man, he be fickle. I best be home while there's still light."

Freddy cleared his throat — whether of the cold or a laugh, Sarah couldn't tell.

"Good rest to you, Mr. Fisher." Sarah curtsied.

"Same to you, Miss Brown." A nod of mutual understanding passed between the two men before he went back the way he'd come.

Gypsy licked remnants of corn crumbs off Sarah's side, making a long sweeping wet spot. She rubbed the dog's ear. The horse nickered, tired and ready for the warm hay.

Freddy nodded toward the barn. "If you're in the walking way — care to help me bed Tilda?"

Sarah flushed under the coverlet. No proper man would've dared ask a woman in her undergarments to walk anywhere. By the same token, no proper woman would've been out alone in the dark in her nightgown to begin with. She turned the situation over like a flapjack. What was the best course of action? She crossed her arms over her chest, pretending to be in deep contemplation as to whether he was worthy of her company.

No one else was awake, so if she chose to

forget, it would be gone, she decided. It was the memory that made it real, and the only important thing to remember from the night was that the Hills and the Fishers were most undoubtedly UGRR stationmasters. Whether she helped Freddy barn up the horse or not was of little significance.

"I was headed in that direction anyhow," she replied and walked to the opposite side, so that the girth of the horse's muscular neck and head was between them. Gypsy trailed behind, sniffing Sarah's footsteps for bread crumbs.

An owl hooted, and the other barn animals bawed and bayed when they swung open the door, bringing with them the chilled air.

Freddy tied Tilda in her stall. The hay crunched beneath his feet. His silence set Sarah's mind to worrying despite her resolve not to care — and she didn't care. At least not in theory. But it needled her: finding her in the garden so indecorously dressed, did this young Mr. Hill see her as unfit? Or worse — juvenile?

To break the silence, she said the thing on the forefront of her mind: "I like Mr. Fisher. He's kind, and it meant a great deal what he said about my father."

"You heard?"

She nodded. "But you needn't worry. I'm

a Brown. We're excellent secret keepers. I know about the . . ." She lowered her voice to a whisper: "Freedom Train — the Underground Railroad. I paint the maps." The last word came out like a hiss, though she hadn't meant it to.

"You painted all the picture maps?" Freddy stared at her a long minute, his face bemused.

Sarah's heart quickened at the unspoken accusation declared in the barn. Danger and fear could be wildly potent, like flint and steel. Useful in some situations. Destructive in others. She was about to turn and flee back to the house when he smiled.

"Impressive. You're very talented."

The lobes of her ears went hot despite the chill of their tips.

Freddy slid his hand along the ridge of Tilda's neck, across her back, and over her hindquarters. "The Fishers," he continued, "are an extension of our family. I'd fight tooth and nail for them." He led Sarah out of the horse's pen, closed the door securely, and locked gazes with her. "I understand the abolitionist mission. A lot of people do. Your father has cut the way, not just for the end of slavery but straight through the heart of this country. However . . ." He looked down to the bridle in hand. "There are those who don't agree with his particularly violent tactics. They stand for the cause but believe there's a better way for action."

He was making a point. The UGRR and her father's raid were not held in matched esteem. While a majority of Sarah wanted to agree, she felt the fiery impulse to defend her father. Wrong or right, it was the eve of his greatest sacrifice. He was due reverence from his child, at the very least.

"Pigments *must* be muddled to create a new landscape," she said.

"Can't that be achieved by brushstroke as well as the painter's knife?"

Sarah couldn't deny that. It did take both. The barn was balmy with the scent of wool and leather tackle, cow's milk and nesting mice in the rafters. Motes of chaff floated by, glinting like sand in a black-bottomed riverbed. Sarah could vaguely make out the contours of Freddy's profile, fine and pale. Color lost to the night shade.

His eyes glistened gold despite the darkness and studied her with equal curiosity. "You're different from your mother and sister. You have your father's spirit."

A strand of hay floated down from the rafter above and landed on her forehead. She reached a hand to whisk it away at the same time as Freddy. Their fingertips brushed, and Sarah's heart took off at a dash. She'd never been alone with a man not her kin. She shuffled backward and tripped over Gypsy. Freddy caught Sarah by the bare arm. The blanket fell away. He steadied her, then draped the blanket back over her shoulders. Her skin crawled with a thousand fire ants — anger, embarrassment, and something else she couldn't put a finger on.

"Mr. Thoreau might approve of a brisk outing to tire the body, but I doubt he'd endorse a girl not sleeping," said Freddy.

Girl. The word bit sharply.

"Quite. I'm *exhausted* by it." She marched out of the barn, keeping two steps ahead of him: through the yard, across the garden, to the kitchen door. There, she stepped out of the boots and turned. Best to say good night now, as she had no intention of being escorted to her bedroom like a *little girl.*

"Good evening, Mr. Hill."

"Freddy," he said. His fair face, full and more handsome than ever, shone bright as Mr. Fisher's Moon Man above.

"Freddy," she repeated. She didn't return the invitation to call her by her familiar name.

"I hope you're able to rest. Tomorrow" — he paused and exhaled — "will be full of tomorrow."

He must've waited in the garden until he was sure she'd reached her room, for only after she'd cast off the blanket and climbed into the bed beside her mother and Annie did she hear his footsteps on the stairs. She sipped the air with each creak. When the door to his bedroom opened and shut, she fought her mind from imagining him a wall away, staring up to the ceiling as she did now. She squeezed her eyes until starlight eddied behind her eyelids.

God, forgive me. I ought to be praying for my father's soul. He had not escaped — would not. It was the hope of a quixotic child to believe he could. No matter how perfectly her map had been drawn, he could barely rise to take a sip of water. How could she have been so foolish as to think he was a saint, capable of miracles, when even Christ bled to death on the cross. At that hour, he was just where she'd left him: in a southern jail cell, dying even as death would soon be noosed to him.

"Drink the balsam, sister," Annie murmured.

Sarah got up and took a swig straight from the black bottle. She gagged at the sharp bite and placed the woody tang from her sick bed. Then she lay with her fingers laced over her chest to bind her heart from its pounding. *Sleep,* she prayed. *This day must end.* Like Freddy had said, tomorrow would be full of tomorrow.

Within minutes, the drug granted her request.

EDEN

New Charlestown, West Virginia
August 2014

and a cannon ball blew my eyes away!
— BOB DYLAN, "JOHN BROWN"

The quote was decoupaged across the neck of Denny's guitar case. A duffel bag stuffed like a man-sized sausage blocked the screen door from fully opening. Eden squeezed through, and it clapped at her back.

He turned, and the first thing she noticed was that he'd grown his hair out. The shaggy whorls spilled over his ears, and aviator sunglasses were pushed up on his forehead. Great, she thought, this must be his new thing. A Dylan phase.

"E!" He opened his arms wide, exposing a tattooed heart surrounded by thorns on his biceps.

That was definitely not there the last time

she'd seen him. Her face flushed hot. "What is that?"

He bear-hugged her, and she was buried in his chest. Pine and nutmeg: he still wore their father's same aftershave. Her stomach dipped at the olfactory memory of father, brother, family, and days she'd forgotten — but here they were.

"Does a little brother need an excuse to visit his big sister?"

Not an excuse but a call first, yes. She suppressed her maternal annoyance that he hadn't told her about coming or the tattoo and hugged him back. She liked to think they were as close as ever. He didn't keep secrets from her. Sure, *she* kept things from him, but she'd been doing that since they were kids. That's what good older siblings did.

When their mother had one of her dark spells and locked herself in her bedroom, playing Petula Clark's single "Downtown" so loud the teacups in the curio cabinet clinked against their plates, she'd take Denny outside to wait for the ice-cream truck on the sidewalk. She still saw him with a cherry bomb ice pop, looking up at her, though now their vantage points had swapped. His chin rested heavily atop her head; the bottom of the tattoo peeked out from his shirtsleeve like the tattered edge of a bullfighter's cape.

She stabbed a finger at it.

"Has moving here turned you into a conservative?" He feigned horror and rubbed the offended spot.

Eden rolled her eyes. He wasn't going to divert the spotlight that easily.

Denny flexed his biceps so the tattoo was more prominent. "What can I say — my body is an artistic masterpiece."

She grinned despite herself and swatted his arm. "All grown and *tatted* up. What would our parents say?"

Denny rubbed his tattoo. "It's for Dad, so I doubt he'd mind too much."

Eden leaned in for a closer look. The ring of thorns formed letters: *Dennis.* Their father. Denny's namesake. A pang shot through her. It was a loving tribute, though their mother would never approve.

Eden shook off the nostalgic ache and changed the subject. His eyes were bloodshot. "You look exhausted." She pointed at the duffel. "Plan on moving in?"

"If you ever invite me through the front door." He whistled, scrutinizing the house from pitch to garden. "Some place. Jack got a good one. Almost feels like the grand, royal abode in Larchmont."

Eden frowned. "You want me to fix you a cot on the porch?"

"Relax. Just trying to get a rise out of you."

He wrapped his muscular arm around her, and she felt like a baked chestnut between cracking levers.

"The place is *très* sweet. I thought I was entering *The Twilight Zone.* Do people still live old-fashioned like this?"

"Afraid so." Eden reached for the screen door.

Cricket greeted them with paws planted and tail raised. Seeing Denny, he gave a bark that resembled a chicken's cluck.

"Who's this?"

Eden scratched at her tight scalp. Where to begin . . . ? "That's Cricket. Jack just got him."

"You sure his name isn't Dumbo? He's got a set of ears."

Eden felt unexpectedly protective. *Don't call my dog Dumbo,* she thought, though she knew Denny meant well.

"What's the breed?" His guitar gave a deep, hollow twang when he set it down. Cricket skittered away.

Predominantly cocker spaniel, she supposed, but with the stubby legs of a corgi, the ears of a bassett hound, and the hair of a poodle. He wasn't the cutest mutt. But what he lacked in pedigree, he made up for in gentility.

"Not a guard dog, obviously," said Denny.

Eden had left Cleo in the kitchen when the doorbell rang, but the girl was gone. The backyard: empty, except for a squirrel feasting on her snow peas.

"Come here, fella, I'm your Uncle Denny." He squatted to let the dog sniff his fingertips. "See, I'm harmless, and I'll even feed you treats behind your mom's back."

Cricket was a dog, and she was far from his mother. Despite herself, Eden smiled.

"I can't believe you finally broke down and got a pet."

"Correction: he's here until we find a family that can take him."

In under a minute, Denny had ingratiated himself with Cricket, who flopped onto his back for a belly scratch. He gazed at Eden upside down, then let his tongue flop out merrily. If only human beings could be so easily satisfied, Eden thought. She stirred the Canine Casserole. Rice kernels browned and stuck to the bottom of the pot, so she figured it must be done.

"You should keep him," said Denny.

She scooped the food onto a plate and placed it on the floor. Cricket waddled over, one ear over his forehead like a sock slugged inside out. She righted it.

Before she could stop him, Denny went to the Dutch oven and spooned a heap into his mouth.

"Denny! That's Canine Casserole!"

He stared at her for a blank moment, then clutched his throat. "Oh shit, did I eat chicken gonads?" He stuck his mouth under the faucet and gargled.

All Eden could do was point to *The Holistic Hound* open on the counter, until the laughter cramp in her side unhitched.

He glanced over the page. Shook his head. "Well, if that's dog food, I don't know what to call the crap I've been living off of in Philly." He helped himself to more.

Truthfully, Eden was proud that her first home-cooked meal was a hit. She wished Jack had been there to see. She *could* cook! Not that it mattered now, really, but he'd be impressed. She realized then how badly she'd needed that moment of success. Even one as small as Canine Casserole.

"You know you got a Chucky doll sitting here, right?" he said.

The doll's head didn't exactly blend in with the stainless steel and Italian marble decor.

"Yeah, I know," said Eden.

That seemed to suffice. He nodded.

"Museum-creepy." Then continued eating rice off the wooden spoon.

When he'd finished, he hoisted his duffel onto his back. "Where do you want me?"

Where did she? The only two beds in the house were occupied. She started toward the staircase, mapping out a convincing story in her mind with each step up. Denny followed; the planks groaned under his weight. He paused at the framed picture of Eden, Jack, and himself on vacation together in Holland.

"That was a fun trip," he said.

Eden nodded, the wheels of her mind busy. She swung open the door of the guest room: tangled bedsheets, pillows askew, Jack's T-shirt balled in the corner, his extra razor and toothbrush in the adjoining bathroom.

"Somebody already here?"

"Jack has *severe* sleep apnea. It's like a foghorn!" It was the best tale she could spin together in under a minute. "He pushed over here for a few nights — to give me some rest. He thinks it may be related to the renovations. Dust particles from God knows how long ago. We put in a new air-filter system and ordered anti-allergen bedding, but he's gone so much with work . . ."

It wasn't entirely a lie. He did snore. He

had offered to sleep in the guest room. He was away all week, working in Austin.

She stripped the bed, snatched up Jack's dirty laundry from the floor, and pulled fresh sheets from a box marked LINENS, with a drawing of a laundry line beside the word. No wonder it had taken them five days to move out of their two-bedroom apartment. Her packers were too busy drawing cartoons on box tops!

While Denny was using the bathroom, she did one last check to make sure everything was normal — at least in appearance.

Denny opened the door. "Eden?"

She snapped up like a child with a mouthful of syrup sucked straight from the bottle.

"What are these?" He held out a box of syringes.

She'd forgotten that she'd put the extras in there.

"Uh . . ." She took the box and turned it over, willing her mind to come up with a perfectly legitimate excuse that had absolutely nothing to do with the truth. "Looks like needles."

Denny furrowed his brow.

She tapped the top. "Everybody has a box of syringes for emergencies." It was such a lame explanation that she had to look away, down at her toes and the braided red-licorice rug.

"Seriously?"

She knew she'd have to tell him the truth. Otherwise, he'd obsess and go seeking answers to his worried thoughts in every nook and cranny. They came from the same DNA pool.

"God, Denny, I really don't want to go into it. Nobody's dying — well, at least not me or Jack." She rubbed between her eyes with her ring finger.

His gaze intensified. She wasn't easing his mind.

"Don't get the wrong idea. We're both sort of fine." She groaned. "It's complicated." She had no desire to talk ovaries, sperm counts, and baby making with her kid brother.

"Are you into recreational drugs?"

Eden cackled at the absurdity.

He didn't flinch, not even to wipe away the drop of her spittle that landed on his forearm. "Because you seem . . . off."

She sat on the bedside, dabbing the tears of laughter that she was sure would turn to sobbing if she didn't plug them. "You hit the nail on the head, Den. I was off. *We've* been off — Jack and me — for a long time."

He sat beside her. "Our bass guitarist had a nasty crack habit. A dime-sized hole in his arm that he kept shooting that crap into. He went to Arizona for a month. Rehab." He eyed her thin arms.

She turned them over for his examination. "I'm not on crack, Den. I'm shooting up totally legal doctor-prescribed hormones, but they probably make me even crazier than cocaine would."

He did the Denny left-right head thing.

"We were trying to have a baby."

It came out more easily than she'd anticipated. She'd expected the word to sting but felt nothing.

"In vitro fertilization. I used the needles for my daily hormone shots. It didn't go well, to say the least, but that's done. Maybe we aren't meant to have children." She shrugged.

She was impressed by her calmness. Her ability to provide a rational, controlled explanation. The telling seemed an unburdening. After years of keeping so much a secret, telling Denny brought her unexpected relief. So she went one step further.

"I'm not sure we're meant to be together. Jack and me."

Denny's chin hung to his chest, his face drawn down like a sad clown's. He'd always been a softhearted guy. "I'm sorry, Eden."

"Aw, don't worry." She laced her arm through his, the heart tattoo against her skin. "If life gives you lemons, well, at least you got lemons to do with what you want!" She swung her elbow lightly into his ribs. "Isn't that what Dad used to say?"

Denny nodded, then grabbed her hand and squeezed gently. "You're okay?"

She smiled as if to say, *Sure, of course, absolutely,* but the words didn't come.

"Settle in and make a list of stuff," she told him instead. "I'm going grocery shopping tomorrow."

Denny pulled his guitar from the case and strummed. "Oh, Mr. Cricket, would you care for some brisket or caviar on toasted rye. *Woof, woof,* you say, I want crème brûlée! Well, let's bake some and give it a try."

The song drifted down the hall, over the banister, and through the house. Below, Cricket snored to the melody while Eden went back to her room and did a search on the Internet for antique Civil War dolls. Until she heard from Vee Niles, she couldn't find out much more about the house, but she could investigate the porcelain head.

Denny had inadvertently made a good point: it might be worth a pretty price tag to a museum. Look at Christie's auctions in

New York City. People waved their paddles and paid out their life's savings for the most inane things with a story: a backscratcher said to have belonged to one of the *Mayflower* pilgrims, Winston Churchill's dentures, John Lennon's toilet bowl, a marble one Kentuckian claimed was Abe Lincoln's lucky shooter — the list went on. If it was something the rest of the world couldn't have, they wanted it. The trick was to find that secret trait — or, at the very least, make someone believe there was one.

SARAH

New Charlestown, Virginia
December 2, 1859

Sarah awoke in a fog, alone in the bed. The light through the window was ashen. Her mouth smacked of pine. She rubbed the sleep from her eyes, then steadied their focus. Chaff clung to her nightgown. She pinched a husk between her thumb and forefinger and rolled it until it dissolved.

Mary and Annie were gone, as were their mourning clothes. Sarah anxiously dressed but found she could not lace the corset without help. She paced the room. "Blasted balsam! Blast, blast, blast."

Horse hooves and nickers sounded from outside. Freddy rode into the farmyard. The barn doors were wide open, and the place where the wagon had been was hollow, only wheel tracks in the soft mud. Sarah pressed her nose to the window for a better look, ignoring the sharp teeth of the frost's bite.

Freddy dismounted on the quick, tied the reins to the hitching post, and marched straight to the back door. Within a moment, a chorus of murmurs trembled through the house. Freddy's low voice and soprano tones. They were in the kitchen.

She threw off the corset, pulled on her plum dress minus the stays, and raced down the steps without even combing her hair. Freddy and Priscilla stood in the foyer and looked up at her in sad bewilderment. She knew she was a sight.

"Good morning, Mrs. Hill." Sarah hesitated in greeting Freddy, then proceeded formally: "Mr. Hill."

Priscilla gestured to the parlor. "Won't you come down and have something warm to eat?"

Sarah politely curtsied. "Thank you, but I was looking for my sister and mother."

"Annie is by the fire."

At that, she hurried into the salon, where Annie sat staring at the flames.

"Sister?"

Annie turned with the expression of a scarecrow after a summer swelter: features that should've given line and form were raw and swollen. "Father doesn't want us . . ." Her eyes brimmed afresh. "He doesn't want us there."

"No, you are mistaken." Sarah shook her head. Though her map had not led him to safety, there was still time, still good-byes to be said, father to daughter. He would have last words for each of them. She was sure! Last lessons of liturgy for Annie, last instructions for Sarah to continue their UGRR work. "Freddy borrowed Mr. Fisher's horse. Everything is prepared."

A tear wormed its way down Annie's cheek and dripped onto the crown of Alice's doll beside her chair.

"Please." Sarah turned to Priscilla. "Where is our mother?"

Priscilla covered her quivering lips with a handkerchief and looked to Freddy.

"Soldiers arrived before dawn," he explained. "Your mother, alone, was requested at the jailhouse."

Sarah choked on her own breath.

"They came with a letter signed by Captain Brown. He didn't want you or your sister in harm's way, so we did as he bid and escorted Mrs. Brown. After an hour within, she exited and explained that she would not be going to the execution field. Instead, she asked my father to take her to a hillside overlook so she could watch in respected privacy. I returned to let you and your sister know of your parents' wishes."

Freddy's gaze had softened to an unbearable kindness, and Sarah realized she was crying, though she hadn't meant to.

Priscilla wrapped an arm about her. "Oh, dear girl."

She smelled of mulled cardamom and cloves, and despite wanting to stand strong, Sarah let herself be undone in the embrace.

"It's for your protection," Priscilla sighed. Sarah's cheek rose and fell against her breast. "He is thinking of your ultimate good."

"Governor Wise and General Taliaferro have issued a warning," said Freddy. "The execution may initiate a bloody battle between the lawful government and abolitionist sympathizers." He frowned. "I'd do the same to keep you safe if I were in your father's shoes."

A bubble of fury burst through Sarah's grief. "But you aren't! By noontime, his shoes will be dangling from a scaffold while you sit here in comfort and family!"

The words burned her tongue, and she immediately regretted blighting him with such bitterness. Of all the people around her this grave hour, Freddy was the only one who continued to share her father's secret mission. It was irrational, hysterical, the words in such contrast to her true feelings that she covered her face with her hands.

Alice and Siby entered the room at her shout. Sarah saw their slippered feet through her fingers: Alice in shimmering peach; Siby in burnt sienna. The colors ran together through her tears like oils on a palette.

"My apologies, Miss Brown," said Freddy. "I spoke out of turn." His boots marched out of the room.

"Please don't cry," begged Alice, on the verge of weeping herself. She came to Annie's side, where she knelt to collect the doll. "You were supposed to help," she told it, then sat the doll on the chaise beside Annie as if waiting for a spell to initiate or be broken.

Priscilla did not release Sarah. In fact, her grip strengthened.

"Sorrow will wear a person down to the grave," said Siby. "I've got black tea, hoecakes, and apple butter to keep your spirits hardy."

"Thank you," replied Priscilla. "Just the tea for now."

The grandfather clock in the hallway chimed out nine times. How could that be? It seemed hours ago that Sarah had risen from bed. Days gone by since she'd been in the barn with Freddy. Weeks since they'd

157

ridden the train from New York, and before that, so long past that it reflected a different life altogether.

The execution was to be at noon. Her father would be standing beneath the same dreary, cold sky for the next three hours. And after that . . . no more. There was nothing she could do. The powerlessness was unbearable.

Alice opened a book of cross-stitch patterns: fern fountains and wheat sheaths, tulips and twig ladders, feather stitching and tiny eyelets.

"Color threads are better for French hand sewing but difficult to come by nowadays. Ma's got strong hair with more yellow than mine. I like using that for close relations. We've sewn wedding veils and baby bonnets, cuffs and collars, toys and samples — everything for near about everyone! Ma says I have gifted hands." She splayed them before Annie. "And now — now we're going to make Kerry Pippin's dress." She flipped through the designs until she came to the one of distinction. "Here." She held the sample with both hands, staring so earnestly at the drawing that it appeared as if she were trying to see through it. "Apple blossoms. Love and new life."

"Heady, unconventional love, by some

interpretations," whispered Annie. "Preference, too."

Alice smiled and nodded in staccato beats. "Just the flowers. The fruits speak temptation." She gave Annie a wary glare.

Annie fingered the edge of the muslin frock the doll wore. "I can help, if you like. Something to pass the time."

"You and Sarah have the most beautiful chestnut hair. Might you lend us some from your brushes?" Alice bounced on the seat cushion until Priscilla patted her knee. Then she covered her mouth with a hand and commenced humming "O Tannenbaum." The sound filled up the room so that there seemed to be nothing else.

"I have a little dark thread left on my spool," said Priscilla. "Why don't you fetch that and the frames, dear."

Alice stopped humming. "But it's not nearly enough for the outline."

"I don't mind," Sarah offered. Her hair was thick and her brush notoriously full. "You can use my hair."

At home, their mother often sewed initials into handkerchiefs and other garments with strands that fell away during her nightly one hundred strokes. Father had liked his socks darned with it. He claimed it kept his toes warmer and was more durable.

Alice rose clapping. She governed her gait to exit the parlor, then raced up the staircase.

Siby came from the kitchen with the tea tray. "Miss Prissy, snowdrops pushed up through Ma's garden." She poured their cups steaming full. "Thought maybe Miss Alice like to press a bunch for her fairy code talk while I's down helping with Clyde and Hannah this afternoon."

Priscilla nodded. "That might work well for all."

"I reckoned." Siby nudged the cup closer to Sarah's hand.

The brew's warmth gave way to malty chicory, and she drank it to the last drop without care for etiquette. As Siby had promised, the heat spread through her, thawing the iceberg of hysteria. Her stomach growled, appetite roused. She hadn't the corset on to bind her belly from the grumblings. She put a palm to it like a hand over a crying child's mouth, but that did little to quell the demand.

"This past harvest made the tastiest apple butter I ever crocked. Best orchard for a hundred miles be right in our backyard." Siby busied herself, brushing unseen dust from the chaise with her apron. "Tastiest on hoecakes fresh outta the fry pan, like they is now."

Sarah's stomach groaned audibly again. The flesh betraying the spirit.

"Maybe I ought to have a little something."

"Teensy bite, maybe so," said Siby.

Sarah looked to Annie, whose visage had returned to the fire.

"I'll look after her," whispered Priscilla from behind her cup.

Before Sarah could argue, Siby was helping her off the settee.

In the kitchen, Freddy stood by the stove, a crock of apple butter in one hand and his mouth full. He choked down what he was chewing when she entered, composed himself, and nodded civilly.

A stack of round cakes, tall as a yellow top hat, stood with a fork run through the center to keep it stable. Siby forked a flap onto a plate, then nodded to the butter in Freddy's hand.

"You going to share that with company or gobble it all yourself?"

"Yes, of course — I mean, no — I mean . . ." He held out the crock to her, then set it down on the stove, picked it up, and set it down again on the oak kitchen table.

161

It was the first fluster Sarah had ever seen in him. Color rose to his cheeks.

Siby lifted an eyebrow high. She set Sarah's plate on the table. "I get you a fresh spoon for the jam," she said, patting Sarah's arm on her way to the pantry.

Freddy ran a hand through his dark hair and shifted uneasily. Sarah felt bad about her earlier outburst. She'd been angry at herself and heartsick at the turn of events. Freddy had just happened to be the easiest target. It was an unfair attack and more reflected her inner turmoil than anything she could articulate. She wished she could explain that to him.

The grandfather clock tolled ten. *Ye know not what shall be on the morrow. Our life is but a vapour that appeareth for a time, and then gone:* her father often quoted this verse. Inspired by it, Sarah had painted a picture using watered-down berry juice — too little left on the bush to make a deeper hue. She saw time that way. Sweeps of muted blue, scented with seasons past.

"I'm sorry, Freddy," she said. "I shouldn't have spoken as I did earlier."

He took a step closer just as Siby returned waving a wooden teaspoon.

"All we gots. Used up the silver last night, and I haven't a chance to polish 'em clean."

Instead of handing it to Sarah, she stuck it straight in the crock, then looked to Freddy. "What? I got seven jars in the cellar. You ain't got to look so displeasured. I'll go git another if you're hankering."

"No, I . . ." Freddy began, but she'd already started back to the pantry.

He turned to Sarah, his neck straining against his cravat. "Miss Brown, please don't apologize. I really oughtn't have said what I did. Today is an onerous one for you. I only want to be of service."

His voice was tender, and Sarah found herself moved.

Alice poked her head through the kitchen door. "The bad fairies have stolen my sewing thimble!"

Sarah thought she spoke in jest, but her face was distraught.

"Mister George just asked me to put these up." Siby held an armful of black drapes, bereavement coverings for the windows. She set the new crock of apple butter on the table. "Come along, Miss Alice. We'll find that thimble. Fairies like hiding in the window nooks."

"I understand if you'd prefer to be alone, Miss Brown," said Freddy with a bow.

"I would not, in fact. And 'Miss Brown' was always better suited to Annie. I'm

163

simply Sarah."

She ought not be so bold with a man, she thought, but propriety seemed a trifling statute given the events of the day, the night before, and the gravity of her father's work left to the living. She'd sworn to him that she'd carry on, and so she would. She'd do more than any of his children, more than all of his sons, more than a woman was expected or allowed. She would be her own new creation and paint the way for others to follow.

Sarah held her breath through each of the twelve chimes of noon, until the room swayed slightly for lack of air. She took that to be the physical sign of her father's passing. Annie cried quietly into one of Priscilla's handkerchiefs. Freddy stood tall with his head hung in reverence. Priscilla said a prayer.

The hearth fire sputtered on a mossy patch. The cleaved log hadn't been seasoned long enough for a quiet, steady burn. The flames licked ghoulishly, calling to mind stories of the burning bush, fiery furnaces, and her father's many biblical references to spirits ablaze.

How did a soul journey from earth to heaven? she wondered. Like in Shakespeare's *Hamlet,* could it be sidetracked to visit family and friends before going on? Given her father's standing as a prophet, she imagined God might allow him to drive up in Elijah's borrowed chariot. It would be something he'd do, if she still had faith in such things.

A loud knock at the door caused them to jump. George wouldn't have knocked at his own home, and Siby would've come through the kitchen; so whoever this was, he was not familial.

Freddy opened the door cautiously, then smiled. "Mr. and Mrs. Niles."

"The bells rang out. Seems the deed is done," said Mr. Niles.

"We've brought funeral biscuits for the Brown women," said Mrs. Niles. "Being as we're the only Scots together in town, I wasn't about to abandon tradition, no matter the soil beneath our feet." She gently handed over a parcel. "Just because this isn't a typical passing doesn't make it less mournful. The *Spectator* ran an article about Captain Brown. Leaving behind young daughters and a wife and losing practically all his sons in this dreadful business."

Annie threaded her arm through Sarah's and leaned into her. Sarah leaned back. It was easier to sit up straight as one link.

"We won't be staying," continued Mrs. Niles. "We left Ruthie at home, keeping after the little ones. She sends her condolences, too."

"I'll be sure to pass them along." Before Freddy could close the door, a woman called out, "Frederick!"

Freddy gave Sarah a sympathetic smile, as if to say, *Our neighbors mean well. Bear with us.* Or at least that was Sarah's interpretation.

"Mrs. Milton."

"I see the Nileses have beaten me to your doorstep." Mrs. Milton spoke robustly. "And the Jamisons are coming down the side street. I won't be taking up a minute of your time, but I had a meat pie I thought I'd bring over. No doubt your mother has Siby preparing sustenance, but extra never hurts." She placed a round pastry atop the biscuit package in Freddy's arm. "I suspected Mildred Niles baked up her cinnamon teacakes, so I made a savory."

"Thank you." Freddy readjusted the pie.

"Tell your parents they're good people for helping the Browns like they are. Real good people . . ." Her voice trailed off.

Priscilla rose and took the gifts from him. Freddy didn't bother closing the door. "Here come the Jamisons with their two young ones."

"Bringing a cider jug and a spruce wreath, too. Can't fault them for kindness," said Priscilla.

"What should we do?"

She looked to Sarah and Annie, then back to him. "We'll have to burn twice the wood to keep warm if we have the door open the whole day." She pulled the collar of her dress up under her chin.

It was true. The windowpanes had fogged, then frosted in a snap. The fire had drawn back on itself from the draft, and Annie's fingers on Sarah's arm had chilled.

"Mrs. Brown plans to immediately return to New York with Captain Brown for a wake and funeral," explained Priscilla, "so as considerate as these gifts are . . ."

"Should I turn them away?" asked Freddy.

"No," said Annie. Her eyes were tearful wide, and Sarah knew what she was thinking: Hebrews 13. Turning a stranger away might be turning away their father, come to them in angel form.

Of course, Sarah didn't think Mrs. Milton and her pasty were really their father, but she agreed with Annie. "We can't turn them away when they've come at their own risk and against the governor's restriction."

After the raid in October, no one in North

Elba had stepped a foot near their farm. When any neighbor had lost a child to illness, a father to unexpected tragedy, a mother in childbirth, or the like, they'd attended churchyard funerals, otherwise leaving the family alone to grieve. Sarah couldn't imagine herself dropping by anyone's home — friend or stranger — with funeral offerings as these southerners did. And yet she was deeply touched by the practice.

Her father was gone. He would not drive through New Charlestown in a fire-drawn buggy, but that didn't mean his spirit hadn't sparked in people.

Sarah stood from the settee with Annie hooked to her elbow. Arm in arm, they went to the front door to meet the Jamisons. After them was Mr. Reedling, who ran the sawmill. He brought a small cured ham. The Smiths, brother and sister, arrived next, apologizing that their parents would not come as they were a slave-owning family and did not agree with the abolitionist agenda; however, their mother had thought it right to send a little currant bread from her oven.

By the time Alice and Siby returned with baskets of vittles from Mrs. Fisher and black friends in households across town, they'd already amassed enough food to feed an army: funeral biscuits, meat pie, currant bread, two jugs of apple cider, corn pie, a purse of roasted pecans, three mourning wreaths, and a jar of pickled beets. The girls had stood by the door all afternoon, receiving and thanking the townsfolk for their sympathies as if they were lifelong residents. Freddy left their side only once, to bring coats, scarves, and mittens. Gypsy joined them, lying across the threshold, half inside, half out. Siby stoked the fire, and it never diminished in its blaze.

The grief that had hardened to bitterness in her brothers was purified like boiled water in Sarah. Her father's death wasn't an end to his mission but the beginning of something greater.

People were capable of more love and benevolence than they realized. The collective public voice did not always represent the individual heart. Yes, there were terrible men doing terrible deeds to one another. Men in this very town who abused others based on the color of their skin. There were prideful men who thought their marrow was made of more golden stuff than others'. Her father had proven to them all: when a beating heart stopped, there was no black or white, only blood-red. The flesh was equal.

It was the character of a man that made him better or worse.

These kindly strangers were evidence that while Sarah's family had lost nearly everything at Harpers Ferry, the good would rise as unstoppably as a river after a storm.

EDEN

New Charlestown, West Virginia
August 2014

The smell of coffee percolating awoke Eden early. She dressed and came down to find Denny sitting alone at the marble kitchen island. He faced the windows where the doll rested, so it appeared from afar as if they were locked in an anxious staring contest.

She cleared her throat.

At the sound, he flinched and his coffee sloshed over the side, full to the brim. Jittery. She wondered how many cups he'd drunk. That couldn't be his first.

"Sorry I'm late," she said, though it was the earliest she'd been out of bed in months. "How long have you been up?"

"Never went to sleep." He wiped up the spill with a paper towel. "Can't turn my head off. Night owl."

Of course. He usually played Mother Mayhem's Café until closing, at midnight.

They'd said their good nights at ten P.M. But something in his tone said there was more to it. Why wasn't he still sleeping now, then?

Eden nodded. "There's a mini TV set in the —" She hesitated over what to call the not-to-be nursery. "The other room. We can move that into yours so you can at least veg out on *M*A*S*H* reruns."

"Grrreat, just what I want — 'Suicide Is Painless' as my lullaby."

She hadn't known that was the name of the theme song.

Denny started to sing, "The game of life is hard to play . . ."

She waved her hand. "Okay. Not *M*A*S*H.* Watch *Gilligan's Island.* That's got a happier beat."

She poured coffee into a mug.

"Your dog walker, Cleo, came over," he said.

"Did she?" Eden was impressed by Cleo's young professionalism. "Nice girl. A little strange. I think she's lonely over there."

Denny nodded. "I got that impression."

"A chatterbox, too. Bossy as all get-out. But I appreciate her capitalist spirit. She doesn't have siblings. No parents to speak of. Lives with her widowed grandfather. I haven't met him, but our real estate agent mentioned he's a banker — Mr. Bronner of Bronner Bank." She tapped her mug with a fingernail.

She was as bad as Cleo, jabbering on like she knew the child better than she did. Or maybe that was just it — she wanted to know her better. She swallowed down the feeling with her black coffee.

Denny stared at the frothy brown ring staining the inside of his cup. "That's horrible."

"It sure is. You aren't a very good barista." She winced at the heartburn beginning to gurgle.

"I mean about Cleo."

Eden thought it sad and unfortunate, but "horrible" seemed overly dramatic. She shrugged. "The only granddaughter of a wealthy banker? She could have it worse. Others do."

"Our father died, but we still had each other and Mother. We still had people who gave a shit."

His profanity was disproportional to the conversation and made her wonder again what was *really* going on. She was about to insist he fess up to what was bothering him when he asked, "So how long have you and Jack been trying to have a kid?"

The question fell like a punch and sent

her flying back. She set her mug on the marble with a clink.

"Awhile."

She steeled herself for the follow-up questions: *What's wrong? Why hasn't it worked? Why didn't you tell me?* Instead, his attention returned to his coffee, leaving her to fill the lull.

"We didn't tell anybody. It's just one of those things." She dumped the rest of her cup down the sink, undrinkable, and watched it coat the steel sepia. She didn't want Denny to be sad for her. "Mother Nature can be a friend or foe — depending on the perspective."

"Fickle bitch," said Denny.

She wasn't sure if it was a cynical or serious statement. His countenance hinted the latter, so she laughed to lighten the mood.

"Suppose so."

He rose then and put an arm around her shoulders, pulling her into a strong hug that felt more take than give. She squeezed him back, and the tension in his muscles slackened.

"I'm glad we have each other." He sighed, and his chest bowed wide in her arms.

She wondered when that had happened: When had he grown so big? She could still smell the sunbaked crown of the little boy whose head fit into the nook of her neck. Only now he was tall as a beanstalk.

"You'd be lost without me," said Denny.

When she pulled back, his scowl was gone. She poked a finger at his sternum. "Completely."

A note sat beside the doll's head. Fat, loopy handwriting:

Mrs. A,
If you want Cricket to eat from The Holistic Hound, then we need A LOT of stuff. We got carrots, peas, spinach, kale, and potato in the garden, but we need brown rice, ground chicken, flaxseed, and canned pumpkin. That's for Cricket, but I really think you should get some other stuff, too. PEOPLE FOOD.

I met your brother. He said he'd walk Cricket at noon if that's okay. I'm headed over to the Niles Antique Mill to ask about that doll, then to the bank during grandpa's lunch break.

BTW, I'm reading your Mexico guide. I like it.

— Cleo

The Niles Antique Mill? Vee Niles had called Eden's cell phone and left a puzzling voice message, apologizing for business hours being off and mentioning something about her father breaking his pelvis. She said she had her hands full but might be able to swing by during her ice-cream-truck rounds in the next few days.

The whole message had left Eden entirely confused and annoyed that she'd have to put her plans on hold. She hated having to jump through hoops when it was very simple: she wanted an official seal that said, yes, this house is a historical monument and worth much more than a common dwelling for two childless, pitiful individuals . . . only the first part in writing, of course. Unlike other items, a home wasn't something you could bring to someone; they had to come to it. So Eden would have to wait for Vee. She still wasn't sure why an ice-cream truck was involved.

"Cleo came over with the note prewritten and was damned determined to get it to you," explained Denny.

"The girl has moxie." Eden liked her even more now. "I told you to make a list, too, Den. Otherwise, you and Cricket will have the same prix fixe menu."

"You know what I like. My tastes haven't changed in twenty years."

"Cheerios, chicken fingers, and Capri

Suns?" she countered.

He pretended to seriously consider the items. "Not a bad start. Maybe some salted nuts and beer, too." He scratched his stubbly jawline. "Aw, throw in bread, milk, meat, and cheese. Let's pig out!"

Before she could fend him off, he slid his hands beneath her armpits and lifted her above his head in a movement like a military press — one, two, three times — while Eden fussed at him to put her down this instant.

She grabbed Cleo's list and her car keys from their hook, then slipped into a pair of red sequinned sandals that her mother had sent from Santa Fe for her birthday. Hearing the jangle of keys, Cricket padded into the kitchen and sat his haunch on her toes, sniffing the sparkling sandal straps.

"Keep a watch on this guy while I'm gone," she told her brother. "He's trouble."

Denny scooped up Cricket and held him like a ukulele. Almost at eye level now, the dog fixed his gaze on her, and something inside her flexed like a river reed in the wind.

She cradled his furry jowls in her palm and gently scratched. "I'll be back soon, buddy."

Denny strummed the dog's stomach with his left thumb. "We're going to go for a walk. Clear our heads."

"Keep him on a leash," instructed Eden. Did they even have one? She added that to her shopping list. "Don't let him eat or drink anything funny. Or go tromping through mud puddles. Take a plastic baggie with you. And —"

"Look both ways before crossing the street — got it, got it, Mom. I'll take care of your little darling."

"I'm not — he's not . . ." she began, then stopped and let it be.

Eden got as far as the street corner. With her left hand on the steering wheel, she'd typed "Milton's Market" into her car's GPS and run into the curb twice, so she'd stopped to fiddle with the touch pad. After all her effort, the system flashed back a noncommittal "Unfound." If it couldn't confirm the address, she'd rather it said the place didn't exist at all. "Unfound" was some kind of directional purgatory. It made her the idiot who couldn't see the forest for the trees. The place was findable. But without the GPS map's verification, she sat at Apple Hill Lane, one foot on the brake, debating right or left.

Children squealed and dashed through a neighborhood yard sprinkler. Eden was checking the rearview mirror for cars coming up behind when a flash of silver spokes wheeled by: Cleo! Her saving angel to lead her by Schwinn.

She quickly lowered her window, but Cleo was pedaling faster than the retraction. So she pushed open her door, her foot still holding down the brake.

"Cleo!" she called out the crack.

The bike cruised back around and came up at her side. "What's up, Miss A?"

Eden was glad she'd risen up the ranks from Mrs. Anderson.

Cleo braced her legs on either side and leaned a handlebar against the car's polished paint. Eden tried not to let it grate on her nerves.

"Hey there, where're *you* off to?" She wanted to come off easy-breezy, not like what she was: a frenzied hot mess. The girl had already been subjected to that unflattering first impression, which she hoped to replace.

Cleo's hair was pulled up in a ponytail that, though high, seemed too loose or too heavy to stay upright, so it flopped to one side. She lifted her wrist to Eden and tapped a purple plastic watch.

"Lunchtime."

Was it noon already? Eden checked the

car's digital clock. Technology had already let her down once.

"Didn't your brother give you my note?" Cleo gestured back up the road. "Just come from the Antique Mill, but the Nileses were at a doctor's appointment. Mr. Niles fell off a barn. Got himself totally Humpty-Dumpty. Broke. You meet Vee yet?"

"Yes and no." Eden cleared her throat. Her foot was starting to cramp, so she put the car in park. "Actually, I'm headed to Milton's Market for your list. You said the bank is nearby. Do you want a ride?" She smiled, praying Cleo would take her up on the offer and play personal navigator.

Cleo leaned in close to examine Eden's leather backseat. Her cheeks smelled like tomato flowers on the vine.

"My bike won't fit."

Eden hadn't thought that far. "Okay." She forced a grin.

"I'm going to be late." Cleo put a foot to the pedal and started off.

Eden followed. She expected to see some sign of commerce, some signal that her destination was a block away, but no, just more tree-lined streets and neatly gabled houses. She slowed to stay covertly one car length behind; only it wasn't covert at all.

Cleo turned. Eden turned, too. Another

left, followed by a quick right. At a four-way stop, the girl surprised Eden by swooping around perpendicular to her car.

"This is the street." She pointed ahead. "But it's easier to park behind Milton's. There's a lot up one block."

"Thanks, Cleo," said Eden. "For showing me the way."

"Even a bullfrog can't get lost in New Charlestown. Ain't but one big street, really." She took to her pedals again, slowly circling. "Get some deviled eggs while you're in Milton's. Best in the world! The deli only sells them for special occasions. Got some now 'cause the Miltons — Mack and Annemarie — had their first baby on Sunday."

The child who is born on the Sabbath Day is bonny and blithe and good and gay, Eden recited to herself, each word like an old seam splitting anew inside her. She envisioned Annemarie Milton singing lullabies to her baby, mother's milk wet on its lips. The back of her neck prickled. Eden wanted to turn around, go home empty-handed, lock her bedroom door, and crawl into bed. She studied the heat rising in waves like a mirage on the tarred pavement, feeling nausea.

At her lack of response or movement, Cleo

181

doubled back to Eden's side.

"Did you hear what I said — about the parking lot?"

Eden nodded, her eyes brimming firewater, her throat dry as bone.

"I'll find you after I check in with Grandpa," Cleo called over her shoulder, then raced down the street, wheels spinning at a pace.

Eden watched until she vanished beyond a row of parked cars. *Such an odd kid,* she thought, and it made her smile.

Milton's Market was more than she expected, with a cheesemonger station, a butcher, a bakery, and a deli, in addition to the aisles of cans and prepackaged items. Everything was clean and neat, with gingham awnings over each of the designated areas. She picked up everything on Cleo's list, plus snacks for Denny. She took Cleo's recommendation and got a dozen of Milton's Devilishly Divine Eggs. The swirled yolks were toothpicked with miniature "IT'S A BOY!" flags. Quaint, like being at a Milton family picnic.

As the cashier tallied her bill, Cleo walked in.

"You found it," she said to Eden. Then: "Hey-ya, Mack."

"Hi there, Cleo," he replied.

Eden hadn't taken the time to notice the name tag prominently displayed.

"Mack — as in Mack *Milton?*"

His had been the second name on their real estate contract. Right after Morris Milton. While she'd never met either man, their designation as "the sellers" was the counterpart to Jack and her, "the buyers" in the home-purchase negotiations.

"The one and only." He grinned.

She extended her hand. "Eden Norton . . . Anderson. We just moved in, you know."

"The Apple Hill house, next door to the Bronners. Great property." He shook warmly. "Annemarie's going to be jealous I met the new neighbors before her. She's been after me to bring y'all some welcoming cider doughnuts."

"Those are my favorites." Cleo made a *Mmm* sound.

Eden demurred: "Very kind of you, but really I ought to be the one giving congratulations. I hear you have a new baby in the house."

Mack beamed. "My first. Matthew."

"All the Miltons got *M* names. It's a family tradition," explained Cleo.

"Ah, I see," said Eden. "Cleo's been giving me the New Charlestown Milton primer. Matthew and Mack of Milton's

183

Market. Then there's your brother, Mett, at the café and your dad, Morris . . ."

At that mention, Mack stoned up. Eden had spoken the unspeakable, and it seemed to flash-freeze the air around them.

"Gotta jet!" Cleo jumped to Eden's side, swooping up the brown grocery bag. "Children's Story Hour is 'bout to finish. I got to swap a book. Ms. Silverdash is expecting us."

This was news to Eden. She rolled her lower lip to hide her surprise.

"You best be off, then. Good meeting you, Eden."

"You, too. I'll be eager to meet the rest of your family — and introduce my husband, Jack."

If they stayed in town and together long enough. It was a conventional slip — the habit of introducing herself as a couple. But the Anderson duo had never been problematic. In fact, Jack and she had been quite stellar as a pair, loving and successful in their careers. They'd boasted at dinner parties that it was like finding their other magnet half. *Click.* On that principle they'd stood strong. On that principle they'd wed. It was the attempt to insert a third that had caused separation. Just like a magnet, the dyad forces of attraction could extend only so far.

Cleo pulled Eden's sleeve toward the exit. Her Schwinn leaned against a parking meter a few yards away.

When they reached it, Eden sighed. "I guess bringing up a family feud doesn't make the best nice-to-meet-ya."

Cleo shrugged. "It's not like it's a secret anyhow."

She placed Eden's grocery bag inside her front basket, flicked up the kickstand, and rolled the bike along the sidewalk by the handlebars.

Somewhere, an unseen ice-cream truck's song jingled the tune "Follow the Yellow Brick Road." *Follow, follow, follow, follow,* Eden hummed to the *tick-tick, tick-tick* of the sherbet-colored reflectors falling up and down Cleo's bike spokes. She was off to meet Ms. Silverdash.

SARAH

North Elba, New York
December 23, 1859

Before dawn, Sarah and Annie had cut snowy evergreen branches and holly clusters from the woods behind their house. It wasn't fair, they decided, to stamp out Ellen's Christmas joy for the sake of funeral propriety. Black drapes hung over all the windows and mirrors, and the Lake Placid winter had blustered up a blizzard, banking snow thigh-high. They were glad they'd buried their father as soon as they'd returned. If they hadn't, they might still have his coffin in their parlor that very minute.

The Alcotts had sent a copy of Charles Dickens's *A Christmas Carol,* which Sarah enjoyed — except for the beginning with ghost Marley in his chains. She was in the midst of reading it to little Ellen, skipping the particulars of those pages. *A ghost named Marley came to warn Scrooge of three spirits' visitation . . .* She kept it simple. That was all that was required to understand the rest of the story.

Sarah and Annie tied the cut pine boughs over their door lintels with scarlet ribbon. The fragrance reminded Sarah of Virginia and Freddy and kind neighbors come with wreaths in their arms. She pressed her sappy fingers to her lips and nose.

Annie caught her, hand to face, inhaling deeply. "I know," she said. "It reminds me of that horrible day, too." She sighed as if their father had died all over again. She'd been gloom and doom since returning from the South. "Will we ever be able to smell jack pine again without cringing?"

Sarah worked the holly stems into the evergreen needles. It was a wonder to her that a scent could evoke such opposing responses. She didn't wash the sap off until it was time to help her mother cook.

Mr. George Stearns and Mr. Franklin Sanborn, two of her father's Secret Committee of Six, were traveling down from Canada, where they'd taken refuge after the raid on Harpers Ferry. They were men of great wealth and influence for whom Sarah had painted a number of pictorial maps on papyrus paper, including the very one that directed their journey to the border of "Heaven" — the code word for Canada. With southern justice recompensed by her father's blood, the men were returning to their families and stopping at the Brown farm to pay their respects. Sarah planned to pass them a note vowing her unwavering assistance to the UGRR as soon as she found the opportunity. Before dinner, she hoped.

The women had mustered what foodstuffs they could: a Christmas mold and butter cookies. Sarah helped Mary assemble the dinner: shreds of roasted guinea hen, boiled eggs, and savory jelly to bind it into a single quivering mass. They put a cheese shroud over it and placed it outside, in the cold root cellar, to set up. Meanwhile, Annie and Ellen cut hearts and stars from rolled sugar dough to bake on buttered tins. Ellen giggled and nibbled raw strips.

Mary kissed the top of her head. "Not too much or you'll spoil your appetite."

Since their mother's return from the execution, her stutter had vanished. None of the women had immediately noticed, too caught up in the whirlwind of attending to John's body and preparing for the journey home. But when it finally dawned on them that she was speaking without lisp or hesitation, the girls were shocked and somewhat afraid. Mary couldn't put a finger to when the miracle had occurred, but she was convinced it was one.

"Your father entreated to the Almighty on my behalf. A gift to temper a curse," she said.

Whatever the cause, it cheered Sarah immeasurably to hear her mother speak in smooth succession. Even this mundane moment in the kitchen felt finer than any that had come before. A Christmas mold and butter cookies were not the feast of years gone by, when her brothers and their wives had gathered together to hear their father give glory. No, they'd never have a house or table so full again. But that didn't mean there weren't blessings to be counted.

Sarah couldn't be like Annie, carrying the weight of the past around her neck like the chains of Marley's ghost. She was different from her blood kin. Her life and actions had already deviated from the traditional path.

She thought of Mr. Thoreau and his nature walks at Walden Pond, his grand ambling adventures, and then Freddy's face in the dim barn. She flushed at the memory of her brazenness, her naïve hope that her father would rise like a phoenix with her map as his tinder.

"You're red as a beet, child." Mary stopped to put the inside of her wrist to Sarah's cheek. "Feeling poorly?"

"No." She turned her face away from the stove. "Just excited for a little Christmas."

Her mother smiled. " 'Go your way. Eat the fat and drink sweet wine and send portions to anyone who has nothing ready, for this day is holy to our Lord. And do not be grieved, for the joy of the Lord is your strength,' " she quoted, the words as melodic as a lullaby, a carol of the season, and so it fell on Sarah's heart as much as her ears.

Ellen danced her secondhand dolly along the kitchen table and hummed "God Rest You Merry, Gentlemen." No painted mouth or embroidered smock of chestnut hair like Alice's; Ellen's doll was made of muslin and stuffed with beans. Sarah decided she'd buy it a shiny ribbon sash for Christmas. Ellen would like that.

Her mother moved on to finishing the tallow candles. A hung line of dipped wicks hardened in the window draft, waxy icicles that reeked of gaminess.

"Must we use those?" asked Sarah.

"It's either these or we eat in the dark," replied Annie.

"They'll leave soot on the ceiling, and

we'll be up on chairs through the New Year cleaning."

The point resonated with their mother, who paused in mid-dip. "We'll put lamps over them. Like the Hills."

Both Sarah and Annie stopped and stared at each other. It was the first time Mary had spoken of their time in the South or the execution since returning to New York. They'd assumed it was a subject not to be broached.

"What was their town's name?" Mary tapped her chin. "Charles Town, was it?"

"No, that was the old town where Father was jailed," said Annie, continuing to plunge tapers into the greasy white fat.

"New Charlestown," corrected Sarah. "The Hills live in the *new.*"

"*New* Charlestown. Yes, that's it." Their mother wiped her hands on her apron. "We received a letter from there this morn. It slipped my mind in the preparations for Mr. Stearns and Mr. Sanborn."

From her pocket, she pulled a square letter, sealed with the letter *H* in thick red wax:

To Missus Brown, the Misses Brown,
and Family
North Elba, New York

191

Sarah cracked the seal. Inside was a card with a black-and-white lithograph of Queen Victoria and her family around the royal Christmas tree. Painted by James Roberts some years ago, the image was common enough, but Sarah had never seen it reproduced on such luxurious paper and with such attention to detail. She could make out nearly every toy hanging between the branches, the dollies and jesters and horse-drawn carriages, and the children's dimpled faces and the king's and queen's glad expressions.

Like Dickens's Ebenezer Scrooge being shown around by the Ghost of Christmas Present, Sarah felt as if she were staring through a window into another's life, one happy and full. She held the card up to the firelight, attempting to imprint every corner of the illustration on her mind's eye, breathing in the smell of expensive ink and paper and miles traveled.

"Go on, child, read it to us." Mary had moved over to the cookies, patting the top of one to check its spring, then pushing them deeper into the oven's mouth.

Sarah cleared her throat. While alive, her father had been a staunch proponent of proper elocution. From her first recited word, she'd been taught to sit or stand with a straight back, chin raised, a full breath in the lungs, and clear diction on the tongue. She didn't know how to read any other way. She took the rhetorical position, with one arm holding the card at a proper distance so she could follow the sentences uninterrupted.

" 'Dear Family Brown,' " she began. " 'Despite the brevity of your visit and its dire nature, you left no less of a lasting impression on our household. You are greatly admired.' "

Sarah paused for effect and speculation as to who exactly was admired and by whom. Before the wonder-flies in her chest had a chance to beat their wings, she continued: " 'Though we know it will be arduous in light of those missing round your table, we pray that the peace of Christmas be upon your house and bless those within. Alice has included something for Miss Annie Brown, as she shares Alice's affinity for floriography. Freddy asks after Missus and the Misses Brown's healths. He hopes that you are engaging in many — many good nature walks for consti—' "

Sarah stumbled over the words, embarrassed that Priscilla was penning Freddy's coded greeting, though it pleased her that he'd dared to include it at all. She understood his true meaning — about their secret meeting in the barn and discussion of the UGRR.

" '. . . constitution. Fondest tidings, Mr. and Mrs. George Hill, Freddy, Alice, and, by special request, Gypsy. Postscript: Siby and the Fishers have asked that I pass along their merry tidings, as well.' "

"How kind of them." Annie pinned her last dripping candle to the window line, then came to Sarah's side with renewed interest.

Inside the envelope was a perfectly pressed set of snowdrops. The blooms flared from long-stemmed buds that'd been cut precisely to fit the envelope's dimensions. They reminded Sarah of fairy staffs.

Annie held one gently between her fingertips. "They say God sent Adam and Eve snowdrops as comfort after they were cast out of the Garden of Eden. Their message is hope and consolation."

Mary leaned closer to see. "I've always thought snowdrops a strange flower. Blooming summertime in the midst of winter."

"Like a specter," said Annie.

"Like a miracle," corrected their mother.

Priscilla's penmanship reminded Sarah of miniature snowdrops in a row, looping petals at the end of narrow lines. She drew her finger across the sentences, feeling the grooves of the pen in the ecru paper and wanting to paint the lines grass green and the letters eggshell white. How lovely that would look. She wondered if Freddy had been by Priscilla's side as she wrote. Gypsy at his knee. Alice sewing apple branches with the strands of hair she'd left behind. Siby's corn-bread pie in the oven. Her chest tightened. She trusted them more than any other family she knew, more than her own in some ways.

A spiteful newspaper commentator had written that her father ought to have been sentenced as those in the Far East were. There, treason was considered a plague of the mind, infecting those in close contact; thus, the man, his co-conspirators, friends, and family were all guilty by association and condemned to a similar fate. She thought it the most dreadful thing to wish upon people he'd never met. She'd thrown the article in the fire. The words had curled and shriveled to ash.

The Hills had welcomed them graciously, without a hint of scorn. The entire town had shown kindness despite so many reasons not to. For that and more, Sarah was devoted.

"Are the Christmas cookies done?" Ellen asked.

"Patience is a virtue," Mary reminded her.

Ellen puckered her mouth incredulously and sat on the stool, tapping out the seconds with her feet.

Mary pushed aside two hanging candles and looked to the dusky sky. "Mr. Stearns and Mr. Sanborn could arrive at any hour, and look at us — a waxy mess of Browns." She turned to Annie. "Save the leftover fat for soap and fetch the mold from the cellar. Sarah, dust the decanter. The men will want a sip against the chill. Then hurry up and change, girls. Rinse your faces and run combs through your hair. Use my good perfume to ward off the tallow smell. Just a dab on your wrists, mind you."

"Imperial Tea Rose." Ellen slurred it into one word: *Impeewee-all-tee-rose.* "Oh please, me, too?"

"Absolutely not," said Mary. "Only for older girls."

Ellen bit her lower lip, on the precipice of tears, until Sarah pulled the tray of cookies from the oven. Golden hearts and stars, twinkling-hot butter. One bite and Ellen had forgotten the rose perfume, smiling and humming carols as she munched. Sarah wondered when a person outgrew that —

the ability to be unshackled from memory and desire, past and future. To live purely in the present moment. She hoped that unlike Scrooge in *A Christmas Carol,* one could achieve it without being haunted.

Sarah slipped the Hills' Christmas card into her front pocket. It'd be lost or ruined in the kitchen. Her mother would be grateful for its safekeeping when she went to do her weekly correspondences. Perhaps she'd ask if she could send a reply along, too, and maybe, just maybe, Freddy would cordially write back.

North Elba, N.Y., January 14, 1860

Dear Mrs. Priscilla Hill,
Thank you so kindly for the beautiful Christmas lithograph and greetings! This comes with my mother's note of gratitude, but I wished to send my own as well.

To Alice, please thank her for the beautiful pressed snowdrops. Nothing could brighten Annie's disposition until they arrived. We are grateful for the cheer and the deeper meaning of their bestowment. Annie plans to place them in a silver frame. I've included a sketching I did: a scene of apple blossoms that reminded me of Alice and warmer days to come. As well, herein is another coil of hair from my brush for whatever purposes it may provide in needlepoint artistry.

We are all in good health, as Freddy so inquired. Nature walks are excellent practice no matter the climate. They have been medically proven to clear the mind and improve the body's stamina. I hope to engage in more as the season warms.

Please tell Freddy that I would be glad to loan him my personal signed copy of *Walden* should he care to broaden his education on the subject. Thoreau was a trusted friend of my father's. I could post the book straight off on the promise of noble stewardship. I shall have to send him my new address, however, as Mother has consented for Annie and me to attend Mr. Franklin Sanborn's private school in Concord, Massachusetts.

Mr. Sanborn visited at Christmastime and, over dinner discussion, insisted that Annie and I continue our scholastic pursuits under his keen tutelage. Father would've insisted, too, he argued, and none could call it untrue. Mr. George Stearns has generously offered to be our patron.

Annie will stay in North Elba until our widowed sister-in-law, Martha, gives birth to brother Oliver's child. I am to be sent ahead to Massachusetts by enclosed cabriolet. It will be my first time traveling as a passenger of such modernization. Mr. Sanborn and Mr. Stearns have assured Mother that I will be delivered forthwith with nary a speck of mud on my boots.

That is all the news from here! Again,

our sincerest thanks to you and Mr. Hill for your hospitality. I have yet to taste corn bread or johnny-cake as delicious as Siby's. While some might say the northern grains are different, I'm sure it is my cooking that is the obstacle. I haven't the Fisher family secret. Please give Gypsy a good pat on the head for me. She is possibly the most agreeable dog I have ever met. We pray the New Year brings great blessing to the Hill household.

Sincerely,
Sarah Brown

EDEN

Ms. Silverdash's store reminded Eden of a book: seemingly skinny through the spine, but open the front door and it was wide and full, and smelling earthy like a midsummer night's forest of paper and glue. In the front window, books of varying sizes and colors had been stacked so that they formed a miniature village replicating New Charlestown's Main Street. Rainbow-swirled trees made of carefully folded atlas pages lined the boulevard; colorful ribbons from shredded maps were strung across buildings of city guidebooks; a red octagon the size of a quarter stood tall on a Popsicle stick with the word READ instead of STOP.

But Eden *had* stopped to marvel at the meticulous construction. She hadn't initially noticed the display when Cleo had parked her bike under the store's sunshade and taken up the grocery bag. The too-bright glare of midday and a HELP WANTED sign taped to the glass obscured the view.

"Ms. Silverdash is an artist," Cleo explained. "She makes dioramas. Summer's was called *Follow the Reading Road.* Last winter, she used only silver and white book covers and stationeries so it looked like Main in a blizzard. She'll unveil the fall one soon, during the Dog Days End Festival. She's still deciding on a theme, she says."

Eden was impressed. Bookstore owner, historian, and artist.

"Come on." Cleo pulled at Eden's elbow. "They're finishing up the Children's Story Hour."

The air changed as they moved deeper into the store, made rich and hearty by the oak bookshelves and pine floors. Braided ficus trees shaded the checkout desk with an arch of leaves. Philodendrons draped the bookcase like tangled Rapunzel locks.

Cleo slid the book she carried onto the desk: *Ghost Stories of Harpers Ferry.*

"You like scary stories?" asked Eden.

Cleo rolled her eyes. "Ghost stories are nothing but unsolved mysteries. Ms. Silverdash knows a lot about everything, but she knows an *awful* lot about Harpers Ferry and New Charlestown. Like Tom Storm's ghost,

for instance. You know about him, right?"
She absentmindedly squeezed the fleshy
leaves of a jade plant beside the register.

Eden didn't but was sure she was about
to find out. "Tom Storm's ghost?" she
repeated, and Cleo took it as an invitation.

"His mother was a slave and his father
was a white plantation owner in Virginia.
He was a freedman, but his wife and kids
were still slaves. Their master told Mr.
Storm he could have his wife and two
daughters if he came up with fifteen
hundred dollars. So he worked and saved
up to the exact penny, but then the master
raised the price on him!" Cleo's voice cre-
scendoed. Remembering herself in the
bookstore, she quieted.

"So like any man in a rotten spot like that,
he decided to do it his own way. His wife
and daughters came up on the UGRR —
the Underground Railroad. He met them
somewhere in New Charlestown. But the
night they were supposed to be forwarded
north, an awful hailstorm — just like his
name! — hit, and a posse looking for blood
came to the station house where his family
was hiding. The baby girl started to holler,
so to save his family, Storm got the towns-
men to chase him through the forest. They'd
been drinking and were so riled by the

stormy night that instead of capturing him for the bounty, they cut off his head and tore up his body, then dragged the pieces to Harpers Ferry for the hogs to finish." Her eyes were wide as purple pansies.

"No ghost story can top that! It's historical. To this day, the name of the road from the Bluff down to Harpers Ferry is Storm Street, and some swear a black man with a scar across his throat walks the way at night." She crossed her arms over her chest and lifted her chin. "Like I said, I don't believe in all that heebie-jeebie stuff. My Grandpa says it's not Presbyterian, but . . ." She dipped her head forward and lowered her voice to barely a murmur: "If my kin got ripped up by crazy townsfolk, I'd come spook, too, so nobody'd forget!" She nodded. "That's my theory on the case of Tom Storm's ghost."

Eden leaned an elbow on the checkout desk. Rapt. "So the ghost isn't a ghost but one of Storm's relations coming back to remind people?"

Cleo straightened her shoulders, pleased that Eden got her hypothesis. "Exactly."

One hundred and fifty years was a long time to hold a grudge. But revenge was like a Virginia creeper. Once it took root, you might never get it out of the ground. Maybe

Cleo was spot-on.

"Is that what you want to do when you grow up? Figure out history's unsolved mysteries?"

"And be a veterinarian. I decided that this week. I thought I only liked cats and horses, but I *really* like dogs, like Cricket."

The child could change her mind again tomorrow, but for today, Eden took the aspiration as a personal compliment.

"The only animals I don't like are snakes and spiders," Cleo went on. "Some people have them as pets but, luckily, nobody in New Charlestown. I checked with Dr. Wyatt. He's our vet. I told him about Cricket, and he said that puppies need a bunch of shots. Has Cricket had his? If not, Dr. Wyatt is the best — and only — in town."

Eden hadn't thought they'd keep Cricket long enough to need a vet or vaccinations, but now . . .

"I should probably call him."

"I'll give you his number when we get home — unless I forget."

We, home. Eden liked the way it sounded.

Painted butter yellow and edged in periwinkle, the Reading Room door swung open and out tumbled a set of twins throwing kindergarten punches at each other.

205

Behind them were three women in serious discussion. One of the women held an infant on her hip; another, the hand of a boy who sucked his thumb while simultaneously picking his nose with his forefinger.

The two mothers bantered back and forth while Ms. Silverdash nodded along. She had a chestnut bob that glinted of reddish dye but came off handsomely. She held her shoulders straight like a dancer, giving the appearance of stature despite her petite height. Her skin was tawny olive, her cheekbones high, with a round nose accenting her face.

"We could have a *Wind in the Willows* party with themed snacks and goody bags," said one.

"And costumes!" said the other.

"I think that would be a splendid party for one of you to host at your home," Ms. Silverdash suggested.

The mothers' excitement was snuffed.

"Oh, I assumed . . ." the one with the boy began, then looked down at the toddlers biting and pulling each other's hair on the ground. "Todd works such long hours. When he's home, he likes it quiet. So . . ." She turned to the other woman. "Maybe at your house, Laura?"

Laura scoffed audibly. "You *know* my

house isn't big enough to have this many kids inside — that's why all of our birthday parties are outdoors!"

They both fidgeted uncomfortably, but Ms. Silverdash took no notice. "Next time we'll begin something new — a fairy-tale anthology. Charles Perrault or Hans Christian Andersen." Seeing Cleo and Eden, she smiled widely. "Please excuse me, ladies, there's a new face I'm eager to meet."

Instead of extending a hand to Eden, she wrapped both arms around her. "May I presume you are Mrs. Anderson?"

She smelled like a giant bouquet.

"Welcome! Cleo has spoken so highly of you."

Cleo's cheeks blushed beneath her freckles, and she busied herself with checking the Harpers Ferry book pages for anything she might've left between them.

"Nice to meet you, too. Please, call me Eden."

Ms. Silverdash tapped her chin. "Eden," she repeated. "A beautiful name. Biblical. The Garden, of course."

Yes and no. "It was my grandmother's."

"Ah, a legacy name — even better."

Laura uncoupled her twins. "Doug, Dan, stop it right now or you'll both get the paddle."

The boys continued to grunt and slap at each other.

"Mama, I tried to stop them," defended a girl only slightly older, as if she, too, were subject to punishment.

Laura handed the girl the baby and knelt down between the boys. "You are *family!*" she said, implying it to be more than enough reason to behave.

One of them, Doug or Dan, balled his fist and went for the other, missing entirely and thwacking his mother on the chin.

Laura rubbed the rosy spot, then shook her head. "You wait until your father hears about this." She stood. Her chest was splotched angry pink.

The other mother clucked her tongue and smoothed a hand over her son's head. "Maybe a party isn't such a good idea. All that sugar — gets the kids keyed up." She checked her wristwatch. "We've got to go. William has tennis lessons next."

Ms. Silverdash cleared her throat and laced her fingers together, narrowing her gaze at the twins with such authority that both turned and didn't blink the entire time she spoke. "Daniel and Douglas, you may quietly sit on this step until your mother is ready to leave. You know what the Fur Fairy says: 'Books don't enjoy a fracas. It gives them a spine-ache.' "

One boy followed the other to the step they'd just tumbled down, and they sat, frowning with crossed arms.

Laura sighed and turned to Eden. "I'm Laura Hunter. Sorry about . . ." She waved her hand in a little circle, then fingered the raspberry on her chin. "The smart egg is my eldest, Johnny, twelve, in the gifted and talented program at school. Sometimes I wonder if I should've stopped at one." She chuckled.

The girl by her side readjusted the babe asleep in the nape of her neck. The movement caught Laura's attention.

"I'm kidding, of course." She ran a hand over her daughter's shoulder.

The girl ignored her mother and looked to some point farther in the store's bookshelf forest.

"It's okay," said Eden, though she knew it wasn't.

She'd once been that girl, holding baby Denny close, knowing well that their mother wished for a different life — a life that didn't involve them. Seeing it play out in front of her seemed to upheave a river stone from the mud of her chest. Eden couldn't even create one child, good or bad. Her fingers went numb, and she had to look away to keep the tears at bay.

Thankfully, Cleo changed the subject for all of them. "Speaking of eggs, we can't stay long. Miss A's got Milton's deviled in the bag."

"A New Charlestown celebration treat. The town is growing so much this summer," said Ms. Silverdash. "I hope you enjoy Mack's eggs — your dog, Cricket, too. I've read that the yolks are beneficial for a shiny coat. High in omega-3s."

Eden patted the grocery bag on the checkout desk. "Cricket has you to thank for his meals. *The Holistic Hound* has been incredibly helpful. I've never cooked much before."

"We made the Canine Casserole," said Cleo. "It got two paws up."

"Of course it did!" Ms. Silverdash pulled Cleo to her waist in a hug. "A little love in the recipe makes everything come out right." It was the kind of adoring embrace Eden could remember her mother bestowing on her only a handful of times.

Baby Hunter caught the hiccups in her sleep and awoke with a wail. Laura pointed to her twins. "You two, let's go. We've got to swing by the market before naptime. Come on, come on," she urged, ushering them up. "Say good-bye to Ms. Silverdash."

Instead of speaking, the boys grunted with a wave. Good enough for Laura; she pushed them toward the door. "Nice meeting you, Eden. Cleo, give my best to your grandpa. Bye, Emma." She led her procession out, her purse spanking her rear end as she went.

Cleo frowned at their exit. "On the Nature Channel, I saw a pack of wolves calmer than those Hunters."

Ms. Silverdash laughed, the sound like a Christmas bell. Eden caught a giggle from it.

"Oh, we shouldn't be laughing," said Ms. Silverdash. "Nothing funny about a woman who has more blessings than she recognizes." She lifted the ghost book. "Did you enjoy this one, Cleo?"

"Very much!"

"I thought so. It's one of Mr. Morris's favorites. Given your latest inspiration for veterinary practices, I thought this new series might be of interest." From a nearby shelf she pulled a thin paperback. "*A Diplomatic Dilemma: A Detective Spot Mystery,*" she read.

As Cleo inspected the cover, her enthusiasm dwindled. It featured a cartoon detective dog with a pipe in his mouth. "A kid's book?"

"I read the first chapter and nearly kept it

211

for myself," Ms. Silverdash assured her. "Spot, the dog, picks up on the clues we humans simply aren't capable of perceiving. He uses his masterful skills to direct his human companion, one Detective O'Hannigan, to the perpetrators. They say there's a dog barking in ninety-nine percent of novels. It's about time one got the opportunity to speak the words on his mind. The Fur Fairy agrees."

Ms. Silverdash was an excellent saleswoman. By the end of her pitch, Cleo had begun reading and even Eden was curious.

"But you let me know if you think it's too juvenile."

The girl's eyes ran left to right, left to right; then she shut the cover and slipped the book under her arm. "I'll give it my undivided attention."

A bowl of starlight peppermints sat beside the register. Cleo took one, unwrapped it, and popped it into her mouth. "So . . ." She moved it around until it lodged in her cheek. "I was thinking about the Dog Days End Festival. Last year, I was in charge of making sure the pies and cakes and baked things were in the correct contest categories."

"You did an excellent job."

"I thought so." Cleo nodded. "That's why

I wondered if this year I might have a little more *responsibility.*" She enunciated the word with the peppermint candy secured in her cheek pocket.

Ms. Silverdash smiled. "I think that can be arranged. We're always looking for help, and you're nearly eleven — practically a grown-up."

Cleo beamed at that, and Eden felt she ought to offer to help, too, remembering what Cleo had said about the bookstore being in financial trouble after all of Ms. Silverdash's kindness.

"I saw the Help Wanted sign up front," said Eden. "I don't know if you could use me for the festival or . . ."

Before she'd finished, Ms. Silverdash was clapping her hands. "Saints be praised! I've been looking for someone to lead the Children's Story Hour. I hope today didn't scare you off. Once the story starts, they are angels. It's the before and after that can require a little motherly discipline. I'll be here the whole time. It's an hour, Monday, Wednesday, and Friday. I can't pay you much but . . . you'd be a godsend!"

It lit something in Eden to have pleased Ms. Silverdash, and before she had time to think twice, she agreed. It was the easiest job interview she'd ever had.

213

"*And* the shop is pet-friendly," added Cleo.

"Indeed, we have our own resident, the Fur Fairy of Children's Story Hour."

Ms. Silverdash went into the Reading Room and returned carrying an antique stuffed animal as loved apart as the fabled Velveteen Rabbit. While possessing a bear snout, big brown eyes, and floppy dog ears, it had a human body and wore a faded lace-collared dress embroidered with bough blooms.

"The Fur Fairy has been here since the first hour. The shop might vanish into the mists if she were to leave." Ms. Silverdash winked. "The children obey her every command, including sitting for an hour without fuss. That, alone, proves her power. She'll be at your assistance now."

And so the deal was made. Eden was to be the new manager of the Children's Story Hour starting that very Friday. The happy high of pleasing Ms. Silverdash carried her all the way to her car.

It wasn't until Cleo had finished putting the groceries in the backseat that Eden realized what *exactly* she'd committed herself to: three days a week, she, a childless woman, would be surrounded by children. What did she know about kids? Look at the

Hunter twin: he'd hit his own mother. What would they do to her? Anxiety gripped her, and she knuckled the steering wheel of the parked car.

Balanced on the banana seat of her bike, Cleo knocked on the driver's side window. "Miss A, you okay?"

Her head eclipsed the summer sun, outlining the curve of her cheek against the white sky like the silhouette portrait Eden's mother had done of her as a child. She said it was the most beautiful likeness she had of Eden and hung it on Eden's bedroom wall. Eden had studied it for hours. The image seemed an impersonator with a concealed expression. She made up stories about it, imagining countless frightening countenances in the darkness.

"We didn't talk to Ms. Silverdash about the doll," she said finally.

Cleo shrugged. "She'll be there tomorrow and the next day."

Eden nodded but didn't move.

Cleo cupped her hands around her face and pressed her nose to the window. "Do you know the way or do you want to follow me again?"

With only the windowpane between them, Eden could make out each starry freckle on

Cleo's skin. She relaxed her grip. "I'll follow you."

New Charlestown, Virginia, February 8,
  1860

Dear Sarah,
My mother kindly passed on your words
of the January 14 letter. Instead of sending my reply through her, I thought it
best to correspond directly. I hope you
don't think me impudent. From our
time together, I feel confident that
formal pretenses are unnecessary.

Thank you for your offer to lend me a
personal, signed copy of Thoreau's book
— no doubt treasured by you and your
family — and I'd readily accept if I
didn't already own one, which, although
lacking the hand of its creator, is beloved
and dog-eared from much reading. This
was how I knew you were a person of
great mind when we took our short
nature walk together. However, if there
were another book of your high recommendation, I would eagerly receive that
lending.

Mr. Sanborn's school is of noble
distinction! One of the many principles
our fathers agreed upon: the education
of the mind. You must tell me how it is

to ride in a modernized cabriolet. Father and Mother say they are quite popular in London, where, years ago, they paid sizably to be carted from one street to another. Your benefactor understands what precious cargo is being transported. As you witnessed here, the horse and wagon is still our standard mode of travel. The railroads have yet to build their lines to a majority of southern cities, but soon enough they will see they must — for the natural advancement of our country. I am fascinated by the northern innovations and would be delighted to discuss that subject and literature, as those seem to be our two favorites.

We are well in New Charlestown. Your enclosed apple blossom illustration sparked a new interest in Alice. She has begun construction on a diorama likeness of your orchard on which to stage doll performances. She, like you, has a proclivity for the arts.

Might you continue to send us illustrations? All would be tremendously useful as examples.

I am at the aid of my father at the New Charlestown Church and our community endeavors. Having completed my academics ahead of my peers, I now have the time to live the example set forth in *Walden* and the good Holy Word.

Affectionately your friend,
Freddy

P.S. Gypsy has pressed her nose to the page corner. Her greeting to you.

Concord, Mass., March 1, 1860

Dear Freddy,
I've arrived at Mr. Sanborn's private school and was happy to receive your letter. You are a man of literature! From what I'd always been told, I believed there was a blockade of lettered thought at the Mason-Dixon Line. I'm glad that hasn't affected the Hill household.

Per your request, I've sent my copy of *Flower Fables,* written by Louisa May Alcott. Louisa is tremendously gifted in the written word. I stayed with the Alcotts in Massachusetts a short time before moving into the school's dormitory. With so many girls in one home, we did little more than play checkers, read Louisa's fables, and dream. Our studies must've poorly shown because as soon as lodgings became available, Mr. Alcott counseled it wise to move. He doesn't believe girls sleeping head to toe is beneficial for the mind or body. Being that Abigail May's feet stink of sardines, I wasn't disappointed to have a room of my own. Such a luxury I've never known.

It has a window that looks out to the actual Walden Pond. A dream! Even in the depths of winter. Just as Thoreau described. The colors of the sun mirror back a rainbow of different worlds, depending on the time of day. Misty greens in the morn. Stark cobalt at noon. Yolky yellow come sunset and shimmering blue as a crow's breast by night. I wish I could send a painted scene and not just these words. Boston sits just on the hazy horizon. Seen best by evening. The twinkles of streetlamps hover like stars. I'd been to Massachusetts before but never on my own. It feels as if I'm seeing everything truly for the first time.

It would be my pleasure to send sketches of whatever scenes might be best and most inspirational to Alice and friends.

Before I run out of candle, I must tell

of the cabriolet! It was terribly, wonderfully modern. Teamed by black stallions with the steadiest trot I have ever been privy to. The folding wooden doors at the base ensured that passengers were kept safe from the wheel spokes and trail muck. The glass windows atop allowed me to keep vigilant watch of the scenery, like a whip-poor-will flying across the land. Or at least that's how I imagined it, and I'm glad to report, we landed with a happy chirp.

I hope you are afforded the opportunity to ride in such a fine carriage one day. It makes one aware that knowledge and modernization are making so many impossibles possible.

My candle has gone out, and I am penning this by Walden moonlight. I hope you enjoy the book of fables. When you are finished, you may return it here. However, I hope you write me again sooner.

Your true friend,
Sarah

New Charlestown, Virginia, March 18,
   1860

Dear Sarah,
Thank you for the collection of *Flower Fables.* Mother has begun to read the fables aloud after dinner. We are quite entertained by the whimsy. As well, I've read Alice your description of Walden Pond.

Inspired, she's made a new diorama using our mother's vanity mirror as the pond and colored ribbons for the theater curtain. When fanned, they flitter through various cascades of daylight, just as you wrote. She's to put on a production of *Kerry Pippin at Sarah's Walden Pond* this evening, and all wish you were in the audience with us.

Sarah, might you do us the kind favor of drawing something of the bustling city of Albany? Mother has just read a feature article on the Erie Canal, and Alice waits in earnest for some firsthand description. We trust only you for accurate pictorial rendering. Are you familiar?

On sadder tidings, word has come that your sister-in-law Martha passed away following the birth of her daughter, who lived a mere handful of days. Our deepest condolences. Please write and let us know how you are bearing up.

Affectionately yours,
Freddy

Concord, Mass., April 2, 1860

Dear Freddy,

I'm sorry to reply with unhappy salutations, but shortly before your March letter, Annie arrived in Concord bereft and inconsolable. The passing of Martha and baby Olive seems to have cleaved Annie indefinitely. She hardly eats, taking down medicinal herbs of her own collection or balsam tinctures ordered from European doctors. All leave her in a stupor. She tells me she can't study. Her mind is elsewhere, and I fear it might abandon her completely.

I can't share this with my mother or anyone else. They will insist we return home, and I might as well drown myself in the pond as return to making tallow candles and stitching new buttons on old shirts. Oh, Freddy, the very thought has me as woeful as Annie. Of course I miss my family. Please don't think me heartless. But I'm not like them — Mother, Annie, Ruth, and my sister-in-laws, living and gone. I want more.

I'm doing Annie's academic assignments and my own so that no one is aware. I work all day at school, followed by all hours of the night in my own artistic endeavors. Enclosed is the sketch of Albany's Erie Canal port. I had the opportunity to visit the lock system while studying modern architecture. Father was a great admirer of inventive form and function in transportation design. An academic field I seem to excel in now, as drawing by candlelight is the only place I find peace these days. I hope it is of aid!

To be truthful, I am at the end of my blasted rope and don't know how much longer I'll be able to keep apace . . . Please forgive me for cursing, but I am in need of a friend. You, Freddy, know all that I carry and have offered unconditional rapport at my lowest hour. I hope you might do the same now.

Your true friend,
Sarah

New Charlestown, Virginia, April 20, 1860

Dearest Sarah,

I received your letter this morning and am greatly concerned to hear that you've taken on yet another secret burden. Please know that I am here and you may write anything (curses upon curses, if you wish) without judgment.

Damnation! Now, see, you have my own obscenity in written proof and you may use it as you see fit. I trust you, as I hope you trust me. These penned words hold so little in their strokes. I wish you might paint me all that is within you. If only people could journey like your sketches — with a mere postal fee. Perhaps modernization will progress to such a point eventually. Until that time, I will simply have to bring you by train.

My great-aunt Mrs. Nancy Santi, whom we call Auntie Nan, has invited us to stay with her in Boston in June while Father meets with prestigious investors of our parish's great calling. If you and your sister are not otherwise engaged in academic activities, Father has asked that I pass on his formal invitation to dine an evening that is most convenient to you. Auntie Nan has insisted that you stay as honored guests at her home in Beacon Hill. While Father attends to business, I would thoroughly enjoy the company of the Misses Brown.

I pray that between the date of your letter and today, Annie's disposition might've seen some improvement. If not, I hope this news of our visit is received favorably.

Affectionately yours,
Freddy

P.S. We recently finished Miss Alcott's collection. Alice and Siby have taken to calling each other Thistledown, Lily-Bell, Sunbeam, Leaf, Summer-Wind, and all manner of fairy flower names imaginable. They call you Ripple, the Water-Spirit, in the light of your current stewardship over Walden Pond. Also, we thank you for the drawing of Albany. Alice has dubbed it Ripple's City Port. It has proved pleasingly popular with all.

Concord, Mass., May 6, 1860

Dear Freddy,
I've immediately written to Mother so that she may, in turn, write straightaway

to Mr. Sanborn with her permission for us to visit you and Mr. Hill next month! My father had many friends in Boston. I am certain Mother will approve. It will be so good to see Mr. Hill and you, Freddy!

Mr. Sanborn has announced that the poet and artist Mary Artemisia Lathbury of Saratoga is coming in July to teach a painting salon and summer biblical dramaturgy. She is a woman of great leadership in our work to uplift the nation. I am elated and humbled to study with an artist of such celebrity. I pray she will help me elevate my drawings from sketch to canvas, so my work might be shared further in our friendship circles. Do not fear, however; her arrival will not conflict with your June invitation. Even Mr. Sanborn appears greatly enthused by the news of your father's visit to Mrs. Nancy Santi and our visit to Beacon Hill. He said it was divinely timed.

Lastly, I'm glad the Hills are enjoying the *Flower Fables* book. If you are finished reading by next month, you may return the book to me in person and save the postage. I'm flattered to be likened to Ripple, the Water-Spirit. She was no stagnant fairy. What honorific have Alice and Siby bestowed upon you? Perhaps one of the good Elves living in haystacks of Fairy-land. What mischief and adventure we're sure to have — a water sprite and a barn elf set loose in Boston.

Affectionately your friend,
Sarah

P.S. Annie is still unwell, but I believe this trip is the medicine necessary for all.

EDEN

New Charlestown, West Virginia
August 2014

When the Nileses' white ice-cream truck with the cherry megaphone pulled up Eden's driveway, she was convinced her *Twilight Zone* reality had progressed to a full-fledged Stephen King movie.

But as the state historic preservation officer for New Charlestown, Vee was Eden's only hope of getting the house on the National Register of Historic Places, the seal of authenticity that could blast their real estate value through the roof. Eden had done her homework.

The national criteria required a property to be evaluated for age, integrity, and significance to historical persons, events, activities, or developments. The renovating architect had said the cornerstone was dated 1850. So age was in the bag. While the house had been completely gutted during the renovation, she'd argue that the face and bones were the same, which she hoped would suffice for integrity. Last was significance. Such a subjective quality: one man's trash was another man's treasure — wasn't that the saying? She was sure she could spin barn straw into gold bullion. If there was truly a historical connection, however, all the better.

So horror film or not, Eden was opening the door.

"Mrs. Anderson?" Vee asked from behind the screen.

"Eden, yes. You must be Vee Niles?" Eden nodded to the truck with *Niles' Neapolitans* printed in giant cursive above the frozen-treat chart.

"Sorry about the truck," apologized Vee.

She was younger than Eden had anticipated, Denny's age. Her dark hair was swept up in a French twist, revealing a pathway of diamond studs in her left ear. At one time cartilage, nose, and facial piercings had been the markings of a certain kind — rebels and radicals silently dissenting from social constraints. But those days were long gone. Vee was proof, with her designer jeans, tailored collared shirt, and ear constellations.

"I could only swing by during my route.

Dad usually runs the truck while I work the antiques shop. But back in June he was pulling an old road sign out of a collector's hayloft and fell. Broke his pelvis. He's been home healing ever since, leaving me to run the front door and the midway of this summer circus. The truck's been driving New Charlestown streets since before I was born. I couldn't let the kids down."

Eden understood. "We had a Good Humor truck in the neighborhood I grew up in. My brother, Denny, and I used to wait on the corner every afternoon."

Vee smiled, for the first time. "Exactly. It's tradition."

Eden opened the screen door and motioned her in. "Nice to meet you, and thanks for coming over."

Vee checked her chrome watch and stepped inside. "I can only stay a few minutes."

"Oh? Can you make an appraisal that fast?"

Eden had picked up the house, put on makeup, and asked Cleo to take Cricket on a very long walk, then brush him out and give him a bath. She figured that would keep her busy awhile. She was giving the girl twenty dollars for the extra services. The thought of coordinating a time when

231

no one was home again and everything was presentable exhausted Eden. She'd hoped to have the deal signed, sealed, and delivered in one visit.

"I've already done most of the houses on Apple Hill. I can tell pretty quick about a property. It's the application that takes weeks to complete." Vee took out her clipboard checklist and clicked her ballpoint pen while surveying the ceiling beams. "And that's before you give it to me and the Jefferson County Historic League. After our evaluation, we send it to West Virginia Division of Culture and History. On their authorization, it would go to the National Register Review Board and, if *they* approve, to the National Parks Service in Washington, D.C. The National Parks folks are real quick, though. They have a forty-five-day guaranteed turnaround."

"Forty-five days!" Eden gasped.

Weeks of protocol and stops at three bureaucratic desks, culminating in a forty-five-day review in Washington, meant it'd be months before she'd even have the paperwork embossed. Never mind putting the property on the market, finding a buyer, endorsing her half of the sales check to a private account, hiring a divorce lawyer, and renting an apartment in the city.

Vee ignored Eden's anxious twitching and knelt to run a finger along the grooves of the floorboards. "This the original wood — just varnished up?"

"Yes."

Vee stood and jotted on her clipboard, then walked straight down the foyer into the kitchen. "Oh my," she murmured under her breath. "You sure did a number on this place."

A hot flash made Eden's neck sweat. "Upgrades. So the house could be livable — by modern standards."

"I see." Vee tapped a fingernail on the chart. "I assume the large stainless steel range hood was not part of the building's original integrity, right?"

Eden put a hand defensively to the brick. "The whole wall was a kitchen fireplace. Our architect suggested we keep the chimney and use it for ventilation. It's all cosmetic, really."

"Of course. It's just that the more modifications, the harder it is for the house to qualify as a historical site. You understand. If the only antique item remaining in a building is a crossbeam, how can it legitimately be on the National Register map beside the White House?" She scribbled.

Eden didn't want it beside the White House or any other house. She wanted it beside dollar signs!

"It was built a hundred and fifty years ago. That's got to gain it some distinction."

Vee made a sweeping check across her page. "Yes, but that's only one-third of the criteria. Being old, alone, doesn't make a place significant . . . and with such extensive renovations, it's practically rebuilt new."

She frowned and started toward the door. "I'm really sorry, Eden, but unless you have more . . ."

In desperation, Eden snatched up the doll's head. "We found this in the pantry cellar." The head clanked in her hand.

Vee turned at the sound.

"It's a porcelain doll's head. The little girl next door, our dog-sitter . . . Cleo Bronner . . . was going to ask you and your father about it since you are the experts in town."

Vee came closer. "An antique European doll." She put the clipboard down on the counter. "May I?"

"Please." Eden hoped she didn't come off as too earnest.

Vee turned the head over carefully, ran her fingers along its ceramic neck, considered the crack, and gave it a soft shake.

"There's something inside," said Eden. "The chip from the top, probably."

Like a surgeon in the field, Vee set the doll down facing up and went to the crown. "Might you have a pair of tweezers I could borrow?"

Eden raced up to the bedroom and returned with her pink Tweezerman set. Vee inserted the slanted tips with Eden leaning forward beside her, both holding their breath while she slowly, slowly pulled a tiny metal item through the crack.

"A key?" Eden couldn't have been more surprised if she'd pulled out an elephant.

Vee laid it out in her palm. "A rather modern key. It doesn't match the head, which I'm quite certain dates to around the Civil War. Given that the other houses on Apple Hill Lane are of that time . . . and you say the doll was hidden somewhere?"

Eden nodded emphatically. "The head. Not a whole doll. And yes, in the cellar."

"Can you show me?"

Eden led the way. No longer needing to search for the notch, she quickly pulled up the floor door.

Vee brightened. "A root cellar. Used for keeping meats and vegetables cool before icebox refrigerators. Typically found in the basement or just outside the kitchen. I've never seen one hidden in the servants' or slaves' quarters before."

"Slaves?" The word assaulted Eden.

"Yes. The kitchen, pantry, and laundry room were where the slaves lived and worked to serve their masters. Most of the homes in town have root cellars, but only one other I know has one inside like this. And none of them are this big — large enough to fit a person or *persons.*" Vee gingerly lowered herself into the space. "Also, I've never seen a door hinged to match the floor so perfectly. It's almost as if . . ." Her voice lifted with squelched excitement before she popped her head back up through the opening. "Was there anything else you found in here?"

Eden shook her head.

Vee spoke from the opening, frowning: "But it doesn't match up. These dolls were expensive back then. I haven't seen too many in our area that didn't already belong to a museum or serious collector."

Eden's heart double-pumped. She liked the sound of "museum" and "serious collector." Did "expensive back then" mean *very* expensive now?

"Most were destroyed. Southerners smashed them up because abolitionists were using dolls to bootleg medicine, messages, maps, weapons, and everything in between to plantation slaves. Then, when the war started, both sides thought the trick so good, they used it to shuttle spy messages across enemy lines. So soldiers pretty much took a bayonet to every child's toy they found. A doll massacre."

"Maybe that's why it was put in the cellar." Eden had squatted down so that she and Vee were eye to eye. "To keep it from the — massacre, as you say."

"Maybe, but it still doesn't explain the key. From the shape, make, and material, it is most certainly of the twentieth century. That's forty to fifty years postdating the toy. In addition, a key like that doesn't fall into a doll's head by chance. Someone had to purposefully put it inside."

"So . . . *someone* who lived here in the last hundred years had a Civil War doll and a key they wanted to hide."

"That's my guess. But the bigger question is *why* and what lock does the key open?"

"Must be something *significant.*" Eden emphasized the word.

Vee hoisted herself to her feet and held a hand out to Eden, helping her up off the floor. "I would agree." After Vee closed the door, the two walked back to the kitchen. "There are rumors, town folklore for the most part, that there were people in town who worked the UGRR, the Underground Railroad, and somewhere in New Charlestown was a crucial UGRR station house."

"Like Harriet Tubman, Frederick Douglass Underground?"

"Like John Brown abolitionist Underground, yes. They say his family might've stayed here the night before his execution. I do antiques and appraisals, but Emma Silverdash is our town historian. She owns the bookstore on Main. We've been researching together for years but never found substantial enough evidence to say one way or the other. Old Man Potts moved into this house right after World War II, and hardly anybody set a foot inside until his passing, when the bank took over during probate. Then the Milton business . . . and all that bad blood between father and son. Mrs. Milton had her stroke around then, so basically the place sat empty until you folks. It's entirely possible the doll has been down there since the turn of the century."

"I know Ms. Silverdash!" said Eden. "Cleo just introduced me yesterday. In fact, I'm to lead the Children's Story Hour starting tomorrow."

Vee's officialdom gave way to a delighted smile. "I went to Story Hour when I was little. There were a lot more kids back then. A lot more people at the bookstore in general. You don't know how good of you this is. Business has been hard on her, with everybody buying books online these days. Plus, you know, the bad economy."

While Cleo had hinted at Ms. Silverdash's financial troubles, hearing it from Vee solidified their truth. Eden wanted to help. It was the one place she could make an immediate difference, and she needed that as much as Ms. Silverdash might need her.

"I'm going to be late to my next stop if I don't get moving. You've passed my initial appraisal review, so here." Vee handed Eden the application on her way out. "This is the National Park Service's Form 10-900. It requires you to give detailed historical and architectural descriptions with proper bibliographic references. Ms. Silverdash and I can help if you need us. You have my number."

Just as Vee's ice-cream truck took off down the street, Cleo came in the back door.

"Cricket did his business, stretched his legs *a lot,* got brushed out and washed up to smelling like a Golden Afternoon — or at least that was the name on the shampoo bottle."

Eden couldn't wait to tell her chief detective about the crack in the case.

SARAH

Boston, Massachusetts
June 1860

The half a dozen beagles of Beacon Hill yodeled their greeting when Sarah entered. The good-natured animals nosed at her skirt and licked her boots in welcome before the mistress of the house called out, "Come in, young ladies! Don't be afraid."

A potbellied beagle pawed at Auntie Nan's hem until she pulled it up by its short front legs. The dog nestled in her arms, accustomed to the perched position.

"The little ones are merely saying hello." She extended her free hand to Sarah the way the men did in business agreements. "I'm Mrs. Nancy Santi, but I've been a widow for more years than I was ever a missus, so those who know me well call me Auntie Nan. I insist you do the same, as I fully anticipate we are to be good friends."

She winked at Sarah, who found her altogether astonishing. She'd never known a woman to behave in such an assertive manner.

"Now, which of the Miss Browns are you?"

"Sarah."

Annie curtsied, as was the proper etiquette. "And I'm Annie Brown, Mrs. Santi."

"A pleasure to host you both at my home — or, as the locals refer to it, the Hound House."

She laughed — with pride or contempt at the gossipy moniker, Sarah didn't know her well enough to decipher.

"Here at your feet are Matthew, Mark, Luke, John, Magdalene, and this here is old Rahab, the harlot." She lovingly jostled the dog in her arms. "She's been with me fifteen years, mama to the pack. And a fine pack they are, old girl." She scratched the dog atop its head, and it yawned in hedonistic gratitude.

"Delighted to meet you — all." Sarah curtsied to the hounds.

Annie sniffed indignantly, and the dogs replied in kind. She was perpetually offended these days. Sarah had catered to her melancholy for as long as she could, but her sister had become nothing short of bitter wormwood. She no longer liked to be touched or enjoyed any optimism — spoken, sung, or written. Sarah missed the old Annie. The sister who was always close by, smelling of garden herbs and dried flowers. Now whenever Sarah took a step near, Annie took one away, so that there remained an iron column of coolness between them.

In contrast, Auntie Nan radiated warmth like a phoenix. George and Freddy flanked her like wings, and Sarah's cheeks heated through in their company. It'd been months since she'd seen Freddy in person, but their letters had grown ever more familiar.

Sarah knew it wrong to think so fondly of the Hills. They were part of a memory that should've been agony. But she would not live like Annie, sad and tormented.

"The kind Misters Hill." Sarah extended a hand in similar fashion to Auntie Nan.

Seeing it, Annie's neck and shoulders stiffened to a crucifix.

"My dear." George took Sarah's gloved hand in both of his and held it. "Marvelous to see you again. Mrs. Hill and Alice were terribly disappointed to miss visiting. Alice made me vow to give you each one of these."

He pulled a small account book from his vest pocket. Inside the cover were two pressed shamrocks. "From our garden. Alice hopes you are well and happy. As does everyone in New Charlestown."

Sarah pressed the petite clover to her nose, the barnyard and Virginia sunshine faint but distinct.

Annie, too, seemed briefly transported. She tenderly stroked the four-leaved keepsake. "Please, thank Alice for us."

Freddy stepped forward, his fair skin made ruddy by the southern sunshine, a colorful version of the winter phantom. Sarah was glad for it. She'd already amassed one too many specters in her life. No more of the dead. She wanted life.

He bowed. "Welcome, ladies."

Auntie Nan ran her fingers under Rahab's chin but kept her eyes on Sarah, watching closely. "Now, now, let's not keep the girls standing in the foyer forever. Winifred! Wini—" she called.

A plump, matronly woman in a maid's uniform appeared.

"We'll take tea in the doll parlor." Auntie Nan set Rahab down on the ground. "Boys, fetch the luggage. Winifred has a bad back, and I had to let the butler go after I found him guzzling my best brandy. A jolly fellow, but now we know why."

Winifred nodded. "To be certain."

"I've had two of my favorite rooms made

up," Auntie Nan continued. "Annie will be in my garden room. And Sarah in my Italian art room, as it contains a number of paintings I think she might enjoy. I hear you are a young *artista*." She winked at Sarah. "Be off, men. It's time for women's gossip." She fluttered her hands at George and Freddy, then wrapped one arm around Sarah's waist and the other around Annie's, ushering the girls into the interior, which smelled of rosebuds and bergamot.

"Do you like Earl Grey? I order it from a fine tea shop in Scotland. The proprietors procure the leaves through an Italian grower. So it has the zest of Italy and the refinement of Great Britain and is therefore the *perfect* blend."

She laughed to tears. A private joke.

Seeing Sarah's bemused expression, she explained: "The Hills being of Scottish descent and my late husband being Italian. An inventor and tradesman" — she lifted a hand to the chandelier overhead — "with a taste for extravagance."

She twisted the wedding band she still wore on her finger, and Sarah was struck by a realization: Auntie Nan was still in love with her husband, despite his passing, no children, and years of widowhood. Unlike her own mother, who'd pledged her life to her children and was too old to remarry, Auntie Nan had been relatively young when her husband died. With her own financial stability and youth in her favor, she could've started anew with anyone she pleased. She could've had a houseful of children by now; but instead, she had the hounds. It moved Sarah, bittersweet as it was. She understood that her life would be devoid of such romantic paradigms but . . . for the moment . . . could imagine no greater love than fidelity through that ultimate separation.

When the parlor curtains opened, Sarah gasped. Dolls. Everywhere: lining the shelves, in glass bookcases, on the settees and chairs and ottomans round the room. Arranged like elaborate flower petals on the side tables, colorful skirts flared, row after row to a pistil center puppet standing tall. Some, like Alice's Kerry Pippin, made of fine porcelain heads but many made of wood and soft muslin. A rainbow army of vestiges: children, dogs, cats, penguins and owls, horses and centaurs, creatures of myth and reality and every fusion between. All the painted eyes stared straight at them.

Auntie Nan seemed not to notice the collective force of their watchfulness. She sat on one of the two sofas unoccupied by miniature figurines and motioned for the girls to join her. One of the beagle pups sprang to her lap, with another soon by her side. Matthew, Mark, Luke, John — Sarah couldn't tell which, but she prayed that all of their namesake saints might preserve her.

The girls perched side by side on the edge of the divan. Annie's head turned slowly, taking in the room, then stopped with a nod at the table by their knees: an eddy of dolls with whiskers.

"I dare say, I've never seen anything like these before."

"And you won't! I procure from around the globe and had those custom-made by an astonishing European artist. I sent him a drawing of Rahab's litter, and he created those for me. Admittedly, they look more like cats than pups." She smiled and patted the dog in her lap. "I'm a collector."

Sarah and Annie nodded.

"My husband introduced me, and the hobby remained long after he took his leave. Each room of the house has a theme. After I filled up the rooms at Beacon Hill, I purchased a country estate with enough space to last me through the end of my days. I've got a doll parlor there, too. In fact, I'm waiting on a new order of fairy dolls from a Welsh toymaker — an innovator, really. Head to toe, they are no bigger than a foot.

A smaller doll is so much easier to carry from place to place, don't you agree? It's difficult enough for a mother to carry her baby in her arms. I imagine even more cumbersome for a child to carry a doll of life size. The fairies are the perfect solution, so I purchased every one in his workshop. They should be here any day now."

"But what does a person want with so much of one thing?" asked Annie.

Only Sarah could hear the accusation in her tone. *Gluttony, greed,* it whispered.

"I don't keep them all. Just the few I find most interesting. The others, I give away."

Winifred rolled into the parlor with the tea cart. "The last of the petticoat tails," she announced. "We'll have to send out for more shortbread."

Auntie Nan nodded. "I leave the pantry inventory to your exceptional keep."

"Best that way, ma'am," said Winifred. "Otherwise, we'd be eating one kind of food three times a day for months."

"On the contrary, Winifred! My hobby is proof that I am a woman who loves variety!"

Winifred blustered good-naturedly, then poured the tea. "Here you are, misses." She handed them each a cup of Earl Grey with a sugar biscuit on the saucer.

While Auntie Nan went on about the diversity of dolls she'd amassed from China to Paris, Sarah sipped and crunched, sipped and crunched, until the shortbread was gone and her teacup drunk.

"Should we shield our ears from the secret talk of women?" George asked, peering furtively from the parlor curtain.

"The talk of men is far more mysterious and befuddling." Auntie Nan beckoned for them to come in.

"Spot of tea, sir?" Winifred offered.

Freddy waved a hand and murmured, "Thank you but no." He caught Sarah's eye and smiled.

Her cheeks burned. A biscuit crumb came loose from her back molar, and she gulped it down.

George pulled his pocket watch from his vest and inspected it. "Auntie Nan, don't we have reservations at the Atwood and Bacon Oyster House?"

"Yes! The time got away from me. I haven't even showed the girls to their rooms." She clapped, and it set off a flurry of motion.

The hounds awoke, yapping and sniffing, as if they'd just become aware of the newcomers again. Auntie Nan led the pack to the second-floor landing.

"Sarah." She swung open the bedroom door to the glimmer of lemon wallpaper scalloped in gold.

The bed linens and furniture were done in a matching daffodil, giving the room the illusion of being sun-gilded no matter the hour or season. Every available wall space was hung with oil paintings, landscapes, and still lifes: orchards in endless bloom; ripe plums betwixt bread loaves; allegorical figures at play along a lush river valley. Sarah had never seen a chamber so grand.

"And now, Miss Annie," Auntie Nan sang from down the hall.

Sarah turned to find Freddy still at the doorway. "I hope you'll be comfortable," he said.

"Quite." Sarah clasped her hands at her waist securely and looked at a painted landscape on the wall closest to him.

It featured three figures: a half-naked woman breast-feeding her child and a young man gazing on. Her mother might've requested a room change. Her father would've insisted. Sarah thought the painting exquisite. She could nearly hear the gurgle of the brook and feel the thunderclap of the lightning across the canvas sky. Her heart beat in double time at the fleeting dream that she might walk through the frame into that world — leaving behind this one and all its trappings.

"*The Tempest.*" Freddy pointed from the doorway. His arm, alone, dared broach the threshold. "The painter is Giorgione. It's a replication, but Auntie Nan likes to surround herself with unconventional beauty, whatever its form."

Sarah liked Auntie Nan even more for taking such care to bed her in that particular room. Had it been Priscilla who'd told her of their interests: Annie's penchant for herbs and floriography, Sarah's for pigments and glazes. Or someone else?

She went to *The Tempest* so that only a breath of air separated her from the canvas. The paint whirled across the scene's sky and wicked up gently in the grasslands. The skin of the woman's breast and body was smooth and pink and matched her child. Replica or not, notable talent had been involved. Her fingers twitched to touch, but she kept her hands at bay.

"I think your aunt is one of the finest women I've ever known," she said, still staring into the open expressions of the painted figures. "I admire her."

"Of course you do. She'd turn all of Boston on its head if she could. She's not one for bowing to decorum, either."

Sarah met Freddy's stare and that fiendish grin she recalled from the barn that night in New Charlestown.

"But you are," she said. It came out more as a question.

"In some cases, yes. You can't influence the masses for good if you shock them with a slap. At least that's how my father interprets the Holy Word."

Sarah raised her jaw up firmly. "That's not what *my* father believed."

"No." He looked away. "How best to spread the message is as subjective as how best to eat an egg, I suppose. But we can agree on the basics: it must be cracked open, yes?"

A laugh popped up Sarah's throat. "Agreed." She looked back at the canvas. Thick, opaque colors. Egg tempera paint.

"My mother fries them in a skillet until the edges are curled crisp," she said. "But once, on a visit to one of my father's wealthy associates, they served soft-boiled eggs in silver cups. I thought it the most decadent and delicious meal. Like a mouthful of silk ribbons." She could nearly taste it again. "It was later discovered that while the man owned no slaves of his own, he'd bought the eggs from a slave-owning farm. Father said we'd been tricked and possibly poisoned." She shrugged. "Maybe so, but they were still the best I've ever eaten. Laid by a hen well cared for. I was grateful to the slave who nurtured it. My mistake was telling my father as much. He washed my tongue with Epsom salt water."

"Hurry, dearests!" Auntie Nan's voice echoed down the hall. "Winifred, help the Browns dress." She paused at Sarah's open door with George by her side and a beagle in arm. "My goodness, has this young man had you pinned in conversation? Frederick," she lightheartedly admonished, "give a young lady a minute's peace and help your old aunt feed the babes before we leave for dinner."

Freddy nodded respectfully to Auntie Nan. "Poached," he said before exiting. "That's my preference."

"Isn't poached soft boiling outside of the shell?" Sarah curtsied.

Freddy winked with his back to his family, then joined his father.

"Winifred will be up shortly. I hope the room is to your liking," said Auntie Nan.

"It's exceptional. This painting in particular." Sarah pointed.

"Aw, *The Tempest.*" Auntie Nan's large bosom rose and fell dramatically with a sigh. "A favorite of mine, too. So full of passion.

A man and woman eternally divided by a tributary. A mother's devotion. A child's need. A storm of desires in one fixed portrait." Her voice trailed, and she ran her ringed hand over the dog's head, then faced Sarah. "Art is a fairy tale for the eye. This was painted over three hundred years ago, and still it speaks, tells a story, and leads us to our own."

For once, someone had put to *words* what Sarah felt and knew to be true.

"If I could do it all over again," Auntie Nan declared, "I'd pick up a paintbrush. Even if I hadn't the talent, I would've liked to learn to replicate the masters. But then, I might've lived my life in imitation and not as myself. What a bore that would've been!" Her wide smile returned, and she grasped Sarah's wrist with a warm shake. "Now look who's blabbering." She released the girl and marched straight out, closing the door as she went.

Sarah returned to the painting, hearing Auntie Nan again: *A man and woman eternally divided by a tributary . . .* like the River Styx. She envisioned Mr. Santi on one side, gazing across with earnest devotion. Auntie Nan on the other — only she hadn't the child at her breast. Sarah imagined a beagle there instead and giggled alone in the room. It helped ease the pang of regret needling her chest. She'd never be that woman on the riverbank, in life or the hereafter.

At the Atwood and Bacon Oyster House, Sarah had the Virginia roasted fancy oysters, in honor of the Hills. Freddy had the half-shell Capes, in honor of New England. They shared a silent grin and a lengthy discussion of the eggs featured on the menu: boiled, fried, dropped, and served on toast, grits, wheat berries, or alone. No soft-boiled or poached, however. So they stuck to the house specialties and left the eggs for another time. George, Auntie Nan, and, most especially, Annie were flummoxed by their banter. Her sister thought it off-color to discuss food at such length.

"Mother and Ellen barely have enough on the farm for one full meal a day, and here you are, talking eggs and oysters and European tea," she'd seethed from behind her upright menu.

"Blasted, Annie!" Sarah had whispered back. "Who said anything about tea!" Then she'd lowered her paper menu and ordered the same as Auntie Nan: a sarsaparilla, which she greatly enjoyed.

Annie had crackers and milk, and Sarah

thought that far ruder than her egg talk. They were guests of a prominent Bostonian widow and at an *oyster* house, for heaven's sake. One could not simply nibble milk-sodden wafers. When George pressed Annie to try a half plate of oysters, her sister explained that she hadn't an appetite, which Sarah knew to be the truth. Annie had nearly stopped eating entirely since coming to Concord. Her cheeks were hollow as a rotten pumpkin.

To make up for her sister, Sarah ate her oysters with extra butter and lemon, drank her sarsaparilla cup, and hooted laughter without restraint when Freddy's tower of shells toppled over to the floor. The waiter bid them not to worry. It happened all the time.

In honor of summer's arrival, the restaurant's chef had added a new dessert: ice cream. Hand-cranked on a modern freezer machine by the lauded confectionary next door. The specialty of the night was a three-in-one flavor called *Neapolitan:* vanilla bean, chocolate, and strawberry.

"Please bring Miss Sarah Brown the complete Neapolitan," Auntie Nan instructed. "All great artists must have a palette of choices, especially now that you

are to study with Miss Mary Artemisia Lathbury."

The only person Sarah had told of her
salon studies was Freddy. She was flattered
that he'd shared.

George nodded with approval. "I have
sung Miss Lathbury's hymns. A Renaissance
woman."

"The very kind I like," said Auntie Nan.
"One day, I'll commission you, Sarah, to
paint for me. Perhaps a doll with your own
features so I might have the pleasure of your
company always."

"Don't be greedy, Auntie Nan," teased
George. "Annie and Sarah must first return
to New Charlestown. Priscilla and Alice are
on the precipice of transgression. Envy is
one of the deadliest of sins." He turned to
them. "We'd be honored to have you visit
again."

Annie's body went rigid. She'd sworn
she'd never go near the place where their
brothers and father perished. But Sarah
didn't think of Harpers Ferry and New
Charlestown as sharing a locality. She
wouldn't like to see the old Charles Town
jailhouse again, but the Hills and their
neighbors lived in a place apart from the
bloodshed, murder, and civil unrest. When
she thought of New Charlestown, she was

welcomed by the memory of the hearth's blaze, hyacinth petals, and Alice's smiling doll. It was a bastion not only for Sarah but also for those traveling on the UGRR.

And there was Freddy. Beside him, Sarah felt a momentum that carried her unlike any amity she knew. He believed in her, her talents, and the abolitionary mission, and she was certain they could accomplish a great many things to make her father proud.

"We'd love to," Sarah said, accepting.

George thumped the table. "Splendid!"

Freddy beamed.

Annie fidgeted with her black ribbon necklace. Despite the tight knot at her throat, it had slipped down to her collarbone.

The waiter arrived, carrying a silver platter of colorful ice creams mounded in matching bowls. The dishes mirrored one another, giving the illusion that there was twice as much: chocolate, vanilla, strawberry — strawberry, vanilla, chocolate. Reflection after reflection, like the legion of dolls in Auntie Nan's parlor. Sarah ate with unabashed delight. Not a sprig of mint left behind.

So late did they make their way home that only the stars lit their carriage drive; the streetlamps had been capped out. Sarah was sorry to see the night end but full to delirium with the firsts of many kinds.

A tired Winifred greeted them at the door. "Ma'am, the . . . cargo arrived and are waiting to be properly stowed for the night. The dogs are in bed."

Auntie Nan turned and gave George a serious nod.

"It's late. I'll take care of the delivery." He kissed his aunt's cheek.

"Thank you, nephew."

"Good night to you both." He bowed to Sarah and Annie, then quickly followed Winifred to the back servants' quarters.

"Freddy, would you escort Sarah to her room? I'll do the same for Annie, since hers is on the way to mine."

It was dark in the house. Sarah could not decipher halls from walls. Auntie Nan said good night, then escorted Annie up the stairs, talking the whole ascent about the use of mint in digestion. Annie, no doubt, felt torn between her affinity for herbs and her aversion to discussing her benefactor's bodily functions. Sarah couldn't help smiling. Her sister needed to step out of her tight corset, and Auntie Nan was just the kind to snip the laces.

Freddy extended the crook of his arm, and

she took it confidently. Her mind whirled. A delivery at this time of night was no doubt more than toys and fairy business. George's earnest attention made that quite clear. But she couldn't ask outright. Not here, in the middle of the stairwell, with the first-floor shutters cracked open to let in the briny air and who could guess walking about outside.

So instead, she asked, "How is your Gypsy?"

"Up to her usual — chasing the chickens and stealing food from Siby's table."

Aw, Siby. Sarah warmed at her mention. "And the Fishers?"

Freddy's happy countenance dropped. "They are well, considering the troubling times in our southern states." They took the stairs in matched strides, then slowed on the vacant upper landing. He lowered his voice and broached the subject she had hoped he would: "It is part of why we are here now. The business of slavery is causing quite an upheaval, especially after your father's raid and execution."

Sarah stopped. It was a night of boldness, so she spoke in turn: "Tell me, Freddy, what does your parish have to do with the abolitionist mission?"

Freddy smoothed the top of her hand with his thumb. "Neither my father nor I would ever use the *church* for anything but God's holy work. As a *family,* however, we are committed to the equality of all mankind."

His answer was like a bee circling a flower without rest. Sarah furrowed her brow but did not remove her hand. She understood his caution, but he knew exactly who she was: Sarah Brown. It was time she knew him, exactly.

"You and your father work with our friends in the UGRR, do you not?"

Before they could move forward together, she needed to hear him say it without symbology or codes or interpretations. *I do* or *I do not.*

Her heart ticked out the silent beats.

"We help the cause of freedom by many means." He leaned in close, smelling faintly of chocolate ice cream. "The transportation of men and women out of oppression and abuse is one."

"Is Auntie Nan involved, too? Is that what tonight's delivery was — runaway *slaves*?" She whispered the word, a hex on those it tried to irrevocably define.

"I oughtn't speak anymore. Not here and now," said Freddy. "It isn't safe for you."

"I've never known safety in my whole life."

"If I could have it so, I'd protect you for the rest of mine."

"I want to help here and now. Tell me what I can do."

Her heart pounded fiercely. But he ignored her impassioned demand. They walked toward her room in silence. At the door, he paused.

"My father and I are well aware of your proficiencies. You are our chief mapmaker, Sarah. Mr. Sanborn and Miss Lathbury do not put their confidences in just any student. Tonight, what you can do is enjoy the hospitality of my aunt. All is well, my dear."

He kissed her knuckles, and her head spun slightly, high on sea breezes, ice creams, and secrets shared. Before she could stop him, Freddy withdrew down the dark hall, fading with each step until finally gone.

Alone in her room, she paced. The Hills and Auntie Nan were conclusively part of the UGRR. Auntie Nan's collector shipments were a cover-up for forwarding runaways north to Canada. The dolls had to be part of the operation, too. Just as the Jefferson County guard had said: smuggled weapons and messages.

God had already determined that she follow in the path of the Brown men and take up the spear of action. With renewed determination, she vowed to paint her maps more precisely than all of Galileo's star charts. She stared again at *The Tempest,* barely able to make out its dark river winding to the canvas horizon.

Outside, a spark was followed by a thunderclap. A summer storm.

She fell into bed, exhausted from the power of it all. The rain falling off the eaves lulled her fitful mind to sleep, and she didn't stir until Winifred knocked on her door carrying a breakfast tray.

"Morning, miss." She set the serving tray beside Sarah in bed: a pot of tea, buttered toast, and three soft-boiled eggs in silver cups. Beside the plate was a vase with a pink rosebud and her copy of *Flower Fables,* a note tucked within the front cover. Sarah recognized the familiar handwriting.

Dear Sarah,
Thank you again for lending us Alcott's beautiful book. I hope this breakfast makes up for my absence. The delivery we spoke of briefly last night has required our expeditious departure. Auntie Nan promises to return you to Concord in the most elegant and modern of carriages.

Our time together in Boston was all that I had hoped for and more, a pleasure I'd like to repeat as soon as possible. With your family's consent, you and Annie are enthusiastically invited to our home in Virginia this September, should that time frame suit your academic schedule. The trees will be changing their colors. The Blue Ridge is at her most beautiful in the autumn. A landscape for artistic inspiration and one we would all greatly like to see you capture.

Please write me your answer straightaway so I may arrange your travel with dependable friends. We are eager to see you again. New Charlestown awaits you, as do I.

Affectionately yours,
Freddy

EDEN

New Charlestown, West Virginia
August 2014

Eden briefed Cleo on Vee's visit while they mixed up a pumpkin dog-biscuit recipe from *The Holistic Hound* later that afternoon.

"They bayoneted baby dolls. Vee called it a doll massacre."

Cleo gasped, less in horror than intrigue.

"She came by during her ice-cream-truck rounds — you know, with her dad and the broken pelvis, she's had to take on being the driver, too. Pass me the eggs, would you?"

Cleo carefully did so, then finished measuring out the flour. "My grandpa said one of Vee's brothers ought to have come home to help but Montana is clear across the country."

Eden remembered Cleo mentioning Mrs. Niles's death, but she didn't know Vee had siblings. "Brothers?" asked Eden, giving the cracked eggs a good beating.

"Two. They met a pair of barrel-racing sisters at the rodeo, hitched up fast as lightning, then moved out west to start a dude ranch together. Vee left, too, for a while, but she and her husband got a divorce. Her ex moved to Boston, and she came home for keeps. My grandpa says he's sure they had good reason, but he also says it's too easy for folks to get the split ticket from Uncle Sam. Ms. Silverdash says that's not judgment. It's 'eternal optimism.' "

There was truth in what Cleo said. It would probably be faster for her to serve Jack with divorce papers than to submit the National Register of Historic Places form. A sad reality, considering she'd lived with Jack for seven years and in the house for only three months. Time again proving itself an arbitrary critic. A marriage and a house both accrued memories, vaulted secrets, but at what point did you say *I've had enough of walking on splintered wood* and move out? Was it eternally optimistic to think a fresh coat of paint might make it right?

Cleo had left the biscuit bowl to inspect the key, so Eden finished mixing the wet ingredients into the dry, then dumped the dough onto the marble countertop for the rollout.

"Vee's right," said Cleo, turning the metal over. "It's too smooth to be as old as the doll. I think they used mostly rusty stuff — iron and copper — back then. Too small for a human door. Too big to be a toy. And did you see? I rubbed off the dirt, and there's a tiny number stamped on one side."

Eden moved over to her, hands covered in flour. She bent down low to get a good look. "Thirty-four?"

"Only time I see keys with numbers on them is when they're official business or something."

Eden didn't like the sound of that. If the government owned the key and whatever the key unlocked, then it could possibly claim ownership of the doll. She huffed. "Maybe it's somebody's lucky number — like instead of a name."

The theory was weak. Cleo frowned.

Eden changed the subject: "What's the cookbook say is the next step?"

" 'Cut biscuits with dog-bone cookie cutters,' " Cleo read, but Eden hadn't any cookie cutters. Dog, bone, or otherwise.

In a flash, Cleo used a paring knife to trace a perfect bone biscuit in the rolled-out dough.

"You can draw?"

"Ms. Silverdash taught me," said Cleo.

"She does all kinds of art. Not just drawing and painting. She makes her own pottery cups, and she sews the coolest costumes for Halloween. Oh, and what she calls 'floral flair.' She puts pretty flowers together, basically. Plus her dioramas — she'll teach you if you ask her. She teaches everybody 'cause she went to college. Everybody teaches everybody there. It's how it's done."

"Well, those are amazing." Eden nodded to the sketches in the dough.

Cleo looked up at her, hopefully. "You think?"

"Even better than a cookie cutter. It's got character. CricKet BisKets — with capital K's for Cric-Ket and the vitamin K in pump-Kins! Pretty as a magazine ad."

This was her kitchen, she reminded herself, not a marketing pitch room.

"Gourmet CricKet BisKets!" Cleo clapped. "Can we really call them that? Even though we got the recipe from *The Holistic Hound*?"

"A recipe is just a formula for people to follow. What counts is how *you* make it. The final product is going to be a little different for everyone — every time, too." Eden shrugged. "Have you ever seen the numbers on the bottom corner of a painting?"

Cleo nodded.

"That means it's a limited-edition print of the original 'recipe.' A maker's mark of exclusivity."

"Like this?" Cleo carved a *C* into the bridge of one doughy dog bone. *"C* for *Cricket."*

"Exactly! And a fine maker you are, Miss Cleo."

Cleo swished her ponytail back and forth and continued to draw on the rest of the dough.

When she finished, Eden transferred the bones onto a baking sheet and into the oven. Within minutes, the smell had transformed the house. Gone were the bitter solvents and tangy wood varnishes. It smelled like Thanksgiving dessert pies from Eden's youth: apple, pumpkin, peaches, and berries. Her parents always invited friends over to cook on the holiday, and it was the one time a year their home felt whole. Nostalgia for something she'd never had but dreamed of made her inhale as deeply as she could.

Then Jack walked in the front door, a day early from Austin.

" 'Ello?"

To Eden's surprise, his call coupled with the spicy baking scents brought on the sort of childhood glee she'd felt when her father had returned from his office in the city.

"Smells amazing in here." With his navy blazer over his shoulder and a saunter to rival John F. Kennedy's, he came into the kitchen. "What's all this, Eden?"

"We're baking!" proclaimed Cleo.

Jack looked toward Eden with a curious smile. "Are you?"

"Uh-huh. Pumpkin." She held up the spoon like a magic wand.

"You never cease to amaze." He winked, and her stomach fluttered.

"First batch will be done soon. Care to try?"

"Be our unbiased taste tester, Mr. A," said Cleo.

"I'd be honored." He bowed to the women in knightly fashion.

Cleo giggled. "Everything sounds like King Arthur when you say it."

"Jack's got blue blood," said Eden. "It's in his family crest. He's British royalty."

"No joking?" Both of Cleo's eyebrows raised high. "Well, dang, what are you — a prince or stork, duke of somethin'?"

"A York, you mean?"

"York, stork, dork, pork," she rhymed. "Whatever you call it over there."

"Yes, quite right," he agreed.

This made Eden laugh, a light thing that

washed over her like a bubble bath.

"Nothing so grand, darling," Jack continued. "An ancient cousin married a lady far above his station hundreds of years ago. Thus, our family became regality by one drop of noble blood."

"Really — that's all it takes?" Cleo scratched at her nose, leaving a flour thumbprint.

He nodded. "And a wicked smart man he was. I took his example to heart." He gestured with his chin to Eden.

A bolt of lightning shot through her core, and she didn't fight its heat. She couldn't deny the power he had over her. When they were good, they were so very good together.

He laid his coat on the kitchen island.

"Oh, don't just toss that there," she said before she could stop herself. *It might get flour on it,* she thought but had already bitten her tongue.

His grin dropped. "Where do you want me to put it?"

She registered the tone of annoyed tolerance. It put her on the defensive.

"Where everybody else would put their coat — in the closet," she snapped. "It's not like it's a completely *unreasonable* request."

Cleo went quiet by her side. The love spell broken. Jack obeyed and took his jacket to

271

hang it up.

Hearing him, Denny came bounding down from upstairs. He'd gone out to run an errand earlier that day, returning hours later with a Chipotle drink cup in hand. That and Indian food were Jack's preferred take-out options. The closest Chipotle was thirty miles east, in Sterling, Virginia, and she wondered what errand had required Denny that far away. She would've asked but didn't want to henpeck him with questions. He'd been moody since arriving, brushing off her every attempt to corner him about why. Something was troubling him. If he wasn't ready to tell her, perhaps Jack could tease it out.

So Eden stayed silent while Denny greeted Jack and led him away to the living room, despite her desire to call him back: *Jack, I'm sorry, I didn't mean to snap. Look, do you see? The biscuits are done! You promised to taste what I made.*

Instead, the two men went for a walk with Cricket while she and Cleo finished baking. The walk kept them out past *Wheel of Fortune* to *Jeopardy!,* so Cleo went home. She didn't mind missing Pat Sajak but was not about to forfeit her Alex Trebek earnings. With the house empty and the kitchen cleaned, it was just Eden and the doll's head.

She went up to read in bed but couldn't focus, going over and over the same paragraph until the front screen door clattered and ESPN whistled up through the floor. Denny made his way to the guest room after midnight.

She knew she ought to invite Jack back into their bedroom. It was half his. Making him sleep on the couch after a long workweek was plain callous. If she offered him a good night's sleep, it didn't mean she was forgoing her plans. It was merely being considerate. The fact was, Jack had treated her better than what she'd witnessed in ninety percent of marriages. She loved him, and he loved her . . . it just wasn't really working with *them.* At the very least, he deserved a mattress under his back.

She was about to go down and make the proposal when a new thought came to her: *What if he doesn't want to sleep beside me?* How awkward would that refusal be, and it was a very, very plausible response. Maybe they were better apart, as simple as that.

She left him downstairs and didn't sleep a wink herself. Instead, she studied the plaster medallion ceiling. When the bedroom's remodeling plans had been drawn up, Jack had said the cascading texture around the center fixture was called a "skyscape"; it simulated an eddy of stars around the moon at night and rays crowning the sun during the day. It looked like rows of teeth to Eden.

At dawn, she heard Jack talking to Cricket on his way to shower in the downstairs maid's bathroom. She worried if he had a towel. She hadn't put any on the rack. Then she envisioned him standing naked in the steam, beads of water dripping to the floor, and a sensation she hadn't felt in some time awakened and stretched: yearning. Not to lie together and make a child, but for him — just him. She turned on her side, brought her knees to her chest, and stuffed the feeling into a ball as if it were one of those rain ponchos that folded into itself.

At the sound of footsteps on the stairs, she panicked.

Don't come in here, she thought, and then: *Please, please, come.* She couldn't have it both ways. She held her breath when the shadow of feet paused at the door and a hand knocked.

Not Jack but Denny stuck his head into her bedroom, and she was met with too-bright morning light and unexpected remorse.

"Sorry to wake you, E, but I got another

errand in the city. Didn't want to just disappear."

Eden sat up and pushed a fuzzy wave of hair off her face. She must've fallen asleep. Briefly. Somehow.

"Cleo came," Denny continued. "We gave Cricket a couple biscuits for breakfast. Looks like you're the new Queen of Doggy Dishes, sis."

"I'll make business cards." She swung her legs over the side of the mattress and willed them to be strong. Her ankles popped. Her knees tweaked.

She couldn't remember when it started, but it seemed the morning pains had increased over the last few years. Old age was like a creeping vine, spreading long, toothed leaflets over everything. While her body felt a hundred years old, it had the attitude of a snarky teenager, arguing with her at every turn. She rubbed at the smart in her kneecaps and rolled her ankles until they conceded.

"Jack's gone?" she asked.

"Yeah, he left for the office a few minutes ago."

"What's going on in the city —" she began, but Denny was already out the door, calling back, "Gotta run, good luck at work today!"

Whatever business Denny was attending to, it was more than she'd had in the past three months. It was Friday. She was starting at Ms. Silverdash's at noon and was excited to be an active member of a community again.

Eden turned the wooden wand on the bedroom's plantation shutters to welcome the day. She couldn't recall having opened them since moving in. A hoary old maple met her, one tangled arm outstretched to the window. So close, the veins on the bear claw leaves looked like road maps.

A squirrel popped out of a hollow and scrambled down the bark to the garden, where Cleo sat Indian-style between the rows of plants, a breakfast can of Dr Pepper by her side, the *Frommer's Mexico* guide in her lap. Eden watched her move her finger over the pages, turning slowly, transcending the world around her for the one within the pictures. Eden wished she could take Cleo to Mexico, walk with her through the exotic flower stalls, buy her a chocolate-scribbled *garabato,* and see a flamenco performance. She'd like that. It could be reality. It wasn't an outlandish request. Not like wanting to go to outer space, ride a dragon, or break a curse with a prince's kiss. People took family vacations all the time.

But Cleo wasn't her family. She was just the kid next door, like a million other kids next door. The side of Eden's neck stitched with a muscle spasm, and she rubbed at the knot until it went away. Then she showered, blow-dried her hair straight, put on makeup, and dressed in an orange silk sundress she'd worn to the Virginia Gold Cup years prior. Too loose around the hips now — fertility pounds come and gone — it billowed behind her like a cartoon flame. Cricket arched his back high when she came down the steps and sniffed at her furled hem.

She swished the silk gently over his nose. "Good morning, Cricket."

Sluggishly, he trotted after her into the kitchen, where Denny had left a half pot of hazelnut coffee. His barista skills were improving. She filled her mug and mixed in stevia for sweetness.

She'd always believed it immature to drink doctored coffee. In the office, she worried that it gave the wrong message: that she was soft and unable to hang with the big boys. She'd taken silent pride when the mugs were passed round and she'd swallowed the bitter black without hesitation. Meanwhile, the president of her agency added so much cream and sugar to his, it might as well have been a milkshake. The rules were different for men.

Now she admitted to herself that she hated black coffee. Always had. She took a drink of the warm hazelnut and rolled it around her mouth.

Someone had moved the doll's head down from its ledge. It lay sideways, cheek to marble, beside the jar of dog biscuits. Jack or Denny, she assumed.

"Good morning to you, too," she said to it.

Imagining its many years of dark, cold entombment, she turned it upright in the sun. It made her glad her father had been cremated. She couldn't stand to think of him decomposing: flesh to bone, bone to dust. With a finger, she traced the painted waves falling left and right of the doll's forehead.

She was ashamed of her outburst the night she'd found it. Poor Jack. It was a wonder he hadn't packed his bags and sent her divorce papers months ago, as crazy as she'd been. He could have his pick of stable, beautiful women. She'd observed the way flight attendants, waitresses, secretaries, and even the nurses at the fertility clinic looked at him. How their voices lilted with the twang of seduction; how they flipped their hair just so and smiled. It was part of what made him so attractive to her, too. There was power in watching their nymphet expressions fade when he took her hand. She liked being Jack's wife. The idea of him leaving her before she left him first nearly brought her to tears, and she berated herself for being an emotional train wreck once more.

She took a biscuit from the jar and breathed in the spices. She'd make it up to him before she went, so they could part as friends.

Cricket homed in on the treat in her hand and sat obediently.

"I know you already ate, but we only live once — unless you're a Buddhist." She gave him the biscuit. "Buddhism isn't your breeding. The Chow Chows' perhaps."

He manipulated the cookie upright between his paws, his full belly protruding onto her bare feet. She drank her coffee, wiggling her toes in his fur. Outside the kitchen windows, the garden was empty. Cleo was gone. To the bank for lunch, she assumed. It was a quarter till noon.

"Time for me to go, too." She picked up Cricket for a hug. His body was hot, as was the day, so she turned on the overhead fan for him. "Keep a trusty guard on the place, Biscuit Breath." She set him in his cushioned bed and slipped into her strappy sandals. "I'll be back after the Children's Story Hour."

The screen door clapped her back as she left, but it didn't bother her. She was busy wondering when she'd begun talking to Cricket and a doll's head and, moreover, why that came easier to her than talking to her own husband.

She parked in the Milton's Market lot again. Finding a spot on Main Street would've taken more time than hoofing it on foot; but a block into her trek, she was cursing her sandals. Stomping the pavement had caused the straps to rub blisters. She stopped in front of the bank to finger the bright sores and check the clock tower. A minute till.

At her PR agency, she'd chastised younger associates for not being at meetings early. "Promptness is key to client satisfaction," she'd told them. "Time is an easy tribute. It sends the message that the individuals are valued."

She might not have been on her way to a fat-cat CEO meeting, but it was a first day on the job. Though she'd met her only briefly, Ms. Silverdash felt more important to Eden than all those ex-clients put together. So she pushed her feet forward and opened the bookstore door as the clock over the Bronner Bank struck noon.

Then she remembered that she'd forgotten to bring the doll's head.

ATTENTION BOUNTY HUNTERS:

Ran away: Bettia, my Negress; gone off with her two young daughters, ages 8 and 3; headed north, possibly aided by Underground Railroad. Large reward for unharmed return of three, lesser if any are damaged or dead. Contact William Thornton III.

JAILED

Committed to jail: businessman, Mr. John Clifford, for attempting to ship a wooden crate containing a lawfully owned Negro out of southern territory. Also guilty of using various household sundries to smuggle unlawful materials to local slaves.

Residents are entreated to check all items before allowing them into their home or they might inadvertently share a similar fate.

SARAH

New Charlestown, Virginia
September 1860

Sarah and Annie arrived in New Charlestown as a drizzling shower abated. A thick fog fell and stuck to the knolls and roadways, giving the place the appearance of a mystic village.

Annie had agreed to the venture south with Sarah. She claimed it was her sisterly duty to chaperone, but Sarah knew it was more. Visiting New Charlestown allowed them to live temporarily as part of the Hills. They had the kind of family the girls wished theirs had been: stable, unconditionally loving, untainted by loss.

The summer months had flown by, and Sarah was grateful. Despite the gift of softboiled eggs, it broke her heart that Freddy and George had set off without saying goodbye in person or including her in their plans. She was determined to be more than the daughter of a once powerful man. She would prove herself a significant contributor to the UGRR.

Outside the carriage window, the distant Blue Ridge Mountains were just as Freddy had promised: the violet Shenandoah River cut gracefully through the jagged cliffs, blotched with early scarlet and yellow. While similar to the scenic woods of Massachusetts, Virginia held a verdant quality, wet and budding wild despite the autumn season. It made her fingers itch to capture the panorama in sweeps of paint.

Sarah's passion had ignited under the tutelage of Mary Artemisia Lathbury; she had grown both as an artist and as an abolitionist. Over quiet brushstrokes, Mary had instructed Sarah on the furtive means to dynamic ends: "Let the men take up their guns and caucus in political chambers. We'll sing our hymns, sew our quilts, and paint the scenes before our heart's eye, and do far more to galvanize the people than any of their rabbling."

Sarah saw that she'd been too quick to action in the past, reckless in her yearning to strike before stricken and bring justice to her family's name. Freddy had been right. Mary revealed to her that a tempered approach achieved the preferred effects better than the brash blade.

But sooner than Sarah wanted, her teacher was gone, and she was left clutching her canvases, wanting to do much *more* than sit at a desk. For the first time, she was admonished by her professors for daydreaming in class. All she could think of was the Underground Railroad, Auntie Nan's dolls, Freddy, and how she might apply her newly acquired skills for the furtherance of these things.

Appraising the sky outside the carriage, she hoped the sun might burn through the rain clouds so she could explore New Charlestown's landscape. She imagined discovering a setting similar to that in *The Tempest*, a bubbling brook banked by forestland, a perfect route for runaways. Her stomach dipped at the memory and the anticipation of arriving at the Hills' now.

The horses gave a whinny as they pulled up to the front yard, where Siby and Alice stood under scarlet parasols. Two children in nappies played with spades and buckets in the flowerbed. When the carriage man *Ho*'ed the team, the women turned to the street, and their faces lit with smiles.

Alice squealed and twirled her parasol.

"Misses Brown!" called Siby. "Welcome back to New Charlestown."

The children set aside their garden trowels. Though dressed in similar muslin shifts, one wore a bonnet tatted with pink, and the other wore none. A girl and a boy. The boy's bald head was nearly as pale as that of every child ever born to the Brown household, and for a moment, Sarah thought they might belong to a neighbor.

Alice handed Siby her parasol and, taking each child by the hand, led them tottering to the street.

"This is Miss Sarah and Miss Annie," she said, introducing them. "The ones I story-told you about."

Too young to understand or reply, the little girl hid her shy smile in Alice's skirt. The boy looked to his elder sister, Siby, who raised both eyebrows high at him.

"Miss-es," she enunciated.

"Is-us," he repeated.

"That do," said Siby, and he beamed back. "These here be my brother and sister, Clyde and Hannah, New Charlestown's toothsom-est apple dumplings, so says Miss Prissy."

Sarah saw the resemblance. "My pleasure to meet you."

At her words, Alice wrapped both arms around Sarah. "We are happy! Happy, happy, happy!"

Sarah hugged her back. She felt the same.

Alice moved to "Annie-ee-ee!" She stretched out the last syllable and gave a similar embrace.

Annie smiled. Her expression softened to one of their girlhood days. Nostalgia pricked in Sarah.

"Well, well, the Ladies Brown," Freddy said behind them.

So close, Sarah could smell the leather riding tackle on his skin. He must've just come from the barn, she thought, *the barn,* and forced her chin down to hide her blush.

"Mr. Hill," Annie greeted him. "Your family is so good to invite us. I pray we aren't a burden. Our father's last days have made the Browns little more than nefarious newspaper cartoons in the South. I hope we aren't sullying the Hills' good reputation."

Sarah grimaced. Just when she thought she saw seeds of change, here returned the Annie of doom and gloom.

"Indeed, not," Freddy said. "It's our privilege to have you as guests. In fact, the majority of New Charlestown is singing the John Brown song — have you heard it?"

At that, Alice hummed for a second and then began to sing with loud bravado: *"John Brown's body lies a-moldering in the grave, John Brown's body lies a-moldering in the grave."*

Annie gasped and covered her mouth in horror. Even Sarah took a step back.

"Alice," Freddy gently shushed her.

Unaffected, she continued: *"John Brown's body lies a-moldering in the grave. His soul is marching on!"*

Annie dropped her hand, her face perplexed, while Alice hammered out the beat with a splayed palm like the Quakers. *"Glory, glory, hallelujah! Glory, glory, hallelujah! Glory, glory, hallelujah, his soul is marching on!"*

The carriage driver coughed and set their carpetbags on a spray of wild daisies by the fence.

Annie's scowl lifted. "I think it's wonderful."

"Are they really singing that?" asked Sarah.

Freddy nodded cautiously.

To everyone's surprise, Annie tittered a nervous but genuine hiccup. "Father would approve. It's a battle cry. A call to arms." She smiled encouragingly to Sarah. "I like it, minus the moldering part, but it isn't falsehood. The flesh is temporary. The spirit marches on!"

Siby picked up their bags. "I'll take y'all's things inside. Come on, Hannah — Clyde. Don't be underfoot. Miss Alice, you best not catch a chill or there be a spoonful of cod liver before bed tonight."

Alice stuck out her tongue, then took Annie by the arm, humming the song as they went.

"I'll settle up with Mr. Collins," said Freddy.

The driver nodded appreciatively.

Freddy gestured Sarah toward the front door. "Mother and Father are inside. We've been eager for your arrival."

He took Sarah's wrist in hand and slipped his thumb beneath the lace of her glove to the inside of her palm. It lasted no more than a flash of a second. Though she knew not why or how, the current of his secret touch propelled her at full steam down the pathway and through the front door, where the welcoming voices spilled from room to room like water on a riverboat's wheel.

On their third night, Siby served lark for dinner, which George assured the girls was delicious and very common in the South. Sarah had always known them as morning songbirds and had a hard time concealing her chagrin when each was set on the table — headless, skewered, with the breastbones beaten flat. While Annie went to work cutting the roasted bird into bite-sized nibbles,

Sarah could not bring her fork and knife upon it.

As it happened, she'd just painted a pair on her canvas that morning. The fledglings had come to her on a boulder bluff jutted out from the woods, which provided a panorama of New Charlestown and Harpers Ferry. The towns, like two bright eyes, peered up at her from beneath the hairline split of the wavy rivers: the Shenandoah to the south and the Potomac to the north. A face in landmarks.

Her breath had caught when she'd stumbled onto it the day before. The Virginia mist rising from the canopy revealed the perfect map below. She'd staked her claim by drawing a large white circle on the boulder with a piece of sandstone. A marker by which to set her canvas at the same perspective. She'd returned to sketch while humming her favorite of Mary Lathbury's hymns: "Day is dying in the west. Heaven is touching earth with rest. Wait and worship while the night sets the evening lamps alight . . ." Mr. Sanborn and his Quaker Friends had taken the song south on tracts to teach the southern churches and, most notably, their slaves.

She imagined her bird illustrations twittering the melody in flight from southern bondage, following the path of her painted landscape. And so, it now seemed the greatest betrayal to eat the birds, plucked naked and crusted with herbs.

George lifted his knife. "It's quite easy to get between the bones. Don't be afraid."

Sarah wished Freddy were there. A friend of his had been taken into custody, accused of smuggling medicine and reading materials to slaves. So he'd gone to Purcellville to act as a character witness. She'd mentioned her morning larks to him before he and Mr. Fisher set off. A muse of creativity, he'd said. However, their dinner menu made her wonder if it had been a blessing or a harbinger.

She ate around the bird, forking a soft, baked carrot and chewing it slowly.

"Delivery come today," Siby announced while pouring apple cider into their goblets. "From Mrs. Nancy Santi."

Sarah's spirits lifted at the mention.

Alice squealed. "But it was just Christmas!" She turned to Annie. "Auntie Nan sent a yuletide nightgown for Kerry and a matching one for me — made by *dear little* nuns in Britannia! Dear little nuns, she wrote, dear little nuns. And Quaker dolls for Hannah and Clyde, but" — she frowned — "their bodies were lumpy so Pa and Siby filled them up afresh."

Priscilla cleared her throat loudly. "Auntie Nan is bent on spoiling you," she said kindly. Then, to George: "Were you expecting this delivery, dear?"

"Look after that package for us, would you, Sib?" he said, seemingly too enthralled with his plate to be distracted.

A flicker of something moved across Siby's brow, but she quickly curtsied and continued pouring. "Yes, suh, Mister George. I take care of it."

Alice fidgeted in her seat.

"You'll have to be patient, darling," said Priscilla. "Remember the dirty wrappings." She turned to Sarah and Annie and waved a hand as if it were common knowledge. "So many maladies on parcels carried from place to place — typhoid, infections. Siby knows best how make sure the deliveries are safe. Isn't that right, Siby?"

"I gots to wear gloves and a honey-man's bonnet so as to keep from catching." Siby bugged her eyes out to Alice, who turned her face down with renewed deference. "Then I gots to wash my hands and arms with lye soap that gets to itching like a thousand mosquitoes! But it's all worth it to keep our house and kin in good stead."

"And we are forever beholden to you for

it," said George.

"Don't need no thanks, just need for Miss Alice to be a patient missy and eat my good vegetables before they's cold."

Alice picked up her fork. "Be extra careful, Siby. I don't want you getting the wicked asthenia."

"I do promise." With that, Siby left them in the dining room to finish their meals.

Sarah's father would often receive compendia from important men abroad. Books and essays, stationeries that came bound in brown wrappings and twine. He'd never mentioned any such fear of plague. In fact, she recalled him giving her brothers the waxy paper to use for cutout figurines. Sarah wanted to follow Siby and see for herself this so-called pestilence package. She was sure it was nothing of the kind and much more than dolls.

Remembering Mary Lathbury's lessons in artfulness, Sarah slowed her anxious breathing and resolved that whatever this delivery was, she would come to find out — just not in the middle of dinner. Restraint was as powerful as action in the business of secrecy.

Rain came suddenly, beating against the rooftop shingles. The wet chill eked into the rooms without fireplaces. When they'd finished supping, George suggested they

293

move to the parlor, where Gypsy slept, warm and merry, by the hearth.

"We had such a lovely spring thanks to you and the book *Flower Fables*," said Priscilla. "Our favorite was the tale of Lily-Bell and Thistledown."

" 'Once upon a time, two little Fairies went out into the world, to seek their fortune,' " recited Alice.

"Alice has a gift for memorization." Priscilla smiled. "Our relations abroad were good enough to send a copy of a similar fairy style — the Danish writer Hans Christian Andersen." She picked up a book on the center parlor table.

"Ay, a story to settle our stomachs." George lit his tobacco pipe, and the spicy smoke wreathed his head.

Annie settled into the sofa with Alice cradling Kerry Pippin beside her.

Sarah had read only two of the Andersen tales, small hand-stamped translations brought back from her father's efforts to sell his wool abroad. Based on those, her father thought Andersen's Christian efforts respectable but that the whimsy deflected the solid Bible parables.

Priscilla put a finger to the table of contents. "How about the tale of 'The Ugly Duckling' or 'The Nightingale'?"

Sarah's stomach turned. The spirits of the fowl world were out for vengeance tonight.

Alice made a plea for "The Nightingale," as she was fond of singing thrushes. Priscilla had read no more than three words when the front door sprang open with a blustery wind. Freddy entered in a state of panic, Mr. Fisher at his heels.

Gypsy leapt from her curled rug but, sensing trouble, abstained from her usual sprightly welcome. She sat on her haunches, gazing up with a worried expression. George and Priscilla's welcoming grins dissolved. They all stood.

"What is it, son?"

Freddy looked to Sarah and Annie, then sighed and removed his hat. His black hair stuck to his forehead, slick with sweat and rain from a strenuous ride through the storm.

"On the road from Purcellville, a posse of local bounty hunters confronted us as to the nature of the Browns being back in Jefferson County. Bloodthirsty for hard coin. Annie and Sarah are not safe here."

A raw wind swept through the house, causing the fire to suck loudly against the chimney flue. Sarah shivered and drew herself closer to Annie.

"The posse circled round, impeding our

passage," Freddy continued. "They said they knew John Brown's daughters were under our roof and while New Charlestown might've charitably embraced them, the greater southern constituency would just as soon . . ." He stopped and looked to Sarah with such intensity that her earlobes panged.

"Go on," urged George.

Freddy set his jaw. A blue vein pulsed above his eye. "They'd just as soon have them follow in their father's strung footsteps."

Priscilla gasped and came between the girls, putting her arms about them protectively. "George?"

"Don't worry, Prissy. I'll put a bullet in any vigilante that dares enter *my* home."

"Each man packed a rifle, suh," said Mr. Fisher. "Four, by my count, but they's said they's got more than that who's ready to take up."

Freddy balled his fists with capped rage. "Claiming some fool mission to clean the county of Yankee interference. Tried to take Mr. Fisher, alleging him to be a runaway slave, without any warrant."

"But I gots my papers." Mr. Fisher patted his chest pocket. "Never without my free papers. I sleep with them in my pocket. You never knows when some crazy hunter be thinking he snatch you from bed, chop off however many fingers be necessary to fit the description. Never mind if the slave master says you ain't his, they's after money, and by then, you's a hundred miles from home, bleeding buckets."

At the sound of her father's voice, Siby came down the hall, close enough to hear but still in the shadows.

"I'd have shot them through if they came within a foot, Mr. Fisher." Freddy's eyes glowed like embers.

George waved a hand in disgust. "It's the November election. Got everybody spun up. Lincoln versus Breckinridge — about to tear this country apart." He patted Freddy's shoulder to calm him, then moved the curtain to see out the front window. "I reckon this storm will slow them."

"You need me to take up arms, Mister George?" asked Mr. Fisher.

"I'd be greatly obliged for a strong shot like yours. But I'd hate for you to leave Margaret and the children unguarded."

"My family be safe where they is. Men ain't coming for my house, suh. They's coming for yours. 'Sides — Margie ain't never let a man sneak up on her. She sleeps with a scoring knife under her pillow."

George nodded and turned to Siby. "I

think it safer for you to go on down to your ma's for the night."

Siby put her hands firmly on her hips. "Mister George, I been working in your house since I was no bigger than a dandelion weed. You think I'm going to turn feather and run soon as there's a sniff of danger?"

Alice began to cry and pull at her hair. "Don't leave, Siby."

"I ain't going nowhere," Siby said to comfort her and led her away from the ruckus.

George didn't argue.

"I'll keep a lookout on the barn and wood line behind," said Mr. Fisher.

George nodded. "Freddy and I will take the front road."

"We should hide the girls," said Priscilla. "Just in case."

Beside Sarah, Annie was stone cold as a belly-up trout, except for her hands, which did a Saint Vitus' dance. Sarah took her sister's palms and rubbed them to still the tremors. "It's going to be okay, Annie."

"It's like Pa, Watson, Oliver . . . the raid at Harpers Ferry. They're all going to die," she whispered.

Sarah shook her head. "Nobody is going to die. Not us, the Hills, or the Fishers.

Nobody." By saying it, she hoped to make it true.

Priscilla bid them hurry, and they followed her through the kitchen to Siby's quarters and the pantry.

"We have a root cellar here," she explained.

She got down on her knees, frantically feeling along the wall until she'd found the handhold. She gave a pull and the boards came up, revealing not only a door in the floor but four pairs of eyes peeping back at them from the dark.

Annie's knees buckled. Sarah shrieked. It was a surprise to Priscilla, too, and she dropped the door with a bang. Freddy came running at the sound.

"Passengers?" she asked him.

Unlike Sarah's mother, Mary, who emphasized God's domestic role for women and feigned ignorance of her husband's illegal affairs, Priscilla was as active as George in the UGRR. A co–station master! This new knowledge thrilled Sarah, despite the danger at hand.

Freddy looked from his mother to the cellar, ignoring Sarah and Annie. He nodded. "I thought Father told you. Tom and Bettia Storm and their daughters. It was an emergency stop. The older child has a fever that's nearly done her in. We sent word to Auntie Nan. She telegrammed that the goods would be here today."

Priscilla rubbed her forehead. "Yes, I wondered as to the nature of her delivery." She lifted the door gingerly again. "My deep apologies, Mr. and Mrs. Storm. Did I hurt you?"

"No, ma'am." Mr. Storm's voice was anxious but composed. He held a young girl wearing a tattered capote. She hid her face in his neck. "We're sorry to have startled you but are grateful for the safekeeping."

"How's your sick child?"

Lower in the darkness, Bettia cradled her older daughter's body. "Better, ma'am. Miss Siby just give her a cup of remedy, and it 'pears to be working."

"There trouble?" asked Tom.

Priscilla did her best to smile. "We'll take care. You rest quiet. A big journey is ahead."

She went to close the cellar door, but the girl in Tom's arms whimpered: "I's scared of the dark, Pa. I's scared."

The judder in her voice ripped open a seam in Sarah. She recalled the soothing doll of lavender she'd given to the runaway babe those many months ago. Sitting in the pantry was the crate in which Auntie Nan's medicine dolls had been carefully packed.

300

Sarah pulled a shiny porcelain head from the straw.

"May I?" she asked. It had helped once before.

Priscilla nodded.

"Here." She handed the doll through the floor. "A friend to ward off fear."

The child was wary to accept until her father chided, "Honest lady gives you a gift, you best to take it."

She obediently took the dolly. Priscilla closed the door over them.

"The Underground Railroad," Annie whispered.

"Right now, the less you and Sarah know about the particulars, the better. For your protection," said Priscilla.

"Upstairs," Freddy said. He took Sarah's hand and rushed her up the steps and into the master bedroom. There he pulled her close and locked his charged eyes with hers. "I won't let any harm come to you. I swear it."

She believed him — believed *in* him. Her father's thundering theology taught of a belief that could move mountains. She swept back the dark, damp locks from Freddy's forehead. His gaze ran the whole of her face, and she let it without blinking. Maybe if she believed hard enough . . . Her heart pulsed hot through her fingertips to the words and the rhythm of approaching hoofbeats outside.

EDEN

New Charlestown, West Virginia
August 2014

"Hello?" Eden called, limping into the bookstore. The blisters were raw and bleeding round the edges. "Ms. Silverdash?" The squeals of children prevented her voice from carrying.

Inside the Reading Room, the Hunter twins lay with their tummies flat on a rug with the alphabet sewn in a whimsical rainbow from *A* to *Z*. They were pretending to slide down the spectrum. The other children stood beside Ms. Silverdash in what looked to be a heated debate. Eden recognized a majority from her last visit.

"Oh, please, *The Little Mermaid,*" begged the Hunter girl.

"Ew, not love stuff," argued William. "*Puss in Boots.*"

"*Cinderella!*" piped in a sprightly pigtailed new girl. "I love Gus-Gus!"

"Children, children," Ms. Silverdash hushed them. "I warn you, these are not Disney cartoons. These are the *real* fairy tales." She held up two thick books with weathered covers. "Perrault and Andersen. No sing-alongs here. 'The Little Mermaid' does not end happily. Puss in Boots is a deceitful kitty. And Perrault's 'Cinderella' isn't a lesson on magical transformations. It's a tribute to the godmother who helps Cinderella though it benefits her not."

The children quieted, but their arms and legs twitched impatiently.

Ms. Silverdash looked to Eden and held up the book in her left hand. "The Fur Fairy has decided. In honor of our new Story Hour leader, we are to read her namesake — Andersen."

Years earlier, Jack had surprised her with tickets to *The Steadfast Tin Soldier,* performed by the New York City Ballet. The love story between soldier and ballerina had made her cry in the gilded theater. At that point, they'd been trying to get pregnant again for a year with no luck. She'd wondered if her weepiness was a sign of something, but no: just the beginning of the emotional seesaw. The characters on the stage were poignantly familiar: a paper girl, a tin boy, blown by fate into the fire.

Ms. Silverdash extended the book to her, and the children's faces turned like evening primroses to the moon.

Ander*son,* Ander*sen.* To-may-toe, to-mah-toe. It was close enough. Eden took the book.

"Children, this is Mrs. Anderson," explained Ms. Silverdash. "She's moved to New Charlestown from Washington, D.C. We know who else lives in Washington, D.C., right?"

"The president."

"Very good, Will," praised Ms. Silverdash.

By their awed response, Eden's address might as well have been 1600 Pennsylvania Avenue. The world was so big and simultaneously so small.

"I live on Apple Hill Lane now," she explained. "Next door to Cleo Bronner." Seeing as how everybody seemed to know everybody.

She was right. The children nodded with familiarity, and instead of an intrusion, Eden felt included, welcomed, one of New Charlestown's fold — if only in the juvenile readers' circle.

Ms. Silverdash swept her upturned hand toward the rocking chair and the Fur Fairy within. "Mrs. Anderson. The hour is yours," she said, then sashayed out of the room, leaving Eden. Alone. With the children.

Her throat suddenly dry as cotton, she fidgeted with the book, moved the Fur Fairy aside, and sat on the edge of the wooden rocking chair. The whole thing tilted forward precariously. She'd never sat in a rocking chair before. She scooted deeper into the seat until it righted itself.

"So now . . ." She opened the cover. "How about we just jump in. 'The Tinderbox' is up first."

The Hunter girl's hand shot up like a spear.

"Yes . . . uh, I'm sorry, what's your name?"

"Susannah Leigh, but everybody calls me Suley."

"Soo-lee," said one Hunter twin.

"Soo-lee," repeated the other.

Suley looked down at her lap and didn't look back up to ask her question. "What's a tinderbox?"

Eden had only ever heard it used as a description for danger — a ticking bomb, an impending disaster — but this was a fairy tale, and she didn't want to turn the kids off before they'd begun.

"It's like a matchbox."

"My Grandpa Pete collects matchboxes."

"Then you know what the title means."

Eden relaxed into the page turn.

" 'The Tinderbox,' " she began. She'd never heard or read it, either. " 'A soldier came marching down the road: Left . . . right! Left . . . right!' "

The story described three dogs: *one with eyes as big as teacups, one with eyes as large as mill-wheels, and a third, whose eyes were like towers.* Eden imagined three incarnations of Cricket and hoped no tragedy befell the faithful animals. The soldier, on the other hand, seemed like a character of few scruples.

" 'The wedding festivities lasted a whole week, and the dogs sat at the table, and stared with all their eyes.' "

If it weren't for the dogs in the tale, she thought, she might've despised it. A soldier fills his pockets, steals from and kills an old woman, spends his loot, then has the genie dogs fetch him some more, including a princess and a kingdom? That hardly seemed like a good moral compass. And wasn't that the point of these early allegories — to encourage virtuous behavior in the reader?

"The End," she announced and flipped the page to see what Andersen had up his sleeve next.

Despite the ethical ambiguity involved, the children were quite pleased. She read

"Little Ida's Flowers," "Thumbelina," and began "The Princess and the Pea."

" 'Once upon a time there was a prince who wanted to marry a princess; but she would have to be a real princess.' "

While it started much the same as her high school production of *Once Upon a Mattress*, it was far less theatrical and ended abruptly: " 'There, that is a true story.' "

Eden added a disgruntled "True as Santa's sweatshop elves."

The children gave each other side glances. Eden pretended to have spoken to the Fur Fairy — which somehow made it all right.

Ms. Silverdash pushed open the door and poked her head through the purple archway. There was no clock in the Reading Room, giving the illusion of being shut away from the real world — like in Andersen's tinderbox.

"Mothers are waiting. It's seven minutes past the hour, but we didn't hear a hullabaloo, so we figured you might still be in fairy tale."

She said "fairy tale" as a matter-of-fact destination. As if it were on the map between New Charlestown and Washington, D.C.

The children rose and went clamoring toward the exit.

Before reaching it, Suley turned. "Thank you, Mrs. Anderson. You'll be here next week?"

Eden nodded. "We'll continue with 'The Saucy Boy.' "

Suley smiled, and the rest of the children followed her exemplary thanks.

Ms. Silverdash moved aside to let them pass. "Have a lovely weekend, my dears." Then, to Eden: "I had a feeling about you — a natural storyteller."

Eden wasn't used to praise from other women. She couldn't recall the last time her mother had paid her a compliment, and, thus, she was unprepared on how best to respond.

"You could probably teach a parrot to do what I did," she said, deflecting.

Ms. Silverdash ignored the reply and led her out of the Reading Room. The children were gone, but they weren't alone. A silver-haired man sat at a small reading table pushed up against the one shelfless wall in the store. In front of him was an enormous salad, not contained by a take-out box but heaped on a dinner plate so that leaves dangled off the sides. He forked the lettuce as if it were a steak, spearing with force but acquiring little.

"Eden," said Ms. Silverdash. "May I

introduce Mr. Morris Milton?"

He wiped his mouth with a napkin and stood with one extended upturned palm. "Call me Morris."

She shook. Finally, the man she'd heard so much about. "Morris Milton whose name appeared on my real estate agent's contract? Also of Milton's Market and Morris's Café fame?"

He gave a humbled grin. "I'm just a name on paper — the financier. The market is my elder son, Mack's. My younger, Mett, runs the café next door."

"I met Mack the other day. Congratulations on your grandson."

He cleared his throat. "Mighty kind. First grandchild in the family, though I've yet to see him."

"Children have a way of changing even the hardest of hearts," chimed Ms. Silverdash. "Evidenced by history and literature. People will do anything for the good of their child, meet every kind of danger head-on, battle monsters, sacrifice, die . . . even swallow their pride."

Morris sat, pushed at his greens. "Got me *swallowing* this lettuce stuff right now," he said to Eden. "Trying to keep me alive until my grandson is as old, lumpy, and gray as his grandpa."

"And wouldn't that be a blessing," she teased.

"If I have to eat like a turtle, I think I'd rather someone boil me and enjoy themselves a hearty stew."

"That could be arranged," Ms. Silverdash laughed. "Years of eating café food are catching up to you." She turned to Eden. "A body can't have ham hocks, corn bread, and pie to the sky every day and not expect a thing or two to turn funny."

"My daddy and granddaddy ate exactly that, and both lived to nearly ninety."

"Mr. Morr-is," she said, breaking his first name into two exasperated syllables. "Your granddaddy spent the last decade of his life in his bed, pained with arthritis and a weak constitution. Your daddy had eight of his ten toes taken off from the diabetes. God rest both their souls, but why would you ever want to follow down either of those paths? For what?"

"Lemon pie is what."

Ms. Silverdash shook her head but smiled. "There's lemon chicken in that salad. Dig down deep and get a piece."

He dug: a curly stem of frisée dropped to the table, and he left it where it fell. "Must be hiding from me."

Ms. Silverdash threw up a hand. "Fine,

fine. If you're going to keep on like this, I'll go next door and have Mett make you a fried peanut butter and bacon sandwich, but when your heart gives out from the clog, don't expect me to give you mouth-to-mouth resuscitation."

"A man has one little surgery and wakes up to a world upside down — and tasteless."

"Little surgery? You had a heart bypass, Morris!"

"I clean forgot!" He gave his breastbone a dramatic tap. "Well, by all means, bring on the turtle food." He plowed the lettuce until he found a misshapen chicken chunk. "But don't tell me that's lemon pie." He grinned sarcastically. "A yard rock is not a diamond, no matter how well you polish it."

"Rocks or diamonds — it matters little what you're buried beneath. Grave is grave."

Morris looked to Eden. "A touch dramatic, wouldn't you agree, Mrs. Anderson?"

"I'm not the best person to ask. We — I try to eat organic."

"Indeed. Even her dog is on the path of clean health. You should take a cue."

Morris gave a wan grin of defeat. "I'm surrounded." He ceremoniously lifted his fork to them. "The South concedes."

"As well it should." Ms. Silverdash winked. "If you ate instead of talked, you'd fill up and feel better. You know your mood is improved by a full belly." At that, she brought a cup of tea to his table. "Peppermint is good for digestion."

He looked to her then with such affection that Eden cast her eyes to the floor. It seemed strange that they weren't married and never had been. She thought of what Cleo had told her — about Morris marrying Ms. Silverdash's best friend — and it saddened her to think that they'd lived side by side yet divided. She wondered if they'd ever been lovers in their youth. Even just once? It seemed cruel of fate to deny them that. Perhaps even crueler to grant it. After nearly a lifetime, did love still need ordainment? Maybe, maybe not. But Eden thought Ms. Silverdash deserved *something* official. If even just a token of fidelity. Love was a tricky flame to kindle and keep, Eden knew well.

"I ought to be going," she said. "I'll let you two enjoy your lunch break without a third wheel." She bit her tongue after she said it, worried that it gave the wrong suggestion.

"Not at all. We enjoy the company."

Morris nodded. "The bookstore used to

313

be full of people every hour . . ."

Ms. Silverdash sighed. "Times have changed."

Eden felt caged. She wanted to stay to talk to Ms. Silverdash about the porcelain doll's head but was hesitant to bring it up in front of Mr. Morris. He and Mack had been the property owners from whom they'd purchased the house on Apple Hill — and, unknowingly, the relic therein. Their real estate agent, Mrs. Mitchell, had negotiated down the Miltons' asking price, dropping it by more than ten thousand dollars. The doll alone could be worth that much. The house, far more. Eden didn't want to put all her cards on the table just yet.

"I'm sorry. I would, but the dog — my dog — Cricket is waiting. My brother, Denny, is here, too, and my husband, Jack, is home. He's not usually. So anyhow, I best go." She stepped toward the door. "Monday, same place, same time?"

Ms. Silverdash bowed. "It's your Children's Story Hour."

"Nice meeting you, Mr. Milton — Morris."

"Happy to have you folks in the old Potter place. A welcomed new neighbor, even if you subscribe to the turtle diet." He waved a red radicchio leaf as good-bye.

Eden backed out of the bookshop. Her first step on the sidewalk tore more flesh from her foot. The blisters hadn't bothered her for the entire Story Hour, but now they stung. She kicked off her sandals as soon as she reached her car and drove home barefoot. By the time she parked in her Apple Hill driveway, the pain and heat had left her sweaty despite the air-conditioning.

She got out and flinched at the stones underfoot. Leaning against the side of the car, she picked the sharp bits out from between her toes.

"First blisters and now damned rocks."

"I'm sorry," came a woman's voice she didn't recognize.

Eden shot up straight.

A girl stood on the porch. She looked to be in her early twenties. Pretty in a plain way: brown hair, brown eyes, not too tall, athletically built. She had the face of the best friend in every romantic comedy Eden had ever seen. However, unlike her movie counterparts, she wasn't smiling. In fact, she looked downright tragic.

Her sad expression prompted a soft reply: "Can I help you?"

"I'm sorry," the girl repeated and came down the porch steps. "I shouldn't be here." She took a sharp breath and pulled her

315

bangs back behind an ear. Her hands shook. "I couldn't get ahold of Denny. His room-mates said he moved out — that he was at his sister's. They gave me the address." She looked up, on the verge of bursting. "My name's Jessica. I'm Denny's . . ."

The tears came, and she never finished. Denny's what?

SARAH

New Charlestown, Virginia
September 1860

The storm brought wind and torrents of rain that sent the maple tree thrashing its arms against the bedroom windowpanes. Gypsy gave a low, continuous snarl, while the women huddled together in the farthest corner of the master bedroom. Alice cried into the belly of her Kerry doll with Siby softly rubbing her back; Annie, cheek to Bible leather, prayed and rocked herself; Priscilla held a shotgun, its safety on but aimed at the door. Sarah stayed posted by her side.

John Brown had taught his children how to shoot — sons and daughters. One of Sarah's earliest memories was the feel of the smooth wooden stock between her palms. The smell of gunpowder and grease and her father close by. His hand over hers, pointing at a green ear of corn stood up on

317

the fence post.

"Get where ye be aiming lined up in your sight," he'd told her. But when she'd tried to adjust the barrel a fraction right or left, he'd held the gun as he saw fit. "Ready?"

She'd shaken her head, unsure of what was to come and afraid of what her trigger pull might do. Without waiting, he'd jerked his finger down atop hers. The gun flashed and kicked back so forcefully against her chest that it left a yellow bloom that purpled in under a minute. The bullet struck the ear in the side, sending white kernel pom-poms to the right and the cob to the left. Annie had been with her, and her father had shifted his attention while Sarah rubbed at her breastbone and sniffed back the tears. Annie was older and more eager to do whatever it took to gain their father's favor. She'd taken aim at a fat squirrel and shot it right off the tree limb without blinking.

Now the same girl cowered in the shadows, and Sarah wondered when her brave sister had died and this sad changeling had taken her place.

A man called out. Another answered. In the din of the storm, they couldn't recognize either. Priscilla's grip tightened on the gun. Siby hushed Alice's sobs. Annie rocked harder.

The front door opened, and the house seemed to inhale and hold its breath with it.

"Browns!" Sarah distinctly heard.

The air changed: tensed and pulsed. A squealing pitch rang high in Sarah's ears. And then a crack — of lightning or bullet, they couldn't tell, but the four women gasped in unison. Gypsy's snarl broke to white teeth, and she barked ferociously at the window. A child cried. Feet pounded back and forth below. Doors slammed. Angry voices bellowed in the barnyard before hooves hammered the sodden ground, blending quickly into the beating rain. Another crack. The smell of sulfur. No mistaking: a gunshot.

Priscilla's thumb trembled on the release, but her trigger finger was steadfast.

Boots on the stairs. Alice and Annie went silent. Gypsy moved to the door, sniffed and whined. Priscilla uncocked the safety.

The door swung open, and had he not said her name before showing his face, Sarah was sure Priscilla would've shot her son through.

"Mother?"

"Thanks be to the Almighty," she exhaled and set the safety back. "Freddy."

His face was paler than Sarah had ever

seen a man's.

"They've run off — after Mr. Storm." He shook his head. "He tried to lead his family out through the back door, but the bounty hunters had surrounded the house without our knowledge. His daughter dropped the doll. The head broke and cut her badly. She cried out, and the men attempted to pursue. Mr. Storm made himself known to divert their attentions and ran into the woods. We tried to stop him but . . ." He exhaled.

"But Mr. Storm be a free man." Siby's eyes were moons of worry.

"Black is black in the night," whispered Annie. She cradled her Bible. "God be with his soul."

Sarah thought she might vomit where she stood. The room swayed. The doll she'd given the child . . . the doll Mr. Storm had made his daughter accept. A white woman's cursed gift.

"The girls — were they captured, are they hurt?" Priscilla rose and set aside the shotgun.

"The child's cut is deep. It will leave a scar. Mrs. Storm is inconsolable. She said her husband couldn't abide putting our family in harm's way. We hid them in the hayloft and are transferring them immediately."

The Storms hadn't known the bounty hunters were really after Sarah and Annie. Mr. Storm had sacrificed himself unnecessarily. Sarah's heart clutched. "Maybe he'll get away or they'll catch him and go for the bounty but find his free papers and be the fools."

Everyone seemed to look away in unison. What she'd said was naïve. If the posse caught Mr. Storm, they'd hang him from a tree with all damnation pouring down.

Siby headed for the door. "I best tend to the wounded child, the sick one, too . . . and their ma."

Freddy exhaled loudly. "*I* was the fool for inviting you here. It isn't safe in the South. For black or white, free or slave. Child of John Brown or otherwise."

Sarah and Annie might've been the daughters of a convicted criminal abolitionist, but they were young, white women from the North. Any man who dared lay a hand to them, drunk or not, would've incurred the full rage of the "John Brown's Song" singing people.

Better to have stayed downstairs and faced the rabble. If they were hurt or, worse, perished, their lives would've been fuel to the abolitionist legacy. But who would sing songs for Mr. Storm? Who would tell his story?

If only they'd been braver and not hidden like mice in the attic. If only she'd not given that doll to the girl. If only she'd not insisted they come to visit. If only, if only . . . Sarah's knees went weak, and she buckled.

Freddy steadied her. "It's all right."

She shook her head. Everything was far from right. It was her fault. She'd only wanted to help, and instead she'd caused this tragedy.

Outside the rain turned to hail, beating against the gabled roof and rolling down the shingles.

"We must forward them north as soon as possible," said Priscilla.

"Mr. Fisher is harnessing the wagon," said Freddy. "We're taking the Storms to Shepherdstown station. No one will be on the roads in this weather. Mr. Storm ran south, toward Harpers Ferry. We must honor his courage by ensuring that his family reaches safety." He turned to Sarah. "At first light, I'll drive you and Annie to the train depot. Father and Mr. Fisher will stay behind in case the men return. Though, from the look of it, they were so drunk they could barely stay on their saddles. I'm hoping that works in Mr. Storm's favor. Father will call for the sheriff, too. They'll scour the woods. New Charlestown is law-abiding. We won't fall into anarchy as easily as the southern states."

"Have the wicked men gone far, far away?" Alice had nearly vanished into the seams of the room and now emerged with a tear-streaked face.

"Yes, darling," said Priscilla. "Far, far away."

Despite Freddy's words of assurance, George insisted that the women remain upstairs, locked in the master bedroom. Gypsy, too. The storm continued to howl and spit against the windows.

"The cold pushing out the warm," said Siby. "Seasons be violent changing."

She did her best to make everyone as comfortable as possible, draping a Jacob's ladder quilt over them as the air did just as she'd predicted and took on an icy chill. At the glisten of clear daybreak, she woke them, having not slept a moment herself.

"We live to see another day of mercy," she said. "I best be down to make breakfast. Menfolk been up all night. I'll use the last of our coffee bean and chicory, if that be all right with you, Miss Prissy."

Priscilla thanked her kindly, and Siby left them to dress alone.

Outside, the sun shone sharply, melting the pebbles of ice into the grass and the gnarled tree roots sticking up from the land. Downstairs, Freddy, George, and Mr. Fisher sat at the table; their grave voices carried through the house's walls along with the smell of fritters, coffee, and burning oak.

"It's this talk of war that's turned men's minds to savagery," said George.

"I didn't recognize any of 'em — not from New Charlestown," said Mr. Fisher.

They silenced when the women entered the dining room.

Priscilla kissed George squarely. "God be praised. You are safe." She turned to Mr. Fisher. "Is there news of Mr. Storm?"

Mr. Fisher looked down at his empty plate speckled with hush puppy crumbs.

"Mrs. Storm and the girls will be in Philadelphia by nightfall," explained Freddy, though that wasn't the question Priscilla had asked.

Sarah winced at the mention, blaming herself for the girl's cut hand, her cries, her father's sacrifice. The breakfast smells turned rancid to her senses. She had to breathe into her sleeve to keep from gagging.

Siby came through the kitchen door with butter-fried pumpkin. "Figured we could use something sweet to settle our stomachs."

She went to serve Alice from the skillet, but Alice shook her head. "Thank you, but no thank you. Thank you."

Freddy forked a pumpkin cube. "It's good — you'd like it, Alice."

She turned her chin down.

"My secret's a squeeze of lemon," Siby explained. "Nobody be thinking lemon and pumpkins court well when in fact they's just what the other needs to be at they best."

Alice refused still. Sarah couldn't blame her. No one but the men had an appetite.

"I put good love in that cooking, Miss Alice," said Siby.

"I'm sorry," she mumbled back.

Siby frowned and went back into the kitchen. She returned with a doll no bigger than a corncob. Much smaller than the medicine dolls Sarah had seen in the delivery box.

"This one was hiding under the others. Scrawny thing. I fattened her up cotton pretty for you."

A fairy doll. Sarah recalled Auntie Nan's description.

Alice's eyes widened, and her fingers itched to touch. "She's a baby," she whispered. "Kerry's baby girl."

"You've got to promise you'll eat first,"

said George.

Alice nodded. Siby handed her the fairy doll, and Alice adjusted Kerry Pippin on her lap and the miniature on Kerry's so that each skirt mirrored the one beneath: baby, child, adult.

"Her name is Pumpkin," she said. Then, to the doll: "I won't let any bad men hurt you, Pumpkin."

Freddy pushed back from the table and stood. "The northbound B&O departs Washington at five P.M. We should go as soon as possible."

While Sarah recognized the prudence of their hurried departure, it wasn't until that moment that she felt the impact of its meaning: she was leaving with no foreseen date of return; she was leaving with her canvas map incomplete. The byways and secret routes of her larks' final passage up the Potomac River had yet to even be sketched in charcoal. It would be nothing more than a romantic picture if she didn't finish.

She understood the danger at hand, but this wasn't merely a painting. It was her hand of action in her father's great work. It was a way she could make amends to Mr. Storm. Just as Mary Lathbury's songs were taken south to unknowing plantation masters, her painting could be used as a guide for men and women on the Underground Railroad. No need to conceal. It could hang proudly in any southern home. Its message would be readily understood by those who knew the secret codes. She would not leave without the last details seared into her memory.

It was just past dawn, and they had yet to pack. That would take Annie at least an hour. Sarah had to go to the Bluff. And she had to go now.

She stood, her aim set: "I'll fetch my paints."

Priscilla nodded. "Yes, Siby, let's see to the girls' things."

Sarah grabbed her satchel of onion paper and pencils from the parlor, snuck down the servant's hall, through the kitchen, and out the back door. Just past the barn, she heard a whistle. She forged ahead, each footstep sinking deep in the waterlogged apple orchard. At the edge of the woods, she heard it again — this time closer and with more urgency. Gypsy sprinted across the leaf-scattered grass, wagging her tail and circling Sarah. She turned. Freddy had followed.

EDEN

"Damned D.C. traffic!" Denny swung through the front door cursing.

Turning the corner to the kitchen, he came to a full halt, his eyes nearly dropping out of his head like eggs cracked into a skillet.

Eden had invited Jessica to stay for dinner. What else could she do? The girl was a wreck, and she couldn't stand outside on the porch all night. Denny off doing God knows what errand, God knows where in D.C. She was a sweet girl, once she stopped crying long enough to complete a sentence. Eden hadn't dared ask what the tears were about, which might incite them to start again. Instead, she'd handed Jessica a butcher's knife and had been pleased to see that she was far more skilled in cookery than in conversation. She'd cubed the pile

328

of potatoes in the time it took Eden to skin one, then moved on to the carrots, neatly dicing in a rhythmic *chop-chop.*

"The man of the hour!" Eden scooped up the potatoes and dropped them in a pot of boiling chicken stock. "Look who I found at our front door."

Jessica laid the knife down beside the vegetable peels.

Denny stood, catatonic in expression. *Earth to Denny?* Eden nearly said, but she didn't want to come off as a reproachful big sister. Whatever was going on with these two, she was really in no position to help or hinder. Look at her marriage: one big Failure. Capital *F.* But like in hers, the laws of force and nature applied. You couldn't just *stand there* gawking. Two pendulums suspended in ineptitude. Somebody had to make a move. Even if that move was from an external push.

"Jessica came all the way from Philadelphia to visit you, Den." She stirred the simmering broth, banging the spoon more than was necessary. "You aren't even going to say hello?"

His Adam's apple bobbled. "Hi."

It wasn't exactly an icebreaker. Fine: maybe one more sisterly nudge would break the mute spell. "We're making Chicken

Soup for the Doggy Soul for dinner. Your basic chicken noodle, minus the noodles, so I figured we could have a bite without me making two different pots of the same recipe. Is that okay?"

He nodded. "I'm okay."

"I asked if the soup was okay, but I'm glad you are, too."

"Oh, uh, sorry —" He pointed to his gut. "Not feeling right. Unsettled."

"Is it flu season?" Eden turned the gas burner *tick-tick-tick* until it lit. "Jessica's having stomach troubles, too." Eden pointed to *The Holistic Hound,* on the counter. "Soup is the best bet for all."

"She's having dinner *with* us?" Denny looked like he sincerely might be sick.

Jessica clasped her elbows in a self-hug.

That was quite enough. Indigestion, stomach virus — whichever, she didn't care. Denny had been raised better than to be so rude. *She'd* raised him better.

"Denny!" Eden put a hand to her hip and gave him a look that she hoped communicated, *Get your act together, kid.* Jessica was a guest in her house. Sure, it was a house she wasn't planning on keeping, but nobody knew that.

She turned to Jessica. "Jack's the same way when he's not feeling well. The

Washington Post ran an article a few years back. Research proved men have a lower pain tolerance than women. One twinge of physical or emotional stress and bibbidi-bobbidi, they turn into cranky babies." She shook her head. "Some way to treat your girlfriend."

"She's not — I'm not — it's not . . ." he sputtered, and Eden realized she'd officially crossed into annoying-mother territory.

Jessica shrank into herself. "I tried to call, but your cell phone went straight to voice mail every time."

Denny sighed and ran a hand through his hair. "I was at a job interview. I couldn't talk."

A job interview! Eden was torn between pride and the daunting feeling that something terribly serious must be going on for her bachelor play-the-guitar-till-I-die brother to secretly interview for a job in conservative Washington, D.C. Only then did she notice that he wore a borrowed set of Jack's pressed khakis and a button-down shirt.

Denny and Jessica were back to staring across the kitchen.

"Jessica," Eden said, "do you mind babysitting that pan of chicken while I get the rest of the ingredients?"

"Sure," she replied, meek as a lamb. Eden passed her the spatula.

"Denny, you help me." She yanked the cuff of his shirt, and he followed her lead.

Alone with him in the dark of the pantry, she pointed a finger up to within an inch of his nose. "You better tell me the truth. Now."

He leaned back, his head thudding lightly against the wall, then slumped down until he was sitting on the floor. "I'm in trouble, E."

"Well, I figured that since the minute I saw you." She was his sister, for God's sake. They shared DNA. She knew him backward and forward, even if he didn't think she did. The sibling sixth sense.

"What's this job business?"

"I'm trying to get a job — with a solid salary."

"Not to be an age racist, but you are twenty-seven. It's about damned time. You're on the verge of being that old man in some rinky-dink bar smelling like yesterday's sweaty meatballs and playing tunes for tips."

He winced. She was sorry to take a reality pin to his fantasy bubble, but somebody had to do it.

"Is that what you and Jack discussed on

your walkabout yesterday?" she asked.

The two had been close since their introduction. It had warmed her to be able to give Denny the big brother he'd never had, a quasi–father figure. It'd be hard on him when they split . . . *if* that's what she still wanted. Because at the moment, what she wanted most was for Jack to be beside her in that pantry. He'd agree with her entirely and help her figure this out. They were good at teamwork, in the office and at home. Or at least, they had been, once upon a time.

"The job was one of the things."

"And the others?"

He looked up to her from below, the same visage she recalled from their childhood.

"I told him I knew about you trying to have a baby and I —"

A bonfire rose to her cheeks and threatened to come flaming out her ears, eyes, and nose. "You talked about *me*?" she seethed before he was through.

He seemed to eat his tongue, mumbling under his breath, *Jack said this* and *Jack said that,* but Eden couldn't hear past her own mental clamor. Jack hadn't even spoken to her about their failure to conceive, but he'd talked to her little brother? What did he say — how did he feel — did he blame her or did he see that she'd done everything she could? *Every* damned thing. That she desperately wished it had worked. That she was sorry. So very sorry to have let them both down. Her mind whirled.

"Jack's worried about you. He wants you happy. Even if you don't think you're 'meant to be' in the long run, the dude loves you, E. For real."

She shook her head. Of course he'd say that. It was the proper Mr. Knightley thing to say. He had to say it, right?

Denny's hand moved under the notched wooden plank, and the floor lifted an inch. "Is this the pit you found the spook's head in?"

She took a deep breath. "It's a root cellar." She refocused, swapping out Jack's face in her mind for the doll's. "I can't remember if our house in Larchmont had one." They'd been in the pantry too long. Jessica was waiting. Eden didn't want to make her more uncomfortable than she already was.

"No cellar," said Denny. "But we had spooks."

Eden pulled two cans of green peas off the shelf. "I told you before, Denny, no such things. Just bad memories best buried in the past."

She left him there and marched back to

the kitchen. It smelled gamey. Chicken on the verge of burning. Jessica was gone.

Eden pulled the skillet off the burner, then quickly shuffled from room to room until she spotted Cricket outside the closed maid's bathroom, directly next to the pantry she and Denny had been in.

As she came closer, she heard the sound of retching. Eden knocked gently. "Jessica?"

Cricket whined and sniffed the oily air.

"I'm sorry," Jessica mumbled from within. "I was fine, and then the chicken . . ."

At the mention, she coughed and gagged again.

"Do you want me to help?" She tried the handle. Locked.

Denny came out of the pantry. "What's wrong?"

"Jessica is sick."

Then Cricket arched his back and suddenly vomited a pile of twisted green grass at their feet.

"What the hell is going on!" Denny yelped, echoing Eden's very thought.

She knelt down to the dog and smoothed back his fur. "I haven't even served the soup, so nobody can blame my cooking yet."

Jessica cracked the bathroom door, dabbing her mouth with a tissue. Seeing the dog vomit, she covered her nose and turned away.

"Must be a bug going round," she said, but Eden recognized the sallow color of her cheeks against the rose of her lips.

She'd become an expert on the signs. Unless Jessica was a righteous vegan, only a pregnant person would react that way to the smell of chicken sautéing. Eden had had the same problem with bacon.

She looked at Denny, and like lightning, she knew she was right. Moreover, *he* knew she knew.

"Help her sit down," she told him.

Denny obeyed, leading Jessica to the kitchen stool farthest from the offending odor.

"You need to drink something," he offered, and Eden was relieved to see that he wasn't behaving like a complete asshole anymore.

"There's a lemon in the fruit bin. Put a slice in water. It'll help," instructed Eden.

On his way to the fridge, he dropped a rusted coin on the island. "I found this in your cellar."

In light of her new realization about Jessica and after finding a doll's head with a cryptic key inside, a shard of old copper didn't get her excited.

"A penny for your thoughts?" she said sarcastically and moved to turn off the burner. She'd left it on.

Jessica held the object up to the light. It wasn't flat like money but had been tooled with an intricate design. "A button," she said. "See the sheaves of braided wheat on the front and the back loop for attachment? My mom sewed a lot of our clothes growing up."

Eden took a good look. She was right. A button. "Another clue for my ace detective dog walker, Cleo." She put it on the window ledge beside the doll's head, then turned coolly to Denny. "I insist Jessica spend the night."

He nearly dropped the glass of water he was carrying but didn't argue.

"No — no, I couldn't . . ." Jessica began, but Eden was resolved.

"It'll be dark in an hour. You can't drive back to Philadelphia tonight. I won't let you, hon. That's all there is to it. You're staying in our guest room, and I've got deviled eggs if the chicken isn't appetizing. Sharp mustard, salt, citrus, vinegar — savories always helped my nausea."

She smiled kindly. "Thank you, Eden."

With Jessica in the guest room, she presumed Denny would take the couch, leaving Jack . . . He'd have to come back to her bedroom. There was no alternative, and Eden was unexpectedly glad. A Newton's cradle of liaisons. She gave Jessica and Denny a click-push, and on the opposite side, they did the same to her and Jack.

"Come on," Denny said, "I'll show you up."

He put a gentle hand to the small of Jessica's back. A minuscule, intimate gesture weighted with significance: whatever they were now, they'd been close. *Very* close. It wasn't a casual spot to touch. Further validation of Eden's presumption. She hoped the two would be able to talk alone, if not in her company.

While they were upstairs, Eden plucked the "IT'S A BOY!" flags out of the Milton's Market eggs. That was the last thing any of them needed. She crammed the toy-sized banners beneath the vegetable shavings in the garbage.

"Who's home?" Jack called through the front door, galvanizing Cricket to welcoming clucks and tail wags. The dog was obviously feeling better.

"Jack, I'm in here," said Eden, hoping to have a moment alone with him before the others returned, but Denny and Jessica caught him first.

"Oh, 'ello, I didn't know we had guests," he said, looking up to the second-floor landing.

"Uh, yeah, a surprise," said Denny, making his way down the stairs. "This is Jessica."

"Jessica? Jessica," Jack repeated. "Nice to meet you, *Jessica.*"

Eden heard recognition in his voice. Denny must've discussed her on their walk. So the boys were in cahoots on that account, too.

"Nice to meet you. I'm sorry to have dropped in on you like this," Jessica apologized.

"Not at all," said Jack with a too-happy jingle. His businessman voice, charm applied in the tensest of circumstances.

All three came into the kitchen. Eden stirred the soup pot. The ingredients whirled round and round in a dizzying pinwheel. "Oh good, you've met Denny's friend. She's staying for dinner and the night."

"*Really?* An overnight guest. Wonderful!" Jack didn't blink the entire time he spoke. It was one of his subtle giveaways only she knew. "And you cooked, too?"

"Yes, one of Cleo's *Holistic Hound* recipes."

"More dog food?"

Eden frowned but saw by his expression

that he hadn't meant it as an insult. He was making light banter. An attempt to ignore the elephants in the room.

"Gourmet," Denny added.

Cricket sat in the middle of their foursome, sniffing the air again.

"I better give the little guy a bowl of soup for his stomach. Jessica." Eden nodded toward the plastic container on the kitchen counter. "Those are Milton's Market deviled eggs. A New Charlestown specialty, I'm told."

Only she noticed the tiny hole in the center of each where the toothpick birth announcement had been.

Eden hid her displeasure when Denny said he'd sleep in Jessica's room. They were grown adults, and this wasn't 1950. Besides, the damage was already done. From what she could tell, they didn't sleep much anyhow. Their voices murmured long into the night. The old house's walls were too thin. She wondered if Jack was able to sleep downstairs. Cricket, too. Or if it was just she who heard the murmuring. She'd had a similar problem as a child.

On more nights than she cared to recount, she'd woken to the judder of the front door, the weight of the bolt sliding; heavy footsteps that made no noise but reverberated through her bed and her in it, legs stretched out like a tuning fork. She'd thought it was another in a long list of magical spirits: Santa Claus and his elves, the tooth fairy, the Easter bunny, angels, ghosts, shooting stars, and doll houses come to life. Legends of fact and fiction, all of which stirred only in secret, at night. She almost wished she'd kept believing in those fairy tales, never to know.

It had been raining the night she was given the truth. The kind of downpour that pelted the roof in furious waves; the thunder moaned so deep and long that she wholly believed it was the collective cry of dead spirits washed up from the grave. The house trembled with the sound, and the rain smattered the windows like fingers clawing for admittance.

Eden had sat in her bed, knees pulled to her chest, for as long as her stammering heart could withstand. Then the door below opened; the walls of her bedroom fought the draft, her ears popped from the pressure, and the air smelled of wet dirt. She'd been so frightened, she'd run not to her mother or father but to Denny, in his cradle. Too young to protect her, but the sight of him comforted her.

"Don't be afraid," she'd whispered to him. "There's no such thing as ghosts. There's no such thing. There's no such thing."

She'd rubbed his little back until his breath's rhythmic purring gave her the steady courage she needed. Then she'd crept through the shadows, across the hall and down the stairs, where puddles of rainwater mirrored the floor. A black mass glistened in the hallway corner. The dark figure turned, and she gasped.

"Eden, what are you doing up?" It was her father in his rain slicker.

He hung his wet coat on the rack and attempted to lift Eden, but she pulled away. He smelled not of bay rum but of something cloyingly sour and intensely shameful. It made her nauseated, and she felt the sudden urge to protect her mother and brother upstairs. Not from her father so much as from the mysterious unseen that threatened.

She never told anyone that secret, not even Denny. At first she kept it out of fear. Then it didn't matter. Her father was dead.

There were no such things as ghosts. The only phantom was the other man her father was when he wasn't with them. She'd begun wearing earplugs to bed then and didn't stop until she moved into a one-bedroom apartment in college, in a new building with insulated walls.

Now she contemplated driving to a twenty-four-hour gas station to buy a pair. Just when she thought she might actually do that, the voices quieted for an hour, maybe two. At dawn, they returned when Jessica said her good-byes just outside the master bedroom door.

"I have to teach my three-year-old tap class at noon," she explained. "If I don't leave now, I'll be late."

"I'll be back up to Philly as soon as my last interview is done," Denny assured her. "Call if you need me before then. I'll keep my phone on, I promise."

Eden was relieved to hear that he was acting responsibly.

The stairs creaked under their weight, and the screen door gave a clatter at Jessica's exit. Then it was Jack's voice rising up through the floorboards. She wasn't worried about Denny seeing him on the couch. He knew — maybe more than she knew — about their marital woes. Not much she could do about that, but she trusted Jack to give Denny practical advice. He was a gentleman with a true heart. It was one of the qualities that had first attracted her to him. That and the sexy British accent. So very Knight in Shining Armor. She smiled to herself.

The two men below exchanged indecipherable conversation. The front door slammed again.

Eden kicked off the sheets. If everybody else was up . . . Trying to sleep now was pointless. She went downstairs to find Denny on all fours, mopping the floor with paper towels. Cricket licked the pads of her brother's upturned feet.

"Cut it out, dude," he warned. "I don't need you to barf again."

"He threw up?" she asked.

Denny startled and flipped over to face her, hands in the puddle he was cleaning. He lifted a drippy palm and screwed up his face. "Peed."

"Oh?" She came to the last step and sat. If Denny thought cleaning up after a puppy was bad, he was in for a rude awakening.

Cricket pawed at her lap until she took him up. "What's going on with you, buddy boy?" He snuggled his snout into her middle, and she ran her fingers through his fur so that it was whorled like kettle corn.

"Jack went for a jog," Denny told her while he finished cleaning.

"Aw." Her gaze shifted wistfully toward the door. They used to jog together. "And Jessica?"

"To Philly."

"She's okay to drive so far?"

He waved a hand. "Better this morning. Twenty-four-hour virus. You know how that goes."

Enough with the pretenses. "I don't believe the stomach-bug baloney, Den, so you can spare me the insult of insisting that's what it is."

"I — she —" he stammered. "Aw, hell." He ran a piss-tainted palm through his hair. "I screwed up, E. She's pregnant. It was an accident."

"An . . . accident?" While she already knew that to be true, hearing the confirmation pierced her more deeply than she'd anticipated. She remembered the opening line of "Thumbelina": " 'Once there was a woman who wished very much to have a little child, but she could not obtain her wish.' "

"What's that?" Denny frowned, confused by her recitation.

"Nothing. Just a fairy tale." She tried to breathe, but her rib cage was knit tight. "What are you going to do?"

SARAH

New Charlestown, Virginia
September 1860

"Where are you going?" Freddy asked, winded by the pursuit.

Sarah gripped her satchel to her side. "My painting isn't finished."

He looked to the woodland behind her. "You can't intend to do it now. We have to leave for the train — and what if the bounty hunters are camped in the woods?" The vein streaking his forehead returned. "Please, be reasonable, Sarah."

He lifted his palm, gesturing toward the house, but Sarah shook her head. She was going to the Bluff and would make a dash, if need be. He'd have to hoist her over his shoulder to stop her, and he was too much of a gentleman for that.

"I just need to see it one last time. So I can finish the way," she entreated.

He studied her, assessing her resolve, then

lifted an eyebrow high. "The way?"

There wasn't time to stand gabbing explanations. "Yes, for the new map," she whispered. "You didn't think I was just practicing my paints, did you, Freddy?" She ushered him into the shadow of the forest. "From the Bluff you can see the passage from Harpers Ferry north along the Potomac. Mary Lathbury taught me the codes on sampler quilts taken to slave plantations. I'm using those, too. The bear-paw maple leaves, waterways, wagon wheels, stars, animals, shapes, and colors. Don't you see? I must finish! For Mr. Storm, if no one else."

Evoking the name seemed to act as fuel. Freddy marched along beside her.

Suddenly, when they were only steps from the Bluff, Gypsy crouched low in the ferns and bared her teeth in a snarl. Freddy grabbed Sarah back by the waist so that they were hidden behind the breadth of a tree trunk, mossy wet against their backs. He had one hand firmly about her and the other under his coat where earlier she'd seen that a pistol had been holstered. Now he pulled it free. The sight of it and the feel of his body firm against hers sent Sarah's pulse galloping.

Gypsy pounced.

An opossum with black eyes stood on its

hind legs, hissed like a creature twice its size, then scurried off.

Behind Sarah, Freddy's chest heaved with relief. He lowered the gun but did not release her. In the absence of movement, she was keenly aware of the loud rustle of trees, the drip of rainwater all around. The wind moved the grand patchwork of leaves overhead like a kaleidoscope, so that looking up made her dizzy. She steadied herself against Freddy. The rhythm of his heart palpitated through the center of her back. She put a hand to her chest and could not decipher which beats belonged to whom.

"Only an opossum," he whispered in her ear. She nodded. She knew.

Using his free hand, he slowly turned her. "You're safe," he consoled her, drawing her cheek close.

She was trembling. He smelled of barn tackle, lemon, and spice. She lifted her chin to face him, and without warning, his lips were on hers. She didn't pull away. Instead, she leaned in, allowing the flame to consume her. It was all she'd ever imagined — too quickly come and gone. Potent as a drug.

Gypsy bounded back to their side with a yip, and they parted. Freddy flushed. Sarah was sure she did the same.

Her first kiss. In every romantic novel

she'd read, there'd been a chapter break upon the kiss. In every painting, a suspended moment. She was unsure what one said after. But they weren't lovers on a stroll, she reminded herself. A man's family had been divided and he might have been murdered beneath these very trees. It shamed her afresh.

She pointed ahead. "Through there."

Out from beneath the canopy, the sky opened crisp as an apple cut wide. New Charlestown was haloed in the plumes of morning fires. The piercing sun had yet to burn through the haze below. Sarah had never been there so early.

Gypsy nervously paced the wood line, unwilling to venture onto the boulder. Keeping her guard over them, she lay down on a pine-needle bed to wait for their return to solid ground.

Sarah went to the sandstone circle and took out her onionskin paper. She quickly sketched the last portion of the panorama, but her mind was preoccupied with the scene that had just passed: Freddy's mouth on hers; the taste of pumpkin; the smell of rawhide; the leaves singing. She wished she could paint all of those feelings.

Below, a farmer with a wagon full of his harvest drove across the village square.

Sarah could only make out the contents by color: red.

Civil unrest was mounting. The country was on the brink of gashing in two. She in the North. Freddy in the South. It was like Auntie Nan's *Tempest.* Her eyes welled.

"You're right. It's the clearest view of the pass I've ever seen," said Freddy. "Your canvas will be extraordinary." He turned to her. "*You're* extraordinary." Clearing his throat, he ceremoniously took her hand in his. "Sarah," he began.

The gravity of his tone and the formality of his touch made her stiffen.

He studied her fingers. "I know this isn't the time, but I'm not sure when . . ." He faced her with shoulders squared. "I love you, Sarah . . . and I think you love me, too." He looked toward the village in the distance, then back at her. "I want you to stay in New Charlestown. Not in danger, as a Brown, but in safest keep — as my wife, a Hill. I want us to make a family together. That is to say, I'd like to marry you, Sarah."

His stare was earnest; his hands, hot. Her own went clammy.

Hearing that he loved her had nearly sent her flying off the cliff top. Then, in the same instant, she'd fallen. Was that how love felt?

Her seed of belief had sprouted fruit. But

she couldn't harvest such a life. A family: wife and a houseful of children at Freddy's knee. She couldn't give him what he asked for and deserved.

How desperately she wished things were different — wished she could say yes and live the rest of her days painting, working in partnership with Freddy, freeing their enslaved brethren, the two of them loving each other. Just the two of them. But those were the fantasies of a silly girl. To put her own desires before his meant she must love him less. She hated herself — body and spirit — for her failures. If she disregarded the reality, Freddy would come to hate her, too, for not making good on the vision he sought for his life. She couldn't bear for him or their UGRR collaboration to suffer because of an impractical decision she made now.

Sarah pulled her hand free from his and let it drop to her side. Deflated and nearly more grief-stricken than when her father had been put to death, she turned to face the abyss.

Sarah Brown, Sarah Brown, Sarah Brown, who will love you now? She'd proven her mother wrong after all.

"I can't." She choked and felt the air grow cold behind her.

Freddy paused for so long Sarah had to shut her eyes to endure it.

"Don't you care for me?" he finally asked.

She held herself steely. She had to be strong, for him, for her. "Oh, Freddy, why must you go and spoil us."

"But . . . what was that back there?" He was wounded, and it stabbed Sarah equally. "Tell me you don't love me."

She didn't dare turn to him. "Not in the way you deserve to be loved. I admire you greatly, Freddy. You're the dearest person to me."

"Is there no hope that you'll come to love me?"

"Not in that way . . ." Her voice broke. "Don't you see that it would be unkind? We'd become bitter and unfulfilled by the humdrums of marriage."

When he discovered her inability to bear children, how could it be any other way? He'd said he wanted to make a family. It would be cruel of her to allow his affections to continue.

"I can't. You see, I . . ." It was not something to speak of. Her wounded womb, too shameful. "I just can't . . ."

"Is there someone else?"

She faced him. She couldn't stand for him to think she loved another. "No, no one,

352

Freddy. I care for you better than anyone in the world. Let's go on being as we are. Eternal friends."

Freddy guffawed. His jaw set tight. He looked past her to the horizon. "Friendship isn't enough. I want your love. So where does that leave us?"

"Forgive me." It was all she could say.

His gaze cast downward to New Charlestown. "There's nothing to forgive. I'm the fool. I deceived myself into thinking you felt the way I do."

The morning mist had evaporated, and the village stood stark. Below, a shepherd herded his lambs into an alley for the butcher to pick his choice.

Back at the Hills' house, Sarah wept bitterly in the guest room. She wondered if it wasn't better to be born into lack — deaf, mute, sightless, orphaned, loveless — so that you'd never know life any other way. The memory of blessings now absent seemed an unendurable curse. Losing Freddy was agonizing. She understood her sister-in-law Martha's torture and Mrs. Storm's suffering.

Annie entered as Sarah's sobs gave way to labored hiccups.

She studied her, baffled. "Come now, sister, be strong. We can give in to our emotions once safely home." She fussed with their luggage. "I packed your bag."

Sarah turned her face toward the pillow, wishing Annie were a thousand miles away and also glad she wasn't.

"Where did you go?" Seeing a broken leaf clinging to Sarah's boot, she put down the bags and came to her bedside. "Something to do with Freddy?"

Though Sarah thought herself empty of tears, the mention of his name crushed her like a cider press. Annie ran her hand over Sarah's poplin skirt, soothing her in the old ways.

"He loves you. It's as plain as the nose on his face. Is that what happened? You told him of your female inabilities and he rejected you?"

Sarah hadn't ever discussed the subject with Annie or even her mother. She couldn't imagine speaking of it to anyone else, particularly the man for whom she cared so deeply.

"He asked me to marry him." Sarah gulped. "And I refused."

She expected Annie's expression to be one of sympathy and comfort; instead, her sister strode from the bed in a fury.

"You are an *idiot,* Sarah Brown," she seethed. "I thought perhaps he'd confessed his feelings for you. But romantic charms and a marriage proposal are *entirely* different. You *refused*?"

Sarah sat up on the bed. Her temper lit. Anger felt slightly better than grief. "What else could I do!"

Annie came within inches of her face, pointing a bony finger. "Married him, you witless girl. He was your chance. Now you've gone and condemned yourself to spinsterhood when you could've been a wife!"

Sarah reached to grab Annie's finger and snap it like a twig, but Annie pulled away. "I can't have children, Annie!" she hissed.

"So what! He wouldn't know that until at least a year after the wedding, and by then, vows would've been made. You would've been secured in a home of your own with a new family, prosperous in-laws, a husband with an income and a future," she railed under her breath. "You wouldn't be poor anymore, living off the charity of richer men. You wouldn't have to be afraid. You wouldn't have to be a Brown! You'd be a Hill. All that *and* love?" She screwed up her face in disgust, then turned from Sarah to the vanity, where she fingered the plaster water pitcher. "There are those of us who would do anything for that opportunity.

Anything. You're a grown woman, sister. It's time to put away childish flower fables and gallant ideas. They didn't do Father or our brothers any good."

"You would have me lie to him? Trick him into a fruitless marriage for my own sake." Sarah shook her head. "Father would be ashamed of the pitiful woman you've become." She stood then, trembling. "Go back to North Elba. A small, *insignificant* life suits you. Not me."

Sarah's voice was hoarse from crying. The girls stood facing each other: two wounded women speared through by truth.

Then Annie sat on the edge of the bed with her back to Sarah. "Maybe you're right about me. But you're wrong about marriage. You've tricked yourself into believing it some idealistic portrait and only you know its secret. Do you think Mother was besotted with Father when they wed?" She turned her cheek to her shoulder to wipe away a tear. Her voice gave no hint of it. "She confessed to me that she thought him a terrifying old man with hair gone gray and patchy like the trees in December. She wanted spring, not winter. But she was sixteen and already once a widow. Young men want young wives, yet untouched. Had she ascribed to your sentimentalism, she might've lived her whole life in mourning clothes at the impoverished knee of her kin. A financial and social burden.

"Father was a good match, a step up in the world, with money and security. She learned to love him with the respect and gratitude so described in the Word. She gave him a family. She stood by him through joy, struggle, death, and disgrace. She did her duties with honor. We wouldn't be in this world if it weren't for that *insignificant* life."

Sarah bit the inside of her cheek, cursing her words. It never failed that when she unleashed her tongue in spite, it scorched everyone — including herself. She wished she could undo it. She wasn't surprised by their mother's confession. She'd always known her parents' marriage had been one of reverence, not love. They shared very little beyond common children.

"Had they loved each other madly, we might never have been born," continued Annie, adjusting her bodice and facing Sarah with renewed poise. "You've seen the couples doe-eyed for one another. The wife wants to dote on her husband instead of her children, and the husband worries that each new expectancy will harm his wife. Covetousness."

Sarah didn't agree but held her tongue as

recompense for earlier.

"Perhaps your refusal was best for everyone." Annie straightened her shoulders. "Had you said yes, you'd feel you would've been *lying*. And your *lust* for Freddy would've incited you to live in *greedy* affection. Three deadly sins accumulated before exchanging vows. Add your failure to bear his seed . . ." Annie smoothed her skirt and stood. "Forgive me for my words against your decision. We each have our own Pilgrim's Progress to follow." She took up the handles of her carpetbag and quickly left the room.

Lies, lust, greed? Sarah's anger flared. Annie should've been looking into the vanity mirror as she spoke! Sarah hid her face in her palms. She'd never felt so alone.

"Father," she whispered, "what can I do to make it right?"

She wasn't sure if she entreated the human or the heavenly or if they were fused into one now. What she was certain was that for the rest of her life, the question would haunt her.

EDEN

New Charlestown, West Virginia
August 2014

On the couch, Cricket slept against Eden's thigh, making it sweaty, but she didn't move him. His breathing was a lullaby. In and out. In and out. Life abiding. She wondered when that instinct kicked in. It had not been so for her unborn children, yet here slept a small soul for whom it had. It had for Denny and Jessica's baby, too.

Hans Christian Andersen had been kind to grant Thumbelina's mother her fairy wish. If only God would be so benevolent. Listen to her: God, fairies. She scolded herself for blending make-believe and truth; though, really, she wasn't sure where one stopped and the other started.

An accident, Denny had said. As if finding a doll in the root cellar or forgetting to buy more eggs at Milton's were comparable to a pregnancy: an everyday twist of fate. But she didn't want Denny to think she judged him or Jessica. Their lives, their child. She would be there to support him, just as she always had.

After his jog, Jack had quickly showered, then gone to the city. A working Saturday: a big Aqua Systems investor was in town. Combing her fingers through Cricket's fur now, she was grateful she had a chance to compose herself before he returned. She was exhausted from insomnia and needed time to make sense of things. Alone.

The slow melody of Denny's guitar floated down from upstairs, no louder than a tinny music box. He'd always sought a sound track to his life. A logical melody he could follow. She'd leave him to it.

Daylight was waning in the late-August sky. A dust mote swirled golden through a slanting ray. She watched it dance as if on puppet strings, bobbing on the updraft of Cricket's sleeping breath.

The kitchen door opened and shut.

"Jack?" she called out gently, not wanting to wake Cricket.

Cleo's head popped around the living room wall, looking as disembodied as the porcelain doll's.

"Nope. Just me. Cricket's dinnertime — he eat?"

Eden nodded. "Leftover chicken soup and a biscuit."

"Oh, okay — when he's ready, I can walk him." But instead of walking anywhere, she sat down beside Eden. Her sandaled feet dangled off the couch. "I've been figuring," she said decisively. "Mr. Anderson hired me for the week, so technically my duties are done, and I'm owed my paycheck."

"Yes, of course." Eden was a firm believer in honoring contracts. She tapped her chin with a finger. Her wallet was empty, and she'd already given Cleo the twenty bucks from the laundry hamper. She could check all of Jack's pant pockets, but she doubted she'd find enough to make the total sum. Plus, she simply hadn't the get-up-and-go for a treasure hunt.

"Jack's got the cash. Do you mind waiting for him to come home?"

She expected Cleo to nod affirmatively, resolved in her coming salary, which was a heap more than Eden had ever earned tending neighborhood plants and pets at her age. Instead, Cleo frowned and picked Cricket's hairs off her shorts.

"Actually, Miss A, I was hoping we could make a deal so as I can keep on working for y'all. You see, I was on the Internet and started thinking about your idea to sell

CricKet BisKets."

"My idea to *what*?" Eden thought back through the last few days and couldn't recall ever saying as much.

"Sell. CricKet. BisKets," Cleo repeated slowly, as if Eden had a hearing impairment.

Eden pursed her lips. She was curious as to where Little Miss Moxie was headed.

"I looked it up, and gourmet dog food is B-I-G. There's a ton of it everywhere, but there's no biscuits like ours in New Charlestown or within a fifty-mile radius. I Google-Mapped it. No organic pet treats. Sure, you can order 'em from the city or California or something, but they aren't *retail accessible*."

She enunciated the last bit like she'd just read it in an online article. Eden hid her smirk. It wasn't a completely outrageous idea.

"I talked to Mr. Morris and Ms. Silver-dash today," she continued. "Told them all about our pumpkin biscuits and even brought samples from what we baked yesterday. Mr. Morris called them 'Garden of Eden turtle food,' but he thought they tasted pretty good. He said if they'd've been entered in the Dog Days End Festival Baking Division, he'd never have known they were for dogs, not people." Her breath came gleefully fast. "So I jumped on that and asked if he and Ms. Silverdash would let us — you and me — sell CricKet BisKets at the festival. I'd help you do *everything*! And in return for using your kitchen and idea, you wouldn't have to owe me a dime — not even the seventy dollars from this week. We could use that money for logos, packaging, and advertising instead. See, I got it totally worked out!"

"Advertising?" At most, Eden had envisioned a plate of biscuits sold for a quarter each. Now Cleo was talking about logos and packaging?

"I watch the *Shark Tank* show with Grandpa. Good marketing is key. Didn't you say you used to work in advertising stuff?" Cleo screwed up her nose.

Eden was equal parts stunned and impressed. Her public relations wheels were spinning, and she wondered why nobody had snatched up the idea before. While the festival's name was a reference to summer's end, it was also a direct nod to dogs. And she *did* know a company from whom they could order simple cellophane wrappers at warehouse pricing. The owner had done promo materials at the PR agency. Everything from logo-emblazoned quill pens to candy Pop Rocks. If they had an image, a CricKet BisKet mascot . . . In a flash, she saw the whole thing. It wouldn't take her more than a phone call. A local festival. A few dozen biscuits.

Like Cleo said, it could be their shark tank trial analysis. Who knew — if it went well, she might not need the house to sell as premium historical real estate. She wouldn't need the doll to be anything but an old doll. This could be her ticket to financial security. She could be a business owner, like Ms. Silverdash. The Mrs. Fields of the dog cookie world! Well . . . Miss. She and Cleo could share the title: Miss CricKet BisKets.

"It would have to be well done," she agreed. "Nothing half-baked. And I'm going to need your solemn oath to help me."

Cleo bounced on the couch. Cricket woke, yawned, and repositioned himself with his nose tucked into the bend of Eden's knee.

Cleo lifted one palm. "I do solemnly swear *never* to leave you alone in the kitchen and to help you do everything." She extended her finned hand. "Shakes?"

Eden shook. "Deal. And may I say, you have quite the gift of persuasion. I'd take you into a boardroom any day."

At the compliment, Cleo pulled her top lip between her teeth to conceal the grin. "To be a real detective, you've got to know how to get folks to see things differently. The rope in the attic is never just a rope in the attic." She pulled out her pad. "I haven't forgotten the case of the Apple Hill doll's head, either. On Pinterest, I saw some that look like yours, but they all got bodies attached. None with different-colored eyes either. That's just weird."

Eden had discovered just as much in her own searches but was glad to have a corroborating accomplice.

"That reminds me — we found more. A button, we think."

Cleo raised her pencil high, like an exclamation in the air. "Another clue!" She scribbled on her detective pad. Serious business. "In the cellar?"

Eden nodded. "A broken doll's head, a not-so-old key, and a rusty button. If these walls could talk."

"My grandpa says if walls could talk, they wouldn't need us humans. Coming and going so fast. We'd probably annoy them, thinking every minute is the first of its kind."

Eden laughed. Such an odd kid. Cleo was perpetually making Eden see the world in a topsy-turvy way.

"The new evidence is in the kitchen, if you care to take a look, Detective."

"I think I best," she said and went to

investigate.

The screen door clapped before the wooden one swung inward. Cricket bounded off the couch, attuned to the sound of new company.

" 'Ello, 'ello," Jack said to them both.

His salt-and-pepper hair was soft and disheveled by the wind, making him look more awake and vibrant than he had in months. His face was clean-shaven and flushed. From the heat or the haste of homecoming, whatever it was, it pleased her, and she felt the old prickle of affection spill down her spine. She'd missed that — missed him — more than she'd realized.

From behind his back, he pulled a nosegay of petite damask roses shaded blood-red to the lightest pink. True damasks looked like petticoats aflutter and smelled richly of springtime. They were her favorites. She recalled the crushed rose from earlier in the week and was ashamed she'd disregarded it so.

"Take two?" Jack put up his left hand in mock defense. "Just these. No more Crickets, I swear."

Cricket clucked at his name.

"You've gone and hurt the poor guy's feelings." Eden smiled. "Besides, I'm starting to wonder if the dog isn't one of those 'blessings in disguise' I've heard tales about."

A lump formed in her throat after she said that, thinking again of Denny's *accident*. She breathed in the roses' fragrance and bottled the emotions.

"A blessing in disguise — you don't say?" Jack studied her for a moment, then turned to the door. "Did the evangelists come calling today? Have you been converted in my absence?"

She rolled her eyes. "They're lovely."

"Am I forgiven?"

Truthfully, she didn't know if his request was in reference to their argument on Monday, something from the day before, or that morning. So many weeks and months of grief between them; so many hostile words and angry nights. It made her tired to remember: the blame, the bitterness . . . *Can't throw out the baby with the bathwater,* her mother used to say. They had no baby, just bathwater, so could they start fresh? She inhaled the nosegay's scent deeper. Eden and Jack Anderson of New Charlestown.

"Yes," she said.

Forgiveness. She wanted that, no matter what.

Cleo returned holding the button.

"Nice flowers. What'd ya do wrong?"

"Why, you cheeky monkey," Jack laughed. "Only a fool would give an account of his offenses when the noose has been removed!"

"A fool or a righteous man," Eden countered.

"Miss Cleo, which do you think me?"

She plumped out her bottom lip and shrugged.

"It's a coin toss, I know," he said.

"No coins, but I got a button."

Jack gave Eden a puzzled look. Eden waved a hand to imply that she'd explain later.

"By all means then, toss away."

"Call it, Mr. A."

"Tails."

Cleo flicked the button into the air, then caught it to reveal the braided face. "Heads."

"I guess I'm a fool then." He gave a lopsided grin to Eden, and her pulse quickened.

She'd take the honest fool over the self-righteous man any day. Upstairs, Denny's guitar had stopped. Accident, blessing in disguise, fate, fortune, or happenstance — they were definitions of the same: life with no guaranteed happy ending. What fable and history could agree upon was that

everybody was searching for their ever-after,
whatever that may be.

Concord, Mass., December 1, 1860

Dear Freddy,

Please say you forgive me. I know you said no forgiveness was necessary, but I need it all the same. After the profound silence on the journey to the station in September, I told myself that October was a restoration of our friendship. But then November came with still no word. I made myself wait until this first of December to write.

Annie is home in North Elba while I continue at Mr. Sanborn's school. I've worked on my New Charlestown canvas daily. The report of Mr. Storm's gruesome death increased my resolve that this monstrous oppression in our land be forthwith obliterated! My greatest hope is that you will approve of the portrait and I will have been of some use to the greater good.

Please, write me and let me know how it is there. With Lincoln's election and the Black Republicans in power, the newspapers from the South are as unsettling as your silence.

Your eternal friend,
Sarah

New Charlestown, Virginia, January 2,
1861

Dear Sarah,
No happier New Year greeting than your letter. The mail is running slow. I received your December 1st post on the 31st. I suppose I ought to be grateful it arrived at all, given the rumors of mail pilfering.

October was, as you presumed, a period of repair. You know my affections for you, so I needn't explain why. With the turmoil of the elections and the results viewed by a majority as disastrous, November was a wearisome month for its own purposes.

Then Father was stricken with a case of Piles and to his great dismay was condemned to lie stomach-down for over two weeks, on doctor's orders. While not life-threatening, it was not a condition Alice, Siby, or I could attenuate. He would only allow Mother to nurse his "wound," and she fretted over his every discomfort so that we didn't see either until nearly the week of Christmas.

When I said there was nothing to forgive, I meant it. Unconditional rapport means you take no offense in the first place — be it in friendship or otherwise; you seek the good and best in the other person, and as you seek, so shall you find. Isn't that what the Gospel commands? My father and yours would say 'tis so. However, I know how your mind tumults . . . so if you insist, then rest assured in this: we are two of eternal absolution.

Please give my warmest regards to Mrs. Brown, Annie, and little Ellen. I pray this letter puts to rest any discord between us, Sarah. There is already enough in this precarious time. We are faithful to our northern friends as they are loyal to us despite our southern latitude. We look forward to seeing your New Charlestown portrait complete, if you still intend to share it with us.

Eternally yours,
Freddy

Concord, Mass., January 29, 1861

Dear Freddy,

I am nothing short of jubilant! Thank you for alleviating my fear that our time in Virginia might've been the last. I could not go on if that were so.

I'm glad your father recovered from his sickbed. Rubeola, scurvy, smallpox, while more life-threatening, are far easier to battle under the care of loved ones. Even in death, family gathers round. It's the suffering we can't share that torments the most . . .

At the present speed of the mail service, I wanted you to know as soon as possible that your letters henceforth should be posted to me at: Fort Edward Institute, Saratoga, N.Y. I am moving there to study under the full tutelage of Mary Artemisia Lathbury. We got on so well this summer, Mary being a mere five years my elder and already lauded across the country — North and South — for her stories, illustrations, hymnals, and diligent work with our mutual friends.

Please give my love and affection to the Hills and Fishers. And a special head rub to Gypsy, if you please.

Eternally your friend,
Sarah

P.S. I am working on my New Charlestown canvas this very hour and plan to share it forthwith upon completion. Hearing from you has catalyzed my efforts!

EDEN

New Charlestown, West Virginia
August 2014

It was the Friday before the Dog Days End Festival. Eden successfully prepared Bulldog's Buffaloaf for dinner without a burnt smidgen. She ceremoniously placed the loaf on a cake stand between the trays of cooling CricKet BisKets. But with no one to witness, it felt a hollow triumph.

Cleo had just gone home. A *Jeopardy!* tournament was in progress, and she had it in mind to win the last cents necessary to open her own Bronner Bank account in anticipation of the bazillions she was certain they'd earn at the festival booth that weekend.

Earlier in the day, she'd come over with Suley Hunter to lend a hand in mixing, cutting, and baking dozens of pumpkin (Original) and apple (Apple Hill) CricKet BisKets.

"She may be a couple years younger than me, but she's real good at cooking," Cleo had explained while Suley was at the sink washing her hands. "Has to be. Hunter kids would starve otherwise. Mrs. Hunter baked some raisin bread for a church picnic once. Mr. Morris said not even the ants took to it."

Cleo was right. Suley needed no instructions. She joined their baking assembly line like a well-oiled gear. Eden had loved the girls' company in the kitchen. The giddy chatter over butter and flour, pumpkin and apples; the sight of their ponytails swishing back and forth as they stirred. Both eager to create something — to put their magic touch to an adult vision. All grown up, Eden couldn't say she'd grown out of that yearning. Maybe no child ever did.

Denny had gone out for beers and burgers, depressed that even the managers offering the most trivial positions had said they were considering others. He'd been on daily interviews. Positions ranging from a statesman's personal gofer to a dishwasher at the Willard Hotel's Café du Parc. His lack of a college degree held him under the "solid salary" echelon, but he couldn't go back to sharing a dirty apartment with a crew of revolving bandmates and what —

use the hookah stand as a high chair, sing Def Leppard lullabies? Ludicrous.

He was at a logjam: no going back, no moving forward.

"My last hurrah before I'm eating rice cereal," he'd said on the phone.

"At least that's organic."

Eden's attempt at a joke garnered little more than a grunt. She worried about him, but this was one journey he had to travel alone. She couldn't carry him, not even a step. The weight of her own life was all she could bear.

Jack had just flown back from Austin, Texas, and was upstairs changing.

Before he'd left for that week's trip, Eden had roused him from the couch, hoping to finally get him alone after everything with Jessica.

"Jack," she'd whispered. "Jack, wake up."

The early hour had a waning-days-of-summer nip to it and made her long for autumn to hurry in with its cozy way, change the leaves to bright oranges and blazing reds, give the summer of their discontent a new dress. She'd placed his roses in a glass jelly jar on the telephone stand, and they seemed to have blushed deeper overnight.

"Want to walk with us? Cleo has church

this morning."

She'd bent down to the couch to scoop up Cricket, and a wavy lock of hair fell down across his cheek. He didn't brush it away.

"Yes, of course, yes." He stumbled over himself to find his sneakers, then joined them on the porch.

Apple Hill Lane on a Sunday morning was quiet. The congregants had set off to sing their hymns while the rest remained blissfully bedded. For once, there were very few neighbors out on the lawns and porches. Only the sound of sprinklers spattering round and round. A dewy haze clung to the ground, the earth cooler than the ether. Cricket wandered aimlessly through the pea soup, relying on their lead for direction.

"Here." Eden passed Jack a paw-printed leash with matching collar she'd picked up at Milton's.

"Does this mean we're keeping him? In sickness and health, rabies and fleas?"

She couldn't very well sell CricKet Bis-Kets with no Cricket, and she'd grown fond of him. It wouldn't feel like home without him there.

"We do."

"Cricket Norton Anderson," Jack proclaimed, giving him a good scratch behind the ear. "Welcome, little bug man. I don't know how you did it, but you've won the lady over."

They set off slowly down the sidewalk.

"I wanted to talk to you. I think you already know, but . . . Jessica is pregnant with Denny's baby."

He stopped but didn't put on a veneer of shock. She felt grateful. She wasn't in the mood to play games.

"So, he did tell you."

He nodded.

"What advice did you give him?"

"At first I told him to marry the girl. He didn't appreciate that perspective."

She smirked, conflicted between loving Jack's old-school chivalry and knowing that it simply wasn't the way things were done anymore. It wasn't practical, even if morally sound.

"I told him to support Jessica and show her that he accepts full accountability as a participating parent. He said they hadn't decided what they planned to do yet."

Denny had said the same to her the morning Jessica left.

"To be honest, I'm rather pissed at the guy."

"Don't judge him, Jack. He's trying to make good." She put her arm through the crook of his and pulled him forward.

"Not for that reason. I understand even the best of us make mistakes — acting out in ways we regret the minute the deed is done. But you can't undo it."

He cleared his throat, and she knew he must've been thinking of her and her unfounded outbursts over the last many months. He'd stuck by her despite it all. He'd known what she could not say in those moments: that she was sorry.

"I'm angry at him for telling you. I specifically told him to exercise diligence. If I may speak plainly." He exhaled sharply, but his voice was gentle. "You're just coming round to your old self, Eden, and I was afraid . . ."

She rubbed his arm, the muscles taut. "He didn't tell me. I figured it out." He studied her face, and she smiled reassuringly. "After everything we've been through, the irony is not lost. It shook me up a little, I won't lie, but then I realized how egocentric that was. It's about Jessica and Denny and their baby, not me."

For seven years, it'd been about her and Jack and what they couldn't create. She'd allowed self-pity to devour her. No more. Like the tale of Jonah and the whale, it was time to climb out of the belly of the beast.

Jack straightened his arm so that her hand

slid down. He laced his fingers in hers, and they walked hand in hand. Something they hadn't done since they were dating, and even then it had seemed a gesture of high school sweethearts, not people their age. She liked it, though. The security of their woven palms.

Cricket pulled at the leash. Jack gave him more slack. "Do you think Jessica will go through with the pregnancy?" he asked. "I imagine terminating would be easier for someone in her spot."

Eden had wondered the same thing. *What would I do if I were in Jessica's shoes? Would I sacrifice my college education, my career aspirations, meeting Jack, and the rest if it meant I'd have a child now?*

"It's not an easy decision either way. It requires ownership of the outcome. Shaking a fist at nature or God is far easier than questioning what you did or didn't do in the situation."

Was she talking about Jessica or herself?

"I don't envy either of them right now. That's why we have to be there for Denny. Whatever they decide."

No. It came to her suddenly, like a gunshot. She wouldn't trade Jack and all they'd known together for a child. She wouldn't give back one minute of the years or look over her shoulder wondering what could've been. Fear was a deceptive lover, and she was tired of sharing her bed with it. She had Jack. She squeezed his hand in hers, and the idea of ever separating pained her. She inhaled deeply to ease the cramp of remorse.

A yard of late-summer azaleas honeyed the air.

"Thanks again for the flowers."

"I'm glad I got them right this time."

She shook her head and studied the gray concrete sidewalk, mindful to step over the crack of each partitioned square.

"I've been a pill to live with."

"You've been through a lot. The hormones," he pointed out, defending her, even in this.

"Hormones or not, there's never an excuse for hurting the people you love. This baby stuff has made me feel like I lost my mind." She sighed. "I'm just so tired of it all. I want my life back. I want *our* life back."

He stopped walking again and turned to her. "I've only ever wanted whatever made you happy. Bollocks! We tried to make this picture-perfect family develop — whether it was meant to be or not, we didn't stop to consider. But there's no *forcing* fate or joy or love."

Her eyes welled, and she didn't stop them. "We tried — we tried *every* way."

It was the first break she'd allowed him to see in a long time. Instead of looking at her with pity, he cupped her chin. "Doesn't mean we stop believing in unexpected miracles."

She leaned into his hand, wishing it could hold the whole of her. Cricket circled, and the leash tangled them closer.

"Like Cricket," he said, wrapping his arms around her to keep them from falling.

The Presbyterian church's bells rang out a tuneless *bong, bong, bong.* The early service had ended, the next one beginning. Only a wisp of fog was left, the rest burned clear by the coming day. Cricket curled himself over Eden's sandaled feet. Yes, like Cricket, but it was more than that. It was everything about this place. New Charlestown.

An ice-cream truck's song began after the bells had ceased: Vee making her church rounds. And then Eden remembered the National Register of Historical Places application, Cleo and their CricKet BisKet business, the doll and key, and all she'd set in secret motion. Maybe those things weren't the pot of gold at the end of her marriage but a bread-crumb trail in the direction of a new beginning.

Across the kitchen now, the doll's head watched her.

Eden gestured to the meat loaf. "I did it." She took off her oven mitts. "I'd offer you a taste, but seeing as you have no stomach . . ." She pulled out a knife and sliced three pieces, scooping the first, still steaming, onto a plate.

"Supper's ready!"

Cricket's body continued to rise and fall steadily in slumber.

Jack, alone, heeded her call. "Smells good."

He was barefoot and wore dark jeans with a white T-shirt. She rarely saw him in casual clothes anymore, but then she'd rarely seen him at all since they'd moved in. The change was nice.

Her thumb slipped into the warm center of the slice she was serving. She licked it clean and was happy to find that the dish tasted as good as it looked. "That one can be mine."

Jack took the plate and ate with his fingers before she had a chance to raise a complaint.

"Damned good," he mumbled.

"Jack . . ." She shook her head at his

messy hands.

"What?"

She sighed with a smile. What — nothing. What — everything. "Let me get you a fork at least." She went to the drawer, but before she'd turned around, he'd finished eating.

"I'll take another, if I may."

He set the empty plate beside the pan. While she served a second slice, he came to her side of the island, his toes touching hers. And there it was again: Jack's minty cedar smell making her knees go weak.

God, she wanted him to kiss her. Wanted to kiss him. But it'd been so long, she'd forgotten how to be intimate without the goal of conception. She'd forgotten how to make love. So while everything within her pulled like a magnet, her flesh remained rooted to the kitchen tiles. *Please,* she thought, *please help me, Jack.*

Cricket yelped suddenly, swimming his arms and legs in chase, his eyes closed, teeth bared.

Jack reached down to the dog, but Eden stopped him. She recalled a story she'd heard on NPR's *Weekend Edition.* A docile pit bull had attacked a pound volunteer who'd attempted to wake him from a fitful dream. By all other accounts, it was a gentle animal, abandoned by an owner who'd trained him as a guard dog against his better nature. While being stitched up in the ER, the volunteer had begged for the staff not to euthanize the animal. The program host argued that human or canine, the unconscious couldn't be controlled.

"He's dreaming," said Eden. She sat on the ground at a distance and called him gently out of it: "Cricket, you're dreaming. Cricket . . ."

The long eyelashes fluttered, struggling through the malaise. The dog's legs went stiff, extended outward in a good stretch, and then he yawned awake.

Eden pulled him into her lap. "Hey there, baby?" His body was feverish. "Did you get it — whatever it was?"

He licked at her neck and face, and she didn't move him away. Nuzzled him closer instead.

Jack knelt down beside them. "How did you know to do that?"

She shrugged. "I just knew."

Jack rubbed Cricket's neck, and the pup leaned toward him from Eden's embrace.

"You're good at this," said Jack.

"Holding a dog?"

He smiled. "Mothering."

"I'm not a mother." The word still stabbed. She looked down at the furry bundle in her arms. Cricket's tail fanned her with each wag.

"I disagree." Jack's countenance turned serious. "You've changed."

"From shooing poor Cricket out the door to doting, yes, yes."

"It's more than that. It's in how you are with Cleo, too. And taking the job at the bookstore with the children."

"You've never seen me at the bookstore," she retorted for argument's sake. Old habits died hard.

"I don't need to see you with children to see you," he said, and she understood that he meant more than her role as storyteller. "I've always wanted you to have whatever you wanted, Eden. If it was a child, so be it. But that was never a *requirement* of mine. I never envisioned that as an absolute part of my life. Not like I did you."

Tears blurred her vision, and she fought them. She wanted to believe him. Their Apple Hill walk had been the peace talk. Now came the treaty terms: a life together without kids? Could she re-dream her dream? Maybe, just maybe, the future needed to unfold as it might. No dreaming or scheming.

The thought was exhilarating in its lack of obligation, unburdened by personal responsibility to make the broken pieces something whole. Eden realized then that she'd been trying to put life's puzzle together based on what she thought the picture should look like, without a master guide. She'd been maddeningly unsuccessful and had made a mess of everything. Worst of all, she'd convinced herself that Jack blamed her. In reality, it was she who pointed the finger at them both.

She'd been reaching for a child at the expense of her husband. It had made her miserable and lonely with the lie that only a baby could fill the void of her embrace. Jack had taken the thrashings, the cold silences, her inability to express her inner sorrow, every angry remark, and every bitter hour for years. Because he loved her even while she doubted her love for him. She'd considered them cursed, but now . . . She kissed him.

In their bedroom, their bodies took to each other instinctually. It was the first time they'd made love in New Charlestown and the first time in years that Eden had given herself without contemplating the outcome, good or bad. It was like it'd been at the beginning — no, it was better. Because in it was all they had lost and all they were gain-ing. In it was forgiveness and the promise of possibility.

Fort Edward Institute, Saratoga, N.Y.,
  April 14, 1861

Dear Freddy,
Please send word as soon as humanly
possible! No time for formalities — we
are at war! God help us. I am breathless
with worry and won't sleep a minute
until I receive news from you, Freddy.
I'll spend my nights in fervent prayer for
protection over you and all those I cher-
ish in New Charlestown.

Love,
Sarah

New Charlestown, Virginia, May 4,
  1861

Dear Sarah,
We are well in body, if troubled in spirit.
I'm sorry this letter comes at such delay.
I pray you have not been sleepless for
these many weeks.
  Mid-April, a northeast storm hit our
village with more merciless clout than
any militia attack. The roadways were
blocked by fallen trees and flooding. We
were cut off from all except our own

until the waters recessed and passage over the hilltops was cleared. We emerged to a world transformed, war and Virginia's secession.

Harpers Ferry is now under the rule of Virginia's new Confederate forces, slaveholders. New Charlestown was spared the infiltration of military forces due to our location betwixt the river ravines and storm damage. However, this moratorium will soon end, as armies on both sides are being called to arms.

Lincoln has suspended Habeas Corpus, sanctioning Yankees to judge and punish as they see fit. The Rebels have implemented similar practices. Soon every man will feel just in taking life on insult alone. A civilized nation has been degraded to anarchy. Mother believes we are living in the biblical Apocalypse. Father and I don't align with her. This is revolution, not rapture! And for that, we are ready to march with force to see our ways changed for the better. We will enlist in the Union Army.

Now, I have news that I do not write easily but I must send given the haste of this war. There is a girl here named Ruth Niles. She and her family are long-standing members of our church congregation and friends of shared trust. Her parents came to pay their respects the day of your father's passing. Ruth is the eldest of five siblings and so is familiarized with the duties of child rearing and running a household. A good girl. Father and Mother think it a sensible match and the Niles are highly enthusiastic, but . . . I feel as if I'm betraying her devotion with every thought of you.

Mother has repeatedly brought up your name in conversation, gauging my reaction, I believe. She knows, in the way only a mother can, to whom my true heart belongs. She's petitioned to take more time deciding, but unfortunately, time is not a luxury we are afforded. If Ruth and I are to wed, I must do so before I join the northern ranks. She would move into the house with Mother, Alice, and Siby while Father and I are away and would be of great comfort to them.

My biggest hesitation is the hope (as impractical as you may think) that you might reconsider my proposal. I pray for it every waking hour. I'm at an impasse, Sarah. I can't turn left or right, forward or backward. If you were to say that you merely needed time to think, I would immediately cease discussion of marrying another.

I love you. I feel no reticence in writing this because it is as true today as it will be a hundred years from now. However, if you are certain you hold no feelings for me, I will follow in the way convention leads and marry for companionship rather than love. Tell me what you wish, Sarah. I will do as you ask.

Eternally yours,
Freddy

Fort Edward Institute, Saratoga, N.Y.,
   May 25, 1861

Dear Freddy,
Marry Ruth Niles. She will bear you a good family, a future seeded with happiness and legacy. It would break my heart forever to see you grow old alone. Please, dear friend, you deserve a full life and home, as is God's will for every man. Marry, and quickly. I hate to think of you marching off to war without some adoring kiss good-bye, someone beckoning you to return safely. Of course, I wish you the same, but I recognize that

my friendship is, as you said, not enough. You merit more than enough.

Tell your family that if they need anything from us Browns, they need only send word, and we will be at their calling. I remain in Saratoga with Mary Lathbury. Please write me here from your military post, though I will harbor no ill will if you feel you cannot. It goes without saying that I am stricken . . . I will be praying daily for sovereign protection over you and your father.

Eternally your friend,
Sarah

New Charlestown, Virginia, June 30, 1861

Dear Sarah,

I am wed.

Though much of New Charlestown came to be witnesses, somberness pervaded the ceremony, knowing it to be the last village gathering without enmity between neighbors.

Father and I leave tomorrow for the District of Columbia, where thousands flock for Union enlistment. Those joining the Confederacy troops are off to Richmond.

Ruth is settling into the house with Siby and Mother. Alice, for whatever reason, has not taken kindly to her sister-in-law, though she's known her all her life. Mother believes it's the upheaval of everything — at home and across the land — that's affecting her mood. She will adjust. There is no alternative.

It would greatly gladden my heart if you'd be so good as to write Alice now and again. Your letters bring her much joy. If you have time left over, I, too, would be uplifted to hear from you, as my affections are unchanged.

I will send my military post address when I have one to provide.

Eternally yours,
Freddy

EDEN

New Charlestown, West Virginia
August 2014

They opened the bedroom window afterward. The night air was cold, steeped with the smell of fallen leaves and coming autumn. The breeze spilled goose bumps across their naked skin as they talked over the maple tree branches pattering the window. The ceiling medallion was no longer an eddy of monstrous teeth but a harvest sky of constellations in motion. Outside a nightjar began to call, *Whip-poor-will, whip-poor-will.*

They'd been talking for over an hour with Eden tucked into Jack's arms. She pulled slightly out of his cupped embrace to check the clock.

"Denny will be home."

Jack kissed her before rising. "I'd best wash up." He collected his shirt and pants and started for the bedroom door.

"There's a bathroom in here, you know." Eden pushed back her tousled hair. "It's nice. A waterfall shower."

"Oh?" He stopped. "Quite right. I remember ordering that fixture. It advertised, 'The supply of Niagara with the grace of a summer rain.' "

She laughed. "Well, it marked itself up a bit. You be the judge." She nodded to the master bathroom. "Please, don't go, Jack."

Even in the dim of the room, she could see his glad expression. He bowed and dropped his clothes back to the floor.

Eden wasn't ready to leave the warmth of their bed and snuggled back into the rumpled sheets. She felt like a teenager again, minus the twinge in her hips. Perhaps not that young — mid-twenties, she decided — and played with a curl of her hair, spinning it round and round her finger like yarn on a spindle.

He left the door cracked so that a sliver of light cut clean through the darkness. The shower began.

"Jack Anderson, Jack Anderson," she whispered to herself, and then: "Jack and Eden. The Andersons of New Charlestown."

There was a rising magic in the incantation, as if *they* were finally made true by it being spoken aloud. She gazed out the window at the gypsum moon. A V of geese sliced through it.

Suddenly, Jack's cell phone pealed from the floor. She leaned over the mattress edge and dug it out of his jeans pocket. An incoming text. Austin area code.

Having once been Jack's public relations attaché, she was familiar with the majority of his business contacts. The only people in Austin were big-ticket Aqua Systems investors. It might be important. So she pulled up the message and read:

Pauline: I'm sorry we couldn't get together this trip. Sounds like you had a busy week. Are you back Monday? Lulu and I are waiting on you for our next dessert date. The Hot Kiss cake ball was definitely my favorite. Love, P

Pauline? Lulu? The smell of Jack's shower was potent. Reminiscent of that rainy night when she'd discovered her father creeping back from his mistress's bed. She thought she might throw up.

The shower turned off. Jack came out, towel around his waist. The light silhouetted him, and steam rose from his skin. A ghoulish brume.

The breeze had taken an icy edge, stinging her nose.

"It's freezing," he said and closed the window.

She pulled her knees to her chest and wrapped her arms around them to shield herself. "The phone." She was surprised by the firmness of her voice. "A text . . . from Pauline."

Jack gave her a quizzical look, then reached for it.

"If you would, please take it outside," she said. She got up, pulling the sheet with her, picked up his jeans and shirt, and pushed them at him. "I mean, outside the house."

He scrolled on the phone; then his face went stark. "It's not what you think."

Her caustic laugh snapped the air. It was the best she could do to keep from crying. "Classic, Jack."

"Lulu is a child — Pauline's daughter!"

A distressing picture blossomed: Jack. Child. Mother. No wonder he didn't need her to have a baby — he already had one. An illegitimate child. An affair. How could she not have seen the signs?

His crumbling poise was more proof. Jack never lost his cool.

"Eden, please, it's not at all what it sounds like. She's an old friend I knew when I was twelve — before my parents' accident. I ran into her and her daughter on the plane months back. They live in Austin. We had cake balls."

"What is that, some kind of sick code? Hot Kiss cake balls? Please, Jack, spare me the spin-doctoring. Remember, I'm the one *you* once hired for it. I was a pro at turning bullshit into gold!"

"Cake balls are cake balls! It's not a euphemism. It is what it is. A Hot Kiss — bugger — I don't know why people put silly names to desserts time after time. Sex on the Beach drinks, Eton Messes, monkey breads!"

"Spin, spin, spin." She was shaking, enraged and hurt. "You know what is the same no matter how or when or what you name it? Adultery. And when a woman signs 'Love' to a married man, there's more than meets the eye. It's code for 'There are real, *big* feelings involved.' "

"It's code for Americans being too blasted chummy with each other!"

"I'll give you ten minutes to get your stuff, and then I swear to God, I'll call the police if I have to."

He calmed himself and pinched the bridge of his nose. "Eden, darling, I admit, I shouldn't have been meeting up with them without mentioning it to you. But I swear on my life, it was entirely innocent. She's going through a nasty divorce, and her daughter is suffering miserably —"

She'd heard enough and didn't care what trials this woman and her daughter faced. Suffering? What the hell kind of *cakewalk* did he think she'd been on?

"Get out," she growled, and he backed away onto the upper landing, covering himself with his balled-up jeans.

"Eden, this is madness."

She slammed the door. How dare he try to make her feel like she was — "Madness!" she yelled through the wood. "You'll see madness if you don't get your ass out of this house. You have eight minutes now."

The stairs creaked under his weight. Still standing in nothing but the bedsheet, she pressed her ear to the door and listened: Jack said something to Cricket; shoed footsteps clapped the floor; the screen door banged. Eden had wrung the sheet so tightly in her hands that it bound her like shackles. She loosened them. Her nail beds were shaded blue and cold from lack of circulation. She pulled on her robe and cracked the door.

Below, Cricket whined, but otherwise, the house was silent. Jack was gone. She came down and sat on the bottom step, taking Cricket into her lap and rubbing her fingers over his warm belly until they regained feeling.

"We forgot to feed you," she whispered. "I'm sorry. It won't happen again." She stood and carried him into the kitchen, where his plate of Buffaloaf sat on the countertop and the oven was still slightly warm.

THE AMERICAN TELEGRAPH COMPANY

TO MISS SARAH BROWN
RECEIVED AT SARATOGA, N.Y., JULY 5, 1862
FROM NEW CHARLESTOWN, (NEWLY RATI-
FIED) WEST VIRGINIA

FREDDY WAS SHOT IN THE SEVEN DAYS'
BATTLE. HE IS HOME. INFECTION HAS SET IN
HIS LEG. WE HAVE DONE ALL THAT WE CAN,
BUT HE WORSENS WITHOUT PROPER
MEDICINE. THE UNION BLOCKADE HAS
HALTED DELIVERIES TO VIRGINIA. IF ANY OF
OUR GOOD FRIENDS IN THE NORTH MIGHT
OFFER SOME AID, WE WOULD BE MUCH
OBLIGED. MRS. GEORGE HILL.

SARAH

Sarah had immediately sent word to Priscilla that she would take the southbound train to the capital. From there, a hired buggy transported her across Virginia's battle lines into the new state of West Virginia. Disguised as a Sister of Mercy, she wore a borrowed habit. In the heat of July, the wimple made her head itch considerably, but she would've worn a crown of thorns to get to Freddy.

She wasn't just going for him, either, she told herself. She was aiding friends who had sheltered and protected her at great personal risk. As vital members of the Underground Railroad, the Hills needed the abolitionist community to help them now. She was bringing the medicine Freddy required to stay alive, which would, in turn, help many more. Her father would have done the same.

"If you are determined in this venture, then your surest safety is to travel as a nun," Mary Lathbury had argued. "Rebels and Yankees are assaulting women of every age. They will rule their vulgar molestations as lawful, given the items you conceal."

Beneath the bulky frock, Sarah carried a purse containing three bars of antiseptic soap, a vial of iodine, and another of carbolic acid. It was illegal to bring these across enemy lines. They would be confiscated if found. Sarah's slight frame worked to their advantage. She looked entirely natural padded and swathed in black and white.

Before setting off, she'd consulted the Saratoga nursing brigade and spent a good portion of her weekly allowance to telegram Dr. Nash in North Elba regarding optimal treatment of bullet wounds and infection. None of what she'd learned had been encouraging. Patients had a higher chance of survival if the affected limb was amputated within forty-eight hours. Given that it had been weeks and infection had set in, Dr. Nash advised water dressings and antiseptics. The nursing staff graciously provided Sarah with the various items without asking questions. Two of the junior nurses taught her proper dressing procedure before she boarded the train.

She wrote Annie and her mother a quick letter of explanation and posted it at the station. It would be weeks before they received the news, and by then, she'd be lodged at the Hills'. She didn't want them fretting themselves to illness over her journey or trying to talk her out of it.

She considered the Hill family as dear as her own. Was there a means to be kin without blood or marital ties? George away at war; Freddy on his deathbed; no medical aid; and a desperate Priscilla telegramming: they were alone and in jeopardy.

Harpers Ferry was held by Union forces but had slipped into Confederate hands time and again. Daily rumors swirled of Stonewall Jackson's plans to seize the Shenandoah Valley stronghold for the Confederacy.

Sarah would not sit still in New York waiting for the news of Freddy's death. The very prospect stung her to tears. After all, she loved him — as purely and truly as one could love. Enough to give up her own happiness for his. Her life for his, if it came to that.

Now, as the buggy wheeled into New Charlestown, she gasped at the alien scene. The forests she and Freddy had once ambled within had been slashed to stumps.

Acres and acres of deforestation up and down the once verdant hills. No longer the landscape she'd painted. She saw now that her canvas had been rendered obsolete before Mr. Sanborn and Mr. Stearns had even had a chance to replicate it. The land was naked clear to the two algae-brown rivers snaking through the mountain gorge. Triangular tents pitched where broad oaks, poplars, and maples had once stood. Fronds of campfire smoke spiraled to a canopy across the July sky. Even the sun seemed remote, banished behind a mantle of war.

Passing through the still streets, the horse's hooves elicited the attention of the tent residents. They hung their heads out of the flaps: Negro men, women, and children, with a handful of whites between. A shred of what was once a uniform here and there. Blue or gray, Sarah couldn't tell, so threadbare and sun-faded were the garments.

"Who are they?" Sarah asked her driver.

"Contraband camp. Runaway slaves, mostly. They turn themselves over to the Federals as impounded property. It's one way."

"One way to what?"

"Freedom." He shrugged. "Until the Rebels come back. Then they'll be sent deep down south, shackled and at the command of the slave catchers. Better off waiting out the war on their masters' plantations. Lincoln's going to win . . . eventually. Boatloads of Irishmen arriving every day up north. Fresh recruits putting on kepis for a hot meal and a gun. They got the fighting spirit, y'know. Southerners are fools, thinking they'll get the Frenchies in uniforms. They come into Louisiana port and run as fast as they can into the swamps. Too smart for this mess."

The driver brought the horse to a halt before the Hill house. The white fencing was gone. The lawn, a mess of sprouted onion grass and dandelion heads. A wild garden of beastly eyes. A broom lay warped and splintered across the front porch, barring entry.

"You sure this is the place?" asked the driver.

Sarah nodded.

He jumped off and pulled her carpetbag from the back of the carriage, then helped her down the steps. Navigating her footing in a habit proved more cumbersome than the same task in a corset and hoop skirt. Sarah left muddy footprints all over.

The driver lingered, scratching his neck and watching Sarah. He'd been paid by

Mary Lathbury, and Sarah had nothing more to give him except thanks.

Quickly, she made her way up the front path, moved the broom aside, and knocked. After a minute passed with no answer, she knocked again, louder. There was the jerk of a dead bolt that she hadn't remembered from before. The door creaked open a sliver.

"It's an angel," came a whisper. Then a doll plunged through the crack, and Sarah sprang back, stumbling over the habit's hem.

"Move on, Miss Alice, that no angel." Siby swung the door wide. Alice held Kerry Pippin, both alabaster pale.

"Why, Miss Sarah." Siby's eyes were big as sodden dumplings. "That be you under the hood and church-bride sheets? Baby Jesus, what you gone and done to yourself up north?"

"Sarah's an angel," Alice proclaimed. "Angel come to take Freddy to heaven." She cradled her doll to her chest.

Sarah shook her head, then nodded, then shook again. "Yes, it's me but *no* —" She turned to ensure that the driver was gone. "It's a disguise. To keep safe on the road."

Siby's shoulders fell with relief. "I sees. Oh, Miss Sarah." She embraced her, then collected herself. "Miss Prissy be mighty glad to have you here."

Seeing the affectionate display, Alice moved forward to join in, bear-hugging Sarah and smelling exactly as Sarah remembered. Dried blossoms and churned butter.

"Come in, come in. They's all upstairs with him now. Miss Prissy and Miss Ruthie — Mr. Freddy's missus."

Concealed beneath the holy garment, Sarah flinched at the mention.

"Made up your room, same one as always." Siby took her bag. "I set your things up, then fetch you a cold lemonade. Fresh-squeezed this morn and kissed with honey. Lemons all we got left a-growin'. Rebs cut down every one of them apple trees for firewood. But the lemon, she too reedy tough and like to smoke when burned green." She ushered Sarah and Alice inside and bolted the door.

The windows were swathed in the same black fabric from Sarah's father's execution day. Fear, as swift as a hatchet, cleaved her.

Siby took her hand with a squeeze. "We put those up over a year ago, after a couple Rebs broke in and stole Miss Prissy's china plates. Tore her heart up, but I countin' it as a blessing. I would've had to bury the whole lot anyhow, and I's got enough to do.

The teacups and silver spoons be back there somewheres now." She pulled Sarah away from the window. "Miss Alice, you be kind enough to help me gussy up a tray of lemonade? Bet Miss Sarah would love a flower for cheer."

"Forget-me-nots are in bloom," Alice said directly to Sarah. "Those would suit best."

Siby patted Alice's back. "Remember to look round that the yard is safe 'fore you venture. Be quick and quiet in your collecting."

"Like a butterfly sipping from a dewdrop," said Alice.

"Yessum. Just like." Siby smoothed a lost wisp of hair back into Alice's bun before letting her dart down the entryway with the doll under her arm.

Despite the passage of time and suffering, the house was the same: the lingering smell of baked corn pones; the lamplight falling in glowing arcs; stairs creaking underfoot; the wooden banister, welcome and familiar beneath Sarah's hand as she ascended.

She hesitated at Freddy's door, unable to open it. His bedroom. Now it belonged to him and his bride, and he lay dying within. She closed her eyes for composure. The veil of her wimple seemed to amplify everything: the air moving in and out of her lungs; her

411

heartbeat drumming too fast; the voices emanating from the other side.

Siby returned from putting Sarah's things in the guest room. She didn't ask why Sarah stood motionless. Instead, she put a hand to Sarah's back and gently led her in.

The room was unadorned. No wallpaper or pictures. No soft rug underfoot. No color except the exposed brick in one corner. To the right, by the window, was a hutch with a white washbasin; to the left, a short clothing trunk with a shelf of books above. Taking up the majority of the room was the rough-hewn bed where Freddy lay. His skin was opaque as the muslin sheets; his black hair in frightful contrast; his eyes half-open, though his chest moved in the unsettled rhythm of fevered sleep. His body was too neatly tucked into the bedding to be natural, like a corpse in a coffin. A chill spilled over Sarah. She wanted to rush to Freddy's side, push off the layers, and take away the curse. But he was not hers to awaken.

Ruthie and Priscilla sat next to each other, working hooks through a crocheted blanket, Gypsy amid the skeins of yarn at their feet. The dog lifted her grayed head but didn't rise on all fours until Priscilla spoke.

"Dear heavenly Father — is that you, Sarah?"

Gypsy cautiously pattered over, burrowing under the habit until she found the familiar scent of Sarah's boots. She wagged her tail in greeting.

"It's a getup," explained Siby.

"The Sisters of Mercy nurses." Sarah pulled the veil off. "My teacher insisted. Especially since I'm carrying these." She slid a hand through her armhole to pull free the hidden purse against her belly. She held it up to the women. "Medicine, soap, clean bandages. They're not an absolute cure, but they'll help us fight the infection."

Priscilla stood from the chair and embraced Sarah forcefully.

"Ask and ye shall receive," she whispered into Sarah's ear. "You are our miracle."

Over Priscilla's shoulder, Ruth set aside the crocheted blanket and patiently waited her introduction. Peach-skinned with hair the color of raw sienna paint, she was narrow and plump in the right places. Like an unshelled almond, full of promise. Beautiful, but starkly different from Sarah.

Priscilla wiped away a joyful tear, then brought Sarah to Ruth. "This is Mrs. Ruth Marie Hill."

"My family calls me Ruthie." She warmly held Sarah's hand. "I'd very much like for you to do the same. I've heard so much about you. I feel like we're sisters."

Before Sarah could respond cordially, Ruthie pulled her into an earnest hug.

"Thank you for coming at such danger. You're the bravest woman I've ever known. I can't ever thank you enough."

The girl's looped braids were scented with chamomile, and Sarah couldn't help but like her for the simplicity. The slight calluses of her hands showed her to be a diligent worker, not a girl of pretension. She was as she appeared: honestly kind and sincere in her affections. Sarah was glad Freddy had chosen her.

Gypsy leaned her heavy head against Sarah's knee. The faithful dog understood what it was like to live silently devoted. Sarah scratched behind her ear, and she thumped her tail.

At the sound, Freddy turned his cheek. His fingers fluttered to find purchase. "Sarah . . ."

The women moved quickly round the bed.

"He hasn't spoken a word," Priscilla gasped. She pulled Sarah to Freddy so that their faces were inches apart, her hand in his. "She is here."

The candlelight glimmered in his dark eyes, glassy and still as two water jugs. Sarah could not blink.

"Hello, Freddy. It's me."

"Sarah." His lips moved without sound. The effort beaded his brow with sweat.

She ran her fingers across to wipe it away. His skin was clammy and hot.

"I've come to ask you to go for one of our old nature walks. To the Bluff, perhaps?" Her voice caught.

"I wish I could," he whispered. His bottom lip trembled with the fever chill, and Sarah bit her own to keep back the tears.

"That's what I named my painting of last fall — *The Bluff.* I was going to give it to you as a wedding gift, but I wasn't able to bring it. They were planning to make replications, but seeing how things have changed . . . maybe I'll paint a new one. I've learned so much. It's sure to be better. Would you and Ruthie like that?"

He closed his eyes and nodded softly.

"You're going to get well, Freddy. You will."

"I liked your first."

"Freddy." She squeezed his hand.

He looked at her then with absolute clarity. "There will never be another for me, Sarah."

She gripped the bedside and took in sips of air to quell the reeling. *He's married,* she reminded herself. *Love him, yes, but he's wed to the better woman.*

"I won't paint another stroke unless you promise to get well."

He looked at her as if reading her every thought, then nodded, once.

"Water dressings," Sarah announced and stood, swiping the corners of her eyes dry. "We must keep the infected area clean at all times. Siby." She turned. "Will you bring us new water — boiled first? And clean rags."

"Yessum," Siby replied and left the room to fetch the items.

Sarah pulled off the cumbersome nun's tunic, leaving the black serge frock beneath, and rolled her sleeves to the elbow.

"Ruthie, Miss Priscilla — we need to undress his wound, wash it out with soap and water, apply antiseptic, and redress it."

Priscilla pulled away the sheet to expose Freddy's injured leg. Old bed linens had been shredded to make bandages. Sarah recognized the printed buds from the blanket she'd used in the barn on her first visit. The bindings were soaked through with chartreuse pus but no blood.

"Was the bullet removed?"

"Yes," said Ruthie. She clasped her hands tight, her knuckles white. "At the field hospital."

"Good. That's good," Sarah said consolingly. "It means we're battling the infection alone."

Alice entered with a tray: lemonade in a pitcher, one glass already poured, and a posy of forget-me-nots tied beside it. Seeing Freddy exposed and the women in motion, she put the tray on the trunk and stood against the wall.

Siby returned with a kettle and poured a steaming stream into the washbasin. Sarah soaked the new bandages, though the water scalded her hands. Freddy had fallen back under the fever, grimacing as they moved his body but otherwise unresponsive. Sarah hesitated. For as much bravado as she put forth, she'd never nursed a bullet wound and had never seen the naked flesh of a man.

Growing up, she'd cared for her siblings through croup, dysentery, fevers, chest colds, wandering pains, and everything in between, but the maladies of the women and men were always segregated. The division did not yield from biblical edict. The Sisters of Mercy did not discriminate and had no doubt seen a fair share of bare humanity, regardless of sex.

Sarah gleaned courage from the borrowed nun's dress she wore. *You can do this,* she told herself. *Freddy needs you.* Across from her, Ruthie watched her husband and wrung her hands.

Sarah unwrapped the soiled bindings. Each one spongy damp and reeking of pork gone sour in a summer smokehouse. Her throat seized, and she had to turn her face away.

"When was the last time these were changed?"

"At dawn," replied Ruthie.

The Saratoga nurses had made it clear: clean, water-soaked dressings needed to be reapplied hourly until the wound stopped seeping discoloration. Infection bound up in infection would encourage gangrene, which could spread into the whole body. Sarah prayed it hadn't reached that point. If so, there was little they could do. Dr. Nash had told her to look to the colors of the eyes: the truest indicator of a patient's prognosis. If the whites were yellow and streaked, the infection was already in the blood. Despite the dark shadows and his shifting lucidity, Freddy's had been clear.

With the bandages removed, she examined his flesh closely. The skin encircling the bullet wound was rotted to the bone, but the entire limb was not necrotic. A small maggot writhed and fell to the side of Freddy's inner thigh.

"God help us," said Priscilla.

Ruthie gagged audibly.

Siby reached to kill it, but Sarah stopped her. The nurses had prepared her for this, too.

"The maggot will eat the dead, infected flesh and leave the living. It's good."

"Bugs eating under your skin be a good thing?" Siby asked in horror.

Sarah nodded. "The hospitals are using maggots on soldiers. It works."

Priscilla brought a lace handkerchief to her mouth, stifling her cries.

Ruthie's cheeks were flushed, her upper lip lightly glistening. "I trust Sarah." She nodded reverently to her. "Tell us what to do."

Sarah dropped the dirty bandages to the floor. Gypsy sniffed the pile, then lurched away, circling around to the other side of the room.

Carefully and contrary to her natural proclivity, Sarah lifted the maggot between her thumb and forefinger. "We need to collect these to put back in the wound after washing."

Siby dumped the lemonade Alice had poured for Sarah back into the pitcher and held the glass out for Sarah to drop the grub into. It sucked at the syrupy residue.

At the sight, Alice began to wail, "Worms'

meat! They have made worms' meat of me! I have it, and soundly too. Your houses!"

Ruthie's hands shook, and she covered her ears.

"Worms' meat! Worms' meat!" screeched Alice.

Priscilla went to her daughter, but Alice threw her off, accidentally pushing her into the brick wall, which scraped her chin to bleeding.

Siby put both arms around Alice with firm care. "Hush now, baby girl. Them's good worms, like the kinds we find in the garden helping the flowers grow strong." She rocked, and Alice quieted.

"A plague. A plague," she whispered without taking her eyes off Freddy.

"You okay, Miss Prissy?" Siby asked.

Priscilla dabbed the blood with a handkerchief. "I'm fine." She smoothed her skirt and came to Alice, still bound in Siby's embrace. "It's too much. I should've known better." She kissed her daughter's forehead.

Alice's words had become a mumble, and she swayed to the recitation's rhythm.

"She plumb wore herself out. Best I put her to bed, then fetch more water and clean rags?" Siby started out with Alice nearly catatonic in her arms.

"What was she saying?" Ruthie asked, still shaking.

"*Romeo and Juliet*," said Sarah. "It's one of Shakespeare's tragedies."

EDEN

New Charlestown, West Virginia
August 2014

There lingered a dense valley fog on the Saturday morning of the Dog Days End Festival. A passing cold front traveling with the Potomac River had been trapped between the bluffs and caused the air over New Charlestown to curdle cool with condensation.

Normally, Eden would not have been up and out so early as to see the ole buttermilk sky, but it was no ordinary day.

"I couldn't sleep a wink!" Cleo had said at the kitchen door. The muddled morning light spun her hair to soft gold, while her eyes retained the indigo of night.

Eden hadn't been able to sleep, either. In the restless, lonesome hours her mind had wandered to Jack's fidelity during the past many years of weekly business travels and, moreover, her father's infidelity while doing the same. Both betrayals wounded so deeply that she howled into her pillow while holding herself like a cross-stitch to keep her heart from spilling out of her chest.

Her muscles had twitched and itched so intensely after the purge that she'd changed the bedsheets at midnight, convinced some colony of mites or itsy-bitsy spider had taken nest between the layers. Still unable to calm her body or mind, she'd busied herself with a mental checklist for the festival day ahead: a gingham tablecloth; a cash box and receipt paper; change of ones and fives; the big box of Original Pumpkin CricKet BisKets; the smaller batch of Apple Hills; the logo banner with a prominently featured cartoon caricature of Cricket; and Cricket, of course. She went over the details while keeping the name on the tip of her tongue to the back of her mind: *Jack.*

He'd rung Denny to plead his case. Smart man, he knew just how to get to her. When Denny got home, she'd listened to him tell the same story Jack had in the bedroom. *Old friend. Fallen on hard times. Daughter. Just coffee and cake balls. Americans and their flippant overfamiliarity.* It could be true. So much of her wanted to believe it was.

"Think about it, sis," Denny had said before leaving for Philadelphia. He was going back for Jessica's first ob-gyn appointment. Until he heard about the job interviews, he'd resigned himself to playing sets at Mother Mayhem's again. A jar of tips was better than nothing, he figured; plus, he wanted to show Jessica he was serious. He was there for her.

"Don't make any hasty decisions. If Jack was having an affair, you probably wouldn't know about it. He's British. They got two-timing down to a science — look at Henry the Eighth, Prince Charles, James Bond, Alfie."

"That's your list of successful womanizers? Nice, Den. Real nice. Not helpful."

"My *point* is that he'd do a much better job covering it up."

Like our father, she thought, understanding it to be true. But it was just that which grated on her: the concealment all these months, harmless or not. It wasn't like he'd met Pauline once on a whim. The text had read: ". . . this trip. Sounds like you had a busy week. Are you back Monday?"

Eden wished she'd taken his phone, called the number, and told Pauline to keep her pick-a-pecking, divorcée thumbs to herself. Damn it, Jack was her husband! The vision of him warm and smiling in her bed made her chest seize up. It was a betrayal of the most intimate nature: secrecy.

Not able to keep her mind from him, she'd gotten up and spent her energies on the tedious National Register application. Another night of insomnia. She was getting good at not sleeping. At dawn, she'd gone down to the kitchen. Cricket had followed from his pillow bed, then sprawled belly to the ground while she placed logo stickers and tied ribbons on CriKet BisKets.

Eden had never seen a dog sleep so much and in so many odd positions. She'd read in a Baby 101 book that in deepest rest, infants sleep in cramped positions mirroring their gestation in the womb. So a crooked arm, tucked leg, twisted torso, or limbs akimbo was simply the unconscious body remolding to old comforts. She imagined Cricket deep inside his mother, arms and legs stretched out like a furry star. It made her smile and chased away the sadness for a time.

She'd perked a pot of thick coffee. Yearning for the something she didn't want to put her finger on, she'd poured a mug and sat on the kitchen mat with Cricket like a rag doll against her. The strength of the drink and his feverish form made her head and body tingle. She cuddled both closer to ward off the chill.

Like an ever-present sentinel on the windowsill was the doll. Its eyes — one black, one green — unblinking. She'd promised to bring it to Ms. Silverdash at the festival today. They'd collected strong facts, but the full story of a thing was not to be found in records. Only people could give her that.

She'd raised her cup. "To a gal with a good head minus the shoulders." She'd tried to laugh at her own joke but found it more pathetic than witty. She could hear the playground gossip now: "Threw her husband out stark naked, lives alone in that haunted house, chatting to dogs and toys and making magic biscuits that are probably laced with hemp — that's marijuana, you know. Because she's into that organic hippie mojo. I've seen a voodoo doll's head through her kitchen window."

A one-way ticket to being that crazy old lady. Every neighborhood had one. The saddest part was that she couldn't fully deny the assertions.

It was then that Cleo had knocked on the back door. Crazy or not, they had biscuits to sell.

On their drive to Main, the car cut the fog like a knife through cookie dough, parting it sluggishly.

"It's *Brigadoon*," Eden said, flapping her windshield wipers at nothing and leaning forward into the steering wheel. "Where's Gene Kelly tap-dancing?"

"Briga-what?" asked Cleo, buckled in beside her.

"It's an old movie. Ask your grandpa. It's about a town that appears from the mist every hundred years."

"Oh," said Cleo. "Well, there's no tap dancing around here. Just flat-footing. We get this all the time. In September, the fog's so bad kids get grace-period passes 'cause the school bus drives right by without seeing them." She blew a patch of condensation onto the window and traced a dog bone: two hearts with their tails bridged together. "Dog Days End. It's the last of summer," she explained. "I start fifth grade on Wednesday."

Eden had completely forgotten: school. The smell of damp, fallen leaves, lunch boxes, chalk, and breakfast orange juice on children's lips. It made her nostalgic and sad that Cleo would be gone for a majority of the days now. From the backseat, Cricket gave a cluck as they turned onto Main. At least she'd still have him to keep her company.

The street was blocked off on both ends

and busy with morning vendors preparing their booths. Eden parked in the Milton's Market lot and carried their wares to the storefront fairway. Ms. Silverdash and Mr. Morris had set up the CricKet BisKet tent in front of the bookstore and café.

Two silver-haired women in heels and pearls cornered Mr. Morris, holding pies like swaddled newborns.

"All the farmers say the best fruit of the season was lemon," explained one.

"Hogwash, Myra, peaches took the prize this year," countered the other.

"Peaches! Heavens, no. My Bill found a worm in his just yesterday."

Mr. Morris *tick-tocked* between the two. "Ladies, ladies, the pie entry table is in front of the bank. Same as every year."

"Well, I would greatly appreciate your escort, Mr. Morris." Myra stiffened her shoulders. "Make sure no thumbs are stuck in the front-runner's submission."

The other woman raised an eyebrow high, but before a retort was given, Mr. Morris led them forward. "Step this way." Passing Eden and Cleo, he mumbled, "*Dog* Days, they got a word for this sort."

Eden laughed.

Cleo gave her a mischievous look. "I know what word."

Paying no mind to the fruit dispute, Ms. Silverdash greeted them: "Eden, Cleo, and our fur man of the day!"

Cricket trailed listlessly on the lead.

"We've made him eat too many trial biscuits. He's nearly as puffed up as old Barracuda," said Cleo.

Ms. Silverdash swept Cricket up into her arms. "Well, I declare!" She ran her hand beneath his full belly. "These must be good eating."

"Thanks to *The Holistic Hound.*"

"Speaking of . . ." Ms. Silverdash set Cricket in the cushion she'd brought out for him. "I placed a special order."

On a card table perpendicular to the head booth was a display of books: copies of *The Holistic Hound, How to Train Your Puppy,* and the complete Detective Spot Mystery series. Atop a raised pedestal in the epicenter was the Fur Fairy, the guardian angel of the bookstore and a most appropriate guest in their Dog Days End booth.

"Surprise!" cheered Ms. Silverdash.

Cleo clapped her hands. "It's like we have our own store!"

"You do." Ms. Silverdash fingered the promotional packaging with the animated logo. "You two have done a marvelous thing here. Just marvelous."

Eden beamed at the compliment. She had to admit, she was proud of all they'd accomplished together.

Ms. Silverdash and Cleo whipped the gingham tablecloth high in the air, and as it fell over the table in smooth checkers, the fog went skittering. Within a minute, the sun cut clear and true through the atmosphere. Ms. Silverdash shielded her eyes with a palm and looked to the sky.

"True to form — going to be a bluebird day. Always is on Dog Days End. No matter what threatens." She winked and patted Eden's arm.

Mr. Morris returned with Vee by his side.

"Doctor says my dad's pelvis looks pretty good. If we're lucky, he'll feel well enough to leave the house in the next couple of weeks. He and our dogs, McIntosh and Nutmeg, were sorry to miss the festival. He's heard so much about the new Anderson folks." She grinned at Cleo, then turned to Eden. "Dad is mighty keen on meeting you and your Cricket."

"Maybe I'll get the chance to introduce myself to him sooner," said Eden. "I finished my house application last night. I could swing it over to you."

Vee smiled. "That would work perfect. I didn't want to get my hopes up if it didn't pan out, but Emma and I've been working on that street for years. It'll be nice to have another home block-checked."

"Are we talking about Apple Hill Lane?" Ms. Silverdash was finishing arranging a bouquet of blue forget-me-nots in a vase.

"Between Dad and the store, I haven't had a minute to tell you. Eden is submitting an application for the National Register of Historical Places."

At that, Ms. Silverdash's eyes twinkled brightly. "Splendid news! That house definitely belongs. It's special, no question."

"Did she tell you what else they found?"

"The case of the Apple Hill doll's head." Ms. Silverdash winked again. "Cleo's been leading our investigation."

"Yes, the head, but what I thought more interesting was what was inside of it."

Eden hadn't had a chance to discuss the key or the button with Ms. Silverdash yet. So much kept happening at once, and her brain had turned to pudding from sleeplessness.

"Miss A! Vee, Ms. Silverdash!" Cleo called. "Come quick, look at this!" She held up the bookstore's Fur Fairy, pointing at its back, where the dress was fastened with two copper buttons of a braided wheat pattern.

Eden's heart flapped like a bird. They

431

brought the Fur Fairy to the box where Eden had stashed the relics from her house. Cleo held the rusty button up to the others. A match. She squealed, and Eden hugged her to her waist before either could exercise restraint.

"What is it?" asked Ms. Silverdash.

Eden lifted the porcelain doll's head and the key. Ms. Silverdash gasped.

"We — the Andersons — found the doll and this button in their root cellar!" gushed Cleo. "This is what's called a *breakthrough*!"

Ms. Silverdash's mouth remained open. She put a hand out to touch the face, then curled her fingers back into her fist.

Mr. Morris returned and, seeing her expression, grew concerned. "What is it, Emma?"

"The Fur Fairy . . ." Cleo treaded lightly, troubled by Ms. Silverdash's lack of articulation. "It has the same buttons, and look —" She gently pulled down the embroidered smocking around the stuffed dog's collar to reveal a ring of tight, antique stitches. "Somebody's sewn the dog's head on, but it's got a person's body — like it was once a baby doll. Given the matching button . . ." She scratched her nose and nodded to herself. "I deduct from the clues that we have located the Fur Fairy's original noggin." She rapped her knuckles on the table like a gavel.

Eden held the Fur Fairy beside the china head; the proportions were spot-on. "It does appear they belong to each other — but how?"

"The Fur Fairy was my great-grandmother's," whispered Ms. Silverdash. "Mrs. Hannah Fisher Hill." She fingered one of the dog's cloth ears. "Hannah and her family lived in New Charlestown over a century ago. My family's past has always been a mystery. It's why I'm such a history buff. I want to know what everybody else saw fit to forget."

She looked toward Mr. Morris, who cupped her hand in his. Then she turned back with her chin raised.

"My great-grandma Hannah and her twin brother, Clyde, were sent west during the Civil War, then came back a decade later. I've spent years researching and tried to make it my college thesis, but the evidence was so sparse. All I had was a theory — that they were on the Underground Railroad — based on a handful of badly weathered tintypes and coded letters between her father-in-law, my great-great-grandfather Freddy, and a woman named Sarah. And this — the Fur Fairy." She straightened the collar so it looked like the petals of a pressed flower. "I knew it was a thing of treasure. When everything else was buried or burned, it was passed on. My Grandpa Silverdash said that during the war, his grandfather worked the Underground Railroad around these parts and dolls like these were used to smuggle messages, maps, and various contraband across battle lines." She gingerly lifted the dog's skirt to reveal the railroad of stitches extended down the torso.

Cleo leaned in close. "Have you checked inside?"

Ms. Silverdash placed the skirt back down. "Nothing but cotton. I restuff her every few years. A lady must keep freshly padded." She smiled. "But the dress and buttons are original."

Cleo's hair was down for the special day, but now she gathered it up in her professional ponytail and secured it with the rubber band from her wrist. "So . . . to the clues — how did Hannah's doll get the buttons? And how come the head swap?"

Ms. Silverdash shrugged. "I can't say."

Cleo gave an exasperated sigh and threw up her hands. "The case of the Apple Hill doll's head remains open!"

"Well, partially." Ms. Silverdash smoothed the cheek of the china doll with her fingers.

"You've helped me solve a lifelong unknown. I am the great-granddaughter of a slave child sent west on the Underground Railroad, and the Andersons' house on Apple Hill Lane was most probably the station." Her eyes flickered with tearful joy. "That's quite something to discover about one's self and town! And all because of you — New Charlestown's ace detective — and Eden."

Eden put an arm around Cleo and gave her a confident squeeze, then placed the Fur Fairy back on the book table. How and why the head and body had been separated was still unclear, but they were certain they'd once been a match. The doll's story was developing from the darkness. The original face might've been lost for over a century, but the Fur Fairy had lived on — been loved by Ms. Silverdash's kin and made into lore by the children of Story Hour. She could not be her original human creation. Fate had bestowed much more magic.

"Don't forget this." Eden extended the key. "If the doll belonged to your family, then this does, too."

"That's what was inside the head," said Cleo. "It's got the number thirty-four on the side."

Ms. Silverdash held it up to the light, with

Mr. Morris inspecting it beside her. "Looks to me like an old bank box key," he said.

Cleo thudded her palm to her forehead. "I should've thought of that!"

"There could be more documents, letters, answers about my family's heritage and the Underground Railroad!" Ms. Silverdash was practically shaking with excitement.

Whatever was in that box was Ms. Silverdash's, and Eden was happy to have played some small role in returning the items to their rightful owner. If the house had been part of the Underground Railroad, then it would unquestionably be added to the National Register of Historical Places. It was a win-win for all parties.

"See, Morris," said Ms. Silverdash. "This is providential proof! The Andersons were meant to move into that house. Everything worked out just as it was supposed to."

"Proof that *we* were right," he muttered.

Ms. Silverdash frowned. "No, Morris, evidence that all seedlings push their way to the surface. To everything there is a season. It's nature's way."

Mr. Morris looked down Main Street to Milton's Market, where a marching band warmed up, tooting notes and thrumming snare drums.

"Thank you, Eden and Cleo." Ms. Silverdash dabbed the corners of her eyes with her embroidered handkerchief. "You don't know what a gift you've given me." She pocketed the key with a pat. "I'll be at Mr. Bronner's bank first thing Monday morning, and you can bet I'll report back every speck I find in the box."

"I'll tell Grandpa to be expecting you." The band's *rat-a-tat* increased. "It's nearly starting!" said Cleo.

"Indeed." Ms. Silverdash turned to Mr. Morris. "You ought to take your position with the other tasting judges so Mayor Smith can kick off the festivities. And I must get to the shop window, tout suite!"

"The new diorama!" Cleo clapped. "Ms. Silverdash unveils *Fall* when the band passes the bookstore."

"I hope you enjoy it. I was inspired by blooms of late. The first Milton grandchild and . . ." She smiled at Eden. "New families of New Charlestown."

Eden blushed, flattered but apprehensive of the honor. If she and Jack didn't work things out, they'd be a town miscarriage of sorts.

Ms. Silverdash looked around the tent approvingly. "I believe this is the beginning of a tremendous venture."

Eden took stock: dog treats in rows neat

as stitches; cash box polished to a silver shine; Cricket sleeping beneath the table; Cleo in her Sunday best, a CricKet BisKet logo pinned to her Peter Pan lapel; Fur Fairy keeping watch over books and BisKets all. Check, check, check.

Time for the final touch. Mr. Morris brought his stepladder from the café and unfurled the banner across the tent's top:

CricKet BisKet Dog Treat Co.
Sponsored by Morris's Café and the
Silverdash Bookstore

Cleo and Eden had kept the tagline a secret. Mr. Morris and Ms. Silverdash beamed up at it, arm in arm, like proud parents. Cricket's doggy caricature shone down on them, bright as the North Star.

"You're famous," Cleo told him and scratched behind his ear.

Eden was elated. It had turned out better than she'd envisioned, and there were very few things she could say that about. She wished Jack could've seen it all. She chastised herself for thinking of him. She'd been hostile for so long, it felt almost natural. However, perpetual heartache wasn't a legacy she wanted to continue.

If she was honest with herself, she'd been

as secretively traitorous to their marriage as he. Perhaps even to a worse degree. She'd been unnecessarily cruel; volleyed hateful words; shut him out when he tried to reach her; schemed to divorce him while accepting his gifts of a beautiful house, roses, puppies, and unwavering kindness.

Throwing Jack out was the ultimate cliché: cheater gets kicked to the curb; wife cries herself to raging strength, then raises a fist in vindication and moves on to self-sufficient success while the two-timing husband wallows in the awareness that he's lost the better woman. Hadn't she seen that tiresome run-on story a thousand times? It was the made-for-TV movie of every week. Fine for the Lifetime channel, she thought, but she refused to be a platitude. Jack was not her father. *She* was not her mother. She would not live the rest of her life in bitterness — either way.

She loved Jack. She hadn't *liked* him very much the last couple years, but even while she questioned everything else in their relationship, she couldn't deny loving him. She felt guilty for that. It wasn't what she was supposed to feel, according to social standards.

But her life wasn't a public relations agency's campaign. There was no *public* in personal relations. So she'd be turning thirty-seven soon and hadn't had a child. So what?

She'd quit her PR career to move to West Virginia and was actually happier than she'd been in cosmopolitan D.C. Who was judging?

She liked eating *Holistic Hound* dog food more than any fancy restaurant meal she'd ever had. And?

She was hopelessly in love with her husband, despite the fact that he might have had an affair . . . She stopped. Her breath caught. How could she say such a thing? Feminist blasphemy.

Yet it was her truth, and that was really why she'd come to New Charlestown — to find *her truth.* She'd been transformed by Cricket, Cleo, Ms. Silverdash and Mr. Morris, the children of Story Hour, and this town that Jack had put his faith in from the start.

The crowd gathered. Families sat east and west on the street's curbs, squinting under the fullness of sunlight. Ms. Silverdash was right. The sky was blue as a robin's egg, with only a brushstroke of haze on the horizon. The fog was gone, with the day opening bright and clear and free of regrets. All save one.

Eden pulled up Jack's number on her cell phone. The trumpets and clarinets, tuba and drums had come together to form a triumphant melody, a resounding trill of excitement that matched the bubbling chatter of the townsfolk. A woman in a wide-brimmed hat, leading a fleecy poodle on a leash, came to their table. A customer.

No time to talk now. Later. Eden put her phone away.

"Dixie loves treats," said the woman. "I'll take two Original Pumpkin and an Apple Hill."

And so they made their first CricKet Bis-Ket sale — before the kettle corn vendor had popped his kernels and perfumed the air sweet-and-salty; before Mayor Smith had inaugurated the Dog Days End, wearing a red top hat in honor of her redbone coonhound, Little Ann; before the panel of baked-goods judges had been introduced and Mr. Morris bashfully sat behind the PIE CHIEF nameplate; before the band had marched down Main to fanfare and a giant town sing-along of Big Joe Turner's "Low Down Dog"; and before Ms. Silverdash had unveiled the *Fall* diorama, a miniature Main Street constructed from pages of ornate floral illustrations: mauve-hued balsams and green firs etched with gold and bronze

441

stems. So vivid that when Eden lifted her gaze from the miniature to the real, the trees and doorways along Main seemed to shimmer with gilding, too.

SARAH

New Charlestown, West Virginia
September 1862

It took a week for Freddy's fever to break.
Two more for the wound to cease weeping
and stinking putrid. The only one to venture
out for supplies was Siby, under cloak of
night. Her family didn't dare come up to
the Hills'.

The unrest between the occupying forces
had made the Fishers' freed papers
inconsequential. Free or slave, they were a
Negro family living in their own house. Siby
reported that her father stayed up all hours
walking the property with his shotgun,
though they knew if he shot a white man,
he'd be hung regardless. Better he hang
than let evil befall his wife and children, he
told them. Siby's mother argued that she'd
rather him alive than territory claimed. She
set her mind to cooking off every fruit and
vegetable in her garden rather than see it fill

a Rebel's stomach. Siby brought over the johnnycakes, jarred lemon custard, potato and corn pies, molasses beans, and more.

Though they'd alerted their Underground Railroad friends that they'd have to halt transportation and deliveries while George and Freddy were on the battlefield, the Hills' house remained a green stop on the UGRR maps and pictorials; thus, they continued to receive secret knocks. Priscilla refused to turn away any hand of need. So they gave out knapsacks of Mrs. Fisher's vittles to contraband slaves and those fleeing north by starlight.

Freddy took only soft grits through August. While he was detached from acute danger, Sarah wasn't sure they'd be able to save his leg until the morning they found the maggots wriggling out to forage for better feed and the abscess scabbed over. At the spectacle of worms crawling down the bed linens, she'd announced him on the road to recovery. Priscilla kissed his left cheek, Ruthie his right; Alice held up her Kerry Pippin like a saint's statuette and paraded about the room singing a hymnal. Sarah dared only to bring her hand to his cheek.

"I made you a promise to get well. Now you've got to keep yours and *paint,*" he said, his bearded jaw tickling her palm.

By early September, Freddy was out of bed. His leg had healed, but he was left with a substantial limp. Mr. Fisher whittled a cane out of an oak branch to Freddy's height specifications, but Freddy was still getting used to his slow amble and instability. He fell often, and they heard his curses from inside the kitchen.

"I never knew he was a man of profanity," remarked Ruthie while churning butter with Sarah.

Sarah laughed. "He wasn't, but I always knew there was a rogue down in him."

Ruthie looked at her curiously, and Sarah realized she'd spoken out of turn.

"Don't we all have a bit of rogue in us?" she amended.

Ruthie continued plunging the milk without responding.

Sarah observed that while they were kind to each other, Freddy and Ruthie's relationship was unlike George and Priscilla's and more like her own parents': side by side yet distant. Ruthie cleaned, cooked, and waited on Freddy's every need. Freddy called her "good wife," complimented her on her food, and thanked her for darning his shirts and socks.

In the evenings, Priscilla read aloud

George's letters, when they came, or various war reports from the *New Charlestown Spectator.* Freddy's leg made it impossible for him to walk without the aid of his cane, never mind carrying a rifle in battle march. He was finished as a soldier. That fact comforted Sarah and the women as much as it shamed Freddy. He didn't speak of his experience on the front lines or his furloughed status.

Instead, he talked of the New Charlestown Church and inquired of Sarah's studies in Saratoga: literature, art, and the abolitionist work. The latter he never brought up in Ruthie's company, despite having called the Nileses trusted *friends,* code for UGRR advocates. Similar to Sarah's father, John, Freddy saw fit to keep this vast part of his life a secret from the woman who should've been his closest confidante, his wife.

Sarah and Freddy walked the barnyard and barren orchard each dusk to exercise his leg. Only then did he openly speak of the Underground Railroad. Sarah's suspicions about Auntie Nan's dolls were correct. Where once the UGRR had used them to smuggle supplies to plantations, now they were even more critical to the anti-slavery efforts. The dolls carried Union messages and diagrams demarcating allied homes across battle lines trusted to shelter runaways and Union spies.

"So the Freedom Train continues to move?" Sarah had pressed on one walk.

"Unofficially, yes," said Freddy. "Though it's much more difficult for passengers to determine which towns are occupied by which side. It could make the difference between life and death, and the Rebels are catching on quick to the dolls. We had a whole crate gutted, the maps destroyed in shipment. So now we send only by carriage. Mr. Silverdash is our conductor. It's risky but no more dangerous than carrying live baggage. Still, they've nearly got us entirely blockaded."

Suddenly, it came to Sarah like a cloudburst. "What if the maps weren't inside the dolls?" Her pulse quickened with the bolt of the idea. "The Rebels have figured out our hiding spot. So we let them continue to spend their energies inspecting shipments and shredding toys. Maybe even plant misleading information inside the dolls while the truth remains as plain as the noses on their faces."

He stopped walking at the line of apple tree stumps. "How so?"

She put a gloved finger to the patterned tree rings and followed them round, fat to wide, flood to drought, year after year. The last ring, nothing but splintered bark.

"Paint the maps on the dolls' faces." She pointed up. "Like the man in the moon."

It was that time of twilight when the sun garishly clung to the day's frayed edges while the moon budded translucent and quiet to the east. Both fighting for the same sky.

"The Rebels will be looking for the veiled secrets. They'll miss the obvious. Like the slave songs and my landscapes. Hair can be painted to look like river waters. Eyes, UGRR stations and hospitable towns. Freckles and rouge spots as safe houses between. A nose, a trusted church, and so forth. Even if soldiers remove the doll's body, the real message — the way north — would remain."

Freddy tapped his cane against the tree stump. "It just might work!"

Her stomach fluttered at his approval, and she beat it down with a thought: "Unless the head broke."

Like it had for Mr. Storm's daughter. She winced at the memory and suddenly felt her idea terribly foolish.

But Freddy continued: "Only the porcelain ones." His mind turned faster than Sarah's now. "We can still use the dolls

Auntie Nan sent as templates but make all replications on wooden heads."

"Yes!" Sarah agreed; then she thought of one drawback. "But paint on wood is prone to erosion. On a natural substance like that, it could disappear altogether with time."

"We don't need them to last a hundred years, Sarah." He smiled. "If slavery remains that long, the dolls have failed in their mission."

He was right. Immediately, they put their plans in motion. With Alice's permission, Sarah tested her facial map skills on Kerry Pippin. She repainted the hair in dark waves — the Shenandoah and Potomac merging at the center part; the right eye filled in black for Harpers Ferry, occupied by Rebels; the left eye bright green for the Hills' station house. The New Charlestown Church nose left white and stately. The lips drawn together, whistling the slaves to free Ohio. The pink swirls of her cheeks extending too low on either side — Quakers in Pittsburgh and a safe house in the Appalachian Mountains.

When she showed the doll to Freddy and Priscilla, they marveled.

"It's brilliant," said Priscilla.

"Paint every doll we have here," said Freddy. "We'll send a batch with Mr. Silverdash so they can be duplicated by our northern friends."

He went to the post office early the next day to telegraph word to Mr. Silverdash. At noon, he returned, calling Sarah's name as he hobbled across the lawn, Gypsy at his heels. She came from her room, where she'd just finished painting a dozen doll visages. Her head was reeling from the paint fumes.

"Sarah!" Freddy stood at the bottom of the staircase, panting from the effort of his walk from New Charlestown Square and clutching a sheet of newspaper.

Priscilla and Ruthie appeared from the parlor, Siby and Alice from the kitchen, so that everyone was gathered, looking from Freddy at the base to Sarah at the top.

"Gracious Lord." Sarah wiped charcoal from her fingers with a rag. "Whatever are you shouting about?"

"Hollering like it's Resurrection Day," said Siby.

" 'For the Lord Himself will descend from heaven with a shout!' " sang Alice.

"Sarah, we must pack you and send you home as quickly as possible. This very hour," he explained.

Sarah's heart shot to a gallop. Her knees buckled. She grasped the banister. This was the second time she'd been hastened away, and it brought back pained and panicked memories from the last. "Home? Today? Impossible. Freddy, I don't understand."

He held up the paper in hand. "They're coming. The Rebel army is marching here now. I can't protect you like a man ought." He shook his head and stomped his cane. "The best I can do is send you to safety. Siby? We've got to pack her. Now."

"Yes, Mister Freddy." Siby took the stairs in double time, rushing past Sarah to the guest room.

"Wear the nun's disguise," he instructed.

Sarah remained on the landing, staring down at Freddy, her mind wheeling as she tried to find some logical argument, but all that came out was "I — I don't want to go."

"Please," Ruthie implored. "Must she?"

Freddy nodded, and it launched everyone into action. Sarah had grown accustomed to being part of the family's workings, but now it was as if she were a fish caught in a ferry's wheel, bumping from paddle to paddle and nearly being squashed.

Priscilla and Alice helped her dress in the habit. Freddy hitched up the wagon with Ruthie's aid. Within the hour, the women were crying round her and bidding her farewell. Freddy sat with the reins in hand as she climbed in, the white guimpe hung around her neck like a flag of surrender. Old Gypsy gingerly pulled herself into the back of the wagon. Seeing all was secured, Freddy clucked his tongue and the horse started to trot. They were off, and the autumn sky had never seemed so piercing blue. It reminded Sarah of her father's eyes.

She assumed they were headed to the capital's train depot, like last time, and so was surprised when Freddy pulled off on a side road leading to a wooded farmhouse. There waited a weatherworn, covered carriage pulled by a team of horses. The coachman wore a soldier's kepi hat with two spoons instead of guns crisscrossing the brim. A bandana concealed his face. Freddy halted the horses.

Without hesitating for invitation, the man hoisted the crate from their wagon bed. "Hey there, Gyps," he said from beneath his mask. Then, to Freddy: "These them?"

Freddy nodded. Priscilla and Siby had packed the dolls Sarah had finished painting, minus Alice's Kerry Pippin.

"Mr. Silverdash, may I introduce Miss Sarah Brown."

Mr. Silverdash gave a nod while securing the box with ropes.

"A more trustworthy man, I know not," said Freddy.

They were the words Sarah's father had spoken about Freddy's father. Her stomach knotted; she missed both men. How much had changed since that first introduction. How much heartache she and Freddy had endured.

"I wouldn't rely on anyone else to take you safely."

Mr. Silverdash tossed her carpetbag into the carriage, then climbed atop.

"If I could," Freddy continued in a whisper, "I'd take you all the way to Saratoga myself. No words of gratitude are enough for what you've done." He looked down at the cane lying sideways at their feet. "Despite what you've said, Sarah, you must've loved me at some point to care for me as you have — to stay by my family's side. But, you see, I'm . . . broken. I pity that Ruth must spend the rest of her days as a nurse wife, and glad that you are free of such a burden."

Sarah rubbed away a tear. It mingled with the paint on her fingers and stained the white of her habit.

"You could never be a burden to anyone. Ruthie loves you. She will give you many children, Freddy. That . . . I could not." Her breath caught.

Now was not the time or place, but life

was no fabled Once Upon a Time. There was no time and place but the present.

"You see, that is why I turned you down. I cannot bear children. I am broken, too."

The words had been heavy as lead bullets on her tongue but did not strike as such. Freddy's gaze remained unchanged: earnest and affectionate.

Mr. Silverdash cleared his throat loudly. "Best be off, my friends."

Freddy took her hand, his pulse radiating hot beats through her skin. He lifted her palm and kissed the inside of her wrist. His lips, soft and true as the year before. She would conjure that feeling for all her days.

"I would've loved you even more," he said.

Sarah's vision softened about the corners, her fortitude over the last many months dissolving.

Mr. Silverdash gave a signal, and his horses whinnied and pulled, eager at their bits.

"You must go now," said Freddy.

She climbed down from the wagon and took a last glimpse at him before entering the carriage, where there was but a fraction of room for her between stacks of paper-wrapped packages. Once she was wedged into the padding, the men exchanged mumbled words outside and the wheels set to a harried pace. She knew not which direction they went. The windows were covered. All she could do was lean back and pray — for Freddy, the Hills, and New Charlestown, with the enemy on its way; for these parcels and their harbored secrets to arrive at their good purpose; for her and her dolls to do the same.

FROM THE
*NEW CHARLESTOWN SPECTATOR:
A JOURNAL OF CIVILIZATION,*
SEPTEMBER 16, 1862

WE ARE CAPTURED.

All residents are hereby ordered to remain in their homes, which are now under the direct command of Confederate General Thomas "Stonewall" Jackson. Residents holding slaves must provide the appropriate paperwork for their property and be registered. Without proper registration, all assets will be confiscated and returned to the Southern States.

EDEN

New Charlestown, West Virginia
August 2014

They sold out of the Original Pumpkin by half past noon, when the New Charlestown Humane Society did its Dog Days End walk. Seeing the animals, Eden had announced to the crowd that for every dog adopted, the adopting family would receive a month's worth of CricKet BisKets free. Vee added that they'd be delivered to the families' doorsteps by the Niles ice-cream truck, to boot. The last of the Apple Hill treats sold then, and Cleo took the names and addresses of the adopting families.

By the time trumpets had announced that the judges had the results of the baking contest, all that was left under the CricKet BisKet tent was a book on potty training puppies. Every *Holistic Hound* had sold, and Eden had secretly purchased the complete Detective Spot Mystery series for Cleo.

Eden liked the idea of Cleo being able to dog-ear the books' pages without the constraints of a borrowed copy. There was something to possessing without fear of loss that made a thing even more precious. "For keeps" was a powerful notion.

Ms. Silverdash had stashed the collection while Cleo chatted up the Humane Society dogs. When the girl had returned to find them gone, she'd sighed, "I didn't even get to give my book review of *A Diplomatic Dilemma.*"

Eden had hidden her smile, knowing full well that the series was nestled beneath the giant jade plant on the bookstore's checkout desk.

Now Ms. Silverdash taped the WILL RETURN SHORTLY sign to the shop window, careful not to obscure the view of her new diorama.

"I can't wait to hear who won," she said. "Though I'm sure I'll be hearing about Morris's bellyache for the rest of the night, too. He has no willpower when it comes to pie."

It was the last event of the Dog Days End: the baking contest awards ceremony. The crowd had gathered before the grandstand. Little Chrissy Smith, the mayor's thirteen-year-old daughter, won in the Crumbles

Division for her Coffee-&-Currants Swirl. She skipped up the steps, where her proud mother presented her with the blue ribbon and a hug. Vee's strawberry Creamsicle blondies (a nod to an ice-cream bestseller) took a third in the Dessert Bars Division. Ham Mercy Cheddar Biscuits won in the Biscuits and Rolls. A three-tiered "Hey Diddle Diddle" cake took first in Frosted Cakes. The entire nursery rhyme had been elaborately piped out in buttercream.

"Too pretty to eat," said Ms. Silverdash, and Cleo remarked, "I'd eat it."

They quickly went through the Cookies, Candies, Yeast Breads, Muffins, and Cheesecakes in whatever order the corresponding judge caught Mayor Smith's eye. Finally, Mr. Morris was up.

He stood, bloated and sugar-weary, to announce the Pie category. The two women, Mrs. Myra Lemon and Mrs. Peachy Perfect, as Eden had dubbed them, sat front and center, their backs ramrod straight.

Mr. Morris nodded to them, then looked broadly over the crowd as he announced fourth, third, and second. "And the first-place pie for this year is . . . Suley Hunter and her" — he checked the card in his hand for the correct title — "Ida's Rose Water Cream Pie with Sugar Petals. Unique and delicious."

"Hans Christian Andersen!" Ms. Silver-dash exclaimed.

The fairy tale — "Little Ida's Flowers"! Eden clapped wildly and gave a hoot. Something she'd never done before, but it came out as thrillingly as she'd always imagined.

Suley timidly took the bandstand, her cheeks ablaze. Mr. Morris presented her with the blue ribbon and the fifty-dollar check given to all winners. She stood beside him holding each in hand, stunned by the *snap-flash* of the *New Charlestown Spectator* cameraman. Eden had to bite her lip to keep from hooting again, but once she'd started, she couldn't hold back. Her joy and pride opened like one of Ida's flowers.

Laura Hunter, your child is a prize, she thought and beat her palms together until they itched. "Suley!"

The girl locked eyes with her and smiled wide.

When the crowd had subsided to a low chatter, Mayor Smith cleared her throat. "Our last award is for a new division. Truth be told, the baking committee was ashamed that they hadn't thought of it decades ago. It was unanimously voted into all future Dog Days End Festivals and will no doubt become one of our most popular categories. It is my real honor to present the inaugural blue ribbon for the *Dog* Days Baked Good to Ms. Cleo Bronner and Mrs. Eden Anderson for their CricKet BisKets!"

Cleo hollered almost loud enough to break the glass windows up and down the street, and her glee set off a cacophony of cymbals and cheers and clapping. She led the stunned Eden by the elbow to the bandstand, where she shook hands with Mayor Smith, then held up the ribbon at the microphone.

"Thank you, New Charlestown! But we couldn't have made one CricKet BisKet without the help of Mr. Morris and Ms. Silverdash. So I'd like it if they'd come up here, too!"

Mayor Smith's eyes bulged with surprise. Mr. Morris was already on the stage. To compensate for her initial shock, Mayor Smith enthusiastically ushered him forward beside Eden and Cleo while Ms. Silverdash made her way so as not to cause a further fuss.

Before she'd reached them, however, Cleo grabbed the mike once more. "Oh — and Mack and Annemarie! We got our organic ingredients from Milton's Market on special order!" She pointed down into the crowd, where Mack stood bewildered beside a pretty blond woman wearing a Baby Bjorn, the soft head of a sleeping infant mushroomed at her breast.

The crowd chanted, "Miltons, Miltons, Miltons," but Mack remained rooted until his wife grabbed him by the arm and led him up the steps. The two men hesitated; then Mack extended a hand, and Morris took it. Without waiting a second, Annemarie lifted her son right out of his swaddling and handed him to Morris, who flushed with pride. Mack put an arm around his father and then, surprising everyone, Ms. Silverdash. The family stood linked across the stage with Cleo at the far end, waving the blue ribbon like a wand.

The crowd cheered even more.

Cleo leaned into Eden's side. "Where's Cricket? He deserves to be up here, too!"

Cricket? In all the busyness of the day, Eden had nearly forgotten the little guy. Concern burst like popcorn in her chest. How careless of her — to neglect him for so long. She chastised herself and ached to leave the stage, hold him close, and cook him the finest *Holistic Hound* dinner in celebration. None of this would've happened without him.

Frantically, she scanned the CricKet Bis-

Ket tent from afar and was relieved to spot the pumpkin-colored fur of his tail just where she'd seen it this morning. But even as she was relieved, something about the sight worried her. He slept more than any animal she'd ever seen, but usually he reminded her when it was time to eat, drink, or sniff out some patch of weeds to mark as his own. A whine, bark, nuzzle to the leg, lolling tongue — something to gain her attention. But she couldn't recall him moving an inch today.

Eden made a beeline for the booth, fighting the crowd, which was dispersing with happy chatter. When she reached the empty tent, she knelt by his side and put a hand to his back. "Cricket?"

He turned his head, and for the briefest moment, she thought all was right. Then she saw his stomach, distended to a tight football despite his having had no food or water since early that morning. At lunchtime, Mr. Morris had brought her bottled water from the café. She grabbed it and gingerly poured it into Cricket's mouth. He sputtered and pulled his body away like a beached sea lion. His nose was frigid. His gums, gray as chimney smoke.

He needed a doctor, a veterinarian. She should've taken him to one when they first got him.

Cleo returned. Seeing her distress, she set the winning ribbon aside and came to the ground. "What's wrong?"

Eden moved Cricket's fur to expose the ballooned belly.

Cleo touched it with a gentle finger. "Rock hard. Did he eat a shoe or something?"

Eden shook her head. "Not that I know of. He hasn't moved all day."

"We need Dr. Wyatt." Cleo's voice sounded pinched.

Vee came from the throng of people heading to their cars, now that the last festival event was complete. Surveying the scene without saying a word, she pulled out her cell phone. "Hey, Dr. Wyatt, it's Vee Niles. We got an emergency. No, McIntosh and Nutmeg haven't eaten more raisins. It's the Andersons' pup, Cricket. Great. Be over at your place in the hour." She thumbed it off. "Him and my dad are golf buddies. You'll get stuck in traffic if you try to get your car out with everyone else. They used our truck to block off Main. I'll bring it up."

"Thank you, Vee," Eden whispered, grateful for new friends.

She pulled Cricket into her lap, and her own gut panged at his whimpers. "It's okay, baby boy, Dr. Wyatt is going to find the trouble. Don't you worry. Mama's here."

She rubbed gentle circles up and down the swelling. His soft, dark gaze fixed on her face.

The festival was over. The Presbyterian church's bells rang, heralding the Saturday five o'clock service. But this time Eden didn't bid them be quiet. She prayed. She hadn't prayed in years. Conversations with a doll's head and her dog were totally acceptable, but communication with some superior entity had always fallen a bit too far on the fantastical side. When she and Denny were growing up, their mother had administered prayer as both righteous spells and wicked hexes that never came to pass. So Eden had little faith.

Now, however, she had the overwhelming conviction that someone was listening. She hadn't the practice to make an eloquent speech, like the priests of her mother's church. So she simply prayed, *Make him okay, please.* And hoped it was good enough to rise from the valley to heavenly ears.

New Charlestown, West Virginia,
   October 6, 1862

Dear Sarah,
The Rebels are now in control of this
region and all correspondence therein. I
pray Mr. Silverdash was able to bring
this news to your goodly hand. No doubt
you have read of the Battle of Harpers
Ferry. The Rebels did a sweep of the
Federal contraband. We had an hour's
lead before they arrived on the streets of
New Charlestown. Just enough time for
Siby to bring Clyde and Hannah up
from the Fishers'. Mr. Fisher refused to
abandon his home, and Mrs. Fisher
refused to abandon him. So we hid their
three children in the root cellar. Mother
covered it with her hooked rug and
prayed the Rebs would take the pantry
foodstuffs and be gone. We should've
known they would be greedier. They
made no attempt to conceal their
repulsive lust.
   They bound me and forced me to the
floor, tying Ruth and Mother's hands as
well. So when they came at Alice, there
was only faithful Gypsy to defend her. I

heard the blast of the gun before her growl had settled to the floorboards. The soldier in command shot her straight through the muzzle. She dropped with teeth shattered like bloody kernels of corn. It was a demonic sight, a demonic act.

Alice gave a banshee cry and came forward — toward Gypsy, I am certain, but the Rebels mistook it as aggression. A young soldier hit Alice over the head with his musket. She fell with her skull open as wide and wet as Gypsy's ruined mouth.

I try not to hate him — the ignorant boy, terrified by the dog and the fervor of Alice's mourning. He should've been home helping with the harvest crop. We all should've been reaping our fields and preparing wood for winter hearths, but we aren't. We are here, embroiled in this hell. I know I can speak openly with you, Sarah. I cannot with anyone else.

I failed to protect my family. I see the scenes in my mind like tintype images burned by light. Writing you is my soul's only salvation. Please forgive me for this lack of decorum between married man and unmarried woman. Though we know each other's secrets well enough.

Our old ways are no more. This war has shown the underbelly of humanity. The scales of righteousness have yet to be balanced.

Raised in churches across the South, these Rebel men left us our "properties" — as they put it — realizing that they had gravely injured the simpleton daughter of a clergyman. Siby has not left Alice's bedside. The head wound seems to have completely unraveled the tapestry of her mind. She speaks in vowels we cannot understand, moaning through the days like an infant. With no physician to give us counsel, we fear that every hour could be her last.

We continue to hide Hannah and Clyde. They tiptoe about the house like ghosts and spend countless hours in the cellar, playing make-believe with Alice's neglected dolls. The dolls' cropped hair reminds Hannah of her own. With their light skin and light eyes, Mother swears the two children could pass as white. Maybe in another place and time, but here, they are known for what they are and we don't dare take the risk. The best we can safely continue to do is forward your map dolls to southern stations. Your painted templates were made with perfect timing, Sarah, and have since been copied to great success! I thought you ought to know of that small but mighty victory in the light of all this unhappy news and more . . .

In the roundup, Mr. and Mrs. Fisher were captured and sent south to the slave markets. The Confederates are now using their home as a makeshift storehouse. With no foods to be found in the garden, they slaughtered Tilda — too old to carry a soldier into battle or pull a load of weaponry. They roasted her flanks over a bonfire and feasted as if she were a fatted calf. The smell lingered for days.

We have not had word from Father since the capture of Harpers Ferry. If you hear news of his whereabouts, we would be eternally grateful.

I have been consigned to serve as a man of God to the Confederate soldiers in New Charlestown. I shirk at these duties. Ruth daily reminds me that in the end, all men face the heavenly host without uniforms. She is right. But my heart has turned cold as a river rock. It is a weight in my chest. No warmth or rhythm. Just there, until I can find a private hour to write to you. Only now do I feel a pulse. Only with you, Sarah. Forgive me for being bold, but it is written in Proverbs: "A man of many companions may come to ruin, but there is a friend that sticks closer than a brother." Or sister, as the case may be.

Love,
Freddy

Fort Edward Institute, Saratoga, N.Y.,
   November 1, 1862

Dear Annie,
Yesterday I received word of the Hills in Virginia. It is even more terrible than our worst fears. Oh, sister! I am bereft. I cry and curse the blasted Rebels. I could not hide my grief from Mary Lathbury, so I have shared all of this with her. She graciously reached out to her friends actively involved in bringing information safely across enemy lines. I pray they will provide a good report of Mr. Hill so I might, at the very least, provide the family a bit of solace.

Give my love to Mama and little Ellen. Keep vigil in North Elba. Those who despise our name will stop at nothing to see us and those we hold dear laid to the grave.

Your loving sister,
Sarah

North Elba, New York, November 20,
   1862

Dear Sarah,
The poison of slavery has spread
everywhere! I was offered a teaching
position in Virginia, but within a week of
my acceptance letter, threats came to
our door — in North Elba. Even Father's
city on a hill has grown venomous with
the spies and bounty hunters! If we are
not safe here, how much more danger
awaits a Brown in the South. So I've
canceled my obligation, though I wonder
if the school will receive either letter.
   President Lincoln's preliminary
Emancipation Proclamation has proven
to be little more than fancy speech. As
the Holy Word proclaims, it is not
enough to speak of good intentions. One
must correspond in deeds. Lincoln is no
Father. And we Browns are not
guaranteed welfare as we await a
deliverer.
   Look to the Hills for example. Shall
we sit in our kitchen, baking bread and

burning wood, until a rogue guard rides up to steal and murder? No. We would be fools and deserving of a cruel fate. While I grieve for the Hills, I will not wait for a similar doom. We must learn from these friends and move to ensure that our family is protected.

Mother, brother Salmon, and I have discussed and feel it best if we go west together. She asked that I send this correspondence to you after she had written Mr. Stearns, Mr. Sanborn, and Ms. Lathbury, which she has. It is arranged. You will return to North Elba immediately, and we will set off to our people in Iowa.

I understand it will be difficult for you to accept this decision with charity. Be mindful that your artistic studies in Saratoga are of trifling substance if your life and the lives of your family members are the cost. Look to Father for example.

If you fight us, it will only delay our inevitable departure and put all in peril. The sin of vain selfishness will bring ruin, Sarah. I tell you this as a loving sister so that you might be spared heavenly judgment. Be obedient and come home. Remember, you are a

Brown. Not a Hill.

Your faithful sister,
Annie

EDEN

"Hello?" Jack had answered, and the sound of his voice had broken Eden's last defensive stronghold.

She opened her mouth to reply, but nothing came out. Too much to say. Too much unsaid. Her heart ping-ponged from spleen to gullet like a pinball game.

"Jack." She coughed.

He went straight in: "Eden, I promise you . . ."

"Jack, please." She needed him just to listen. "I've been at Dr. Wyatt's office. He's the town veterinarian," she explained, and the rest tumbled out hot and fast. "It's Cricket. He's not a puppy, like we thought. Dr. Wyatt says by his teeth, he's probably four or five years old. And he's sick, Jack. They took an X-ray and found a mass the size of a grapefruit in his belly. It's monstrous! Lymphoma — cancer." She stopped to catch her breath and sobbed instead. "He's dying. Dr. Wyatt gave me a bottle of steroids to make him comfortable until the end. But I've been on steroids. They're *not* comfortable!" And then her voice turned off like a blown flame, and she cried silently in the dark of the house.

She'd never allowed herself to cry like that. Ever. Not when they lost their unborn babies. Not when she was going through fertility procedures that made her sweat, grimace, and go white as a bedsheet. She'd held herself steady and occasionally allowed herself stifled sobs of regret or hormone-induced hysteria. Even when she saw Pauline's text and cried into her pillow — they'd been angry, driven tears. Now she wept like she had as a child, raw and vulnerable, uncorked until she was emptied.

"I can be home in half an hour," said Jack. "Do you want me to come?"

"Please," she whimpered. "Come home. We need you."

Exactly twenty-three minutes later, just before midnight, he arrived. She'd sat on the couch with Cricket asleep by her side, watching the neon numbers on the digital clock blink away each minute. Gone. Gone. Gone. Each moment lost.

The screen door opened and clapped at his back, and she had never been more grateful for the sound.

"Eden," he called into the darkness.

Not seeing her, he started to call again, but she was up and straight into his arms, squeezing the "Ee" out of him. God, she'd missed him. In one night and at the risk of losing him entirely, she'd missed him so much more than he'd ever know.

She pulled back so that their faces aligned. The hollows of his eyes were eggplant dark. She knew hers were, too.

"I shouldn't have thrown you out like that. You deserved to at least tell me your side. You deserve *more . . .*" The word seemed to catapult her into another racking round.

He held her close, her face leaving a watermark on his shirt like an image from the Shroud of Turin. He should've been furious with her. She'd thrown him out exposed and without listening to a single word; grown adults didn't behave like that to each other. People who loved each other didn't act with such disregard. But he only held her closer and let her be just as she was.

"Since the moment I met you, I've loved no one else. I couldn't," he said into the crown of her head. "I've never needed anyone but you. You are enough. *More* than enough, Eden. I'll do whatever you need me to do for you to feel complete. Pauline is everything I never want you to be. Lonely, heartbroken, and desperately searching for happiness. I shouldn't have met up with her for coffee. I shouldn't have taken her and her daughter out for dessert. She was just an old friend who knew me when I still had a family." He sighed. "A boy with parents, I mean . . . I was afraid you'd take it wrong if I mentioned it. I should have told you from the start."

"I wouldn't have listened. I *haven't* been listening for years. I've had baby on the brain." She had to take responsibility, too.

A tear wormed its way down her cheek, and he thumbed it away.

"If you want a baby, we'll get a baby. By hook or by crook! If you want to return to the PR agency, I'm your biggest advocate. If you want to leave New Charlestown, we'll go back to the city, too. Whatever you want."

He was freely giving her everything she'd schemed for herself. Only now, a panic rose up.

"I don't want to leave. I want us to stay here." She pulled out of his embrace and looked at Cricket on the couch. "I want him to be buried in the backyard, close by, when it's time. We won't leave him."

Jack pulled her back with a nod. When she spoke, her breath ricocheted off his throat and returned warm.

"I never looked into the faces of the babies we lost. I never made them dinner or sang them a good-night lullaby or held them when they were sick. I never heard their voices or saw their eyes light up at a sunny day. I never mothered them, truly, even if I carried them inside me. In his way, Cricket let me be his mother. Is that weird to say?"

He shook his head.

"We got this amazing little gift, and I don't want to give him back." At that, her body collapsed inward like a broken teacup.

He let her cry without offering trite condolences. She'd been the recipient of the gamut of them when her father died, each a hollow bell of no solace. From the pillow-embroidered reflections — *Better to have loved and lost* — to the biblical — *You must be strong through the Valley of the Shadow of Death* — they did little but force the sufferer into a position of gratitude: *Thank you so, so much for your kindness.* When all you felt was . . . loss. Deep, unrelenting loss. That kind of despair frightened people. Friends, neighbors, acquaintances feared it was catching like a virus, so they'd put on sterile gloves to hand out the *Our thoughts are with you* when really their thoughts were sprinting away as fast as possible. It was too painful to recognize: mortality.

Jack understood, though. He'd lived through the same when his mom and dad had died. Pauline had known his parents. How could Eden blame him for seeking out their memories? Even to the extent of cake balls. She had Denny, but Jack had no siblings to share a *Remember when* with.

She held him. "I don't want to go back to how things were," she whispered.

"We won't," he promised. "We'll make a change."

She buried her nose into his chest. Breathing in that only-Jack smell.

"I want to leave Aqua Systems," he said suddenly.

She leaned back to face him, shocked but not angry. Before she could formulate a question, he answered.

"This isn't the life for us. I want to be with you. Where you're happy, so am I."

She furrowed her brow, but a smile threatened her mouth.

"Only how will we afford the house and the fertility bills? Everything's on credit cards. One of us has to have a stable income."

"I believe you are on your way to illustrious fortune, Mrs. CricKet BisKet."

Mrs. Yes, she thought, *Mrs.* works much better.

He went on to tell her that he'd been contemplating his resignation for months. He'd researched agricultural companies he admired in the D.C. metro area, particularly his father's former employer, Cropland Geni-Corp. He'd e-mailed the vice president regarding his father's old formulas, sitting patiently in a bank security box. It had gotten his foot in the door. The VP had replied that CGC's president wanted Jack to come to the office to discuss the prospect of the formulas being reinstated and the research continued with an ultimate goal: unveiling a new line of products establishing their company as a leader in eco-friendly innovation. This, of course, was contingent on the right man spearheading the project. The right man holding the patents. Jack.

He'd thought it best to tell Eden after the meeting — wait until the ink was dry on the contract. He hadn't wanted to get her hopes up only to disappoint her. However, he now realized that he wanted and needed her by his side for this journey — as a partner, not a passenger.

Eden was dazzled all over again by this man and his ambition. This was the Jack she'd met all those years ago at the agency. The confident man she believed in and admired. She'd been a weight to his life over the past many years, but no more. They'd be allies and help each other achieve more than they'd ever dreamed of. She saw their future clearly, bright and unblemished as a perigee moon.

The kitchen clock chimed, and Cricket awoke at the sound. Seeing them, he wigwagged his tail, his shaggy shadow mimicking the motion on the wall. It was Sunday, and the Anderson family was exactly where it ought to be. Together. And Eden slept.

Decorah, Iowa, May 15, 1863

Dear Freddy,
I can't tell you how regretful I am for my many months without communication. Regretful that I have kept you in worry; regretful of this war; and most regretful of this blasted Iowa! I mourned every line of your previous letter. Immediately upon receiving it, I was removed from Mr. Sanborn's school and sent west with my family — to Decorah! We have been confined here all winter.

I learned there is a worse fate than death. Being buried alive. The snow piled higher than our windowpanes so that we couldn't tell if it was day or night. Not that it mattered. Whatever the hour, the cold kept Annie, Mother, Ellen, and me bunched together in bed like a mass grave from the battlefront. Sometimes I'd wake and think little Ellen dead beside me, her body so small and chilled. It was a monstrous season that nearly turned us into beasts with it. The cramped quarters had us either bickering or mute.

Only Salmon ventured out, in bear fur

and rawhide lacings. Though his family's home was less than a mile from ours, it would take him half the day to traverse. We didn't see my sister-in-law Abbie in all those months but were told she lost a child she hadn't known she'd been carrying. The ground was too firm for burial, but they couldn't put the dead out in the snow. Wolves would catch the scent. So they kept the thing in the cellar. Imagine! The only merciful act of this wretched Decorah is that it froze the lost baby and kept it from decomposing. Though when they unwrapped it for interment, the sight of its bodily shell removed of spirit distressed Abbie to a state of irreparable fragility. Salmon has worried himself into a whooping cough over her — and for good reason. This land would split a mountain if the rock dared open itself to a teardrop.

At home, I imagine our farm's strawberry plants bursting with blossoms. My throat aches at the thought of their fruits. We've been eating canned applesauce for months. It was the main staple put to pantry by our kin, the Days, who greeted us upon arrival, then vanished into the drifts. I'll retch if I'm forced to take one more spoonful.

Blasted gruel. I yearn for the crisp snap of fresh garden harvest, but we are adrift in eternal winter.

My only gladness comes in knowing that the dolls accomplished what we hoped! Thank you for giving me that gift of knowledge, Freddy, and I'm grateful that our friends were able to bring your uncensored words safely to my doorstep. I pray these reach you in equal keeping.

Is there any happy report from New Charlestown? I've imagined it so often I've nearly convinced myself of hope's reality: that Alice has awoken from her injury with a smile; that the Fishers have been returned to their homestead; that your father and mother are reunited; that the Hills gather round the table eating Siby's wheel of corn bread heaped with fresh butter. That the warring has reached cessation during our dreadful hibernation and, therefore, some good has come from it. These thoughts bring me comfort, even if they are a fable of my own creation.

Mother and Annie have finally given over to reason. We will not last another season like this. A cousin has come from California. He speaks of a place called Red Bluff, which, he assures us, has yearlong sunshine and temperateness. We are making arrangements to move westward.

Eternally yours,
Sarah

P.S. In a land apart, I anxiously await further news from our trusted friends. While my paints and pigments are packed in the wagon, as soon as we are settled in California, I will be at our services once more. Please send word again when it is safe.

Fort Hall, Idaho, June 20, 1864

Dear Freddy,
We survived the Oregon Trail only by God's mercy — and the United States Cavalry. I have never been so exultant to see rifled men on horseback. Better than a host of angels. Blasphemous as that may be.

Between Topeka and the Idaho border, we spotted a Rebel party approaching at haste. We made all possible speed. At Soda Springs, we collided with a company of Morrisites. Having seceded from the Mormons, the group was under the protection of the Union troops. We explained that we were the John Brown family and feared that slave-loving Rebels were after us for blood. The soldiers took up their weapons and dispatched the posse straightaway!

They will accompany us into the Sacramento Valley from Fort Hall, and we are forever grateful. Salmon, Abbie, and little Ellen suffer from coughs that will not abate. Mother is drawn and frightfully thin. Annie has gone back into a similar hollow of despair as witnessed in Boston. And I — I no doubt look as wildly desperate as I feel.

Our military escorts have informed us of the war's progress: General Sherman's advance on Atlanta. Grant's campaigns in Spotsylvania, Cold Harbor, and Petersburg. While I am bolstered by Yankee success, my heart is grieved to know that bedlam is near you, Freddy.

Mother says in times like these, we must put our hands together and pray fervently. I understand the compulsion and agree in principle. However, the fact remains that knitted hands did little to stop Father's execution. I couldn't bear if something happened to you. So I write boldly in the hopes that this letter reaches you, even if you are unable to reply.

Please, take all precaution in your work with Mr. S. If not for the good of your young wife, your mother, and your stricken sister — for the good of New Charlestown, which will need men of leadership when this awful war is done.

I yearn for better days when we walked the Bluff together, the sound of the wind through the forest canopy, and the smell of wet ferns. I sometimes wonder if I didn't dream that place and time. Did I — did we?

Eternally yours,
Sarah

EDEN

New Charlestown, West Virginia
October 2014

Cricket died the morning of the first frost. A lacework of crystals wove tight across Jack and Eden's bedroom window, and the icy leaves of the maple dropped overnight from the weight.

Jack had gotten up early for work, preparing for his first week as the new vice president of marketing for CGC's Green Line, based on the Anderson formulas.

"Eden, darling," he'd called her from deep sleep with a shaky voice. "I think it's Cricket's time."

They'd sat on the floor at the base of the staircase, Eden in flannel pajamas, Jack in his suit, and rocked Cricket through his last labored breath. Then Eden had kissed his cold nose before Jack had wrapped his body in a blanket and taken him to Dr. Wyatt's office for cremation.

Cleo had been at school, and Eden was glad for it. It broke her heart to tell the girl the news when she got home that afternoon. They sat on the couch together, and Eden held her until the tears subsided.

"They say Grams went fast," Cleo whispered. "One day she was reading on the porch, and the next day, gone."

Eden hugged her tighter, the girl's caramel hair smelling savory sweet against her cheek.

"I'm not scared of dying," Cleo continued. "Everybody's got to. There are worse things than dying . . . like being alive and unwanted. Even if his life was short, Cricket had you and Mr. Anderson. I asked my pastor, and he said family stays with you for always, even in the hereafter. So it's good that he found you, and you found him. He won't ever be alone. That'd be worse."

Eden rubbed Cleo's hot back. She liked to think that Cricket felt loved — that their spirits were tied together for eternity.

"My mom left me with my grandpa when Grams died," said Cleo. "She went to California. Rehab. Only after she got well, she never came back." She turned her face down to her lap, pick-pick-picking at the stitching of her school skirt until Eden was sure she'd undo the whole seam.

Finally, here it was: Cleo's mom was an

489

addict, living on the other side of the continent. True, it was none of Eden's business, but Cleo had trusted Eden enough to make it her business. She wasn't just some kid next door. She meant a great deal more to Eden now. Eden took Cleo's hand away from the hem and held it, sweaty in her own.

"I don't even know if she's alive or not. I have a picture from when I was a baby, but she was sick then . . . I don't like to look at it much. I've been trying to put the clues together." She raised her eyes to meet Eden's. "Grandpa says he doesn't know where she is, either. He hasn't heard from her in years. She just disappeared. Only nobody vanishes like a ghost."

Eden repeated her own words of comfort with the addition of Cleo's, far wiser than she'd ever know. "There are no such things as ghosts. Only unsolved mysteries. Like the doll's head."

Cleo leaned into Eden's arms.

"That case is still unsolved."

"Well, sometimes we aren't meant to have the whole story all at once," said Eden. "Only the part God, fate, history, or whatever sees fit to reveal at the time. I'm sorry I can't solve the mystery of your mother for you. I wish I could. And not even the world's greatest going-on-eleven-years-old veterinarian-detective could've known Cricket was so sick."

Cleo inhaled sharply, and Eden smoothed the sweaty strands off the girl's forehead. She knew what it was like to feel guilty for something out of one's control.

"We can't force life to do what we want when we want it. We can't change yesterday or control tomorrow. We can only live today as best we can. And it just might turn out better than expected."

Saying it made her believe, too. Something bubbly warm rose up from her toes to her cheeks, and before she could stop it, she'd kissed the crown of Cleo's head. *I wish you were mine,* she thought. *If I were your mother, I'd have come back. If I were your mom, I'd never have let you go.*

Cleo hugged her. "I'm glad I got you, Miss A."

"I'm glad I got you, too, Miss Cleo."

Cleo helped Eden choose a clover-covered spot straddling the backyard's property line. They bought an apple sapling in Cricket's honor and dug a hole to plant it with his ashes. A whole Cricket in a jewelry box of cinders. It seemed too little remains of a body and soul — even a little one of mostly fur.

She thought of her father's ashes sealed

up in the gold urn her mother had picked out. The inscription read, *To some you may be forgotten, to others a part of the past. But to those who loved and lost you, your memory will always last.* It had been on the list of remembrance poems the funeral home suggested. Eden had thought the poem trite at the time. A quatrain that read like a nursery rhyme. She'd been young and heart-stricken over so much left unsaid, father to daughter. His memory would last, yes, but it was muddled with doubt and disappointment. Now she realized that the poem was about choice. The "you" in the stanza was dead. It was up to the living to decide: to forget entirely, to put behind, or to recognize the love and carry that into the future.

Cleo came to Cricket's burial in her church patent leathers and a calico dress that made her eyes glow like periwinkles. Mr. Bronner came, too, and brought an evergreen wreath with a miniature bronze angel tied to the front. Eden felt regretful that their first meeting was for such a somber occasion but was moved by his thoughtfulness. She hung the wreath on the front door, and from the moment she did, the door remained open.

Children and parents from Eden's weekly Story Hour delivered homemade condolence cards smelling of finger paints and glitter glue. Vee and her dad arrived in the ice-cream truck with freshly baked cinnamon cookies, a Niles family recipe. Mr. Niles insisted that it was a tradition as old as the town. He'd healed enough to walk with a cane and used it with Dickensian flourish, *tap-tapping* it as an exclamation point to his gregarious chatter. Eden liked him immediately. As did Jack, especially when they learned that prior to breaking his pelvis, Mr. Niles had been in Scotland, shopping for antiques and visiting relatives.

"Your Cornwall is on the opposite end of the isle, but I'll share a stout with you anyhow — this being the wake of a good dog gone too soon," he good-naturedly quipped. "I got two Labradors. Lost their father, Braeburn, ten years back, and I still get choked up missing that old boy."

Jack and Mr. Niles sat outside on the porch swing, talking for the next hour while Vee disclosed to Eden another gift. Her paperwork for the National Register of Historic Places had been approved by the National Register Review Board and was on its way to the National Parks Service in Washington, D.C., for final review.

In addition to the information Eden had collected on her own, Ms. Silverdash's bank box had provided irrefutable evidence of the home's authenticity. It contained a notarized Last Will and Testament of Mrs. Hannah Fisher Hill, with a detailed description of the Hills' home as an Underground Railroad station managed by her father-in-law, Frederick Hill, and his parents, George and Priscilla Hill. A family tree had been drawn out listing Hannah's parents as the freed slaves Hank and Margaret Fisher; an elder sister, Siby Fisher, and a twin brother, Clyde Fisher; and Hannah's husband, George Hill II; their children included sons Henry and George III and daughters Betty and Camilla, Camilla being Ms. Silverdash's grandmother.

Based on the new findings, Mr. Bronner, in corroboration with Judge Jamison, declared Emma Silverdash the official beneficiary of the remainder of the bank box's contents: fifty thousand dollars' worth of gold bullion dating back to 1867.

Ms. Silverdash had thrown a bookstore party with a buy-one-new, get-one-old-free sale to celebrate and thank the town's patrons for their unwavering support during troubled times. Morris's Café catered the event, but Mack and Annemarie brought the star dish. Celebration deviled eggs, of course. Father and son had reconciled.

"The minute Matthew arrived, I understood," Mack told Mr. Morris.

"When it comes to family, there's no dividing, just multiplying," Ms. Silverdash had chimed in. "That's history's math!"

And they'd all toasted to that with creamy mustard eggs.

That was only the week before. Now the Miltons, including Ms. Silverdash, came to Cricket's burial together, bearing pumpkin pie and skillet corn bread, a book of prayers, and bags of groceries to keep the Andersons' pantry stocked for weeks.

Eden hadn't felt this kind of kinship anywhere before, not even around her childhood table. It was the family she'd always hoped for but never envisioned. There was only one person missing.

"Denny?" She phoned him from the kitchen, where she'd placed the doll's head back on the windowsill beside potted violets from Suley Hunter. "It's done. We buried him."

She'd called him immediately when Cricket had died but had only managed to sniffle and croak into the receiver.

"I wish I could've been there today," Denny let out a long exhalation. "My boss at Mother Mayhem's said if I jumped ship again, there'd be no coming back, and I still haven't heard from any of the job interviewers. How'd it go?"

She told him everything. About the Miltons coming with Ms. Silverdash, Mr. Morris's pies, Vee's funeral biscuits, the National Register of Historic Places, Cleo and Mr. Bronner finishing up the last of the lemonade tea while Jack and Mr. Niles swapped memories of England.

Denny was silent through it all. At the end, he said, "Jessica had an abortion. I just found out."

So suddenly did his grief unmoor Eden that she didn't have a chance to steel herself. Hearing his breath come ragged on the other end, she wept, too — for him, for the babies here and gone, for Cricket, for herself and the unfulfilled hopes she'd bottled up through the years. And though she couldn't see him, she felt Denny's crushed heart.

"Come home," she told him. "Come home to New Charlestown."

Red Bluff, California, September 20,
1864

Dear Freddy,
We have arrived. Our cousin did not
exaggerate. It is autumn and yet the
flower beds overflow with wild roses and
sedum. Alice could have her pick of
every fabled bloom. The forests are not
oaks or maples but pines growing so tall
and narrow, they look like Goliath ar-
rows pointing to the sun. And oh, the
sun! I write you now bathed in it and
shivering off every thought of Decorah.
I close my eyes and it pinwheels right
through my skin. It's our Promised
Land, this California.
We have begun to search for a
homestead. There is no shortage of land,
and the locals have put on their fanciest
hats to show us around. The town's
newspaper correspondent has come calling every afternoon to interview us.
Somehow, I've been dubbed the family
spokesperson. Mother goes mute on the
man's arrival. Annie hides in the kitchen,
conveniently indisposed with the mak-
ings of sorrel soup. And little Ellen is

497

more likely to tell the neighbors about the menagerie on her circular needlepoint frame than anything of significance.

The town is small but contains the necessities: post office, general store, bank, courthouse, a gun shop and hardware store, church on one end and blacksmith on the other. While Salmon and Abbie intend to find land to raise sheep, Mother, Annie, Ellen, and I are searching for a simple home in town. We'll first need stable employment. What the locals don't realize is that while we are rich in name, we are poor in finances, having used nearly all we had to make this journey.

The Red Bluff schoolhouse has advertised for a teacher, as have a number of the surrounding townships. Annie and I aim to secure two of those positions straightaway, given our scholastic backgrounds. Once again, we're ever grateful to Mr. Sanborn for his patronage of our education. It is proving a powerful asset to our family's survival. I am also told that there is a large contingent of society ladies with a desire for stylish sewing, embroidery, stamping, and paintings from the East.

I'm devising a way to turn my art into purse pence since it is not being used for other measures at present.

Truest, trusted friend, we are desperate for news of you and your family, having not received any for so very, very long!

Eternally yours,
Sarah

P.S. Enclosed is one of the thousands of miniature pinecones underfoot here. Thimble-sized, as if carried by Louisa May's fairies. They have renewed my curiosity. Magic may exist after all . . . or at the very least, the hope of magic.

New Charlestown, West Virginia,
   October 20, 1864

Dear Sarah,

I have written dozens of letters over the course of the last year with the hopes of sending the latest as soon there was a safe opportunity. However, Harpers Ferry, New Charlestown, and the surrounding townships have swapped hands of opposing military jurisdiction so often (Lee, Jackson, Milroy, Early) that as soon as the ink had dried on a letter, another battle would erupt and we'd again be divided from our northern friends. This war has turned into the generals' card game, and we, the people, are petty coinage on the saloon table.

Added to our confusion is the deteriorated state of the Confederate forces. Their uniforms are little more than tatters, stolen bits from fallen Union troops, so that we aren't ever assured of a soldier's true creed. A man in Federal garb could turn out to be a Confederate in disguise. The Yankees are no better. They come as they please and take whatever supplies we have. Any attempt to stop them is perceived as proof that we are southern sympathizers. My unsolicited Confederate appointment as minister to the troops has been used as evidence against me, despite my papers of Union furlough. Neither side trusts us, and we trust no one except our faithful friends and New Charlestowners.

Father perished at the Battle of Gettysburg. I'm sorry this news reaches you so late and, yet, abruptly. Provisions were made to bring his body home. He now rests in our own New Charlestown Church cemetery, beside Alice, who did not, as we hoped, recover from her injury. Mother has been in mourning for the entirety of this war. Her grief has aged her tenfold. Despite the rumors of peace each season, the war continues. I wish this letter could be as our old ones — full of literature, art, and happy memories — but times have changed. And while we are changed, too, I still count you, Sarah, as my truest confidante.

It is with that in mind that I send this weighty request and write more candidly than ever before . . . as I intend to pass this letter directly into the good hands of Mr. Silverdash and our ✥ friends.

From the reports of slave catchers and the years between, we hold no false optimism that Mr. and Mrs. Fisher will return. Hannah and Clyde Fisher have been hidden in our home since the war's onset. They are as much our family as our blood relations and, in many ways, more. I would sooner give my life than see these two children come to any harm. Keeping them hidden was an easier task when they were young. However, at nearly five years old, they are growing at great pace. Soon even their one safe haven will betray them, proving too small for their bodies should the Confederates come for inspection.

Ruth has had her hands full with our firstborn, little George, nearly a year old. She is weak from nursing and her own lack of proper nutrition, so Siby has taken on the task of caring for her and my ailing mother. Hannah and Clyde are mostly left to themselves and spend more hours than is healthy beneath the pantry floorboards. They need the sunshine you described.

Since your departure, Mr. Silverdash has become a formidable legionnaire of the ❖. His work extends to the free state of Ohio. Despite Lincoln's Emancipation Proclamation, the routes have remained covertly active. Most of the lines move north to Canada, but there are those striking out west — to you in the Sacramento Valley.

Hannah and Clyde are at hourly jeopardy. I have argued for Siby to go with them, but she refuses to leave Mother. She will only give her consent for the children to flee if you, Sarah, are their destination. Please, discuss with your family and send word as soon as possible. Whatever your decision, I will remain . . .

Eternally yours,
Freddy

THE OVERLAND TELEGRAPH COMPANY

RECEIVED AT NEW CHARLESTOWN, W. VA.,
NOVEMBER 19, 1864
FROM RED BLUFF, CALIF.

FREDDY, WE RECEIVED YOUR LETTER OF
OCTOBER 20 AND ARE REPLYING POST-
HASTE. SEND. WE HAVE BEEN IN TOUCH WITH
THE ALCOTTS. AN OHIO QUAKER THEY CALL
MR. HAYMAKER IS FAMILIAR WITH MR. S AND
IS AT OUR SERVICE. ETERNALLY, SARAH

SARAH

Red Bluff, California
February 1865

Sarah sat up in bed reading to Hannah and Clyde, tucked to either side beneath the pictorial quilt. " 'Once upon a time, there was . . .' "

The two had arrived on the first of January, like New Year gifts. Clothes in ribbons with foreheads glinting of sand from the journey across the western plains. They'd been timid of every face, wary of even the kindest touch, and clinging desperately to their few belongings.

For Clyde, that had been the Hills' translation copy of the Hans Christian Andersen stories: the pages dulled to moth's wings; one sentence penciled inside the front cover: *These help him sleep. — Freddy.* Clyde had carried the book under his shirt all the way from Virginia to California, so that even now, he slept with arms crossed over his chest in a security stitch.

Hannah had arrived clinging to Alice's Kerry Pippin. Though bibbed in an embroidered smock of apple blossoms, the doll was a macabre sight: headless, filthy, and gutted of her softness. Sarah knew why. She took a knife to the seam running down the middle while her mother and Ellen bathed the twins. Within was a rolled bundle of unmailed letters from Freddy dated over the course of the last year and a tintype encased in a gold-etched frame: Freddy, Ruthie, and little George.

It was her first glimpse of Freddy's child. Her first glimpse of Freddy or Ruthie since she'd left them. Freddy's hair was dark as ever, his eyes matching in sepia. Her whole thumb fit over his face, and she'd pressed it there a long moment.

Both Ruthie and he were far thinner than she remembered, and the seriousness of their expressions didn't match Sarah's memories. She wondered if it was a permanent change of wartime or a temporary one of the camera lens. She prayed the latter. Her worry was lessened at the sight of little George, who appeared to have no concern for either his parents' stony stares or the stark canvas against which they sat. He was plump, smiling with open mouth, and stretching a blurry hand toward his mother's cheek. Sarah imagined him touching it a blink later. The tintype stood on her bedside table so that the children could see their kin whenever they wished.

Despite its lack of face, Sarah had washed Hannah's doll, restuffed it with lavender and cotton, then sewn it up in even stitches. She'd been practicing her needlework extensively and had advertised her services in the local paper. To her delight, she'd received a number of orders for embroidery, stamping, and design and had accrued quite a following of customers among the Red Bluff society ladies. Every penny was welcomed, and she worked her fingers raw each night after long days at the schoolhouse. She and Annie had acquired teaching positions. The employment had afforded them the financial stability to purchase a two-bedroom home of their own in town while her brother Salmon and sister-in-law Abbie started a ranch in Bridgeville.

Mary attempted to have Hannah share a room with Ellen, but the twins refused to be separated. So Ellen begrudgingly went to her mother's bed while Annie slept on a rollaway and the twins took roost with Sarah.

Now, by the light of a paraffin candle, Sarah finished reading and closed the book. Hannah squirmed against her while Clyde's breath came even.

"But, Miss Sarah, I's not yet tired," Hannah whispered, no louder than a broom's sweep.

Sarah wrapped her arm around. "You must be part nightingale, Han."

"No I's not. I's all girl!" Hannah pulled her doll over her face to muffle her giggles.

Sarah moved it aside tenderly. No more hiding or codes. Let a smile be a smile, safe in its own truth. She sat the toy upright on her lap and adjusted its headless lapel.

"You know, this baby needs a face."

Hannah stared thoughtfully at the empty space above the shoulders. "Siby say we have to leave it in the hiding place 'fore it breaks and cuts us on the railroad train," she explained.

Sarah grimaced. She wondered where Mr. Storm's girls were now, grown up in freedom but fatherless. The sorrow of that night still haunted her, along with so many other moments she wished she could change.

She hugged Hannah closer. "Nothing will break or hurt you here. I'll make sure."

" 'Cuz ain't no soldiers in Red Bluff?"

"That's right, and because you're part of our family now, too." Sarah leaned her cheek to Hannah's head, smelling the rose shampoo Annie had made from the rambles of wild bushes encircling their porch.

The child raised a fawn finger to the painting on the bedroom wall: the Bluff, with a villager's wheelbarrow of red harvest in the center. Sarah had been sure to retrieve her original painting from Mr. Sanborn before she left Concord. It was all of New Charlestown she could claim as her own.

"I miss them's at home," said Hannah.

"Me, too," Sarah sighed. "It was the hardest thing for them to give you up, but I'm glad to have you with me."

Hannah grinned, covering her mouth with her hand. Sarah pulled it away. "You have the prettiest smile. Don't hide it. It brings me joy."

Hannah lifted her face to Sarah. "Mister Freddy says God be having a joyful heart even when he's sad 'cuz joy be like a garden. Once it take root, ain't nobody — not even soldiers! — keep it from growing when the sun come out," she said, proud to have remembered the sermon.

Sarah's chest pinched. "That's from the Gospel. Mister Freddy gave you the Word." She rubbed the skin above her heart with a thumb and returned to the doll. "So you see how important it is that we give this girl a new face. It's up to you. You tell me what kind you want, and I'll sew the finest one I can."

Hannah nodded eagerly one, two, three times. "I think she smiles like Gypsy," she said at last.

"Gypsy? How do you know Gypsy?"

Hannah had been too young to have any memories of the loyal dog.

She shrugged. "Everybody know Gypsy. She be the Fur Fairy watching over us. Siby say so."

Sarah thought this odd, but who was she to contradict? Whether real or imagined, the sentiment was true.

"Then it's settled. We'll give her a Gypsy smile."

Hannah beamed but quickly sucked her lower lip under her teeth. Remembering the talking-to, she let it go, and Sarah was pleased to see her growing more comfortable — even in something as minute as a grin.

"We'll start sewing tomorrow, but for tonight, sleep."

Hannah pulled the quilt up in agreement, then turned on her side, facing the table. "Good night, Mister Freddy, Miss Ruthie, and little George." She kissed her hand and placed it to the tintype. "Good night, Miss Prissy and Siby," she whispered. "Good night, Ma and Pa, wherever you be. Good night . . ." She yawned.

"Good night, Miss Hannah," said Sarah. "I love you."

"I love you, too, Miss Sarah," she whispered, halfway to dreaming. "Good night, Fur Fairy." She hugged the doll to her chest, and her breathing fell into rhythm with her brother's.

Sarah kissed her own hand and did as the girl had, hoping her father had been right in his preaching. That believing as a child could manifest miracles.

Good rest to all you, my beloveds, she prayed, and she glanced one last time at her painting of the Bluff before snuffing out the candle.

NPS Form 10-900
(Rev. 10-90)

United States Department of the Interior
National Park Service

NATIONAL REGISTER OF HISTORIC PLACES

1. NAME OF PROPERTY
Historic name: Hill, George and Priscilla, Underground Railroad Station Home

2. LOCATION
Street & number: 8 Apple Hill Lane
City or town: New Charlestown
State: West Virginia
Code: WV
County: Jefferson

3. STATE/FEDERAL AGENCY CERTIFICATION
As the designated authority under the National Historic Preservation Act of 1986, as amended, I hereby certify that this nomination request for determination of eligibility meets the documentation standards for registering properties in the National Register of Historic Places and meets the procedural and professional requirements set forth in 36 CFR Part 60.

In my opinion, the property meets the National Register Criteria. I recommend that this property be considered significant nationally.

Signature of certifying official/Title: *Alanna White*
Date: *10/17/2014*

State or Federal agency and bureau:
West Virginia Division of Culture and History
(State Historic Preservation Office)

In my opinion, the property meets the National Register criteria.

4. NATIONAL PARK SERVICE CERTIFICATION
I hereby certify that this property is:
☒ entered in the National Register.

Signature of keeper: *Patrick Peabody*
Date of Action: *12/1/2014*

EDEN

New Charlestown, West Virginia
December 2014

A light and steady snowfall quietly transformed New Charlestown from autumn gold to winter silver. Eden and Jack had gone to bed under a gentle flurry and awoken to a scene resembling Ms. Silverdash's newest Christmas diorama.

Jack had said good-bye with a quiet kiss to her forehead and a morning song: "Christmas is a-coming, and the geese are getting fat." He'd pulled open the bedroom blinds so she could see the shimmering branches.

"It stuck," she'd whispered, then pulled the blankets up warm around her chin and breathed in his musky sleep smells still lingering in the bedding.

Later, he'd texted: Made it to office fine. D.C. is operating full-speed. Wear your Wellies there.

Which she did, and she was glad for dry feet as she drove to Main, wheels crunching on leavened powder. A handful of cars had ventured out by quarter till noon. Most were parked near Milton's Market — people collecting last-minute staples so they could hunker down in comfort. Her tires were the first to leave tread marks before the bookstore.

She wasn't sure if any of the children would come. A cancellation of that Friday's Story Hour was certainly prudent, but Ms. Silverdash would not close the shop unless snow blocked the door from opening. And despite the enchanted feel, there was no more than an inch on the ground. In Eden's old Adams Morgan neighborhood, the salt trucks would've come through before dawn, churning the white to gray sludge so that by morning rush hour they'd merely have to scrape their car windshields and go on as usual. She liked that it was not the usual here. Nothing was anymore.

They'd finally cleaned out the nursery bedroom, unpacked the brown boxes in the kitchen, and given everything a place to call home. All the baby gear had gone up to the attic for the time being, and the house seemed renewed by it. They'd started a CricKet BisKet website, with orders coming in by the dozens from as far north as Connecticut and south to the Carolinas. With Jack's help and Mr. Bronner's advice, they'd trademarked the products and were looking into broadening their sales through a manufacturing facility. Cleo had agreed to have her company shares siphoned into a college savings account, and Eden was thrilled to contribute to her good future. It would've pleased Cricket, too, she thought.

The Nileses offered up their ice-cream truck, retired during the cold months, to the CricKet BisKet services. Eden had suggested that Denny come work for the company. She'd have to hire someone to deliver goods nine to five anyhow, so why not him? He needed to get out of Philadelphia. His wildness had been tamped down by the Jessica affair. No more rock-star gazing.

On Vee's suggestion, he'd placed an advertisement in the *New Charlestown Spectator* for after-school and weekend guitar lessons and had become quite popular with local high school students looking to "make it big." Their youthful idealism appealed to him, and to his surprise, he was a natural teacher. Between the two jobs, he earned enough to rent the one-bedroom apartment over Morris's Café

515

and had moved to New Charlestown permanently.

It had been Mett Milton's place until he'd announced that he'd been accepted to L'Academie de Cuisine that fall. Annemarie Milton had stepped in as café cook until Mett's return. She brought baby Matthew to Ms. Silverdash's each day while she worked between Morris's and Milton's Market on Main. Mr. Morris and Ms. Silverdash relished having the grandchild in their keep and doted on him endlessly.

Now the youngster sat on Ms. Silverdash's hip, merrily sucking his pacifier with a cheek pressed to her shoulder.

"Looks like just the Hunter twins today," she said. "Snow or heat, storm or clear blue, Laura's children never miss Story Hour."

Eden sat in the rocking chair. No matter what became of CricKet BisKet Dog Treat Co., she'd decided to retain her storyteller role at the Silverdash Bookstore. One hundred and sixty-eight stories in the Andersen collection, and they were on 104: "The Pen and the Inkstand." But Eden paused, thinking it unfair for the rest of the children to miss out.

"What if we read something else today — a special treat for you boys being good for your mama?"

Doug and Dan exchanged grins.

"Fur-furry!" said Doug.

Dan nodded. "Fur-furry!"

Eden could easily tell them apart now. Doug's nose was lightly peppered with freckles, and Dan's was not.

"Ask the Fur Fairy?" She pointed to the dog doll stationed on her bookshelf throne.

The boys looked from the toy to Eden's lap, where a real puppy slept. Both pointed to the latter. "Furry," articulated Doug.

Eden smiled approvingly. "Very good. Ladybug is furry." She cupped the napping pup to her chest.

Ladybug's head bobbled unsteadily at the change of position. She blinked her long eyelashes, once, twice, then gave in and closed her eyes again. Puppy breath came milky sweet. She was nine weeks old. A King Charles spaniel that looked like she could've been Cricket's sister. Eden and Jack were smitten. The week before, they'd picked her up from a Harpers Ferry family with a litter and had hardly put her down since.

"It seems she's too sleepy to weigh in. How about you boys take the Fur Fairy to pick a book?"

They returned with *Maurice Sendak's Christmas Mystery,* a story puzzle in a box.

Eden moved from the rocking chair to the reading rug, sitting Indian-style with Ladybug snuggled in her lap. She read while the boys pieced together the final solution. At the end, they skipped excitedly around her and the puzzle image singing "We Wish You a Merry Christmas" in vowels and consonants she couldn't understand. She didn't correct them — sometimes the spirit surpassed words and memory.

By the time Eden arrived home, the sun had risen high and bright, making the icy tree boughs wink spectrums at every turn. Coming through the front doors, she was greeted by the rich smell of braised chicken. Ladybug yawned and sniffed the air, eyes wide with appetite. The day before, Cleo had brought over her Gram's slow-cooker Crock-Pot. Eden had never used one but was quickly impressed.

"It's just your style," Cleo had explained. "You throw whatever ingredients you want in and turn it on."

"Incredible. Where's this been my all my life?"

"In our house. Under the fry pans."

Eden had thanked her with the promise of her first official sit-down family dinner. Cleo, Mr. Bronner, Denny, and the Niles were coming over, and Eden was eager to impress. She lifted the top off the slow cooker. A plume of steam rose, hearty as a bite.

Ladybug pawed at her foot.

"Just be patient a little longer, baby. Daddy's not home from work yet."

The phone rang. She put the lid back on and scooped up the pup as she answered. Ladybug rolled to the side and let a paw dangle over her arm.

"Hello?"

"Hello, Mrs. Norton Anderson, it's Dr. Baldwin at Cherry Grove Fertility Center."

Her fertility specialist. It'd been so long, she'd nearly forgotten.

"Oh! Hi, Dr. Baldwin, how are you?"

It caught her off guard, like revisiting a place you used to call home but didn't anymore. There you'd shared a kiss, there a tear, over there your first taste of jam on bread, on those steps you tripped, in the sun you stood here. Yet it was entirely foreign. You couldn't wait to leave and go back to where you now belonged.

"I'm fine, thank you," Dr. Baldwin replied, then continued formally: "I'm calling because the last we spoke, we were going to give you and your husband time to . . . rest." There was a shuffle of papers in the background. "I'm looking at your chart, and it seems we have four frozen embryos. Fertilized and viable. We've previously discussed your age and blood-work levels, and your cervix is already showing signs of early atrophy."

She winced at the description. She'd forgotten how businesslike the clinic's physicians could be. A kind of factory feel that, in the past, she'd interpreted as a sign of good practices.

She hugged Ladybug closer to feel something alive — flesh and blood, breathing, real.

"If we are going to implant, sooner is best. Time is critical if you wish to carry the child yourself." Again with the raspy papers, like leaves being raked into a pile. "Given your medical history, I would suggest two or three for the first go. That would leave one or two as backup if the others don't bear out."

Eden ran her hand through her hair. What if . . . Hope sprouted fast and green, but she was more cautious now.

"So we'd restart hormone injections, schedule doctor appointments, do everything we did before, and what — wait and cross our fingers?"

"Yes. Maybe your body just needed to

recalibrate. I can't predict the future . . . I'm just a doctor, not God." He chuckled at his own comparison.

Right, thought Eden.

"I can pass you over to the nurse for an appointment?"

"No, I need to talk to my husband first."

"Of course. Call the front desk whenever you're ready, and they'll set you up."

Easy as pie. Only it wasn't. Eden bit the inside of her cheek, thanked him for calling, and hung up. The words echoed: *atrophy . . . time is critical . . . recalibrate . . . the future . . .* Her head swam. She sat down on a kitchen stool.

Normally she'd engage in a mental Rubik's Cube of how it could go: imagining the possibilities one way and then the next, turning the pieces over and over until a row made sense. Now, however, all she saw was the glittering layer of snow outside the windowsill where the doll's head had once been.

After Cricket's burial, she and Cleo had made rehabilitating the doll their mission. Vee had helped them locate a muslin body from her supply of antique toys. They'd repaired the cracked skull with porcelain glue and painted the face afresh, keeping the features the same, the eyes different colors.

Ms. Silverdash was officially able to authenticate both the head and the body as from the Civil War era; furthermore, the peculiar facial painting was in fact part of an elaborate Underground Railroad code. An unsuspected map for runaways. The only doll similar to this one had been unearthed in a safe house outside of Cincinnati, Ohio. Unfortunately, its face had faded to near disappearance on a wooden head. The National Underground Railroad Freedom Center's forensic anthropology team hadn't been able to determine who the artist might've been, but its use as a UGRR code carrier was unmistakable. Now, through Eden's discovery and Ms. Silverdash's letters, they were certain that the Sarah of correspondence was none other than Sarah Brown, the daughter of legendary abolitionist John Brown.

Eden wondered how many lives Sarah's dolls had helped save — not just the people who'd carried the mapmaker's secrets but their children and their children to follow. Ms. Silverdash had let Eden read the letters between Sarah and Freddy, and Sarah's passionate words matched the piercing gaze and tender smile of the painted doll. An uncommon woman for her time, a mighty woman for all time, thought Eden, and she cherished it as legacy.

Unwilling to part with the artifact, no matter the price, she set the refashioned doll beneath the hallway telephone stand, greeting all guests to the Andersons' home.

"Hey, Miss A!" Cleo swung in the front door. School was over. Everyone would be there in an hour.

"Smells *awesome.*" Cleo went to the crock and tapped the lid. "Works like a charm, right?" Confident of the answer, she didn't wait for Eden to respond, slinging her backpack off and pulling *Frommer's Mexico* from within.

Cleo had chosen the guide for her final book report before the winter holiday. Eden had helped her put together the class presentation, complete with a rainbow poncho (from Eden's closet), a grand bouquet of tissue-paper blooms (produced in their living room), and Mexican scribble cookies (baked in the Andersons' oven).

"Public Relations 101: it's not about the product. It's about the product's story. The experience of a shared dream," she'd explained to Cleo while tying bright tissue paper into floral bunches. "Emotion is the most indelible memory. You give that to your class and they'll remember Mexico forever. It's the Once-Upon-a-Time effect."

Whether you were promoting books or dog biscuits, the principle applied to any kind of audience. People didn't just want shampoo; they wanted Rapunzel's beauty to make a prince scale a tower wall. Legend.

"Like this." Eden had put a red flower behind her ear. *"Viene con migo, muchacha,"* she'd said in her best Spanish accent, then mimicked the flamenco dance she and Jack had seen in Puerto Vallarta.

"Zorro! Zorro!" Cleo had joined in, skipping and blading *Z*'s in the air.

Now the girl waved the guidebook. "I got an A plus! Mrs. Blakey said it was the most stylish book report she's ever had."

"Bueno!" Eden pulled her into a one-armed hug, and Cleo leaned in fully, kissing Ladybug's head.

She stayed in Eden's embrace while the pup licked her nose. "You got carrot breath. Must've liked those puppy biscuits."

A spin on the CricKet BisKet recipe: adding pureed baby carrots and whole flaxseed, double-baked extra crunchy for teething. Ladybug had devoured their trial batch.

The front door gave its signature groan and clatter.

"E, it's us." Denny and the Nileses arrived

at the same time, exchanging hellos and laughing.

Hearing the jingle in Denny and Vee's voices, Eden felt something flicker inside her. They complemented each other, she thought, but before she could surmise further, Ladybug swam her arms and legs toward the new arrivals. Eden put her on the ground to scamper down the hall.

"There's the bug!" Vee cooed.

"Are we still making Green Bean Amandine?" asked Cleo. "It's my favorite."

"Sure are. Wash your hands and get your apron on, Señorita A Plus. You can snap ends for me."

Denny entered with a family-sized box of gingersnaps. Mr. Niles carried a bottle of Cairn o'Mohr, and Vee a giant drum of Neapolitan ice cream. Eden had asked them to bring dessert, but this was enough for an army.

Ladybug pranced figure eights about their feet.

"We followed the star and come bearing gifts." Denny bowed. "Gold, frankincense, and myrrh of the culinary sort."

"If you're a wise man, we're in trouble," Cleo chided from the kitchen basin, behind a veil of bubbles.

"Oh, lookee here," Denny said in a mock-gangster accent. "A little *wise*-gal, eh?" He gently pulled Cleo's ponytail.

Eden's cell phone rang with a new text: Coming home!

"Jack's on his way."

"Grandpa, too," said Cleo.

Vee set the table, and Mr. Niles poured glasses of tart apple cider while Eden transferred the chicken onto a platter. Denny put on a CD he'd made of himself singing classic carols to the strum of his acoustic guitar. Eden thought it the most beautiful sound she'd ever heard and told him so. Music filled the house with earnest cheer. She and Cleo hummed along as they lit tapered candles in the dining room.

"Once-Upon-a-Time effect?" asked Cleo.

Eden nodded. "Exactly."

She'd talk to Jack about Dr. Baldwin's call later, when they were alone. Decisions had to be made, but for now, her house was full and happy and just as it should be.

HANNAH

Before their carriage had come to a full halt, the front door on Apple Hill Lane swung open and out came the Hills, one after the other, in a neat column of beaming faces despite their black mourners' armbands.

"There's Miss Ruthie and little George — not so little anymore." Clyde pointed through the window.

Hannah peeked around the carriage curtain to see. The ringlets over her forehead caught in the bright sun and shimmered in sunset hues. She adjusted her feathered hat so the violet wisps fell away from the brim and she could get a better look. She'd ordered the dress and matching bonnet from a boutique in San Francisco, where her mother had taken a job as an adjuster for the U.S. Mint.

Her mother never wore a corset, so Hannah hadn't expected her to appreciate the cinched waist, lace trimmings, bustle, and bindings.

"The new fashions are nothing but fluff, puffs, and ruffles." Her mother had shaken her head, then smiled admiringly. "You do look lovely, Han."

Hannah had grown to be a beauty. Her skin was the color of a doe's belly; her eyes like early spring buds hinting green through the russet; lips so naturally colored, they made flowers seem pale. A true California rose, everyone said, sun-kissed and blossoming. Her brother, Clyde, mirrored his sister's bronzed complexion, handsome features, and good nature. Red Bluff folks commented that the Fishers' kin — lost in the war — must've been of Italian or Spanish descent. The details of their heritage remained a family secret.

Shortly after Hannah and Clyde had arrived as babes, Sarah had begun teaching immigrant workers' children and local orphans. On the side, at first, but soon those students outnumbered the residents' children at the schoolhouse where she was employed. So the Red Bluff Ladies League (many of whose members were avid clients of Sarah's, regularly purchasing her needlework designs and paintings) had decided that something must be done. They'd opened an additional school, with Sarah as the primary teacher, and assumed that her compassion must have compelled her to adopt the twin Fisher pupils. *How benevolent. A pillar of our community,* they said. Never imagining the dangerous journey the two had endured or the family losses they'd suffered as children of freed blacks.

Their home in California afforded them safe distance from the wounds that remained raw and open long after the surrender of the Confederacy and the Thirteenth Amendment's abolition of slavery. John Brown's life's calling had been attained, but the hand of action could change only so much. It couldn't cleanse the blood, no matter how copiously it had been spilt. While the country had legally made all men equal, they'd heard enough reports to know that bigotry festered and continued to kill with equal malice.

It was for this reason that Hannah and Clyde had remained in the West all these years. Their aunts Annie and Ellen had both married California men. But Sarah had remained unwed, raising the twins and caring for their ailing grandmother Mary until she passed away.

As a girl reading fables, Hannah had once asked if Sarah had ever been in love and, if so, where had her prince gone? Sarah had said simply that God wrote her story differently. He gave her two magical children worth ten thousand kingdoms, and that was more love than could ever be written of. Hannah saw the truth in that.

Freddy and Ruthie had seven children: five boys and two girls. The Hills had faithfully kept in touch through letters since Hannah's earliest recollection. They felt as much a part of her life as anyone. Their first son, little George, was now grown. Having graduated from the University of Virginia's School of Medicine that spring, he was beginning his medical practice in New Charlestown. Freddy and Ruthie's eldest daughter had married a clergyman under Freddy's pastorship. The couple had refurbished the barn into a second house so they could live close by. The rest of the children had made homes on the roads branching off the newly denominated Main Street.

A government mapmaker had come in accordance with the Ninth Census for the publication of the *Statistical Atlas of the United States.* The Hills had been honored when the official had christened their street

Apple *Hill* Lane.

While Priscilla had died a decade before, faithful Siby had remained by the family's side. She'd searched out her parents in the Deep South after the war ended, but the trail had gone cold at the North Carolina state line.

"If they's alive, they'll come back. If they's dead, they's spirits already here," she'd said.

The Fishers' home had been recompensed to Siby. She swore the ghosts of old Rebels had taken roost within and wouldn't spend one night under its eaves. With Freddy's help, she'd sold the property for a goodly purse. He invited her to continue on with them. The Fishers and Hills were family, and they couldn't imagine living without her.

And so Siby had stayed and been mammy to Freddy's children and eight grand-children. The Fishers' finances sat safely in the town bank through the carpetbagger years, producing a mighty investment. Not trusting currency that could burn or change insignia, Siby insisted the funds be converted into gold and kept in a lockbox, which she bequeathed to Hannah and Clyde. It was the news of her death that had called the twins back to New Charles-town. Hannah and Clyde were Siby's only blood kin, and they remembered their elder sister lovingly.

Sarah had helped them pack their belongings and had bid them good-bye at the train station. She wouldn't go with the twins, despite Hannah's pleas. She said she wasn't the same young woman she'd been. The journey back was too great. Her life was in California, and there she'd stay, beside her mother, sisters, and brother unto death. The twins couldn't argue with that. It was this same familial devotion that had drawn them back across the continent now.

Outside, Freddy and Ruthie were the last to come down the Hills' front steps. The house had a new face, different from the one Hannah remembered: a stately white porch with overhanging eaves and a black gable roof. The older couple was framed by it and by their children fanning out before them in the yard.

"It's just like one of Mother's paintings," said Hannah.

Clyde agreed.

The year they'd started grammar school, their new teacher had organized a bake sale to raise funds for winter coal, board chalk, and the like. Hannah and Clyde had come to Sarah meekly and asked if she wouldn't mind them calling her "Mother," since they hadn't one to name the way the other students did.

Sarah had first written to Freddy for Siby's permission. As soon as the letter of approval arrived, she'd agreed to the moniker. Both children had danced around her using "Mother" in various references: *What story will we read tonight, Mother? The supper stew smells good, Mother. How are you, Mother? Where is Mother, Clyde? I don't know, I'll call her: "Mother!"*

Sarah, too, had been overjoyed, so much so that she couldn't hold her sewing needle steady. So she'd put away her embroidery work, and though they had school the next day, they'd taken their baskets to the orchard and feasted on ripe, round peaches by moonlight.

Hannah and Clyde had gone to bed with full bellies and sticky lips, but Sarah had stayed awake, painting a still life of their celebration basket. The children discovered it beside its inspiration the next morning.

"I can't tell one from the other," said Clyde at breakfast.

"I want to eat it!" Hannah had swiped her finger across the wet fruit in the corner.

"If you eat that, you'll have an awful bellyache," Sarah had cautioned. She had cleaned Hannah's finger, then pulled both children to her waist. "No painting can fill you up. It's not real — just one moment. A memory for when peaches aren't in season."

She'd taken an actual fruit from the basket and bit it, exposing the dewy flesh, then passed it to Hannah. Hannah had eaten it to the stone and remembered always.

The carriage door swung wide. The chilly river breeze swept through the cabin with the earthy scent of pine.

"Welcome!" Little George acted as footman. He had his mother's russet hair with the confident stance of his father.

Despite the hospitable greeting, Hannah sat rooted. Clyde gave her an elbow nudge, and she bashfully extended her hand.

While Clyde was thoughtful and reserved in word and deed, Hannah was the first to plunge headlong through whatever door gave her entrance. It was unlike her to be timid.

She stepped out and stood with her hand in George's, looking up to his golden eyes. The corset bindings strained tight, and although she held her breath, her heart fluttered wildly beneath the laces. She'd never felt anything as potent. She could not let go.

"Litt— George," Clyde interrupted, extending his palm.

George released her then, and she willed her knees to hold steady.

"I'll always be little George to family," he greeted. "Welcome, brother Clyde. Sister Hannah." He turned to her and smiled.

Her head spun.

Then came a flurry of arms, faces, and embraces. Variations of the familiar mold: Freddy in the eyes, Ruthie in a brow, Freddy again in a mouth, Ruthie in a curl. The grandchildren looked alike, too. One fair child cradled a beautiful doll, which drew Hannah's attention.

"I had a doll like that when I was a girl," she told her, "only we had to change her face to a magical one."

"What happened?" asked the child. "Why'd she change?"

Hannah smiled. "I had to leave her old face behind."

"Because she became a Cali-for-ya girl?"

Hannah nodded.

"Grandpa gave her to me." She thrust her doll forward. "She's from Boston. Her name's Nancy."

"She's pretty," said Hannah. "But not as pretty as you."

"I think you're the prettiest lady I ever saw."

Hannah kissed her cheek, and the girl kept

close to her side.

They moved through the crowd of Hills to Freddy and Ruthie. The couple embraced Hannah and Clyde as if they were children returned.

"We've missed you terribly these many years," said Freddy. For a moment's pause, his gaze skimmed past them to the empty carriage, as if looking for someone more, then quickly returned. "It's good to have you home. Son, please see to their luggage."

"My pleasure." George bowed to Hannah, and her breath caught.

Ruthie put an arm around her shoulder. "Come have tea and cornbread pie. It's not as good as Siby's, but I hope it has her blessing, with you two back at the table."

Within the house, a dog barked a welcome as the Hills escorted the twins down the brick pathway lined with forget-me-nots and ruby balsams, still blooming in the un-conventionally warm winter month.

U.S. Patent and Trademark Office

U.S. DEPARTMENT OF COMMERCE PATENT APPROVAL

1. NAME OF INVENTION:
Original CricKet BisKets®
Adapted from *The Holistic Hound.*
Makes 50 dog bone–shaped CricKet Bis-Kets®.

2. INGREDIENTS:
2 1/2 cups organic whole-grain flour
2 tablespoons organic ground flax meal
2 large organic eggs, beaten
3/4 cup canned organic pumpkin puree or
   fresh pumpkin baked soft and mashed
1/4 cup cold water, give or take a splash

3. INSTRUCTIONS:
Preheat oven to 350° F. Grease two bak-ing sheets or line with parchment paper.
   Combine flour and flax meal in a bowl. In a separate bowl, combine beaten eggs and pumpkin until smooth. Add wet ingredients to dry. Then add cold water, a tablespoon at a time, until the dough comes together to form a spongy ball.
   Roll dough out to 1/4- to 1/3-inch thick-ness. Draw signature biscuits using knife

(two heart tops with bridge between) or 2-inch dog-bone cookie cutter. Place cut biscuit shapes on baking sheets. Use tines of fork to embellish: gently stick into middle, wiggle, and remove; carve logo initial *C*. Reroll scraps and repeat until dough is used up.

Bake 20 to 25 minutes, until the tops of the biscuits have dried out completely. Remove from oven and flip biscuits over. Return to oven, rotating trays front to back, and bake another 20 minutes, until crunchy as hardtack. Let cool on wire racks. Store in an airtight container until ready to ship to customers or give immediately to eager pup patrons.

4. ADDITIONAL INVENTIONS BASED ON ORIGINAL:

* Apple Hill® CBs: substitute 3/4 cup applesauce for pumpkin puree in original recipe and spelt flour for whole-grain flour; add 1 teaspoon of cinnamon.

* Miss Cleo® CBs: add 1/2 cup organic blueberries.

* Ladybug® CBs: substitute 3/4 cup pureed organic baby carrots for pumpkin puree

in original recipe; add 2 tablespoons whole toasted flaxseeds.

AUTHOR'S NOTE

Mapping Sarah with Sarah

According to the moleskine journal I tote just about everywhere, the first scratch of an idea for this novel came on June 5, 2011. I couldn't get a woman's voice out of my head. She kept saying, *A dog is not a child.* At the market where I was buying peppers, at night while listening to my husband snore, while brewing my tea and baking biscuits, while walking my dog through our neighborhood . . . she called to me from the steps of the Apple Hill house.

When I finally wrote down the phrase on June 5, I swung open the front door and out came a dozen hastily penned pages of contemporary New Charlestown. As with my other novels, I knew the names immediately: Eden and Jack Anderson.

It's funny how characters come full-formed to an author. Our duty is to dig, gently but fervently, to unearth the narrative around them. And so I excavated the fictional landscape. I knew the Andersons lived near the true Harpers Ferry and Charles Town cities in West Virginia. I Googled home addresses: Liberty Street, Duncan Field Lane, Washington Street. All were lined with Queen Anne homes featuring elaborate porches and gabled roofs. Beautiful architecture. The real estate listings said they were facades to older foundations dating back to the 1800s. My story wheels had begun to turn. I had a place, a vision of the setting.

I immediately began outlining Eden's chapters, but it wasn't until September 2011 that John Brown's name appeared in my journal. A genealogy tree transcribed from the Internet wormed its way down the page alongside another scene I couldn't get out of my head. Scribbled illegibly as if I might blink and forget: *Jail cell. Warden. John, hung before noon. Wife. Daughters.* Then there she was, Sarah Brown.

Her character details spilled out like a cup running over. Freddy, Ms. Silverdash, Cleo, and the Miltons, too. All seemed to crowd my imagination, hollering to have their names added to the playbill, to be remembered.

By October, I'd begun historical research

on the Brown family, Sarah in particular. I was fascinated by her nearly forgotten life. A gifted artist, early feminist, abolitionist, friend of the famed Alcott family (Louisa May and the rest), familiar with all the leading men of the Underground Railroad and John Brown's Secret Six Committee, highly educated, a minter, an orchardist, a teacher of orphans, devoted to children not her own, called the most beautiful of John Brown's offspring, and yet never wed, never engaged, even as all of her siblings married off. It grated on me — not knowing her story.

So I began what would end up totaling over three years of mapping Sarah across the country. In Concord, Massachusetts, I visited Orchard House, where she stayed with the Alcotts while at Franklin Sanborn's private school; Boston, where she visited "Friends" of her father, John Brown. In Harpers Ferry, West Virginia, I walked the town from beginning to end, the railroad tracks to the riverbank. With my own dad by my side, I went into the firehouse where the infamous Harpers Ferry Raid met its bloody finale. There, Sarah's brothers and other raiding men died together, slave and free, black and white, all dust now.

In the swelter of that 2012 summer's day,

we were silenced by the ominous substance of history underfoot and rising up in the Virginia heat. Then my dad said, "All those sons — those boys . . . dead. A tragedy." His words gave me goose bumps.

A hundred and fifty years later, a father stood mourning lost futures. I have two brothers, Jason and Andrew. As a sister, I can't imagine the pain of losing them. Call me selfish, but if I were in Sarah Brown's shoes, I'd just want my family back — even though the cause was righteous, her loss was considered the catalyst for the Civil War and a nation's emancipation from slavery.

I visited Charles Town next. The old courthouse where John Brown was imprisoned, put to trial, and hung still stands stately and white across the street from the clock tower bank, town hall, and steeple church. So quaintly Americana and yet its history is steeped in violence and heartache. It was there that I clearly saw Sarah and Eden, side by side, as an iconological mirror.

I continued to follow Sarah's trail from West Virginia across the continent to Red Bluff, California. The gracious director of Archives and Collections at the Saratoga Historical Foundation Museum opened the doors to me off hours for a private research

Author Sarah McCoy at the Saratoga Historical Foundation Museum.

visit. She patiently answered my litany of questions, provided me all the documents the museum had on hand, allowed me to take photos, walk the rose-brambled grounds, and stand before Sarah's paintings.

The five on display are the only publicly remaining artworks by Sarah Brown: pencil and crayon portraits of John and Mary Brown; oil paintings titled *Peaches, View of Mt. Diablo,* and *Carmel Mission.* Between her art education and commissioned pieces, there must've been more. But like her life, they seemed to have come and gone without detailed chronicling and, so, they're buried beside the people she aided as an abolitionist, the orphans she nurtured, the family, friends, and local community to whom she remained devoted.

I walked the town of Red Bluff, too. Though 3,000 miles apart, its Main Street was nearly identical to Concord, Harpers Ferry, and Charles Town, with residents going about their daily errands, children following along, and businessmen waving hello to one another just as they did in the nineteenth century. I went to Sarah's gravesite, sat beside her on a bed of pinecones, and listened to the autumn leaves whisper. I say confidently that I felt Sarah there in Madronia Cemetery and believe she was a guardian angel to the writing of this novel. With me in my darkest hours was a woman who made an unconventional life into an extraordinary legacy. I gained strength in the faith she displayed. I was inspired by her as a creative, independent woman.

But please understand, I didn't set out to write a biographical account of Sarah Brown or a romanticized version of the facts. My role as the storyteller was simply to use the tools of my craft and imagine what Sarah's life might've looked like, how she felt, her struggles and joys, what she might've dreamed, even as I dreamed her into existence. I did my homework for years: researched newspaper articles, letters, distant Brown relations alive today, Sarah's real-life art, Underground Railroad artifacts, symbols, and codes, bootleggers, baby dolls, and a colossal amount of John Brown information available in library archives.

The pictorial symbols I described are factual to the documented Underground Railroad and Slave Quilt codes. I united those cryptograms with the speculated use of children's dolls to smuggle contraband, spy messages, and medicines to slaves in antebellum America and during the Civil War. Most informative to my story development was the debate surrounding the "Nina" doll on display at the Museum of the Confederacy in Richmond, Virginia. The family who donated "Nina" claimed her to be an example of the doll-smuggling theory. Passed down through the generations as legend, she gained celebrity today due to her ambiguous past. "Nina" fueled my imagined trajectory for Sarah and Eden.

Admittedly, I took liberties with some of

the historical events and facts. I was more concerned with capturing Sarah's heart and future impact on Eden in the present day than on writing an official profile. This book is wholly my own invention.

As a writer and a reader, the most satisfying part of mapping any characters (historical, contemporary, real, and fictional) is the emotional journey taken beside them as they discover their independence and develop into stronger people. I believe we become stronger from these characters' pasts, presents, and futures. We learn to view the world and all of our lives, here and gone, as one giant map. Paths, decisions, history, and destiny interconnect even if we can't blatantly see the linking tracks. But, given distance and a stilled perspective, they are unmistakable and ultimately divine. This is what Sarah and Eden demonstrated to me. I hope their stories, two in one, proved the same to you, my esteemed community of readers — present, future, and perhaps even one never-to-be-forgotten woman from the past.

ACKNOWLEDGMENTS

My eternal thanks to . . .

The courageous women (family, friends, neighbors, strangers, those here and gone) who openly shared their intimate struggles, fears, physical pains, and emotional battles in defining and creating a "family." Equal thanks to the men who supported and loved these women through every hour. This novel is in honor of all of you.

Mollie Glick, my super agent (it's official, you have the keychain), literary match, and dear friend. Emily Brown, a wicked smart addition. Kristin Neuhaus for trumpeting this book across the globe before I'd even finished the last word. And everyone at Foundry for being nothing short of phenomenal.

My Wonder Woman of an editor, Christine Kopprasch (certified by scandalous apron), Maya Mavjee, and Molly Stern for being lionhearted champions. To my

Charlie's Angels fierce team at Crown: Jay Sones (a.k.a. Charlie), Annsley Rosner, Sarah Breivogel, Rachel Meier; and perpetual Angels: Meagan Stacey, Emily Davis, and Kira Walton. To Bonnie Thompson for having the eaglest of eagle eyes (yes, I verbed a noun in not-quite homophonic alliteration) and Mary Doria Russell for the brilliant introduction.

Katie Alexander, the Saratoga Historical Foundation's Archives and Collections director, who was wonderfully kind to open the museum off hours so I might stand before Sarah's paintings, stare, dream, take notes and photographs, ask a thousand questions about the Brown family, and generally consume her entire afternoon. My visit to the Saratoga Historical Museum was instrumental in knowing Sarah's life in California.

The Madronia Cemetery staff for allowing a Virginia lady in Texas boots to sit beside Sarah Brown's grave, collecting leaves and pinecones, running my fingers over her etched headstone, and mumbling awed hellos without shooing me off as a lunatic vagabond.

The following institutions and collections that served as tremendous resources: the University of Virginia's John Brown Archive and newspaper scans from the *Staunton Spectator;* the University of Missouri–Kansas City's compilation of John Brown's transcribed letters; the West Virginia Division of Culture and History, the Virginia Military Institute Archives, the Virginia Foundation for the Humanities, *Harper's Weekly* archive; the Miller-Cory House Museum for their list of colonial herbs and usages; Alice Keesey Mecoy's blog "John Brown Kin"; the John Brown Wax Museum, the Harpers Ferry National Historic Park, the Harpers Ferry Historical Association, the Jefferson County Museum, the National Museum of Civil War Medicine, the Jefferson County Public Library; PBS's *History Detectives* program with special thanks to historian Gwen Wright; the Museum of the Confederacy, the Louisa May Alcott Orchard House, the Saratoga Historical Foundation, and the EVMS Jones Institute for Reproductive Medicine.

I must give due reverence and credit to the writers who dug into history for me and presented the information in packaged books, essays, articles, and other primary sources. I could not have written this book without their precedential work and the comfort of having these authorities stacked across my writing desk: *The Browns of Ma-*

dronia by Damon G. Nalty; *The Californians: After Harper's Ferry: California Refuge for John Brown's Family* by Jean Libby; *Stitched from the Soul: Slave Quilts from the Antebellum South* by Gladys-Marie Fry; and to the fiction that informed and lit my imagination: *Cloudsplitter* by Russell Banks; *Cold Mountain* by Charles Frazier; *Little Women* by Louisa May Alcott; and *Fairy Tales* by Hans Christian Andersen.

Immeasurable thanks to friends who shared their innermost heartaches and joys — and never once balked at my pointed questions, inane bantering, or irrational tears. Thank you for your uncensored, treasured friendship and for allowing me to be part of your families: Christy and JC Fore, Stacy Rich and Eric Schatten, Mary and Courtney Holland, Kristin and Jason Romesburg. Your little ones, my honorary nieces and nephews, are proof of modern miracles and ancient promises.

Significant thanks to my shining-star person, Christy Fore. Without you, my creative process would not be complete. I would not be complete. I could go and on . . . as you know and have e-mail evidence, but I'll leave the gushing to our secret correspondences. Much love to Kelsey Grace and Lainey Faith (because they deserve to have their names in this book, too).

Endless thanks to bookish friends who have supported, loved, and cheered me from coast to coast and around the globe while researching and writing this novel: truest "Peppah Sister" Jenna Blum, Caroline Leavitt (cowgirl boot blinger), Beth Hoffman (#Happydale), Emmy Miller (goddess momma), Robin Kall Homonoff and my honorary MOT family (Emily, Burt, David, Ari), Chris Bohjalian, Jen Pooley, my SSS (you know who you are, Lovin); Edan Lepucki, Patrick Brown, and D'Bean for proving that writer parents are über-cool (organic pomegranates and yoga pants forevah!); Therese Walsh (T-ea sis) and my Writer Unboxed friends; Kathy Parker, Marcie Koehler, and the Best Book Club beauties; the independent bookstores and book clubs across the nation and globe who've crusaded and cheered my work, you are the fuel to my rocket ship, unquestionably.

To my family, no acknowledgment or reverence or gratitude is enough. You are the underpinning of my spirit. Without you, I'd be a lost button. Your daily support, prayers, and eternal love through sunshine and rain are the true definition of *family:*

my dashing younger brothers Andrew and Jason McCoy, my best friends and heroes; my grandparents Wilfredo and Maria Norat, Grandma Mona Louise McCoy, and all my relations, near and far. Special thanks to Aunt Gloria O'Brien for showing me the beauty of an adoption family. Titi Ivonne Tennent for truly being a second mother, singing "Going to the Chapel" in the car on my wedding day, three-way hugging me from sobs to laughter that October 2013 afternoon, and so much more. You are my magical God-mommy.

Most of all, thanks to my parents, Eleane and Curtis McCoy. I am humbled and grateful beyond life and breath to be your daughter. Mommacita, you know the true beats of my heart. Daddio, to whom this book is dedicated, you are the reflection of agape. Thank you for driving me to West Virginia and walking Harpers Ferry corner to corner in the blistering heat with a smile and equal zeal for my characters. We'll never know why they moved that old firehouse, but we'll always have KFC buckets of chicken on the road trip.

To my husband, Brian (a.k.a. Doc B), we've been riding this trail together since high school but over the years of writing this book, your courage, unflappable good nature, and faith have led us to blessed new territory. Daily, I'm awed by your talents and compassion, and bolstered by your abundant love. Thanks for asking me to the prom those decades ago and for telling me I'm always enough — sometimes a plenty handful. Play that K-Ci & JoJo cassette tape. I thank God that I finally found you.

ABOUT THE AUTHOR

Sarah McCoy is author of the *New York Times, USA Today,* and international bestseller *The Baker's Daughter,* a 2012 Goodreads Choice Award Best Historical Fiction nominee; the novella "The Branch of Hazel," in *Grand Central;* and *The Time It Snowed in Puerto Rico.* Her work has been featured in *Real Simple, The Millions, Your Health Monthly, Huffington Post,* and other publications. She has taught English writing at Old Dominion University and at the University of Texas at El Paso. She calls Virginia home but presently lives with her husband, an Army physician, and their dog, Gilly, in El Paso, Texas. Connect with Sarah on Twitter at @SarahMMcCoy, on her Facebook fan page, or via her website, www.sarahmccoy.com.

The employees of Thorndike Press hope you have enjoyed this Large Print book. All our Thorndike, Wheeler, and Kennebec Large Print titles are designed for easy reading, and all our books are made to last. Other Thorndike Press Large Print books are available at your library, through selected bookstores, or directly from us.

For information about titles, please call:
   (800) 223-1244

or visit our Web site at:
   http://gale.cengage.com/thorndike

To share your comments, please write:
   Publisher
   Thorndike Press
   10 Water St., Suite 310
   Waterville, ME 04901

LARGE TYPE
McCoy, Sarah
The mapmaker's children

NOV   2015